INSIGHT GUIDES

USSR

The New Soviet Union

CCCP = Соноз Советских Социалистических Республик
SSSR = Soyuz Sovetskih Socialisticheskih Respublik
USSR = Union Of Soviet Socialist Republic

Produced by Wilhelm Klein
Art Direction and Design by Villibald Barl and Hans Höfer

A P A
PUBLICATIONS

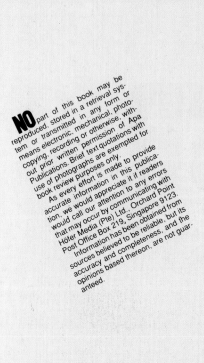
USSR
The New Soviet Union

First Edition

ABOUT THIS BOOK

In Insight Guide to the Soviet Union, the world's largest country, covering 1/6th of the globe's land mass, seemed to be a logical project for APA Publications to undertake to add to the ninety-nine destination titles selling in the bookshops of the world. Still, it was a provoking thought back in '88.

Two years earlier, Mikhail Gorbachev had initiated the process of *perestroika* and, just as important for the APA project, the process of *glasnost*, which - for the first time in many decades - permitted Soviet authors to write from their hearts without the fear of being censored or reprimanded.

The concept seemed simple: to work closely together with writers from the USSR, authors competent to write about subjects which are beyond the reach of most western journalists. Easier thought than done at a time when much more than the Berlin wall divided east and west and when people on both sides were still beset by a "fear of touching"!

It was only while the book was being shaped that a new spirit took hold of the Soviet Union; during the two years that the book was being written, both the internal process of democratization and the ethnic and national independence movements matured.

Capturing the soul of a people

This book needed a spiritual guide, someone who comprehends the east as much as the west, someone who has long been at home in the projected common European house, someone whose voice supersedes language. **Yevgeny Yevtushenko**, Soviet Union's foremost poet and free thinker, has become that guide.

To pursue a project as challenging as this, **Hans Höfer**, APA's entrepreneur-publisher, assigned **Wilhelm Klein**, author and editor of various Insight guides, to be the project manager for what was to turn out to be APA's 100th guidebook. Klein brought a few indispensable assets to the endeavor. Back in the early 70s he was co-editor of a Neo-Marxist magazine in Germany and as such is well acquainted with the philosophical and social implications of the present process in the USSR. Even more important, he roped in his friend, Yevgeny Yevtushenko, as *mentor spiritualis* and contributor to the project.

In many meetings, at Yevtushenko's home in Peredelkino near Moscow and at Klein's home in Dreieich, Germany, they laid the groundwork for the production of this vanguard volume of east-west understanding.

At Yevtushenko's suggestion, the next contributor to be approached was **Konstantin Likutov**, Deputy Editor in Chief of Novosti Press. Three books and numerous articles on relevant subjects made him an ideal participant in the project. He has traveled the world and edited books published by Alexander Bovin, Chingiz Aitmatov and Yevgeny Yevtushenko. For this guide he wrote about the geography, the people and the politics of the USSR and about the Caucasus.

Dimitri Volkogonov, a bestselling author whose book *Triumph and Tragedy* has been published in over 20 countries, wrote the section on Stalin.

Vladimir Grigoriev, fluent in three languages and a well-known journalist, wrote the sections covering the Baltic and the Western Republics.

Yevtushenko and Klein

Igor Zakharov, who studied philosophy in his hometown of Leningrad, was secretary to the Politburo member Alexander Yakovlev. He wrote the chapters on Soviet history and Leningrad.

Yevgeny Filiminov works for Intourist as a specialist on tourism in Central Asia. He wrote that chapter and the section on the ancient Silk Road.

Alexander Platkovsky comes from a well-known family of journalists. He reported for the Komsomolskaya Pravda from Pyongyang and has canoed down some of the Siberian rivers. Siberia constitutes his main professional interest. The "Wild North", the "Wild East" and the "Transsib" texts come from his pen.

Gely Ryabov is a State Prize Laureate and scriptwriter. He dedicated many years of his life searching for documents on the execution of the Imperial family. This is also his theme in this book.

Vladislav Govorukhin spent his childhood in the GDR and translates from English and German into Russian. He is now a senior editor of the press agency APN and has traveled extensively within the USSR. He wrote about Moscow, his hometown of choice, and about Kiev, the hometown of his wife.

Alexander Proskurin, a graduate of the Moscow State University's department of Journalism, has written numerous articles and seven books on subjects from daily life in the USSR to the Cosmonauts. The latter is also his theme in this Insight Guide.

The exception to the rule

One writer in this circle of eminent Russian journalists and authors does not come from the USSR but from Germany. For the sake of giving a diversified view of a country as controversial as the Soviet Union, **Dr. Karl Grobe** - one of Germany's foremost liberal journalists, a "Russia watcher" by vocation and calling, wrote the "view from outside" for this Insight Guide. His other contribution, "The Third Russian Revolution", makes this book more than just a guidebook; it fosters understanding of a contemporary drama taking place in front of our very eyes.

There are several others without whom this book could not be what it is. **Leonid Ivanov**, a post-graduate student of Russian language in Moscow and contributor to Apa's *City Guide: Leningrad*, came for a few months to Germany to complete the Travel Tips section, which contains inside information on subjects and regions as yet untouched by western publications.

Then there are those numerous photographers, Soviets and foreigners, who documented what unfolds so impressively over 350 pages of the book. And last, but not least, there are the many fine maps and ground plans drawn from new sources within the Soviet Union, all together representing the most comprehensive resource for the reader who wishes to acquaint himself with the "New Soviet Union".

-APA Publications

Likutov   *Govorukhin*   *Dr. Grobe*   *Zakharov*   *Volkogonov*

HISTORY AND PEOPLE

PLACES

MAPS

TRAVEL TIPS

Russia Cannot Be Understood With The Mind

by Yevgeny Yevtushenko

A tourist visa to the USSR enables you to visit a great many different countries - all known collectively as one country. A tourist visa to the USSR gives you right of entry to a multi-storey Tower of Babel, swaying under the burden of many religions, languages, customs and, in recent times, political parties. Not so long ago this tower seemed like a gray Communist monolith surrounded by labor camp searchlights, barbed wire and ideological watchdogs. Then, all of a sudden, from various floors of this tower came the sounds of mutinous poetry and of protest rock songs, calling for freedom, of political speeches proclaiming the preeminence of universal human values over the class struggle. It was in the stone throat of this tower that the two Russian words *perestroika* and *glasnost* were first heard.

A Tower of Babel
or a Tower of Pisa?

Some felt that the Tower of Babel would rush to the aid of its concrete sister, the Berlin Wall, if it were ever in danger. But the Tower of Babel did not even stir when rioters in jeans started tearing down its concrete sister. In fact, if the truth be known, the tower secretly smiled to itself because it disliked its younger sister, if only because it had been forced to feign love for her.

But while, only yesterday, many in the West ecstatically welcomed the collapse of the Berlin Wall and the swaying of the Soviet Tower of Babel, today many have lost at least some of their enthusiasm and now anxiously wonder what the outcome of it all will be, whether the balance of peace is going to be shattered, and whether other people's collapsing walls might damage their own.

The upsurge of interest in the USSR and in everything going on here is accompanied by a certain apprehension, and this is being felt equally in tourism. Some people do not fancy the idea of walking about a swaying, crumbling Tower of Babel decked out with all sorts of contradictory slogans like "The Party is our driving force!" and "Party, give us a go at the wheel!" While Gorbachev is showered with flowers and words of praise in the USA, during the recent May Day parade in Moscow he was forced to leave the Lenin Mausoleum because some of the vociferous cries reaching his ears were far from complimentary. Something out of the question since Stalin came to power is happening: people are being allowed to criticize the head of state without being arrested for it. People who are used to thinking of the USSR as a frozen block of conformism find this hard to come to terms with. To understand what is happening in our country, just imagine an incredible scene like this: the giant body of a frozen mammoth is lifted out of a refrigerator, and all the germs inside start squirming to life - not just life-giving germs of freedom but also those of chauvinism, nationalism, great and small, and social envy verging on hatred.

The first alternative elections, the first real parliamentary debates, the first glimmers of civic freedom; uncensored at last, the press is fighting for the right of the truth and democracy but on its pages all these dangerous germs are also dancing their revisionist Dance of Death...

And look at that meeting of two or three hundred anti-Semites in Red Square next to the Kremlin's ruby stars and the black government limousines which keep sidling out of the Kremlin. Nearby a demonstration of half a million Muscovites is protesting against anti-Semitism and bureaucracy. The miners' strikes and the carnage in the Caucasus may scare away the fainthearted but one of the few true joys of life is being an eyewitness to history in the making.

For the benefit of those who have not been to the USSR yet, let me explain some of the problems facing our national Tower of Babel. On no account should the nationality question in the USSR be modeled on the American one. The United States is a country of emigrants, and its states, unlike the Soviet republics, are divided up territorially and not by nationality. A hundred years ago the Russian Empire already had more or less the same geographical outlines as the USSR of today, also occupying one sixth of the earth's surface. Just one "tiger's paw" of the Soviet Far East is about the same size as the whole of Italy's "boot".

Many foreigners still call the USSR "Russia" in the old way, and all its citizens "Russians". This is a hurtful mistake, which gives an inferiority complex to the national minorities and a no less unhealthy complex of unacknowledged superiority to the nations whose culture is older than Russian culture. Discussions are now being held in parliament and the press on the need for an internal Soviet passport. At the same time there is a

energetically arguing that the eradication of the nationality clause from documents is an affront to their national pride.

When a poet recently wrote, "My nationality is Soviet", he caused a storm of protests in the republics. The dictatorship of Stalinism introduced the tactless notion of the Russian people being the "elder brother", and this naturally hurt the pride of many nationalities. Paradoxically, though, the Russians - the "colonizers", that is - sometimes turn out to be living not better and often even in far worse conditions than the nations they have "colonized".

In a Central Asian village on one of those sunny spring days when the almond trees are

debate about the clause in educational course and employment questionnaires where you have to indicate your nationality. In the past, and even today this clause has been used in a discriminatory, chauvinist and, in particular, anti-Semitic way. Meanwhile some nationalities, especially the Caucasians, are

Preceding pages: "Those who do not labour do not eat"; a young face on Gorky Street, Moscow; Orthodox churches are veritable treasure chests; everlasting comradeship; on guard; Caucasians love to wear big caps. Above, the popular Aquarium Rock Band.

in full bloom, I once saw cotton-pickers in striped padded coats and skullcaps drying one hundred rouble notes on the ground. You could not imagine such a thing happening in Russia. This makes the Russians also feel inferior, and the poisonous seeds of chauvinism find fertile ground in hearts which have been enraged by life's injustices.

Speaking irritably about the attempt of some republics to secede from the Soviet Union, one Russian writer even threatened that Russia herself would secede as well. This, of course, is absurd. Without Russia the Soviet Union is unthinkable. Just now

Gorbachev's political opponent, Boris Yeltsin, the recently elected president of the Russian republic, is raising the question of her sovereignty but he does not mean to tear to shreds the territories which, after much difficulty, Ivan Kalita, Ivan the Terrible and Peter I succeeded in sewing together with threads of blood.

For the peoples of the USSR the Russian language is as irreplaceable as a means of communication as English is the world over. Without it how could the peoples of the USSR who speak over a hundred and fifty different languages talk to one another?

The Avarian poet Rasul Gamzatov comes from a mountain people numbering around 300,000. His books of poetry are published in his native language in editions of up to 50,000 (a record per head of population!) But several million copies of his books have been printed in Russian translation.

The small and, from a technical point of view, very poorly equipped Georgian film studios, Gruzia Film, is one of the best in Europe as far as the quality of its productions is concerned. It was here that one of the greatest films in the entire history of filmmaking was made: Tenghis Abuladze's *Repentance* which won the Grand Prix at Cannes. But would the Georgian film studios have survived if there had not been such a powerful multi-national market in Russian inside the USSR? Heaven forbid if nationalistic ambitions, unappeased by the legal right to sovereignty, make our people break off economic and cultural ties.

Is the common European home we long to create really possible if it is completely split up into separate units and there are no doors between, say, the Georgian and Russian rooms or the Russian and Lithuanian rooms? After destroying the wretched Berlin wall, the symbol of the ideological forced division of kindred spirits, surely we are not building new walls between our peoples?

The Tower of Babel concept may prove fatal not just for a political system but also for many specific people alive today. I prefer the idea of a Tower of Pisa. Especially as it is inevitably linked with tourism. And tourism does not only mean money. Tourism into and out of a country is part of a policy vindicating man's freedom to travel whenever and wherever he likes.

So then, welcome to the USSR, to our complicated Tower of Babel which one day, I hope, will turn into a Tower of Pisa - leaning to one side perhaps, but not collapsing.

Russia has to be seen

The 19th-century Russian poet Fedor Tiuchev once wrote four lines of poetry containing a complete formula for Russia, that vast power which will always remain an enigma for foreigners. It goes like this:

> *Russia cannot be understood*
> *With the mind,*
> *Nor can she be measured*
> *By a common yardstick*

> *A special character she has:*
> *In Russia one can only have faith.*

To this I would add - Russia has to be seen. And I would say so even if I were American and not Russian. But please don't think this is part of an advertising campaign for the Soviet tourist board. I shall even give you this honest warning: for many years now the service in our country has been ironically defined as "unobtrusive". Rumor has it that the late Richard Burton, who had flown into Moscow for a film festival, flew out again the very next day after waiting 40 minutes for a cup of hot coffee for breakfast. Unfortunately, our waiters have assimilated the smooth, leisurely flow of Russian rivers over the plains.

Foreign tourism in the USSR is relatively new - it hardly existed between the 1920s, when Stalinism became well and truly entrenched, until the 1957 International Youth Festival when Khrushchev, following the example of Peter I, "forced a window into Europe" - this time through the Iron Curtain. Thousands of different-colored representatives of humanity, speaking many different tongues, leapt through this window, tearing their jeans on the Iron Curtain's rusty barbs. The myth about all foreigners being spies

lin's labor camps that Khrushchev released: he also released the grim truth like a genie out of a bottle and neither he nor Brezhnev after him, no matter how hard they tried, could stuff this genie back in again.

We now understood the full horror of our losses: 27 million perished during World War II, and about as many arrested people died of hunger and deprivation after the Revolution of 1917. The Russian proverb - "You can't chop wood without making the chips fly" - proved an understatement: not only chips or branches flew but whole trunks were torn up with their roots. Top professionals in politics, science, art, industry and agriculture were cut down... Why? After all,

with cameras in their buttons, radio transmitters in the heels of their shoes, and pockets full of Colorado beetles was dispelled. And so was the other myth about the USSR being the happiest and most just country on earth.

"I know no other country where man breathes so freely" went the chorus line of one of the most popular songs in the 1930s when every tenth citizen of the country was in prison. It was not only convicts from Sta-

what could a state possibly gain from killing off its professionals? That is true but not in Stalin's state where only human cogs of the state machinery would be needed, not independent-minded individuals.

The economy of a society which counts on submissive, mediocre people, and not on talent, is bound to collapse. So it was with Stalin's system. It started to flounder at the same time as the Iron Curtain. The perestroika program announced by Gorbachev is the result of a terrible awareness of Dostoyevsky's formula: all the greatest ideals are not worth a single tear shed by an innocent suffering

Left, their's is the future. Above, popularity cannot be achieved behind closed office doors.

child.

Perestroika's main victories are moral. After returning from exile in the town of Gorky, Sakharov entered the Kremlin as a People's Deputy of the USSR. Soviet citizenship has been returned to the outstanding musician Rostropovich and the celebrated theater director Liubimov. Books like Solzhenitsyn's *GULAG Archipelago*, which were banned until only recently in the Soviet Union, are now being widely published. Our military intervention in Czechoslovakia and Afghanistan has been officially condemned. Soviet troops are leaving Eastern Europe. Emigration is getting easier. The USSR is gaining moral and material credit from

unfree economy keeps widening. This gap is dangerous because the conservatives are blaming none other than the free press for the economic crisis. But can a doctor's diagnosis be regarded as the cause of an illness?

People are demanding a ban on the showing of capitalist shops on Soviet television because they say it is irritating "ordinary Soviet citizens" who still spend a quarter of their lives in queues. This really does irritate Soviet people but they are also asking themselves why it is they are living so poorly in such a country.

I do not consider that Western countries should give us charitable donations by way of help. Charity corrupts. But I do think that

Western countries. The specter of a third world war is no longer troubling mothers the world over.

But along with these moral victories perestroika has also suffered economic defeats. The government is still fearful of a free market economy, just as a fish reared in an artificial reservoir with concrete walls would be of the open ocean. The bureaucracy is vehemently resisting the idea of a free market because it will lose its privilege - that of granting or withholding its permission and fixing prices at a level that suits its ends.

The gap between the free press and the

the Western world could help us by sharing its positive and negative experience of the free market, and by investing financial support and know-how in joint ventures.

Not so long ago the convergence of the best features of socialism and capitalism, as proposed by Sakharov, was denounced as a "betrayal of the Motherland". Gorbachev is also still treating this concept with far too much caution.

The arms of all aggressive ideologies are elbow-deep in blood. On the other hand, as far as we know, tourism has never arrested, shot or hung anyone...

Nature, characters, food - the life of a country

No country deserves to be examined only under a political microscopic lens. Nature, characters, food - this is what the life of a country is usually based on. There is a saying that every nation deserves the government it gets. A harsh and in many ways true saying but does it always apply? I lived for nineteen years under Stalinism but did my mother and father whose fathers - my grandfathers - were both arrested as enemies of the people, did my parents really deserve Stalin? And what about Pasternak and Shostakovich - did they deserve him?

really be held responsible for these unlawful actions? If so, then surely every American can be held responsible for Hiroshima...

I do not consider Russian chauvinists "normal" Russians, nor, indeed, any other aggressive people with vast inferiority complexes. My mother is a normal Russian. I have never heard her make insulting remarks about any other nationality, and her friends are Russian, Jewish, Georgian and one is even Chinese.

My mother loves guests and no matter how late they drop by, she always manages to make a feast out of nothing. Foreigners are sometimes baffled how it is that the Soviet food shops are absolutely empty but when-

My mother was never famous but just now, in June 1990, she is celebrating her eightieth birthday, and still working as the oldest newspaper kiosk saleswoman in Moscow. During World War II she gave concerts to the soldiers at the front and ruined her voice, and after the war she went out to work and brought up my sister and me single-handed. Of course, she was mistaken in thinking that Stalin did not know about the unlawful actions taking place in the country. But can she

ever they visit someone's home, the table is always stacked high with food. In the West the opposite is sometimes true: the shops are bursting with food but on many tables there is hardly anything when you visit them.

To make up for the lack of foodstuffs in the shops, our people are very fond of making home preserves. On many windowsills you will see large bottles of cherries sprinkled with sugar that are fermenting in their own juice - this is a kind of homemade liqueur. In most homes you will find three-liter glass jars of salted cucumbers or tomatoes flavored with garlic, dill, horseradish and blackcur-

Left, healthy life through aerobics. **Above**, restricted area.

rant leaves, and jars of tangy green apples in a solution of salt, honey and cherry leaves.

To make up for the lack of black caviar, which can only be bought in restaurants for three times the shop price or in the "Beriozka" shops for hard currency, our housewives have learnt to make their own caviar: this is popularly called "poorman's caviar" because it is simply a purée of stewed egg-plants or courgettes and tomatoes. Nearly every cupboard contains a fascinating anthology of homemade jams such as rowanberry, cranberry, wild strawberry and gooseberry and the berries themselves are also preserved whole. There will always be several necklaces of dried Boletus mushrooms hanging in the kitchen. If you were to ask me where to find the best Russian restaurants, I would say, in a friend's apartment.

A friend in any country is a magic key for opening hearts and doors. But are you willing to become a magic key for a Russian visiting your country? Who knows, in the future perhaps all humanity will be part of a vast voluntary firm of reciprocal tourism based on mutual understanding, and not half-hearted, camera-clicking curiosity.

It is wrong to presume that people only discover the truth during parliamentary debates or at philosophical symposiums where everyone always tries so hard to look intelligent. People also discover the truth at friendly gatherings around a table, and the nature of this truth is cheerful as well as tragic. I love my writing table but I also love Georgian tables with their superb wines *Kindzmarauli*, *Khvanchkara*, *Odzhaleshi*, *Tsinandali*, *Teliani*, *Aladasturi* with *satsivi* (turkey in walnut and coriander sauce), *nadugi* (curd cheese with mint), *khasha* (tripe soup with garlic), and hot *suluguni* (Mozzarella cheese) that melts in the mouth.

I also love Armenian trout sprinkled with crimson pomegranate seeds and the world's best homemade vodka which is made from Cornelian cherries (there are at least 35 lbs/ 15 kilograms of berries in every 2 pints/1 liter). I love sweet-smelling Central Asian pilaff and lamb kebabs served straight from the coals which sizzle in your fingers and carry the fresh aroma of the waterfall roaring nearby. And, as a Siberian, what I enjoy eating most is a freshly-caught Siberian fish such as *nelma* or *omul* which has been salted for no more than five minutes, and I will wash

it down with neat alcohol in an aluminum mug or just spring water.

Kvas is a marvelously refreshing traditional Russian soft drink made from dried black bread, yeast, sugar and currants. It is also the base of one of our most popular cold summer soups - *okroshka* - to which you add finely chopped spring onions, dill, parsley, radishes, roast beef and boiled egg with a little salt and soured cream on top. Incidentally, people who sneer at everything foreign and insist that all the best things in life can only be found in their own country, we ironically refer to as "kvas patriots". I cannot stand such people in the arts but when one is talking of the real thing, I must admit I am a real

"kvas patriot" myself and I think it is better than Pepsi and Coca-Cola - and if you do not believe me, try it for yourselves!

I am also a patriot of our wonderfully diverse nature. After all, nature which has created us cannot be held responsible for the bureaucratism we have created. Here are some of the images which spring to life in my mind's eye when I look at a map of the USSR. A seals' breeding-ground on the Komandor Islands: hundreds of gleaming pairs of seals lying on the sand with their flippers round each other, their gentle passionate groans blending in a unique symphony of sound. A gray-whiskered old walrus on a large ice-floe near Dickson Island, listening inquisitively to the strains of the Italian song Santa Lucia coming from a schooner close by. A huge bear standing on the breezy bank of the Siberian river Vitim, trying to shake off swarms of mosquitoes. Mist over Lake Baikal: flashing golden streaks of light reflected across the water's surface as trains speed by. Siberian peasant women in my home town, Zima Junction, on their way back from market carrying frozen white moon-shaped rings of milk. Women miners in the town of Mirni extracting future diamonds from the muddy ground. A ruffled crow perched on a post in the Urals which reads "Asia-Europe" and a little peasant boy peeing underneath, grin-

Afon resembling gigantic candles offered to God to redeem all our sins.

The exquisitely carved stone Tomb of Tamerlane in Samarkand: when, despite Moslems' protests, it was opened in June 1941, black smoke came pouring out and by some mystical coincidence shortly afterwards Hitler attacked the USSR. The grandiose monument over Babii Yar in Kiev where the Nazis shot several tens of thousands of Jews. Leningrad's famous White Nights where every time the bridges are raised Dostoyevsky's specter plunges into the water. The sumptuous St. Basil's Cathedral in Red Square whose architects were blinded on the Czar's orders so that they could never

ning from ear to ear.

A Rumanian circus artiste riding her horse onto the deck of a trapper's schooner in Arkhangelsk to say farewell to her captain sweetheart. The breathtakingly beautiful wooden church at Kizhi which was built in 1714 without a single nail. The books in Yerevan's Matenadaran Library that are so old they have turned to stone. The churches in the mountains of Georgia which look just like faceted lumps of rock crystal. The stalagmites in the Abkhazian caves at Novy

build anything more beautiful.

The lugubrious Lubyanka building - the KGB headquarters - where so many innocent people have been tortured: recently a large crowd - including a small number of miraculously saved ex-convicts and many young people who do not want a similar tragedy to occur again - met by the building with lit candles in their hands and formed a human ring of light.

The Georgians are renowned for their exceptional and unique brand of hospitality. In a Georgian home you must never praise anything: if you do, your hosts are sure to give it to you as a gift (even if it nearly breaks their

Left, faceless images. **Above**, birch groves abound in Russia.

hearts!).

You can tell an Armenian by the eternal biblical sorrow in his eyes. And flickering in the depth of his eyes is the shadow of Mount Ararat that was taken away from the Armenians, the specters of the victims of numerous massacres, and the pain of the Diaspora when they were scattered throughout the world. In our country people say, that an Armenian's eyes are always sad, even when his face is lit up in a smile.

Our unique multinational country is like a classical Ukrainian *borshch* containing everything a practical housewife happens to have at hand. If just one of the ingredients is taken out, no matter whether it is beetroot, onion, carrot, tomatoes or finely minced bacon, the *borshch* will no longer be the same, and will possibly no longer be a *borshch*.

A poet in Russia
is more than a poet

So says a line of my poetry which is frequently cited by critics and readers. For centuries the position of a poet and, indeed, of any artist in Russia has always been special. I have already mentioned the architects of St. Basil's who were blinded. The fact is, in Russia artists learned to see well even when their eyes had been put out and to speak the truth even when their tongues had been cut off. Russia was the last country in Europe to abolish serfdom. Censorship was introduced into Russia soon after Ivan Fedorov printed the very first books, and he was exiled from Moscow by Ivan the Terrible. The czar instinctively sensed the power of the printed word to oppose his authority.

Ever since then, censorship has seldom be relaxed, and these rare periods were generally followed by a return to even harsher censorship, and - with the exception of the few months between the February and October Revolutions of 1917 - it has never been totally abolished. The Soviet government reintroduced censorship after the publication in 1918 of Gorky's book *Untimely Thoughts* in which he criticized the Bolsheviks whom he had supported before the Revolution.

In another poem I wrote: "The history of Russia is the struggle of free thought against the suffocation of thought". This was true before and after the Revolution.

Political systems have changed but censorship has stayed put. Poetry was traditionally the leading genre in Russia, forging the way for the great prose of the future. Why poetry? Because when harsh censorship was in force, it was easier for the poetic metaphor to conceal the meaning's seditious naked blade under beautiful cloths of rhythm and imagery and deceive the Imperial guard, and later the totalitarian party regime. The greatest Russian poet, Pushkin, was the archetype of the formula about the poet in Russia being more than a poet: as he was, at one and the same time, a most subtle lyricist, a rebellious civic poet, the editor of what was in those days a radical journal, and a friend of the Decembrists, who organized a revolt against the czar. Lermontov picked up the pistol Pushkin had dropped in the snow at his last duel while it was still smoldering and gained instant notoriety by hurling the following accusatory words in the faces of the great poet's murderers:

> *And with all your black blood*
> *You will not wash off*
> *The poet's truthful blood!*

He was immediately arrested for these lines and then exiled to the Caucasus where he was also killed in a duel. All the great Russian prose of the 19th century - that of Tolstoy, Chekhov and Dostoyevsky - had its origins in Pushkin, who once, incidentally, gave Gogol the subject of his masterpiece *Dead Souls*.

After a conversation with Pushkin, Czar Nikolas I wrote the following entry in his diary: "Today I talked to one of the most intelligent people in Russia", but at the same time he also gave instructions to the head of the gendarmerie, Benkendorf, to step up their surveillance of the poet. When Pushkin, despairing of getting some of his poems passed by the censors, asked the czar to become his personal censor, he discovered this did not help matters either.

Dostoyevsky, having linked his fate to the Petrashevist revolutionary movement, was sent to do hard labor in Siberia. "Hard labor, what bliss!" wrote Pasternak. At the Pecherskaya Lavra in Kiev I recently saw the gigantic panel in which some fanatical religious painter at the turn of the century had depicted Pushkin, Tolstoy, Dostoyevsky and Nekrasov as condemned sinners writhing in pain in the fires of hell. What finer company could you find than that!

With their appeals for freedom and democracy the Russian classics laid the foundations for the abolition of serfdom and, later, for the Revolution. But the Revolution began by crushing democracy and not developing it. Many were forced to leave Russia, including the leading writers Bunin, Tsvetayeva, and Khodaseyevich, the top philosopher Berdyayev, the singer Shalyapin, and the artist Chagall, to name but a few. The romantic poet Gumiliev was accused of taking part in a counter-revolutionary conspiracy and executed. The exceptionally talented poets Mayakovsky and Esenin who had sung of the Revolution's first steps committed suicide, as though they sensed the intelligentsia was about to be exterminated en masse. Gorky was surrounded by secret police agents and harassed, and there is evidence to suggest his death was caused by poisoning.

After hailing the doctrine of "socialist realism", official literature set about glorifying the party and Stalin. It was a sheer miracle that the last representatives of the old intelligentsia - Pasternak and Akhmatova - remained alive while eminent figures like the poet Mandelstam, the theater director Meyerhold, the novelist Babel and many others were being murdered. The great writers Platonov and Bulgakov were not arrested but their best works were only published after Stalin's death.

The war against Nazi Germany gave writers a rare chance to be printed and yet remain true to themselves but the Cold War afterwards put an end to all their hopes. The dictatorial decrees passed by the Communist Party's Central Committee penetrated every sphere of life, including music, art, literature and film.

After Stalin's death the situation in the arts began to alter and once again poetry became the troubadour of change. Even before Solzhenitsyn or Sakharov appeared on our social scene and a movement emerged to defend human rights, the poetry of our generation raised its voice for the first time against bureaucracy, Stalinism and anti-Semitism. Only then did there appear Dudintsev's first anti-bureaucratic novel *Not By Bread Alone* (1953) which was condemned as anti-Soviet, and Solzhenitsyn's novella *One Day In the*

Life of Ivan Denisovich, the first printed testimony to the hell of Stalin's camps. After being awarded the Nobel Prize, however, Solzhenitsyn was deported from the country.

During the so-called years of stagnation many talented people, such as writers Victor Nekrasov and Joseph Brodsky, artists Oleg Tselkov and Ernst Neizvestny, musicians Mstislav Rostropovich and Galina Vishnevskaya, and film-director Andrei Tarkovsky were forced to go abroad. Now perestroika has given their names and works back to the people. It is symbolic that Ernst Neizvestny, who now resides in the United States, is presently working on a number of monuments to the victims of Stalinism which will one day stand on the sites of former concentration camps.

Because our literary journals have started printing works that were previously outlawed, they are now more popular than ever before. (The record edition of the monthly journal *Novy Mir*, for instance, is 2,700,000). Nowhere else is so much respect shown to literature as it is in our country. Our art galleries are filled today with works by all kinds of artists - abstractionists, surrealists, and hyperrealists. Having cast off their ideological shackles, Soviet film directors are now being continually honored with awards at international festivals.

Like mushrooms forcing their way through an asphalt road surface, new theaters keep popping up. Soviet art has resolutely freed itself of the Party's ideological patronage. In the past the Party commissioned musical works and then used state funds to pay for them. Today musical works are not commissioned and they are not paid for either! Today art has got to fend for itself. After safely avoiding the Scylla of political censorship, art has now fallen into the Charybdis of commercial censorship.

After gaining the right to creative independence, art no longer receives material support from the state. Will it keep going? Will it not get commercialized? To make sure this does not happen, we shall have to remember more often what the 19th-century revolutionary Alexander Herzen once said about the tasks of Russian art: "We are not the doctors. We are the pain."

Yevgeny Yevtushenko
Peredelkino, 5 May 1990

Imagine that you have decided to travel along the borders of the Soviet Union in a train which covers 2,000 kilometers (1,200 miles) a day. Such a journey would take a whole month. The total length of the USSR's land and sea border is over 60,000 kilometers (36,000 miles).

Occupying half of Europe and one third of Asia, the Soviet Union stretches for nearly 5,000 kilometers (3,000 miles) from north to south and for approximately 10,000 kilometers (6,000 miles) from the west to the east. Its territory accounts for nearly one sixth of the earth's land surface - 22.4 million square kilometers (8.65 million sqare miles). It is easier to compare the USSR with continents than with states - it is a little smaller than Africa but larger than South America and three times larger than Australia.

There are eleven time zones within the Soviet Union's territory. When it is dawning in the east of the country, dusk is not yet falling in its west. When it is 5 a.m. on Cape Dezhnev on the Chukot peninsula, it is midnight on Lake Baikal in Siberia, and 7 p.m. the previous day in Moscow.

The USSR has borders with 14 states, which is a world record. In the west it borders on Norway, Finland, Poland, Hungary, Czechoslovakia and Rumania. In the east the Bering Straits divide the USSR from the USA, while the Sea of Japan and the narrow Straits separate the USSR from Japan. The easternmost land frontier is with North Korea.

The southern neighbors are Turkey, Iran, Afghanistan, China and Mongolia. The USSR's northern border skirts the seas of the Arctic Ocean. The sea frontiers account for approximately two-thirds of the total Soviet border - the whole of the eastern and northern borders, and almost half of the frontier in the west.

Surrounded by twelve seas: The twelve seas of three Oceans - the Atlantic, Pacific and Arctic - wash the shores of the USSR. The

seas of the Atlantic Ocean - the Black Sea, Azov and Baltic, have cut deep into the continent and come close to the vital centers of the country. Many first-class resorts are situated on the picturesque coasts of the Baltic and the Black Seas. The most famous of them are Jurmala near Riga, Yalta on the southern coast of the Crimea and Sochi on the Black Sea coast of the Caucasus.

The Barents Sea with its bay, the White Sea and the Kara, Laptev, East Siberian and Chuckchee Seas are all part of the Arctic Ocean. All lie north of the Polar Circle and are ice-clad almost all year round (only the southwestern part of the Barents Sea near the Kola peninsula coast remains free from ice, even in winter, due to the Gulf Stream). Navigation in the northern seas is possible only with the help of ice-breakers.

The Pacific makes contact with the USSR in the Far East through the Bering Sea, the Sea of Okhotsk and the Sea of Japan. In winter the greater part of these seas is covered with ice, except in the south of the Sea of Japan where big ports, Vladivostok and Nakhodka, are situated.

By all reasonable criteria, two huge lakes - Caspian and Aral - which lie deep in the Eurasian continent, should also be classed as seas - they are big and salty and are populated by marine flora and fauna. The Caspian Sea, the largest lake in the world, is rich in various breeds of sturgeon.

The Aral Sea is comparatively shallow. Surrounded by the deserts of Kazakhstan and Central Asia, it has been suffering a dreadful ecological tragedy in recent years entirely through the fault of man - it is drying up fast, and in danger of simply perishing.

Plains and plateaus: Boundless and beautiful plains stretch for thousands of kilometers all across the Soviet Union, both in Europe and Asia.

The East European (Russian) plain extends from the western borders to the Urals, and from the Arctic Ocean to the Black and Caspian Seas.

Its average height does not exceed 200 meters (656 feet) above sea level, and the hilly uplands of the Valdai, Central Russia and the Volga only reach 300-400 meters

Preceding pages: the Pamirs are amongst the world's attractions for alpinists; helicopters in Siberia often become the only means of moving around. <u>Left</u>, a young Yakutian.

(985-1,315 feet). The undulating areas of the plain alternate with nearly flat regions, while the northern part bears the traces of ancient glaciation in the forms of the gently sloping ridges, rounded uplands and lake hollows.

The Urals, which stretch for more than 2,000 kilometers (1,200 miles) from the north southward, are a chain of geologically old and comparatively low mountain ranges, separate the European part of the USSR from its Asian territories.

The immense West Siberian Plain, which is even flatter than the Russian Plain, lies beyond the Urals and extends eastward to the Yenisey river and from the coast of the Arctic Ocean in the north to the steppes of

of several immense "steps" which rise eastward. The first of them is the dissected Central Siberian Plateau fringed by the mountains of Southern and North-Eastern Siberia in the southeast.

Mountains of eternal snow: The vast territory, limited in the east by the mountains of the Pacific watershed, forms the second step, known as North-Eastern Siberia. This mainly mountainous area includes the systems of the Verkhoyansky and Kolymsky ranges. The Soviet Far East occupies a relatively narrow strip of land stretching from the northeast to the southwest. In the south of the Soviet Far East the terraces of the Sikhote Alin mountain system descend toward the

Kazakhstan in the south.

The large Turan lowland lies south of the West Siberian Plain behind the low Turgai Plateau and a vast area of hills and hollows. The Turan region occupies a greater part of Soviet Central Asia, extending from the Caspian Sea coast to the high mountains of central Asia. This area consists mainly of the vast sand deserts of Kara Kum (350,000 square kilometers or 135,000 square miles) and Kyzyl Kum (300,000 square kilometers or 160,000 square miles).

The eastern part of the Soviet Union, lying between the Yenisei and the Pacific, consists

Sea of Japan.

The mountains of the Kamchatka peninsula and the island of Sakhalin are comparatively young geologically. Among these mountains there are many extinct and active volcanoes - they number 180 in total, including about 30 active ones. Mt. Klyuchevskaya (4,750 meters or 15,580 feet) is the highest of the volcanic peaks.

Mountainous landscape is characteristic not only of Eastern Siberia and the Far East. For instance, part of the Carpathians (the part known as the Eastern or Wooded Carpathians) forms a chain of strikingly beautiful mountain ridges with an average height of 1,000-2,000 meters (3,000-6,000 feet) in the extreme west of the USSR.

A powerful mountain belt stretches for thousands of kilometers along the Soviet Union's southern border. It includes the low Crimean Mountains (up to 1,500 meters/4,500 feet) which descend to the coast of the Crimea, a peninsula in the Black Sea.

A vast mountainous area, the Caucasus, lies between the Black and Caspian Seas. The highest ridges of this system are in the Great Caucasus where Mt. Elbrus, a double-peaked extinct volcano and the highest mountain of Europe, is situated. Its western peak is 5,642 meters (18,506 feet) high, and

Communism (7,495 meters) and Mt. Lenin (7,134 meters/23,400 feet). The Pamir, like the Tien Shan, is famous for its giant glaciers which contain immense reserves of pure water - about 2,500 cubic kilometers. The longest of them (77 km/47.75 miles) is the Fedchenko glacier (1,700 meters/5,580 feet wide and the ice in its central part reaches a depth of up to 1,000 meters/3,280 feet) named after the Russian scientist Alexei Fedchenko who lived in the 19th century.

The Tien Shan is a system of high ridges crowned with such peaks as Mt. Pobeda (7,439 meters/24,400 feet) and Khan-Tengri (6,995 meters/22,945 feet) as well as vast and comparatively even highlands and large

the eastern one rises to 5,621 meters (18,437 feet). East of the Caspian Sea the mountain belt begins with the low Kopet Dagh mountain range (up to 3,117 meters/10,224 feet).

Further east the USSR's highest mountains, Pamir and Tien Shan, fringe the deserts of Central Asia. The eternally snowy peaks rise above the clouds to a height of 5,000-6,000 meters (15,000-18,000 feet) above sea level. The highest peaks in the Pamir are Mt.

depressions, in one of which lies the pearl of the Tien Shan highland Lake Issyk Kul. The mountain belt north of the Tien Shan comprises the separate mountain ranges of central Asia and the vast Altai-Sayan mountainous area. In the Altai, the high ridges alternate with the deep river valleys and mountain hollows. Near the southern bank of Lake Baikal the Sayan Mountains adjoin the ranges of the Baikal mountain system.

Half of the country under permafrost: The tundra occupies the Far North along the Arctic Ocean coast. Lying in the permafrost zone, which accounts for approximately half

Left, rich man's dacha in the Smolensk region.
Above, approaching the Pamirs.

of the USSR's territory, and on infertile land which thaws out only to a small depth in the short summer, the tundra consists mainly of moss and lichen-covered flats and areas of low-growing shrubs.

Towards the southern limit of the tundra you will usually find a belt of dwarf birch, willow and pine growing almost level with the ground. South of the tundra lies an immense zone of coniferous and mixed coniferous and broad-leaved forest. This is the taiga which occupies the northern European part of our country, Siberia and the Far East. You can fly in an aircraft for hours and see nothing but the boundless green sea of the impenetrable taiga stretching for thousands of kilometers; the Siberian taiga zone is almost equal in area to Western Europe.

Speaking about woodlands, it is worth pointing out that the USSR accounts for one-fifth of all the forests of the globe and for one quarter of world timber resources. The woodlands stretch across the entire Soviet Union from the Baltic Sea to Kamchatka and occupy one third of the country. The taiga accounts for a major part of the total.

Country of 3 million rivers: The rivers dissect the country's territory like strings of pearls. There are about 3 million large and small rivers with a total length of 9.6 million kilometers (5.95 million miles). Roughly 200 big rivers are more than 500 kilometers (300 miles) long. Some of them, like the Ob in Siberia, flow on the plains and are slow. Others, like the Angara which falls into Lake Baikal - the deepest pure-water lake on the globe and famed worldwide for its crystal clean water boil down the rapids. The Kolyma in the north is ice-clad for eight months a year, while the Rioni in warm Georgia does not freeze at all.

The main rivers of the European part of the USSR originate in the center of the East European Plain and flow in different directions towards the seas. The Dnieper falls into the Black Sea, the Don into the Azov Sea, the Western Dvina into the Baltic Sea, the Northern Dvina into the White Sea, and the Pechora into the Barents Sea. The beautiful Volga, the largest river in Europe, falls into the Caspian Sea. The Volga and its tributaries account for about half of the USSR's total river cargo transportation.

The main rivers of Siberia flow from the south northward. Their list includes the Ob -

the longest river in the USSR (5,410 km/ 3,360 miles), the Lena (4,264 km/2,650 miles) and the Yenisei (3,6053 km/2,2240 miles). The rivers of Central Asia do not reach the ocean. The two largest of them - the Amu Darya (2,600 km/1,615 miles) and the Syr Darya (2,991 km/1,855 miles) - terminate in the drying up Aral Sea.

There is a city in the USSR which is called a "port of five seas", even though it is situated about 1,000 kilometers (620 miles) from the nearest sea coast: this city is Moscow, the country's capital. A network of man-made canals, the best-known being the Moskva-Volga and Volga-Don canals, has unified the rivers of the European part of the USSR into a deep-water transport system which links Moscow with the White, Baltic, Caspian, Black and Azov Seas. It goes without saying that this multiple canal system is of great economic importance, but it also gives those who love to travel a unique chance to make captivating river journeys from Moscow to Leningrad or even to Astrakhan lying in the mouth of the Volga.

From subzero to tropical heat: The climate of the Soviet Union varies. In Siberia there are places where it is colder in winter than at the North Pole, and in some areas of Central Asia it is hotter in summer than on the Equator. Frosts of minus 70°C (183°F below zero) occur in Yakutia, where steam from breath gets frozen in the air. In Turkmenia the temperature of the scorched sand in the sun reaches up to 70°C (158°F) and burns your feet if they touch the ground.

When they start harvesting barley in Uzbekistan, the houses in Petropavlovsk-Kamchatsky are already under deep snow from blizzards. While it takes a larch-tree one hundred years to become a little thicker than a ski stick in the same region, a young bamboo grows by more than one meter a day in subtropical Adzharia.

During the same season you can find yourself in the dark of the polar night or have a rest on the coast of an unfreezing southern sea. On the whole, the climate of the country may be characterized as moderate and continental with large fluctuations of temperature between winter and summer.

Areas with a subtropical climate lie only in the south, in the regions sheltered by mountains from the north (the Caucasian coast, the southern coast of the Crimea, and the Central-Asian valleys). It is very seldom cold there. Early spring flowers appear almost immediately after the autumn ones. Violets blossom at Christmas. Snow sometimes covers them, but only for a very short time.

The sable, the seal and the lynx: The USSR has a diverse fauna. The walrus, the seal, the polar bear, the polar fox, and the reindeer live in the north. Two flocks of fur-seals out of only three left in the world have their breeding grounds on the islands in the northern Pacific.

The forest zone is home to the brown bear (widely used as a symbol of Russia), the wolf, the red fox, the lynx, the sable, the ermine, the elk, the roe deer and the wild boar;

them 250 caught on a commercial scale, live in the lakes, rivers and seas.

Ores galore: The USSR is very rich in minerals. It leads the world in reserves of coal, iron and manganese ores, natural gas, apatite, asbestos and many other minerals.

The known reserves of iron ore make up 40 percent of the world total. Most of the deposits are situated in the Krivoi Rog and Kursk basins in the European part of the USSR. Rich iron ore deposits also exist in the Urals, Kazakhstan and Eastern Siberia.

Manganese ore deposits are located mainly in Georgia and the Ukraine, and non-ferrous metals in Kazakhstan and the Urals.

The Soviet Union accounts for more than

the Far East has tigers and leopards; the southern steppes and deserts are home to the saiga, the dzheiran antelope and the hyena; in the Caucasus there are wild sheep and the Caucasian tur while the mountainous areas of Central Asia are home to the mountain sheep, the red wolf, the markhor and the snow leopard. The red squirrel, the musk rat, the polar fox and the sable (its fur is famous worldwide) are the main animals hunted for their fur. About 1,500 fish breeds, among

Hour of dusk in Tobolsk, Siberia.

half of the world reserves of phosphorites and two-thirds of potassium salt. The Ural mountains are rich in emeralds, rubies, malachite, jasper and other precious and semi-precious stones. In the USSR there are also gold and diamond deposits, mainly in Eastern Siberia.

The major deposits of oil and natural gas are situated in Western Siberia, the Volga area, the Urals, the Caucasus and Central Asia; coal in the Ukraine, Kazakhstan, Western Siberia and Yakutia, and oil shales in the western areas of our country. Turf can be turned out on vast territories.

СОБРАЗ ВЕЛИКАГО
ГДРА ЦРА И ВЕЛИКАГО
КНЗА АЛЕѮ҃ВА МIХАИЛОВIЧА
ВСЕА ВЕЛIКIА IМАЛВА
IБѢЛВА РОСÏI САМОДЕРЦА.

A TIMELESS BRIDGE BETWEEN
ASIA AND EUROPE

"Russia's past was good for nothing, its present is vain and it has no future." This maxim by Russian philosopher Pyotr Chaadayev has been contradicted by statesman Alexander Benkendorf who lived at the same time: "Russia's past was miraculous and its present is more than marvelous, as for the future, it's beyond the limits of the boldest imagination." Between these two extreme viewpoints, expressed more than 150 years ago, there is a whole gamut of opinions of the Soviet Union.

Most history books about the Soviet Union start with an account of the state of Urartu which ceased to exist back in the 6th century B.C. It couldn't have been otherwise, since the USSR is not only the world's biggest country, occupying one-sixth of the planet's dry land, and one of the most populous countries (nearly 300 million inhabitants), it is also one of the most multiethnic states on the globe: more than 100 nations and nationalities live in its 15 Union and 20 Autonomous republics, 8 autonomous regions and 10 autonomous areas, 128 territories and regions. Most of these nations have become part of what is today the USSR relatively recently (in the 18th and 19th centuries and some of them only several decades ago). Before that they had had a history of their own in no way associated with Russia.

Therefore we will dwell here only briefly on facts and events which took place from the Palaeolithic to the 9th century across the entire territory currently occupied by the USSR. Then we will turn to a description of Russian history, from Kievan Rus to the Muscovite state, and from the Russian empire to the Union of Soviet Socialist Republics. More detailed accounts of the history of Central Asia, the Caucasus, the Ukraine, the Baltic states and so on, will be found in the respective chapters following this historic outline.

Man first came to the territory of the USSR, in its present boundaries, from the south way back in the early Palaeolithic, or

about 700,000 years ago. Archaeologists have discovered traces of ancient peoples in the Crimea (the Kiik-Koba cave), Abkhazia (the Yashtuk settlement), in Central Asia (southern Kazakhstan and the environs of Tashkent). Traces of our ancestors who lived 500,000 or 300,000 years ago were found in the Ukraine, not far from Zhitomir and on the Dniester river. In the Mesolithic (the 10th to 8th millennia) people lived all across Eurasia. Moving northwards man reached the coasts of the Baltic Sea and the Glacial Ocean. Many researchers believe it was at that time that people found their way from Siberia to America through the Chukot peninsula.

Legendary Urartu: Urartu, already mentioned, is the most ancient state on Soviet territory. It emerged as an organized state in the 9th century B.C. on the Armenian plateau (in the vicinity of Mountain Ararat and Lake Van) when eight local tribes formed a union in the face of a threat from neighboring Assyria. Urartu was an oriental kingdom headed by a despot who, together with his courtiers owned the entire land; the priests were also very influential. The working population comprised slaves and commoners. Metal production and foreign trade flourished (the route from India to the Mediterranean passed through Urartu). The country engaged successfully in numerous wars. In one year alone, for instance, they captured 46,000 women prisoners and 2,500 horses. Then, around 590 B.C., Urartu was destroyed by neighboring Midia.

A 70 km-long (43 miles) canal, which used to provide water for the city of Tushpu, is the only physical evidence of that ancient state. The canal, however, is still operable.

In the middle of the 1st millennium B.C. small slave-owning states emerged in Transcaucasia, of which Kolkhida (West Georgia), Iberia (East Georgia), "The Land of Flame" Albania (Azerbaijan) - and the Armenian kingdom were the most influential. They had ceased to exist by the beginning of the first century A.D., since some of them had been conquered by the Roman Empire and others were annexed by the Persian monarchy.

Cities along the Silk Road: For quite a long time Persia had tried to conquer the rich states of Central Asia, Khorezm (on the lower reaches of the Amu-Darya), Sogdiana (on the Zeravshan) and Baktria (on the upper reaches if the Amu-Darya). These states possessed extensive artificial irrigation networks and, therefore, highly developed cotton-growing and silkworm-breeding enterprises. The Great Silk Road, which linked India, China and the Mediterranean, cut through those states. In the 6th century B.C. the Persians managed to invade Central Asia; in the 4th century B.C., however, Persia itself was conquered by Alexander the Great. Subsequently the Central Asian states

The Rus: According to ancient Russian chronicles the Russian state took shape in the 9th century. At that time the northern part of the vast territory which is called Russia today was covered by dense forests, lakes and marshes, whereas vast grass-covered steppe lands stretched to the south. The total population of that area was then a mere 1,000,000. The majority of the population comprised various Eastern Slav tribes, predecessors of the modern Russians, Ukrainians and Byelorussians. They lived on the banks of the Dnieper, West Dvina, the upper reaches of the Volga and Lake Ilmen. Further to the east and north was the home of Finno-Ugrian tribes, considered to be the common ances-

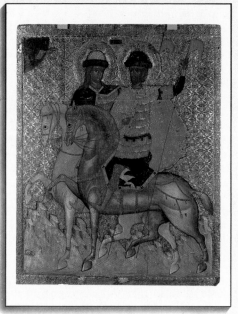

were at different times and to different extents dominated by the Greeko-Baktrian state, the Parthian kingdom and the Kushana Empire.

In the north of the Black Sea zone a powerful Scythian kingdom emerged in the 3rd century B.C. According to Herodotes, Scythians were growing the best wheat in the world. Greek-style slave-owning republics along the Black Sea coast served as middlemen in Scythians' wheat trade. The best known of the republics were Olvia (near Nikolaev), Chersonesus (Sevastopol), Pitius (Pitsunda) and Dioscuriada (Sukhumi).

tors of such different peoples as the Hungarians, Estonians, Mordovians and Finns. To the south-east of the Slavs there lived various Turkic tribes, Khazars, Pechenegs, Volgan Bulgarians. Lastly, the northwest part of the Slavonic lands was the home of the Lithuanian tribe.

Traditionally Slavs lead a settled life and engaged primarily in tilling the land. They almost had no use for iron and practically everything they used was made of wood. They were brave warriors ready to fight to their last. But they did not like to fight in the open, preferring to overpower the enemy by stealth. They used to lure their enemies into the forest and then attack them by surprise. Extremely cruel in war, the Slavs were gentle and hospitable in peace time.

Rurik, Oleg and Prince Igor: According to the ancient chronicles, the Russian state was formed in 862 in Novgorod, where the residents asked the legendary Rurik, a Varangian Rus, to come and rule them. His younger relative and successor Oleg extended his power and ruled over all the Slav lands from Novgorod to Kiev. Under his rule Kiev became the capital city of the principality. From that city Oleg and his heir Prince Igor led successful wars with the Greeks; when he nearly seized Constantinople.

such as present-day Tartu in Estonia and Yaroslavl on the Volga. He also put an end to raids by the steppe nomads of the south and waged successful wars on the Lithuanians and Finns.

By the end of his life, Yaroslav's dominion stretched from Lake Ladoga in the north to the middle reaches of the Dnieper in the south, and from the Oka river in the east to the Western Bug in the west. After his death, however, Rus gradually split into several principalities.

The Tatar invasion: The situation changed drastically in the second half of the 13th century with the onset of the so-called Tatar yoke. The Tatar-Mongols were nomads in-

The next landmark in Russian history is the year 988, when Prince Vladimir introduced the Christian faith to Russia and Greek priests baptized the entire population of Kiev almost overnight in the Dnieper river. The heyday of Kievan Rus was in the 11th century under Yaroslav the Wise who was anxious to promote Christianity and did much to shape the state. He set up settlements in the empty expanses and built frontier cities,

Far left, Rublyov's Holy Trinity icon; **left**, Boris and Gleb. **Above**, Peter the Great interrogating the Czarevich Alexei.

habiting the steppes of Northern Asia. In the early 13th century Jenghiz Khan managed to form a powerful empire by uniting numerous Asian tribes. In 1223 Jenghiz Khan's hordes won their first battle over the Russian dukes and their allies on the river Kalka, which falls into the Sea of Azov, but subsequently retired again to the steppes in the east.

It was not until fifteen years later that the Tatars reappeared in Rus, this time headed by the Mongol Batu. They devastated the northeast of Russia, seized and burned down Kiev and headed further towards the Adriatic Sea. The death of their leader stopped the

Tatars' advance and made them return to the Asian steppes in the lower reaches of the Volga, near present-day Astrakhan, where a new capital of the Tatar khanate (the Golden Horde) emerged.

The Horde's political and financial domination of Rus lasted for more than two centuries. It was the Khan who nominated the Grand Duke, distributed lands among lesser dukes as he saw fit, settled their disputes and collected tribute. However, the Tatars did not interfere in the internal affairs of Rus as long as they were settled peacefully; they were also very tolerant of Christianity. That is why historians' attitudes to the consequences of the Tatar yoke differ: some of

them blame Tatar domination for slavery and the isolation of Rus from the rest of Western civilization; others believe that it was due to the Tatars' efficient and centralized government that the Russian dukedoms did not collapse but instead united to form a powerful centralized state which eventually refused the Tatar tribute, conquered the Tatars and rightly became heirs to this largest Eurasian empire.

Ivan the Terrible: Russia's independence and power were restored under Rurik's 20th generation descendant, Ivan IV, the Terrible. He was born in 1530 in Moscow, which by

that time had become Russia's principle city since, two centuries earlier, Kiev and western Russia had been annexed by Poland. This cruel and ambitious statesman managed to turn Russia into a great power. At the age of 17 this son of Grand Duke Basil of Moscow demanded to be crowned as czar and later conquered the Tatar khanates and annexed their territory.

However, he was equally cruel in respect of Novgorod and Pskov, which were still independent at that time. He also captured a considerable part of the Baltic areas as a result of different successful campaigns against Swedes in the north-west and Poles in the west, whereas in the east he annexed almost the whole of Siberia.

His reforms inside the country were as grandiose as they were ruthless. The feudal system with its multi-level vassal hierarchy was replaced by direct and strictly centralized subordination of subjects to the monarch and his associates. A balanced paternalistic system was set up in the country, with on one hand the czar-father and, on the other, the rest of the population who were considered (and considered themselves) small and silly children who needed to be told what they were to do, what they were to think. It has to be added that Ivan the Terrible was an unorthodox man as far as his private life was concerned: a philosopher who owned the richest library in the country, a syphilitic who married eight times, and a paranoiac who killed with his own hands his elder son and a great number of his courtsmen.

Time of Troubles: As often happens in history, after the death of such a powerful ruler the pendulum swung in the opposite direction and Russia plunged for four centuries into the "Time of Troubles". The inefficient rule of Theodore, Ivan the Terrible's weak and childless son, and the mysterious death of Ivan's youngest son Demetrius, when still a child in 1591, put an end to the 700-year-old Rurik dynasty. Popular unrest, famine, and the Polish invasion in the west, headed by a "Pseudo-Demetrius", facilitated the rise to power of Boris Godunov, a clever but unfortunate statesman.

His untimely death in 1605, the murder of his son (who was slain by a mutinying mob), the Swedish occupation of the north of the country and the Poles' entry in Moscow all made Russia's collapse seem inevitable.

The coming of the Romanovs: In 1613 Michael Romanov, a distant relative of Ivan the Terrible, was elected czar at the age of 16 and thus founded the Romanov Dynasty which ruled the country until 1917. Michael's son, Alexius, who ruled from 1645 to 1676 did much for the country (for instance he returned the Ukraine to Russia), but his achievements were eclipsed by the rule of his youngest son Peter who lived 1672-1725, the first Russian sovereign to accept the title "Emperor" and known to history as Peter I the Great.

Peter the Great: He was indeed a great reformer of Russia who tried to take his country out of isolation and give it, albeit only outwardly, a Western civilization. Regrettably his ways were those of a despot and to quote Karl Marx "for once he used barbarous methods to eradicate barbarism." Over six feet tall, Peter the Great assumed the regency still as a child. However he did not bother himself with state affairs and cared little about etiquette; instead he surrounded himself with foreigners and devoted all his energy, zeal and far-from-common abilities to forming a regular army as well as a navy which Russia had not had before. But his dream of creating a navy was not easy to achieve since at that time Russia owned only the White Sea in the extreme North. Therefore in 1695 he started a campaign in the southern direction in an attempt to take the Black Sea from Turkey.

Initially the war was quite successful and the Russians managed to seize the Sea of Azov, but later it became evident that the forces were unequal and enterprising Peter decided to travel abroad incognito to see for himself all that, in his opinion, Russia needed: fortresses and factories, wharves and banks, schools and libraries.

Opening a window to the west: Peter returned home, after his 18-month travels, in 1698 and immediately set about trying to reform Russia. These were primarily reforms to the original Russian way of life: the czar ordered his court to wear short robes instead of long caftans and by decree he forbade all his subjects, except peasants and priests, to grow beards.

He also forbade parents to arrange marriages for their children and introduced assemblies, or parties, with attendance obligatory for all, even for married women. He

<u>Left</u>, the first wife of Peter the Great, who suffered in custody. <u>Above</u>: <u>left</u>, Catherine I – founder of a female rule; <u>right</u>, Catherine II – the correspondent of Voltaire.

opened schools and printing houses, streamlined the alphabet, introduced the European calendar and started a newspaper. He also sent young people abroad annually as students and apprentices.

In 1700 he declared war on Sweden to gain access to the Baltic Sea which Russia lost during the Time of Troubles. The war lasted for more than twenty years and was eventually won by Russia. On the coast of the Gulf of Finland Peter founded Russia's new capital, St. Petersburg (now Leningrad) built in West European fashion, all of stone. After the signing of the peace treaty with Sweden he accepted the title "Emperor of All Russia". Immediately the Northern War ended, Peter to carry out a military reform, to introduce draft for the peasants and compulsory military service for the nobility. War required money and this entailed a tax reform and various changes in the status of the cities and peasantry. The soldiers needed arms and plants, factories and manufactures started mushrooming. The need for imports led to the rise of the merchants. On the other hand, in his effort to overhaul the social structure and forms of administration Peter left intact the very foundations of the state order.

Under his rule the supreme power of the monarch remained as strong as ever. The serfdom increased and the nobility got new duties with no new rights, the government

Peter started a campaign against Persia and in 1723 the latter ceded to Russia the western coast of the Caspian Sea (present-day Azerbaijan). This opened up a road to the east, to India, which interested Peter greatly. But his plans were never to come to fruition: the emperor died in 1725 before he turned 54.

It would be wrong to assume that in his reformatory endeavor Peter replaced the old Muscovite set-up by the new European order according to a single master plan. All his reforms, be it in the administration or in the social composition of Russia, were necessitated by military developments and needs. War required regular troops and this induced became more centralized, but at the same time more bureaucratic. In a word, Peter effected no revolution and all of his reforms were aimed at perfecting the old order but making it more cultured and European. The only radical reform he carried out was in the sphere of religion. He abolished the patriarchate and thus subordinated the church to the state.

A century of female rule: The 18th century was that of feminine regency in Russia, for 71 years after Peter's sudden death men were on the throne only for four years. First it was Peter's last wife Catherine I (1725-27), a woman of a most obscure origin. She was succeeded by infant emperor Peter II, Peter the Great's grand son (1727-30), whose father had been executed by Peter I for disapproval of his reforms. There was no direct heir and in 1730 Anne, Peter the Great's niece, a widow, was offered the throne on the condition that she curtailed the powers of the monarch. She agreed, however as soon as she was crowned she tore up the "conditions" she was given to sign. The subsequent decade was then marked by her capricious and whimsical character, which was in addition largely influenced by profit-seeking and cunning courtiers of foreign descent. In 1740 Anne's nephew, the baby Ivan VI became emperor, but after a few months he was

strength for the future epoch of great conquests and reforms.

Glorious times: The glorious time came in 1762 after Catherine II, the daughter of an insignificant German ruler, overthrew her husband Peter III, who had been enthroned only a year earlier, and started her 34-year-long reign which brought her the name "Great". She was keenly pursuing Peter the Great's reforms though in a less radical way. She had none of Peter's ruthless straight-forwardness, her ways were mild and charming. Incidentally, there was no need for ruthlessness anymore since people became increasingly aware of the need for reforms. Like Peter the Great, Catherine II was good

overthrown and Peter the Great's daughter Elizabeth was enthroned. The first thing she did was to order all dishonest foreigners banished. She also opened the first Russian university in Moscow, instituted credit banks, abolished internal customs and adjusted the nobles' rights and duties. Elizabeth's calm and popular reign went down in history as a time when Russian society, free from the former provisional rulers, could pull up

Left, religious revival at Optina Pustyn monastery. **Above: left**, Peter the third; **right**, Marshal Kutuzov, who defeated Napoleon.

at picking up assistants and perfect executives. First of all she made efforts to turn Russia into a state ruled by laws, which was especially needed in the provinces where all sorts of abuses were widely practiced due to the lack of control on part of the central government. To this end Russia was divided into 50 provinces *(gubernias)* which in their turn broke down into districts *(uyezdy)*. Each province was to have special administrative institutions, "province administrations" for general supervision and "administrative offices" to oversee industry and construction, judicial bodies were separated from government, and many offices in the above institu-

tions were made elective.

1775 saw the suppression of a large-scale peasant revolt under Pugachev who called himself "Peter III who had escaped death". State-owned surfs appeared in the country and the situation of the privately owned surfs was a little alleviated. "If you want to prevent crime, enlighten the people." To back up these words of hers, Catherine opened dozens of various educational establishments, including some for girls. Many new writers emerged, hundreds of books were printed and magazines were put out. The empress herself was in regular correspondence with Voltaire, Diderot, Baron Friederich von Grimm and other European celebrities; she wrote fairy-tales and comedies, personally drafted laws and patronized art and architecture, theater and opera.

In 1768 Russia started another war on Turkey, its deadly enemy, and three years later won partial possession of the coasts of the Black Sea and the Sea of Azov. Prince Potemkin, Catherine's favorite and advisor for most of her reign, became Governor General of the conquered territories, named Novorossia. Thanks to Potemkin's efforts in 1783 Russia peacefully annexed the Crimea, the last independent Tartar khanate.

Intensive development of the new lands was started: settlers (including Germans) came to the place and peasants resettled from the inland provinces to engage in farming, cattle and silk-worm breeding, wine-making, urban development and in extensive road construction.

In 1787 the Russian soldiers under the brilliant Alexander Suvorov took from Turkey vast lands to the north-west of the Black Sea. As for Poland, another of Russia's long-standing enemies, it was divided between Prussia, Austria and Russia in three stages in 1772-95.

Catherine the Great's son and successor, Paul, mounted the throne in 1796. Barely sane, he had bitter feelings of having been neglected by his mother. His ill-balanced mind and tyrannical proclivities prevented him from playing the role of the "Knight without Fear and without Reproach", that he had taken upon himself; instead he inspired

Left, Russia's dearly loved poet Alexander Pushkin who died in a duel.

dissent in his associates. In 1801 Paul was assassinated by court conspirators. He was succeeded by his son Alexander I who could never forgive himself that his father had been removed from the throne with his tacit consent and felt guilty for his death.

The reign of Alexander I: Alexander had received a careful education at the hand of his grandmother Catherine II who invited F.C. de la Harp, the future President of Switzerland, to be her grandson's tutor. Sentimental and dreamy, Alexander even when very young wanted to reform the entire government, abolish serfdom and make his charges happy. His dreams never came true, though he did a lot of good. He abolished tortures and corporal punishment, encouraged landowners to liberate their serfs, instituted a number of grammar schools and provincial colleges, as well as three universities. He also introduced ministries to oversee the most important sectors of state government and a council of state to draft new laws. Although Alexander himself was a peaceable person, a considerable part of his reign was marked by wars which were mainly waged against Napoleon.

Napoleon's invasion: Initially Russia was involved in wars beyond its national confines as part of the anti-Napoleon coalition. Then, in the summer of 1812, Napoleon gathered soldiers of all the conquered nations under his colors and attacked Russia with a 700,000-strong army. Pulling up forces for a rebuff, the Russians waged a war of retreat, whereby they were luring the enemy deep inside the country where they occasionally went on harassing them. In the invaders' opinion the local population were guilty of "uncivilized" behavior: as soon as they saw the French they hurried away, burning their houses and all they could not take away with them.

All the way to Moscow the French saw nothing but deserted villages, and were greeted by guerrilla strikes rather than the welcome they expected. The Russian troops in the meantime were spoiling for a fight and even began to suspect Prince M. Barclay de Tolly, the commander-in-chief with a foreign background, of high treason.

Alexander I named Prince Mikhail Golenishchev-Kutuzov, an ethnic Russian, in his place, but he too proceeded with the retreat, which was more advantageous to the Russians. On August 26, 1812, after the bloody but undecided battle at Borodino (a hundred kilometers or 62 miles off Moscow), the Russian army retreated beyond the capital, which surrendered to Napoleon.

Napoleon in Moscow: Having entered the city, Napoleon waited in vain for a ceremonial peace proposal. The inhabitants of Moscow burnt the city and fled. The French army had been running out of food, local peasants avoided any contact with the invaders, food supplies from Europe had been disrupted, there was no place for billeting French troops, the roads to the south had been effectively cut off by the Russian army and the desperate Napoleon faced no other option

manner that everyone should own what he had owned before Napoleon started his devastating wars. But Russia added Polish territory to its domains, which had hitherto belonged to Prussia. It would be in place to mention here that several years before Russia had also annexed Finland (from Sweden in 1809) and Bessarabia (from Turkey in the year 1812).

The Decembrist's Revolt: Alexander I, known as the "Blessed", died in 1825, leaving behind no children to ascend to the throne. Everybody expected Constantine, the elder of Alexander's surviving brothers, to ascend to the throne, but he would not accept. Instead Alexander was succeeded by

but to turn back to the west following the road devastated by the French army only a few months before. The French strength was on the wane due to hunger, cold and annoying attacks by Russian hit and run squads. As a result, barely a tenth part of Napoleon's grand army survived the ordeal.

But Alexander I was not content with having driven Napoleon out of Russia and decided to rid the other invaded nations of the French as well. He brilliantly accomplished this mission, and in 1814 Russian troops entered Paris.

The European monarchs then convened at the Congress of Vienna to rule in a noble

his junior brother, Nicholas I. A group of radical young officers, dreaming about a constitutional monarchy or even a republic, decided to exploit the uncertainty surrounding the succession, to their own advantage. In late 1825 the Decembrists, as they were later called, encouraged the guard regiments in Petersburg to revolt in favor of Constantine, against Nicholas, but they were crushed by loyal troops, having failed to enlist popular support. (Many soldiers whom the Decembrists led to the central square to demand "a constitution" thought it was the name of Constantine's wife).

Nicholas I, a tough ruler who stuck rigidly

by the bureaucratic forms of government, tried to halt social and political development at home and also in relations with other countries for which he was rightly dubbed "the policeman of Europe". After a series of successful wars with Persia and Turkey he annexed almost the entire Caucasus and rid Greece of Turkish domination. But he suffered a military and political fiasco in the 1853-56 Crimean War in which Russia had to fight against a Turkish-Anglo-French coalition. The concluding stage of the war coincided with Nicholas' death, and his son Alexander II, after ascension to the throne, embarked on a series of major political reforms which led to a drastic renewal of

opened the way to people of all classes to independent local government in both rural and urban areas.

A third capital reform concerned the law courts. In 1864, Russia established the same system of open court proceedings that had already existed in all European countries. In 1874 new conscription rules were introduced. Active service was reduced from 25 to 16 years and military service was made obligatory for all classes, not just for the serfs.

Acquisitions and annexations: The reign of Alexander II was also marked by a number of annexations. First of all he finished invading the Caucasus. (The earlier Russian ap-

Russian life and earned him the title of the "Liberator".

The emancipation of the serfs: One of the chief reforms accomplished by Alexander II was the emancipation of the serfs. What also earned him the glory of a liberator was the 1864-70 introduction of the district and provincial *zemstva* (county councils) which

Far left, Cap of Monomakh – tzars' crown preserved since 13th-14th centuries; **left**, Triumphal Arch in Moscow – commemoration of victory over Napoleon. **Above**, the battle off Chesme during Russian-Turkish war, 25-26 June 1770.

propriation there was Georgia, which volunteered to join Russia way back in 1801.) Far more important were Alexander II's acquisitions in Central Asia. Thus, the Russian Empire swelled as it was joined by the vast Turkestan Region and its chief city of Tashkent, the Khiva Khanate and other lands on the banks of the Amu-Darya, and also some territories on the eastern coast of the Caspian Sea. The latter became almost entirely a Russian sea.

The Russian army won special accolades in the 1877-78 Turkish war, in which Russia stood up, as she had done repeatedly before, for Orthodox Christians mercilessly oppressed by the Turks.

Having been defeated in every field, Turkey was forced to conclude a humiliating peace agreement on the following terms: Rumania, Serbia and Chernogoria, the Christian states hitherto under the supreme authority of the Sultan, were to become entirely independent; the Slav lands to the north of the Balkans would be united in the newly-established Bulgarian Principality; other Slav-populated lands were to be given a fairer treatment by Turkey; and, finally, Russia would receive some of the formerly Turkish domains in Asia, including those of the Kars and Batum.

The more or less peaceful development of railway line, the longest in the world, which linked European Russia with her far outlying domains in the east.

The early years of the reign of Nicholas II, the son of Alexander III and the last Russian Emperor, were interrupted by the outbreak of the 1904-1905 Russian-Japanese war which Russia lost in disgrace. The catastrophe added weight to the political and ideological destabilization that had long been accumulating in different groups of society.

Years of turmoil and revolution: The tragic inability of the government in general, and of Emperor Nicholas II in particular, to respond adequately to political crises was increasingly evident.

Russian society in the third quarter of the 19th century was brought to an abrupt halt by the assassination of Alexander II.

His successor for the next 13 years was his son, Alexander III, whom some called a peace-maker, others a quiet drunk and stay-at-home, still others, who opposed him, called him the creator of stagnation and political reaction.

Despite the reputation of the Czar, Russia expanded her Asian domains in Central Asia and in the Far East near the Pacific under the reign of Alexander III. Those days also witnessed the building of the Trans-Siberian

These and a multitude of other factors led to the outbreak of the First Russian Revolution whose starting point is associated with the "Bloody Sunday". On that decisive day, troops shot at a peaceful demonstration of workers and their family members who had gathered in front of the Winter Palace in Petersburg to see the Czar, and killed many of them.

Above, members of the 19th-century terrorist group, "The Will of the People." **Right**, the last Russian Czar Nicholai II.

THE ASSASSINATION OF THE ROMANOVS

by Gely Ryabov

It happened in Yekaterinburg on the night of July 16, 1918, in a house which once belonged to Ipatyev. In a basement room eleven guards shot seven members of the Czar's family along with four of their most loyal servants. The victims included six women and a 14-year-old boy. The room was rather small, about one square meter per person - much less than a grave. It was a veritable massacre. Why were they killed? What for? Over seventy years have passed since those tragic days and emotions have calmed down. But have they really calmed down?

*"What if I could enter
that room again,
To stand against that
wall and stop the bullets.
But the bonds of time
are broken and
I can't go there.
I'm covered with dry
blood and can't wash it
away."*

No, the tragedy of those distant days still bothers the peoples' conscience. For a long time the details of the assassination interested the investigators only to obtain facts which would make it possible to find the bodies of the Romanovs - the former Emperor Nikolai Alexandrovich, his wife Alexandra Fyodorovna, their son Alexei, their daughters Tatyana, Anastasia, Olga and Maria, and their servants. However, for 70 years I have been intrigued by many other things as well; for example by the question who actually ordered the assassination of the Romanovs?

Historians insist that this order was issued by the Urals Council. But I am confident that this statement is erroneous. I have in my possession a note written by Yakov Yurovsky, who was in charge of the special house in Yekaterinburg, which I got from Yurovsky's son, Alexander. This is what it says: "Reminiscences of the officer in charge of the special house in Yekaterinburg, Yakov Mikhailovich Yurovsky, Party member since 1905, about the execution of Czar Nicholas II and his family."

"On July 16 I received a coded telegram from

Perm with an order to exterminate the Romanovs. At 6 p.m on July 16, Filipp Goloshchokin issued the command to execute the order." That was when Yurovsky said to the Czar: "Nikolai Alexandrovich, your relatives tried to save you, but failed. So we have to shoot you."

Outwardly, everything seems clear: the Romanovs were executed upon the order of the Urals Council. But was this really the case? First, nobody has ever seen the original of the Urals Council's message which contained the order to execute the Czar's family.

Why was it not preserved along with all the other documents from this house - as was the "correspondence" between Nicholas II and imaginary "plotters" and the log in which all the events in Ipatyev's house were registered?

Yekaterinburg officials reported the execution to Moscow and were worried about the reaction from the center, especially from Yakov Sverdlov, Chairman of the All-Russia Central Executive Committee. If the Urals Council was acting on its own initiative, what was the reason for coordinating with Moscow the text of the report about the execution? Sverdlov received the following coded telegram from Yekaterinburg: "Tell Sverdlov that the whole family met with the same fate as its head." The official version: "The family perished during evacuation." I firmly believe that the decision to execute the Romanovs was taken neither in Yekaterinburg nor by the Urals Council.

After many years of research I have found irrefutable proof that the eleven people shot in the basement of Ipatyev's house were not thrown into a mine pit, as was previously suspected. It took a long search and finally in 1979 I found the place of their actual burial. Their skulls, however, remain in a swamp.

More than 70 years have passed since this murder and it could have been forgotten, except that the people killed were not only the Czar and his wife; their innocent son and four daughters were also murdered. It is in the Christian tradition of Russia to bury all those who were innocently killed. God permit that it will be properly done.

The Russian Revolution

Strikes, acts of terrorism, executions and shootings, seizures of landowners' lands, pogroms, acts of civil disobedience and many other similar forms of political struggle did not stop even after the Czar mercifully gave his country the Constitution of October 17, which envisaged the institution of the Duma (Parliament) with limited authority. The prerogative of forming the government was still reserved for the Czar.

The demise of the First Russian Revolution was followed by the onslaught of reactionary policies and frenzied attempts by Prime Minister Pyotr Stolypin and his supporters to keep the unruly nation on a leash. The increasing political awareness of the masses and growing influence of the Duma were effectively brought to an end by the outbreak of World War I.

The war years were marked by defeats on the front, immense loss of human lives, economic dislocation and the total inability of the government to keep control of law and order in the country. In addition, the Royal family was discredited by Grigori Rasputin, who exerted increasing influence on Nicholas II and his wife Alexandra. Trouble-making by radical political parties and growing left-wing tendencies among the multi-million body of the Russian peasants, who stopped trusting blindly in the sanctity and infallibility of the Russian Sovereign, led to a logical end - the Second Russian Revolution of February and March 1917.

The Bolshevik Revolution: In the following account of the 1917 events, all dates are given according to the old Russian calendar which differed by 13 days from the western calendar adopted in 1918. The revolution of October 25 according to the old calendar bears the name of the October Revolution, although it took place on November 7 according to the western calendar. The collapsed monarchy was replaced by a diarchy, with the powers shared between the Provisional Government and the Councils of Worker-Soldier-Peasant Deputies.

This delicate balance survived till the fall of 1917 when the Bolsheviks, led by Vladimir Lenin, (just back from emigration) won a majority in the Petrograd Soviet chaired by

Leo Trotsky, Lenin's closest associate. A secret meeting of the Party Central Committee held on October 10, 1917, endorsed an armed uprising, and on October 24, Lenin, in a letter to the Central Committee, demanded firm action against the Provisional Government, insisting that a further delay would be lethal. In the evening of October 24, Lenin arrived in the Smolny Institute, the rebel headquarters in Petrograd (modern Leningrad), to preside over the revolt.

On the night of October 24-25, the revolutionary detachments of workers and soldiers seized the central telephone exchange, the post office, the Baltic and Nikolayevsky railway stations, the municipal council and

other key facilities. The counter-revolutionaries still controlled the city center. As the revolutionary guards advanced, the Provisional Government was finally besieged in the Winter Palace. On the morning of October 25, the revolutionary uprising in Petrograd came to an end and the powers of government passed into the hands of the Petrograd Revolutionary Military Committee.

"To the Citizens of Russia": On the same day, the Revolutionary Military Committee published an appeal *"To the Citizens of Russia!"* drafted by Lenin. It said: "The Provisional Government has been deposed. State power has passed into the hands of the organ of the Petrograd Soviet of Workers' and Soldiers' Deputies - the Revolutionary Military Committee, which heads the Petrograd proletariat and the garrison. The cause for which the people have fought, namely, the immediate offer of a democratic peace, the abolition of landed proprietorship, workers' control over production, and the establishment of Soviet power - this cause has been secured".

At noon, the remaining pockets of resistance were crushed and the last stronghold, the Winter Palace, surrendered on the night of October 25 and 26. In the evening of October 25, when the revolutionary troops were still storming the Winter Palace, the

ers, Soldiers and Peasants!" drafted by Lenin, which announced that power had passed into the hands of the Soviets. At its second session late at night on October 26, the delegates unanimously adopted the Decree on Peace, also written by Lenin. The Soviet government thus called on all the belligerent powers to conclude a democratic peace without annexations and indemnities. Also, it abolished secret diplomacy and proclaimed its determination to publish all secret treaties concluded by the czarist administration and the Provisional Government. And it denounced all the treaties concluded in the interests of the Russian landlords and capitalists. Lenin proposed a draft

Second All-Russia Congress of Workers' and Peasants' Deputies convened in Petrograd. Most of the delegates were members of the Bolshevik Party. At its first session, the Congress adopted an appeal *"To Work-*

Decree on Land for the consideration of the Congress. Once endorsed, it abolished landed proprietorship without any reservations and compensations.

All land, with the exception of plots belonging to rank-and-file peasants, had to be confiscated and handed over to the Soviets of Peasants' Deputies. Private ownership of land was banned, so it could not be leased or bought.

Hired labor was also banned. Land had to be distributed between peasant families depending on the number of able-bodied members and local circumstances.

Preceding pages: igniting the civil conflict, government troops firing at a demonstrating crowd in July 1917; the Winter Palace is taken; and Lenin in Switzerland in 1917 ready to guide the Bolshevik Revolution. **Left,** a Komintern magazine. **Above: left,** Bolsheviks' Manifest; **right,** workers recruited to stay on guard in Smolny.

The Second Congress of the Soviets elected the All-Russia Central Executive Committee, and then the first Soviet government was formed - the Council of People's Commissars - appointed mainly from the ranks of the Bolshevik Party, with Lenin as Premier, Trotsky as Commissar of Foreign Affairs, and Stalin in charge of Nationalities.

The dictatorship of the proletariat: By rejecting the calls of other socialist parties for power-sharing with the Bolsheviks, Lenin reaffirmed what had been put in no uncertain terms in the Bolshevik newspaper *Pravda* a day after the seizure of the Winter Palace: "We are taking power relying on the voice of the country and counting on the friendly sup-

the Soviet Union shall be the "leading and guiding force of Soviet society" and that it is the Party that determines the perspectives of society's development and steers the activities of the people.

The Soviet order, as the Bolshevik Party later called its reign, began to spread quickly across the country meeting with little resistance. Yet the consolidation of Soviet power could not be seen as complete as long as the question of the Constituent Assembly remained undecided. The decision to convene a Constituent Assembly, elected freely by all the citizens, to determine the future political system was taken by the Provisional Government, yet the elections, with no precedent

port of the European proletariat. But once we take power, we will take an iron hand against the enemies of the revolution and saboteurs... They have dreamed of the Kornilov (the leader of an abortive attempt to overthrow the Soviets in summer of 1917) dictatorship... We will give them the dictatorship of the proletariat."

To Lenin the dictatorship of the proletariat meant the dictatorship of the Bolsheviks; and the fact that his idea has stood the test of time is borne out by Article 6 of the present Soviet Constitution which says clearly and unambiguously that the Communist Party of

of freedom in Russian history, were held only after the October coup (it is worth noting here that Lenin nearly always preferred to refer to the October events as a "coup" rather than a "revolution", believing it was a more precise and modest term). As a result, the Bolsheviks received 24 percent of the vote, the socialist parties 59.6 percent, and the bourgeois parties 16.4 percent.

The Constituent Assembly: The Constituent Assembly, that was to form Russia's future finally convened on January 5, 1918. Vladimir Bonch-Bruyevich, chief administrator of the Council of People's Commissars, said later that Lenin called a full meeting of the cabinet soon after the first session of the Assembly. After a brief debate "all achieved a unanimous opinion that nobody needed that talking-shop...

It was decided not to intervene with the session and give everybody a chance to talk as much as they wanted, but on the next day not to convene the session again, dissolve the Constituent Assembly and tell the delegates to go back home."

With the historical crack, "the guards are tired", made by the head of a team of sailors who guarded the Tavrichesky Palace where the Constituent Assembly had convened, thus, ended the brief history of the first freely

thing to everybody, all at once. "The face of the truth is scary," wrote the Spanish philosopher Miguel de Unamuno, another witness to those events, "and the people want myths and illusions, wanting to be cheated. The truth is monstrous, unbearable, lethal." Those holding such views maintained that the Bolsheviks gave the people an illusion of peace, land and grain. But reality was different - world war, grain confiscations, famine, and unlimited terror.

Civil war: Finland won back its independence in December 1917 and - as a result of a separate peace treaty concluded by the newly-emerging Soviet republic with Germany on humiliating terms - Poland, Lithuania,

Left, Trotsky – Commissar of Defence. **Above**, meeting of the Council of People's Commissars.

elected Russian Parliament.

Nikolai Berdyayev, a Russian philosopher who had witnessed those events and later emigrated, described Bolshevism as "the least utopian and most realistic theory perfectly matching the situation obtained in Russia in 1917." Others disagreed, saying that Bolshevism achieved an easy victory and encountered little or no resistance precisely because it offered an utopia: every-

Latvia and Estonia also became independent. The subsequent bloody, three-year-long civil war, together with famine and economic dislocation, resulted in millions of deaths. In a desperate attempt to withstand the strains of the civil war, Moscow, which had again been made the capital of the country, announced the introduction of War Communism, a policy which implied full nationalization of the economy, banned trade which was to be replaced by a rigid rationing system and allowed harvest confiscations from peasants.

As a result of such measures and the Bol-

STALIN

by Dmitry Volkogonov

Stalin was dying. Lying on the couch in the dining room at his Kuntsevo estate, he had ceased all attempts to get up, reduced to raising his left arm occasionally as if begging for help. His half-closed eyes could not conceal the despair with which he stared at the door. His lips moved soundlessly, weakly, mutely. The stroke had taken place several hours before. Yet no-one was at Stalin's side. At last his bodyguards arrived, anxious at the fact that there had long been no sign of life in the dining room window. They were not entitled, however, to call out the doctors immediately. One of the most powerful individuals in the history of mankind could not allow such a thing. Beria's consent in person was needed. They sought him long into the night, only for him to consider that Stalin was merely sleeping soundly following a heavy supper. Only ten to twelve hours later were the frightened doctors ushered in to the dying Leader.

The very way that Stalin met his death is profoundly symbolic. It was indeed a cruel twist of fate. Even after several hours in agony, no help was at hand. And this was Stalin, almost a God on Earth, with the power to eject millions of people from one end of the world to the other by merely uttering a few words! He became a hostage to the bureaucratic system that he himself created.

A vicious tyrant: The past cannot be assessed by the simple use of numbers: whether Stalin had more achievements than crimes to his name. The very approach is immoral, since no achievements can justify inhumanity. And what achievements can there possibly be, if this man was to blame for millions of people perishing? Today it is clear that he was a vicious tyrant, whose violence alienated the people from their regime and gave birth to the symbiotic combination of bureaucracy and dogmatism.

What was the cost of Stalin's dictatorship? How many people were sent to their dooms at the behest of the tyrant and the machine he created? I believe that we will never find out for sure.

However, I can quote the following figures, based on a number of interim statistics discovered by myself from archive sources. The "revolution" in the countryside of 1929-1933 resulted in 8.5 to 9 million peasant farmers being imprisoned, exiled or killed. The purges of 1937 and 1938 affected 4.5 to 5 million Soviet people. And in between these two great waves Yagoda, Yezhov and their henchmen did not remain idle; approximately one million were arrested. After the war, and especially at the end of the 1940s, even taking into account that in 1947 capital punishment was repealed, there was a noticeable increase in the number of camps and people exiled or expelled, making up a third wave. Such people totaled 5.5 to 6.5 million. It may be pointed out that criminals as well as political prisoners were dispatched to the camps. Yet until the time that Stalin died, 25-30 percent of those held in the camps had been convicted of "anti-revolutionary activity", according to Beria's figures.

Twenty million victims: In total from 1929 to 1953 and excluding the war years, 19.5 to 22 million people fell victim to Stalin and his purges. Of these, not less than one third were sentenced to death or died in the camps or in exile. This might be a somewhat conservative estimate, but it is based on documents.

What was the cost of victory in the Great Patriotic War? Why was it that with Stalin, the "genius" in charge of our armed forces, our losses were two or three times those of the enemy? For a long time the figure first given by Khrushchev - more than 20 million - has been in circulation. In my opinion, the only thing that Khrushchev got right was the "more than". Historians are now investigating in an attempt to specify the precise number: the people should know how many of their sons and daughters were sacrificed on the altar of Victory.

The number of servicemen, partisans, resistance fighters, and peaceful citizens who perished during the Great Patriotic War seems to vary between 26 and 27 million, of whom about 10 million died in battle or as POWs. Those who were the first to be committed to the war on a strategic scale in 1941 sustained especially high losses, and approximately 3 million were taken prisoner. The cost was only slightly less in 1942.

sheviks' unlimited devotion to Lenin's genius and to the organizing talents of Trotsky who created and led the Red Army, the latter was achieving victories in all fronts by the autumn of 1919. In early 1920, the Entente powers removed the blockade, established earlier, of Soviet Russia and one by one began to recognize its new government, first *de facto* and then *de jure* (in 1924).

By May 1920, the civil war, which had claimed 15 million lives, was nearly over, and the First Constitution was adopted in July. The Kronstadt garrison (consisting mostly of sailors with a peasant background) revolted in the spring of 1921 but was soon suppressed. This last hotbed of the peasant war that had swept the country added impetus to Lenin's plan of transition to a new economic policy (known by its acronym NEP) which envisaged market arrangements.

Before this could be implemented, an unprecedented drought hit a highly populated part of the country in which 20 percent of the population lived. This was immediately followed by a disastrous famine.

Then in 1922, Joseph Stalin, on his way to power, was elected General Secretary of the Central Committee, while Lenin increasingly dispensed with his duties as a result of his grave illness.

The founding of the USSR: The Union of Soviet Socialist Republics was formed in December 1922. Formally, state organization proceeded along the lines of Lenin's plan of a federation of sovereign republics, but in reality Stalin got the upper hand with his autonomization idea, according to which all major decisions were to be made by the central authorities.

Lenin died in January 1924. The powers of government and Party leadership increasingly passed into the hands of a trio - Zinovyev, Kamenev and Stalin who gradually barred Trotsky from power, although he was still left a Politburo member. The reshuffle occurred in 1926, with the Politburo dumping Zinovyev in spring and Trotsky the following fall. Stalin began his ascension to unlimited personal power. The year 1929

marked a turning point. It began with the deportation of Trotsky who had earlier been expelled from the Party and had spent nearly a year in exile. In April, the 16th National Party Conference adopted the first five-year development plan, pursued since October of the previous year. The plan envisaged a crash program for nation-wide industrialization with reliance on domestic strength. In November, Bukharin was dropped from the Politburo, his "right-wing deviations" announced as posing the greatest danger to the Party and the country.

Stalin in power: On December 21, Stalin turned 50 and the anniversary signaled the beginning of the leader's personality cult.

Six days later, at the conference of Marxist agrarian scientists, Stalin announced the end of NEP (which Lenin had described as a serious and ever-lasting policy only eight years before) and the commencement of a painful transition to the policy of collectivization and elimination of the kulaks, or rich and independent peasants, as a class.

Stalin's order to pursue collectivisation of agriculture was executed with zeal and vigor even though the country was swept by a wave of protests. In March 1930, Stalin was forced to publish his notoriously liberal article *"Dizzy with Success"* in the Pravda. The

Right, "Who shot Trotsky" – Investigation by Soviet press into the assassination of disgraced commissar in 1940 in Mexica.

slogan of "total collectivization" was temporarily dropped, but by March 1931 most of the peasant households in the country had been collectivised. The campaign was accompanied by the requisition of grain, including seeds.

Famine struck many regions of the country, killing millions. Millions more perished as well-to-do peasants and members of their families were identified as being kulaks and forcefully deported to the inhospitable and unhealthy northern and eastern regions of the country to die.

A Central Committee decree abolished all school reforms introduced after the revolution. Another decree banned all independent

ment in concentration camps in cases of extenuating circumstances. The new Law on High Treason provided only one punishment - execution. Regular public trials of the "enemies of the people" were held across the country, with the campaign reaching its peak in 1937.

In January 1933, Stalin announced the fulfillment of the first five-year plan within a period of four years. The second five-year plan set forth even more ambitious tasks to turn the Soviet Union into an industrialized nation. In January 1934, the 17th Party Congress convened and was immediately proclaimed "the Congress of the Victors". Of the 139 members of the Central Committee

associations, groups and trends in literature, the arts, music and architecture. An "antireligious" five-year plan subsequently envisaged the elimination of all worshiping institutions by May 1, 1937, and the "purging of the very notion of God".

Internal passports were established, accompanied by the introduction of compulsory residence permits; but the passports were issued only to urban dwellers. A draconian law *"On the Protection of the Property of State Enterprises... and Enhancement of Socialist Ownership"* envisaged shooting as a punitive measure or a 10 year imprison-

elected at the Congress, 98 of them, or 70 percent, would be arrested and executed by the end of the decade.

Speaking in the Red Square, Stalin announced: "Life has become better and more rewarding." The new Constitution, known as the Stalin Constitution, was adopted in December 1936 .

The Second World War: On June 22, 1941, Nazi Germany treacherously attacked the Soviet Union. War became a daily routine of Soviet life for the following four years. Stalin had tried to avoid the USSR's involvement in World War II by concluding a non-aggression pact with Hitler in 1939 (which also resulted in the Soviet acquisition of Estonia, Latvia, Lithuania, the Western Ukraine, Western White Russia and Bessarabia).

Barely six months after the beginning of the war (popularly known as the Great Patriotic War in Russia) Nazi troops occupied half of the USSR's European territory, besieged Leningrad and emerged at the walls of Moscow and on the banks of the Volga, pushing hard to reach the Caucasus.

Victory at last: On December 5, 1941, which marked the fifth anniversary of Stalin's Constitution, the Russian army launched its first counter offensive. The en-

It seemed that the allied euphoria over the joint victory would inevitably lead to relaxations of international tensions. But optimists proved wrong: it was found out that the Western powers were willing to co-operate with the Soviet Union only when faced with a die-hard enemy like Hitler. Stalin's speech to his voters on February 8, 1946, and Churchill's Fulton address marked the beginning of what later became known as the Cold War. The "Iron Curtain" was dropped across Europe from the Baltics to the Adriatic Sea.

The Cold War years: The Soviet Union began licking its war-inflicted wounds. It could not breathe new life into the 20 million dead, but it certainly could and would restore the

emy was driven away from the Soviet capital. But the German offensive continued in other directions. A breakthrough was achieved only early 1943, following a spectacular Soviet victory in the battle of Stalingrad in the lower reaches of the Volga. But fierce fighting continued for another year before Russian troops drove the Nazis from their country's borders. It took another year to crush the Third Reich by storming Berlin.

Left, Nazi atrocities in Minsk 1941. **Above**, Red Army offensive.

1,700 cities and towns, over 70,000 villages and nearly 32,000 industrial enterprises, mines and electric power plants, and tens of thousands of cultural and health establishments which all lay in ruins.

About a third of the Soviet national wealth had been lost in the war. Thanks to the enthusiasm and disregard of all privations and hardships, the people of the Soviet Union rebuilt their country, despite substantial allocations of resources for the maintenance of a military parity with the United States. In 1949, the Soviets produced an atomic bomb and in 1953 the world's first hydrogen bomb.

The Post Stalin Era

The Khrushchev thaw: Stalin died in March 1953 and in September Nikita Khrushchev was elected First Secretary of the Soviet Communist Central Committee. The country was exposed to a long-awaited "thaw". The revival of Leninist legal standards in the Party and government affairs, the well-known report to the 20th Party Congress in 1956 exposing the crimes committed by the Stalin regime (which was, however, not published in the Soviet Union until the spring of 1989), the rehabilitation of Stalin's victims,

The launching of the world's first satellite and Yuri Gagarin's manned space flight, the raising of the Berlin Wall and the Caribbean crisis, the officially sanctioned harassment of the poet and translator Boris Pasternak and the first publication of Alexander Solzhenitsyn's books, the removal of Stalin's corpse from the tomb on the Red Square and sincere promises to build up communist society by 1980 - this odd list of controversial and contradictory events was also associated with the efforts of Nikita Khrushchev.

The Era of Stagnation: Khrushchev was denounced in October 1964, and Leonid Brezhnev ascended to the leadership of the Party and the country. His 18-year reign is

the laws on cutting farm taxes and encouraging agricultural development, the introduction of passports for collective farmers and the abolition of the 1940 anti-labor law prohibiting workers to quit their factories, the establishment of state pensions and a considerable democratization of public life - these achievements certainly go to the credit of Nikita Khrushchev.

In foreign policy, the breakthroughs were also remarkable. The Soviet Union at that time established diplomatic relations with West Germany, ended a row with Yugoslavia, signed the Warsaw Pact and the Soviet-Anglo-American Nuclear Test Ban Treaty.

currently seen as the "era of stagnation". Brezhnev's official biography, published when he was still alive, described him as "the outstanding leader of the Communist Party, the Soviet state and the international communist and workers movement" and as a "leader of the Leninist type and firmly committed to Lenin's principles of internationalism and the selfless struggle for peace and social progress".

Much praise was sung under the Brezhnev reign to the leader's outstanding capabilities, sharp mind, exceptional courage, resourcefulness, exactingness in relations with the subordinates, and intolerance of all manifestations of red-tape. Shining on his broad chest were five golden stars of the Hero of Socialist Labor, the Order of Victory (the supreme military award), the badge of the Lenin Prize for achievements in literature, the Karl Marx golden medal and several dozen other orders and medals.

The truth is, however, that Brezhnev never was a "great" and "strong" personality. Intellectually and temperamentally, he had never ascended to the status of an outstanding personality, even from the point of view of a veteran career-seeker. "If I were asked to give a very brief description of Brezhnev," writes Roy Medvedev, a Soviet historian, "I would refer to him as a mediocre and weak

person. He was in fact a dull and imprudent bureaucrat, harboring no big dreams, nurturing no interesting ideas or plans, and wielding no uncommon style. He did not have even a trace of Lenin's political genius. Fortunately, he lacked Stalin's malicious lust for power, brutal vindictiveness and super human will. His character and intellect made Brezhnev a dependent, indecisive and dull person largely despised by his closest aides. They followed Brezhnev because they knew

Preceding pages: ancient and recent classicism combined. **Left**, Khrushchev advocating for planting corn. **Above**, Brezhnev.

their zeal would be rewarded, but certainly not because they believed he was exceptional." During the Brezhnev years there was a revival of the personality cult and a process of corruption and bribery started among government officials and even among members of his family. The administration grew enormously but was concentrated in the hands of a few party officials.

Assessing the nearly two decades during which Brezhnev served as the General Secretary of the Soviet Communist Party Central Committee, many divide his reign into two distinct phases. The first decade of the Brezhnev era marked the most tranquil and peaceful period in the USSR's history. But then detente was brought to an abrupt end by the Soviet incursion in Afghanistan.

Soviet economic and political influence spread around the world and for the first time in the post-war era it achieved real military and strategic parity with the western countries. Although the Soviet economy slowed down its pace, the Soviet people enjoyed a higher standard of living in the early 1980s than in the early 1960s.

The country was recovering from the shock of Stalin's brutal terror, and yet it was Brezhnev and his administration that stubbornly attempted to revive Stalin's cult of personality denounced by Khrushchev. Dissidents were persecuted, although it is important to mention here that before the 1960s nobody would even dare to think about the possibility of a dissident movement, even less so about one capable of resisting the omnipotent state apparatus.

After Brezhnev's death, Yury Andropov became General secretary of the CPSU Central Committee. He was an exceptionally talented and intelligent person but his time in power was too short to start the necessary changes in society that would have been a prerequisite to revive the stagnating economy. After his sudden death he was replaced by Konstantin Chernenko, a late follower of Brezhnev who tried hard to keep the old conservative group in power. But his days were also numbered and in 1985 Mikhail Gorbachev started to turn the domestic and foreign policy of the USSR around.

Perestroika: Since March 1985, the country has now been pursuing the policy of perestroika that came with the new General Secretary. The way for the reform of the old-established system of the party's leadership was opened when the democratically elected Congress of People's Deputies abolished article 6 of the Soviet Constitution that demanded the leading role of the CPSU. During the Third Congress of People's Deputies, Mikhail Gorbachev was elected President of the USSR, a position that holds unique power and permits him to continue his radical changes.

The economy is now gradually changing from central planning to the rule of market mechanisms. New forms of ownership were introduced, enterprises have been given extensive rights and the idea of profit centers will soon be ruling the different sectors of

industry and commerce. Cooperatives appear everywhere and are fast competing with government run institutions. A new law on land has opened the chance for individuals and groups to own land and become more productive.

With Boris Yeltsin becoming the President of the Russian Federation, by far the largest republic of the union, and the decision that this republic's laws supersede the union laws, a new chapter of internal politics has opened that might change the whole structure of the Soviet Union.

Many informal movements have been founded and unions and public organizations developed new ways to express themselves in a democratic fashion that was unheard of in the USSR until now. Glasnost, the politics of openness, is creating a new understanding of the people's inherent power. New parties are being set up and the future will surely bring a multi-party system to the USSR. Perestroika is not yet over, nor has it become history. It is today's reality.

Mikhail Zhvanetsky, the leading Soviet satirist describes the present situation in the USSR thus: "There, over the hill, they seem to be doing well, but we can't do the way they are doing over there on the other side of the fence. Moreover, we have some big wheels along with us, who keep saying that we can't do the way they are doing it over there, for we have once refused to do so and must now suffer and keep our word... In short, it's banned to do the way they are doing there, but it's impossible to do the way we are doing here. That's why the public watches with awe - the way it watched humorists walking on a tight rope sometime ago - how economists explain why it's impossible to do the way we are doing here and why we shouldn't do the way they are doing there, or else what shall we do with those who are preventing us from doing it. We can't just throw them overboard, we have to feed them, because it was their idea, after all, to do the way we can't be doing any longer. So here is what I think: maybe we should be held by the whole world as an example to point a finger at and say: Look, guys, don't you ever do it the way they were doing it."

We began this historic essay with a quotation from the Russian philosopher-prophet Pyotr Chaadayev. We will end it with another quotation from his work: "We shall acquire genuine freedom... from the day we fully grasp the path we have traveled, when an involuntary admission of all our blunders and past mistakes will suddenly be on our lips and when a cry of repentance and sorrow, filling the whole world, will come from our hearts. Then we will take a place among nations whose mission in this world is not only that of battering-rams or cudgels but one which also generates ideas."

Left, leaving Afghanistan. **Right**, army – "peacekeeping force" in the areas of ethnic unrest.

"We are too much in a hurry with the reform of the political system. We should first provide enough food for our country, and only then engage in democracy", claim the critics of Mikhail Gorbachev, "Perestroika cannot tolerate gradual evolution" advocate the leaders of the USSR; "Far more cataclysms are in store for us on this evolutionary path than on a revolutionary road", say those who call themselves radicals.

These contradictory points of view, which rule each other out, are heating up the discussion. And these views are not the extreme ones. There are people who no longer believe in perestroika, who believe that Gorbachev, like a driver who has lost control of his automobile on an ice-covered road, is leading the country into nowhere, to say the least of it.

It can be seen, however, that perestroika, led by Gorbachev - a master of the art of specific politics - is drawing closer, step by step, to a new image of socialism, though with immense difficulties.

The command system: It is hard to understand or even to imagine what the USSR's political system is, without getting an idea, of the general political situation which has developed in the country over the first few years of perestroika. Perestroika is changing the social and political atmosphere of the USSR very fast, literally from day to day. It was much easier to assess the situation earlier, before perestroika, because of the practically universal power of the Communist Party or, to be more exact, of its apparatus that formed the basis of the political system. The administration-command system, reared by Stalin back in the early 1930s, gave all the reins of government to the Party-state apparatus. The Party committees - from the central to the district one - were levers of this system and served as a kind of drive belt from the "leader" Stalin, then Khrushchev, and later Brezhnev to the faceless people.

Up till recently, the most important political decisions were adopted in the quiet offices of the Politburo of the CPSU Central Committee and after that were unanimously supported and approved in effect, simply registered by the Supreme Soviet - the USSR's parliament - which assembled twice a year for a day or two. There was not a grain of democracy in all that.

The authority and power of the "leader" and his entourage was unlimited. Illustrative of this is the stationing of troops in Afghanistan in December 1979, which even some Politburo members learnt of only from the TV news program.

A new image of socialism: In that situation, the Party's new leadership headed by Gorbachev called for a reorganization of all the spheres of society; specifically, for the reform of the political system. The main idea was, and is, to get rid of the bureaucratic mechanisms of administration and management, to democratize the social and political structures through openness (glasnost) and pluralism of views and - most importantly - to give full powers to democratically elected representative bodies.

Gorbachev believes that this is the sole way to create a new image of socialism, a socialism that is more civilized and humane. In this he is definitely supported by a majority of the USSR's population.

December 1988 saw the adoption of a new law on elections and the necessary alterations in the USSR Constitution. In spring 1989 elections of People's Deputies were held in an atmosphere of unprecedented political activity. The first Congress of People's Deputies of the USSR, which is now the highest body of state authority, took place in May-June of the same year.

The supreme body of state authority: The Congress of People's Deputies consists of 2,250 members elected on the basis of universal, equal and direct suffrage by secret ballot. One third of them, 750 deputies, are elected from the territorial electoral districts with an equal number of inhabitants; they represent the interests of all citizens irrespective of their nationality, social status or place of residence. Another third of all deputies are elected from the national-territorial districts, 32 deputies from every Union Re-

Preceding pages: change of guard, Lenin Mausoleum. **Left**, new era – new leader.

Politics 79

public, 11 from every Autonomous Republic, 5 from every Autonomous Region and one deputy from every Autonomous Area, regardless of the number of their inhabitants. And finally 750 other deputies represent the All-Union mass organizations - the CPSU, the Young Communist League (Komsomol), the trade unions, the cooperative organizations, the associations of researchers, creative unions and public committees, including the women's councils united by the Soviet Women's Committee, and so on.

For the first time ever: The norms of representation of each of them were established by law. It is something new and characteristic of the ongoing reforms that different

held also in some other districts where several candidates had been registered but none of them had received enough votes to be directly elected.

The results of the elections were as follows: 172.8 million voters participated, which means 89.8 percent of the total electorate. People of 65 nationalities won seats in the Congress, among them 352 women. 88.1 percent of the deputies were elected for the first time. 24.8 percent of the People's Deputies work in industry, construction, transport and communication, and 18.9 per cent in agriculture. Workers and collective farmers account for 23.7 percent of the People's Deputies, managers of industrial plants and

candidates for election were registered in approximately three quarters of all electoral districts. Due to this, for the first time ever, the elections in these districts were real elections and not just formal voting, as had been the case before.

In 399 electoral districts tradition prevailed and only one candidate figured in the ballot-paper - most frequently, the local top-ranking official. But perestroika, which had revived civic self-awareness, produced its results: the electors in some districts black-balled these sole candidates, and repeat elections had to be held. Run-off elections were

amalgamations 6.8, and intellectuals 27.1 percent. Seven religious figures won seats for the first time ever.

As many as 1,806 deputies (80.3 percent) are aged 30-60, and 187 are under 30, nine of them being only 21 years old; 1,957 deputies (87 percent) are members of the CPSU. This figure was hotly discussed both in the Soviet and foreign press.

It seems that the electors sometimes voted not so much for Communists as for the people of principle who share their interests, irrespective of their Party membership. At the same time it is noteworthy that in quite a number of areas the Party officials, among them secretaries of the Party Regional Committees, failed to win the people's trust. This is evidence of the rather low prestige of the specific Party leaders who suffered a defeat, especially because many of them lost in non-alternative elections in which they hadn't even a rival. In many cases precisely this fact "campaigned" against the candidate and was the root cause of their flop.

For the first time in history all meetings of the highest body of state authority in the USSR were given live coverage by radio and television. It was also the first time that the huge hall of the Kremlin Palace of Congresses became an arena of hot debate and

the USSR's military budget and the scale of its foreign debt and budget deficit was made public. The People's Deputies held frank and principled debates which were not always characterized by parliamentary correctness. Discussions were held on ways to extricate the country from its critical economic situation, on how to solve ecological problems, how to end the interethnic tension in some areas, and how to improve the living standards of millions of people living below the poverty line.

It was a free comparison of views - sometimes diametrically opposite ones - on the processes taking place in society, and on its past, present and future.

witnessed clashes of view and principle; there were no obstacles either to real discussion, or to criticism.

It was also the first time that the leaders of the Party and the state drew an objective picture of the economic situation of the USSR and the state of its finance for the benefits of the MPs and of society as a whole. It was the first time that data on the size and structure of

Left, hammer and sickle at Lenin museum in Moscow. **Above**, the still accepted Communist triumvirate?

A new political culture: It would be naive to expect that the two weeks of debates in the Kremlin Palace of Congresses could resolve all the problems facing the USSR. They did, however, help to lay bare the major defects and outline the most pressing, top-priority objectives. The approach to a new political culture was an important event. In the heat of the debates held in the first days it so happened that Boris Yeltsin was not elected to the Supreme Soviet (he had won almost six million votes in Moscow during the elections). The fact that Congress found a way to solve this difficult issue was strength, and

Yeltsin finally became a member of the Supreme Soviet.

As well as debating a very broad spectrum of domestic problems and foreign policy issues, the Congress fulfilled the tasks, assigned to it by the Constitution of the USSR, of forming the permanent bodies of state authority and administration and appointing officials to the highest posts in the state .

The Congress of the People's Deputies: After heated debate, the Congress elected the Supreme Soviet of the USSR (a two-chamber permanent legislative, administrative and control body of state authority, each chamber consisting of 271 members), the President of the USSR Supreme Soviet (Mikhail

litical system. The heart of the matter does not lie only in the creation of a new Soviet parliament. The most important achievement is that a real transfer of all state authority to the elected representative bodies, the Soviets, is taking place.

The Supreme Soviet: The USSR Supreme Soviet, created by the Congress (the Congress sessions are convened twice a year, but each session lasts 3-4 months now), continued the work set in train by the 1989 Congress. Evidence of this were the candidates to the posts of Ministers and Vice-Presidents of the Council of Ministers who didn't survive the Parliamentary purgatory and failed to win the approval of the Supreme Soviet.

Gorbachev) and the First Vice-President of the USSR Supreme Soviet. It also approved the appointment of the Chairman of the USSR Council of Ministers, the Chairman of the USSR People's Control Committee, the Supreme Court, the Procurator-General and the Chief State Arbiter of the USSR. The first meetings of the chambers of the USSR Supreme Soviets elected the Chairmen of the Council of the Union and of the Council of Nationalities.

The work of the Congress and of the Supreme Soviet has certainly opened a new stage in the development of the USSR's po-

The Supreme Soviet also relieved students of military service, acting in this issue contrary to the wishes of the military-industrial lobby which is far from being weak in any modern country, not only in the USSR.

By a very insistent, and somewhat chivalrous gesture, the Supreme Soviet raised pensions with effect from October 1989. In the last hours of its first session, the Supreme Soviet made a kind of symbolic gesture by raising the pay of the President and his First Vice-President above their Party salaries, thereby emphasizing that they head the Supreme Soviet but not any other body.

The Party's omnipotence: It is abundantly clear to all that the previous Party practice of wielding a diktat over the central and local Soviets - in other words, the Party's omnipotence - cannot be accepted today. Perestroika has put on the agenda new, democratic mechanisms for interaction; the functions of the Party, and the exercise of power and administration are being separated and transferred to the Soviets. The Soviets consist of the representative bodies of state authority, comprising the Congress of People's Deputies of the USSR and the USSR Supreme Soviet, the Congresses of People's Deputies and the Supreme Soviets of the Union and Autonomous Republics as well as the local

Soviets - from regional down to village level.

In the view of the Party newspaper *Pravda*, the formula of interaction should be as follows: the Party works out the policy and carries it out through the central and local Soviets. The Party organs may implement their political ideas only by way of persuasion and recommendation through the Communist Party members elected to the Soviets.

Left, the pride of Great Patriotic war veterans.
Above, Andrei Sakharov back in Moscow.

Inner-party democracy: We are now witnessing an irony: the Party advanced the idea of perestroika (to be more exact, the idea was advanced more by its new leader, Gorbachev, than by the Party itself) and gave it a good start, especially in the foreign-policy sphere, in developing openness, and in democratizing society, but the Party has also found itself in the rearguard of this process in some seemingly incomprehensible way. There are many reasons for this, the root cause being the fact that inner Party democracy remains at the level which existed prior to perestroika.

A graphic illustration of this was the election of the People's Deputies from the CPSU: 100 candidates to 100 seats! And this took pace in an atmosphere when democratization is making fast headway throughout society. The Party's leadership, headed by Gorbachev, is aware of the gravity of all this and has already mapped out measures to remedy the situation.

The dead grasp the living, the ancient Greeks said. In fact, the legacy of the Stalin dictatorship and the Brezhnev stagnation are still felt, especially in the Party. In the consciousness of the masses the Party is, as before, associated with the Party committees and their apparatus. But the Party is not the CPSU Central Committee, nor the Central Committees of 14 Union Republics, and also not the 159 Territorial and Regional, 896 City and 666 District Committees. The Party has nearly 20 million members, all equal, led by elective bodies ranging from the Plenums of the district committees to the Plenums of the Central Committee and Congresses of the CPSU.

All the aforesaid leads to the conclusion that the political system of the USSR is changing dynamically and, the most important of all, becoming dynamically democratized. The reform of the political system, proclaimed by Gorbachev, is aimed at the maximum democratization of all aspects of life but - it is also perfectly clear that this democratization process must bear fruit that befits a socialist society.

The abolition of the Party's supremacy and the election of Mikhail Gorbachev as President of the USSR, with a priority to represent all strata and forces of society, seem to represent the beginning of a new era in the history of the USSR.

THE THIRD RUSSIAN REVOLUTION

a view from outside by Dr. Karl Grobe

The Soviet Union is in a pre-revolutionary crisis. The rulers have exhausted the alternatives available to them and are not even making progress with tentative reforms. The population is sick and tired of the old system but, as yet, there is neither a program nor an organization to effect changes.

Never before has the abyss between the monopolistic Communist Party and the population been as clearly evident as in the

Those 2,744 delegates who assembled for the Soviet Federation Party conference that had been nominated in the Russian Soviet Federal Socialist Republic (RSFSR). The RSFSR had not had its own party organization since 1925; but from the RSFSR come approximately 58 percent of all communists and in the non-Federation republics, the Russians have always had a disproportionate number of comrades. In the

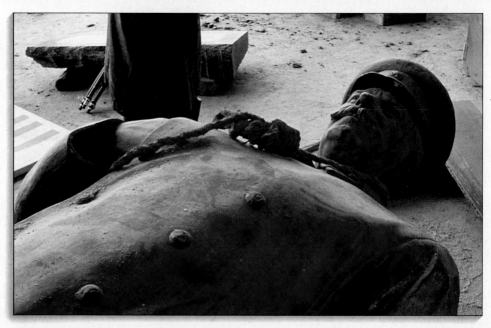

summer of 1990. At the two most important party conferences held in June and July 1990 in Moscow, the adherents of communist orthodoxy managed to get their way in the votes and resolutions (the decisive point was the fixation of the "choice the Russian people made in 1917"). Nevertheless, the election of 1989 resulted for the first time in the setting up of parliamentary committees without a previously determined monopoly of power through the Communist party, and pointedly did not confirm the "choice of 1917". The orthodox wing of the Communist Party lost whenever a counter-force presented itself.

Baltic Republics on the other hand there are, in each case, already two communist parties - a "national" and an "internationalistic" one (primarily Russian).

Of the 2,744 RSFSR delegates, 1,171 were full-time party functionaries, 210 state company directors, 130 state farm directors and collective farm chairmen (Sowchoses), ergo 1,511 persons that had been sent there by the very institutions that they had to vote for. A closed society in other words, counter-balanced only by 563 peasants and workers (of which 200 did not have a voting right - they were only there for appearance sake).

Of course the delegates were not elected by the rank and file members of which there are said to be 19 million (in view of the vast number of party membership books being handed back, this figure was greeted with sarcastic laughter). They had been proposed by state-employed functionaries, the secretariats at all levels.

The bureaucracy thus reproduced itself in the delegates. And it is this bureaucracy that constitutes the problem. The word bureaucracy does not describe a mode of behavior nor does it describe the countless multitudes of those who, as white-collar workers or civil servants, serve the state, but rather the ruling class itself. The genesis and continuous rule

that had taken over from the monarchy in February, had had sufficient time to prove its incompetence.

The hierarchically organized party of the Bolshevists, well-versed in conspiratorial tactics since the first revolution in 1905, took over power, supported by the municipal councils (*Soviets*) in Petrograd and Moscow, on behalf of the working classes. But these Soviets, at the time estimated at three million people of a total population of 150 million, disintegrated during the course of a horrendous civil war and the resultant economic depression.

Within the Soviets, the Bolshevists (who soon began to call themselves communists)

of the bureaucracy is founded on the two revolutions of the year 1917. In February (according to the western calender, March) Czarist Russia had imploded like a balloon that had come into contact with a lit cigarette. By October (according to the western calender, November) the bourgeoisie, the democratic, liberal and constitutional forces

Preceding pages: enjoying pluralism – exposition of paintings in Moscow Bitsa park. Left, the fallen tyrant. Above, Azerbaijanians destroying their Communist Party membership cards in Baku.

eliminated all other parties. After 1920 the Communist Party was synonymous with State power.

A development that had already started in the newly-created Red Army during Lenin's lifetime, under Leo Trotsky, eventually permeated the whole of Soviet society: political commissioners, supervisors appointed by the party, controlled the "bourgeois specialists" (commanders, civil servants) and soon developed identical interests.

"The Party" metamorphosed to become the party of the bureaucracy. According to the last statistics available from Czarist Russia (1897) there were 430,000 civil servants including teachers and physicians. In 1985 when Mikhail Gorbachev took office, the number of functionaries was estimated as being at least 18 million, of which no fewer than 615 had ministerial rank (in Czarist Russia, which was deemed to be inundated with bureaucrats, there were never more than 25 functionaries).

The bureaucratization of Soviet society was effected by two instruments that had been created by the Communist Party itself. One is the *nomenklatura*, a list of official posts solely appointed by the central committee. The second is the (General) Secretariat of the party, the authority responsible for the appointment to nomenklatura posts. The officials of the nomenklatura control all state, economic, judicial, cultural, police, regional and communal power.

The system that defines itself as "socialism" for years cited external dangers as a justification for centralism. In the first four decades after 1945, the Cold War provided the ideological justification. However, by the late 1980s, the size of the military juggernaut proved to be no longer economically viable. Compared to the social product, the Super Power USSR had to spend more than four times as much for military purposes (which also included space programs) as the USA if it wanted merely to keep pace.

The supply of food and basic necessities to the population stagnated, the agricultural production slowly decreased - for the first time a large number of critical intellectuals protested against political coercion and looming ecological hazards. On 12th March 1985 Mikhail Gorbachev became general secretary of the Communist Party with the express order to transform the floundering Soviet Union, which had stagnated under Andropov and Chernenko, back to some sort of efficiency. His first targets were foreign policy measures to slow the arms race and to achieve disarmament. Home policy was to accelerate the growth of the economy. Not *perestroika* but *uskorenije* (acceleration) was the prime economic catch phrase.

To achieve this it was necessary first to break the stranglehold of the bureaucracy; the restructuring (*perestroika*) initially of the command structures became the official program. During the 27th Party Conference in March 1986, the power monopoly of the communist party was once again emphasized and even in the commemorative speech on the occasion of the 70th anniversary of the October revolution (7th November 1987) Gorbachev voiced his endorsement of all aspects of Soviet history. A few critical strictures concerning the personality cult culminated in a firm support of the form of collective leadership that had been customary since 1956.

At least the new leadership took heed of the criticism voiced by dissidents like Andrei Sakharov and began to ease up on former prohibitions and to repeal sentences of banishment. The mass media were encouraged to point accusing fingers at bureaucratic inefficiency. Writers were empowered to start a critique. The idea was not to castigate the system, but to make it more effective.

But one event had already shaken up the structures: the reactor catastrophe in Chernobyl on 28th April 1986. Cover-ups by the Ukrainian party bureaucracy, pooh-poohing maneuvers in Moscow, the resultant uncovering of horrific blunders in construction planning (which had been known to insiders all along), irresponsible handling of high tech, regional sloth, the official oppression of those ecological groups sounding the alarm - all these inadequacies of the bureaucratic state were uncovered by the Chernobyl catastrophe.

The press - all of a sudden wide awake - found catastrophic conditions wherever they looked. The ecological endangerment to Lake Baikal, a reservoir that holds of one third of the fresh water of the Eastern hemisphere; the drying-up of Lake Aral; the resultant medical, social, cultural, economic and ecological costs of the Central Asian cotton monoculture; the destruction of the fertile black earth zone due to excessive exploitation; the prevailing dissatisfaction of the urban population as far as accommodation and lack of supplies is concerned; the privileges of the nomenklatura - all this was vehemently discussed. A general crisis awareness became evident that was rapidly intensified by that section of the press that made use of the new liberties (*glasnost* originally meant "publication" and gradually gained the meaning of "uncovering").

In December 1986 a second explosion occurred - this time between diverse Soviet nations. On 16th December the Kazakhstan Central Committee dismissed the Party leader Dinmuhamed Kunajev and appointed the Russian Gennadij Kolbin. Protest demonstrations resulted. For some days there was civil war in Alma Ata. The relatively mild conflicts in Kazakhstan were the start of a new wave of nationalism that soon spread to all Soviet Republics.

The aim of creating a uniform Soviet nation out of gradually merging nationalities can be considered a failure. As soon as they had been constituted, People's Fronts won

solved relatively easily if they had not simultaneously been an expression of a deep-rooted social contradiction, that was especially accentuated in the under-developed regions of the USSR. The jingo-istic rejection of immigrants, no matter whether they are Slavs or Volga Germans, Lasen, Meschetes, Ingusians or Armenians is directly linked with industrialization, with a lop-sided leaning towards the Central Committee and its lack of consideration of regional requirements. The conflicts are thus an expression of a social crisis itself. The traditional, multi-cultural basar-trade econ-omy of Central Asia has broken down and in the modern economic sectors immigrants are

elections in all Republics of the Union - in each case against the orthodox main stream of the Communist Party - and by summer 1990 most Republics of the Federation had declared their sovereignty in some form. The attempts of the Central Committee (i.e. President Gorbachev) to save the situation by means of a new federation treaty merely constituted a withdrawal skirmish.

The national conflicts could have been

primary source of labor. Only menial work is left for the locals. Women and children work in cotton fields. They are excluded from the decisive administrative functions.

In the Baltic, the Ukraine, Transcaucasia, the highly centralized plan economy was forced through without any differentiation whatever; millions of formerly free (albeit poor) peasants, traders, intellectuals and artisans were physically destroyed in the course of the industrialization process. The economic policy everywhere is virtually a colonial cudgel; and, especially in the southern republics, it has lead to unemploy-

Boris Yeltsin, Russian president in nearest fu-ture, urging democratic powers to unite.

ment figures of around 25 percent - whereby, because of multiple job-sharing and seasonal work, hidden unemployment remains unconsidered.

But even in the RSFSR the social contradictions have escalated to crisis point; pauperization of the kolchos and sowchos peasants, the failure of the planned economy, crisis in the service industries, wastage and excessive exploitation of natural resources - all these have turned the RSFSR into something like an "Upper Volta with atomic weapons" as critical economists have put it.

In compliance with Marxist tradition, Soviet thinking is directed to productivity forces and productivity conditions. Many

China. The question of entitlement to ownership of the means of production, in turn, endangers the social and economic basis of the nomenklatura and is therefore in itself revolutionary.

Initially Gorbachev's party leadership had endeavored to make the existing apparatus more effective, but not to jeopardize the power of the nomenklatura as a social class. The plan proposed as late as the 19th Party conference at the end of June 1988 to nominate a President to preside over the party apparatus must be viewed in this connection. The introduction of a presidential system independent of the party, whose power monopoly was simultaneously eliminated

Soviets have recognized the paralytic inability of the bureaucratic, planned economy to deliver the goods and now demand a transition to free market enterprise. They call especially for privatisation of the forces of productivity and liberation of the peasants by granting them leaseholds for life instead of integrating them into collective delivery plans that are practically synonyms for land-dues payments. Thus in summer 1988 the economist Nikolai Shmeljov criticized the fact that the reform had not begun in the rural area by the liberation of the peasants from the planned economy as had been the case in

from the constitution (article 6) corresponds to the attempt to defend the interests of the nomenklatura simultaneously against the orthodox wing and the radical reformers. It is reminiscent of Bonapartism, the presidential adjudicator role as sovereign "over the parties", whose power is based on "the powers of order". But the powers of order (the army and the KGB) are nothing if not conservative in the USSR.

The 1990 party conference was, moreover,

Participants in the human chain from Tallinn to Vilnius.

90

the occasion for an outpouring of criticism of the system that the leadership had not foreseen. At the end of June 1988, the third revolution began to take shape (or even the fourth if one takes the developments of the year 1917 as constituting two revolutions). The fact that Gorbachev used his political strength to establish a presidential power-apparatus separate from that of the party is directly relevant to this. It was also a reaction to the anything but passive resistance of the apparatus itself and to politicians like Jegor Ligachev who, initially a Gorbachev supporter, was convinced of the necessity of reforms but who now began to realize that the ruling class was endangered by the very dynamism of the reforms.

Boris Yeltsin, a populist fundamentalist who comes from Sverdlovsk, homed in on the privileges and incompetence of the party elite and left the perestroika line pursued by Gorbachev. Despite the bureaucratic obstacles put in his way, he was able to win the elections in Moscow (to the parliament of the USSR) and Sverdlovsk (to the parliament of the RSFSR) with a 90 percent majority and in spring 1990 he was elected (Parliamentary) President of the RSFSR. He soon gathered several of Gorbachev's important advisers around him, people who were disenchanted with the progress of perestroika and who, for the first time, publicly stated their intention to split from the Communist Party.

After the founding party conference of the Russian Communist Party and the election of the hard-liner Ivan Polozkov to the position of republican party chief in the RSFSR this split seems increasingly likely. By nominating Polozkov, the party has decided to continue to prop up the old, possibly slightly reformable, system; however, in the government of the RSFSR, in the city halls of Moscow, Leningrad and other large cities, the radical reformers are in the majority.

On the other hand, a pan-Russian chauvinist right wing - long since thought obsolete - has crystallized around the PAMJAT, originally an environmental protection group. PAMJAT's tendencies to antisemitism and religious bigotry seems especially attractive to Russians living in the more impoverished areas of dilapidated cities. The neo-Stalinist right wing centers around the chemist Nina Andrejeva and the local head of the party Boris Gidaspov.

In summer 1989 a new power appeared. From the miners' strikes in Workuta and the traditional areas around the Donez and near Kusnezk a self-administrative area evolved, almost comparable to the Soviets of 1905 and 1917 and showing the first signs of a socialist party antagonistic to bureaucracy.

The July 1990 Communist Party conference was expected to be a decisive event. It was predicted that Gorbachev himself might be forced to resign as party chief, capitulating a split between the radical and conservative wings.

This did not happen: Gorbachev remained party leader, and succeeded in having his nominee elected as deputy, pushing Jegor Ligachev, the leader of the conservative faction, into the sidelines (some say, to the end of his political career). It was nevertheless a hollow victory for Gorbachev, and many critics say that the conference achieved nothing except more compromise, further procrastination.

Boris Yeltsin made a dramatic walkout, and several leading party politicians, including the mayors of Moscow and Leningrad, Gavril Popov and Anatoly Sobchak, announced their decision to leave the party in order to pursue reform unshackled by the bureaucrats. Faced with growing support for the reformist Democratic Platform party, the days of the lumbering dinosaur, the Communist Party, seem numbered.

Gorbachev has given himself two years to turn the Soviet economy round - a wholly unrealistic timetable in the view of many of his critics. The multiplicity of political parties that is developing could, in theory, be seen as an indication of a profound democratization of the Soviet society. This would be overly optimistic, however.

Democracy is a form of government that allows conflicting interests within a society that is nevertheless founded on a common set of basic values and social structures. The Soviet Union has lost its consensus about society. That, too, is indicative of a pre-revolutionary situation - of a turning point. And the very fact that a breakaway from Stalinist dictatorship and Brezhnev petrification has happened at all is in itself already revolutionary.

THE MANY PEOPLES OF THE USSR

Union Republics, Autonomous Republics, Autonomous Regions and Autonomous Areas:
As the legend goes, once an old man invited his adult sons to visit him and, showing a bundle of sticks, said: "Try to break it." The sons tried hard, but none of them managed to break the bundle. Then the old man divided the bundle into twigs and began to break them one by one. "Look here, my sons. If you are united, no enemy can gain the upper hand over you."

This legend is more relevant now to the

and Tajikistan - are also multi-ethnic states and include Autonomous Republics (they number 20) and Autonomous Regions (8). The Russian Federation has also Autonomous Areas within its territory.

This state-territorial structure is easy to explain. The latest census (January 1989), during which, as during the previous one, a citizen's nationality was put down on the strength of what he said, has shown that the USSR is inhabited by 145 nationalities. But there is no consensus among scientists about

USSR than ever before. The recent developments - the persisting conflict in the Nagorno-Karabakh Autonomous Region, the bloody disturbances, unprecedented in cruelty, in the Fergana valley, the mass skirmishes in Abkhazia, and the complex and largely contradictory processes in the Soviet Baltic Republics cannot but cause anxiety over the unity and stability of the Union of Soviet Socialist Republics.

Today the USSR is a multi-ethnic state incorporating 15 Union (Soviet Socialist) Republics - SSRs. Some of them - the Russian Federation (RSFSR), Georgia, Azerbaijan

the real number of nationalities. Different figures mention up to 400.

A distorted policy: The problem is that, beginning with the 1930s, the Leninist nationalities policy became distorted. It was based on equality of all nations and ethnic groups and on the encouragement of tendencies to assimilate.

The negation, however, of historical, cultural and ethnic tradition, and the identification of national sentiments with nationalism, led to the voluntary "unification" of some small ethnic groups with others to form one nation. Now, even those belonging to small ethnic groups begin to regard themselves as people of a different nationality during the censuses.

In any event, the Russians, who number over 137 million, certainly constitute the largest nation. As many as 22 other nationalities number more than one million each, 50 less than 100,000 and among them about ten number less than 1,000. The Neghidals, who number 500, are the smallest ethnic group. They speak one of the languages of the Tungus group and live in the valleys of the Amgun and Amur rivers in the Khabarovsk Territory. The Aleuts, who live in the Komandorskiye Islands in the Far East, number 550.

eration and Estonia.

More women than men: The number of women in the USSR exceeds that of men by 15.7 million. This excess begins from the age of 30 and, in the demographers' view, is explained by the higher mortality rate among men, and in the older age groups also by the "demographic echo" of World War II in which more men than women perished.

As of January 1, 1989, there were 2,190 towns in the USSR, 24 of them having a population over one million and another 34 having more than 500,000. The biggest cities are Moscow, Leningrad, Kiev and Tashkent. Over the past decade the population of all towns and cities increased substantially, by a

According to the latest census, as of January 12, 1989, 286,717,000 people live in the USSR. The population has increased by nearly 25 million over the decades which had passed since the previous census. The highest growth rates of the population were registered in the Turkmen, Uzbek and especially Tajik Union Republics, and the lowest in the Ukraine, in Latvia, the Russian Federation.

total of more than 25 million. But it dropped dramatically, from 207,000 to 120,000, in the Armenian city of Leninakan as a result of the terrible earthquake in December 1988 which destroyed that city and two small ones, Spitak and Kirovakan.

The Union Republics: Article 76 of the Constitution of the USSR defines a Union Republic as "a sovereign Soviet socialist state". A Union Republic has its own constitution, which it adopts on its own, and its own legislation. The territorial boundaries of a Union Republic may not be altered without its consent. It has an emblem, flag and an an-

Preceding pages, we are all so different and so alike. **Left**, "I haven't met you for ages!" **Above**, at a coop market.

them of its own. As a sovereign state, a Union Republic has, in theory, the right to enter into relations with foreign states, conclude treaties with them, and exchange diplomatic representatives.

In conformity with the Constitution of the USSR and the Constitutions of the Union Republics, they theoretically exercise full sovereignty in deciding questions relating to their internal life: management of the economy on its territories, including planning and budget, ensurance of the rights and freedoms of citizens, social and cultural development, etc. How far this sovereignty can go in reality has, however, been shown by the recent development in Lithuania.

The Autonomous Republics fulfill on their territories functions analogous to those performed by the Union Republics on theirs. They also have highest bodies of state authority and administration, constitutions, capitals, emblems and flags of their own. The territory of an Autonomous Republic may not be altered without its consent.

The idea behind the setting up of Autonomous Republics within the Union Republics was to give smaller nations, who inhabit a certain part of the territory of the Union Republic, the possibility of state development that takes into account ethnic, cultural and specific features of their way of life; to enable them to have their own economic bodies and bodies of state authority and administration and to enable them to develop judicial proceedings, their own press, schools, theaters, and cultural establishments, using the native tongue.

The gap between words and deeds: In theory everything seems to be all right and harmonious, but this is so only on the face of things. The problem is that from the Stalin era the contradiction between words and deeds became almost a national tradition; many provisions of the Constitution pertaining to inter-ethnic relations remained, in essence, on paper. For decades equality of the peoples and their right to sovereignty remained only constitutional declarations. Any attempt to recall this right was easily and quickly stemmed or caused suspicion.

Furthermore, the USSR's existing state system itself is largely scientifically groundless and even illogical. For instance, the criteria giving grounds for the formation of Union Republics were formulated more than fifty years ago. They were based on the geographical distance from Moscow, the numerical prevalence of the nationality which had given its name to the Republic, and the existence of at least one million in population. These criteria are not only obsolete now, they are also altogether too formal. It is logical that the Soviet press has asked more than once why, for example, the Tatar or Bashkir Republics were made Autonomous, while Estonia is a Union Republic, the indigenous population in the former two exceeds by far that of Estonia. In short, the legislation on the problems of inter-ethnic communication - and this is generally recognized - is in a neglected condition and is likely to be altered in the immediate future.

The inter-ethnic contradictions, the sense of offense and resentment and the striving for sovereignty are now burning issues. Perestroika has broken the many-year vow of silence on the nationalities problem, silence which the optimists of the Stalin-Brezhnev epoch tried to present as the highest manifestation of internationalism.

At long last, the joyful song about a "united family" in which happiness, calm and prosperity allegedly reigned has been classed as social myth-making. This song was sang at a time when the forcible resettlement of the peoples - the Crimean Tatars, Germans of the Volga area, Meskhetian Turks, Balkarians and others - and millions of people of different nationalities were ordered to leave their native land and were sent to Siberia and Kazakhstan or wherever else they were commanded to go.

Monoculture and interethnic tensions: The high-voltage inter-ethnic tension, which is dangerous by reason of its short and long circuits, has only one source of power supply: the administrative command system under which, for decades, "solely correct decisions" were adopted and were unconditionally fulfilled. Many problems which traditionally seemed to be ethnic are not such in reality. The developments which took place in the Fergana valley were not at all a bolt from the blue. The clouds of irritation and discontent, which poured a heavy shower of barbarity on the Meskhetian Turks, did not

Kazach hospitality: guests are invited to try bread with salt.

arise in the last one or two years.

It would be impossible to understand the deep causes of the Fergana developments if they were sought only in relations between the two nationalities. Their root cause lies in the imposition of a monoculture: cotton, reigning supreme on three million hectares which are strictly protected against "invasion" by grain and fodder crops, vegetables any other "secondary" crops, exacted a high price in terms of labor and human relations.

The fate of thousands of adults and children have been sacrificed to cotton, which was used by the elite to earn the stars of "Heroes" for themselves. There are hundreds of thousands of strong adults who have no jobs and at the same time schoolchildren work on the plantations from September to December.

Russian workers in the Baltic states: Take the situation in the Baltic area where enterprises, which employ manpower from all over the USSR because of the lack of local labor, were built at the will of the All-Union Ministries. The grudge which the indigenous population has against these honest hard workers, who naturally and rightfully claim apartments, accommodation at pre-school centers and the other good things of life, were pre-programmed. Regrettably, there is a very long list of such examples. The conclusion is that the command economy, which is moreover in a crisis state, causes interethnic conflicts. It seems that those Russians, Estonians, Ukrainians and Kazakhs who believe that if there are plenty of products in the shops, the nationalities issues will be less pressing may well be right. Switching over to regional (republican) profit and cost accounting is a way to remedy the existing situation. The pioneers - the Lithuanian, Estonian, Latvian and Byelorussian Union Republics - took to this road on January 1, 1990. In conformity with a resolution of the USSR Supreme Soviet, they have switched over to self-management and self-financing.

Only time will show how relations between these Republics (and not only theirs because quite a number of other regions are also preparing to switch over to profit and cost accounting) with the All-Union bodies will shape up. Lithuania's drive for total independence seems to be only the beginning of a long and painful process.

As to the All-Union bodies, they will only

coordinate the whole economy of the USSR, its foreign, defense and social policy. If the Republics will have to struggle against bureaucratic centralism it will again be regarded as struggle against Russia.

The Russians' fate has never been light. Russia paid a dear price to enable the other Republics not to feel destitute. Of course, subsidies are not the best method to keep the economy healthy, but they served their purpose. Today, the same problems which exist in many ethnic regions plague Russian cities and villages as well - perhaps, their situation is even worse. In short, the crisis state of society and the common woes press for a resolution that involves pooling the efforts of all

the peoples of the USSR in order to change the overall quality of life in all the Union Republics. Time has long been ripe to create a kind of code of principles governing interethnic relations, a code which the founder of the Soviet state, Vladimir Lenin, spoke of nearly 70 years ago.

The language question: Such a code would contain rules regulating the performance of national customs and traditions and formalizing freedom of religious belief, protecting national monuments of culture, bilingualism, and the right to free instruction of children in the native tongue, everything that concerns the very notion of a "people". There is a claim that "Moscow is to blame" for all the problems of nationalities, for instance in the questions of the language. It is perfectly clear that the national self-awareness of many peoples rebel when their native tongue loses its significance, supplanted by Russian (incidentally, over 15 million people of non-Russian nationalities consider it to be their native tongue); when national classes and schools are closed through the effort of too zealous officials, many of them non-Russians; when one can more often hear the Russian language, but not Moldavian or Estonian, in the streets of cities like Kishinev or Tallinn.

It is true, however, that many Russians who have lived in other Union Republics for decades have not taken the trouble to learn the local language. This is the sole explanation of the non-acceptance by some circles of a Russian-speaking population and of the laws on language adopted in a number of Union Republics, specifically in Estonia and Moldavia. It is symptomatic that the law of the Estonian Union Republic contains an

Left, Moscow policeman. **Above**, Russian environmentalist.

item which says that any person who addresses the state bodies of the Republic must receive an answer in his native tongue. A Russian in the Russian language, and an Estonian in Estonian. Accordingly, those who work in the communal or health services or in the state bodies must know both Estonian and Russian.

Keeping the Union from disintegration: Mighty centrifugal forces are intrinsic to ethnic problems. While solving them, it is necessary to prevent disintegration of the whole Union, especially because many problems will exist for many years. Illustrative of this is the problem of Nagorny Kharabakh, an Autonomous Region in which the Armenians account for 80 percent of the population but which forms part of the Azerbaijan Union Republic as a result of Stalin's "border-making".

The impulses of tension, which emerged with perestroika because of the incorrect or sometimes too emotional reaction to such issues, aggravated the problems. Listed among them are the dramatic events in the Abkhazian Autonomous Republic. As a result of the actions of extremists who demanded withdrawal of the Republic from the Georgian SSR, mass exchanges of fire between the Georgians and Abkhazians, with the participation of up to 200-300 people on each side, took place there in July 1989.

The law on elections to the local Soviets, which was adopted by the Supreme Soviet of the Estonian SSR in August 1989 which envisages a kind of residence qualification, has deprived tens of thousands of people of non-indigenous nationality of universal suffrage. As a result, a wave of mass strikes of the Russian-speaking population swept the Republic and paralyzed its economy.

There is a tight tangle of inter-ethnic problems in the Soviet Union, and it can be untied - of course, not at once - only through the joint efforts of all its peoples. Though the present situation is very grave, President Gorbachev and all sober-minded people are aware of this. Common sense prompts that the state's integrity can be preserved only in a constructive way, through democracy, openness, mutual understanding, cooperation and dialogue; by broadening the rights of the Republics and imparting to the USSR both the content and form of a Union of equal sovereign republics. There is no other way.

"How's life?" - this standard greeting has now largely ceased to be a mere pleasantry to Soviet people, since it usually hints at the hope that any day, now or at least in the near future, life is going to improve. The responses to it are of course varied but nearly always gloomy. Academician Leonid Abalkin, the driving force behind perestroika, says simply: "Our life is no worse than the way we work." Absolutely right. We shouldn't believe those who blame Gorbachev or the government for all the sins on of an accelerating economic reform that should give every "normal" person the chance to live a decent life. They are also to be blamed for the empty shops, the increasing use of rationing, the shortages - both temporary and chronic - of the most essential items such as soap, sugar, detergents, fashionable clothes, decent footwear, and so on. They also bear their share of responsibility for the strikes that so amazed the country in 1989, when 15,000 people were absent from work every day; for spiraling crime, includ-

earth, who are forgetful of their own share of responsibility for what's been done or not done; for squandered hours at work, for reluctance to work productively and creatively. It is easier of course to point the finger at Stalin and his cronies - Khrushchev and Brezhnev - for the failures of our economy, for the growing tension in society. One thing that is obvious, however, is that they are not the sole culprits of our current plight. Also to blame are all the people, both singly and collectively - in other words, society as a whole. They are to be blamed for their inability to work and earn against the background ing organized crime, which has come to present an everyday threat to our lives; for declining morals which takes the form of increasing prostitution and drug addiction.

To reiterate: all are to blame, yet it has to be said that society is still far from realizing this. All around, in buses, at factories, in design offices, in the shop queues that have, alas, virtually become the country's hallmark, one can see a flood of discontent: some are simply grumbling, others are venting their spleen on everything and everyone. Except themselves. It is rare to come across someone who is happy with their current lot and future prospects. Yet at the same time, everyone is satisfied with themselves.

So what is this, an outpouring of social disillusionment or the usual Russian moaning, as commented upon by the great satirist Mikail Saltykov-Schedrin as far back as the early 1880s? "It has to be said," he wrote, "that at the current time in Russia it is rare that you will meet a person that is satisfied... whoever you listen to, they are all complaining, moaning, howling."

His words remain relevant to this day. Yet the present situation, even though patterns of thought and behavior may still be similar, differs fundamentally from that of a hundred years ago.

a united "We"?

Perestroika, the way out? Nonetheless, the roots of the worsening political crisis are to be found in the economy. Only now, after years of perestroika, are we beginning to understand that from Brezhnev's regime of stagnation we have inherited an economy that is virtually in ruins, with shortages of labor, materials and finance - not to mention a devastated (fortunately, not everywhere) natural environment.

Does this mean that perestroika has nothing at all to show for itself? On the contrary, initial results give cause for hope. Declining growth rates have been halted, and the economy has, so to speak, adopted a more human

The disillusionment felt by some is not merely confined to not having the food or footwear that they would like. Today a clear antipathy towards socialism can be detected in the population of the USSR. The country is undergoing not only an economic crisis, but a crisis of ideals. Will society once again be able to rally round on the basis of ideals? Will it be able to gather the separate "I's" into

face. For example, more housing is being built, there are more hospitals, kindergartens and schools. For the first time in many years the death rate has fallen and average life expectancy has risen; injuries at work and at home are down. But still...

The budget deficit continues to grow, and inflation is on the increase. As a result, confidence in the rouble has been undermined, which, inevitably, has led to consumer panic. Despite rising incomes, in 1988 they rose more than during the preceding two years put together, and far outstripped the growth in productivity. Living standards for the greater part of the population have fallen: over 40 million people, or 15 percent of the population, live below the poverty line (which is still set at a very conservative 75 roubles a month). This applies mainly to pensioners, single mothers and families.

Perestroika has made the lives of the people more splendid. Only now, after decades of tyranny under Stalin and stagnation under Brezhnev, can the millions of Soviet citizens, feel relatively free, both economically and spiritually.

Glasnost, the mind set free at last: Glasnost is probably Gorbachev's greatest achievement to date: it has truly revolutionized society. No more is anyone surprised to see how all,

In Moscow during the First Congress of People's Deputies the Lenin Stadium in the Luzhniki sports complex became the scene of such activity, as up to 200,000 Muscovites and others gathered there every evening. Numerous deputies, including Sakharov, Yeltsin, Yevtushenko and others came here straight from the Kremlin in order to discuss with their voters matters that the Congress of People's Deputies had been debating a scant hour previously.

Ideas, views and suggestions bubbled forth that could be put to the Congress the next day. This was the place where the deputies had their work and opinions assessed by the electorate.

from humble workers to academicians, can openly speak their mind about the country's past, present and future. No one is surprised that it is permissible to criticize the country's leadership, be it in the newspapers, on the television or at the Congress of People's Deputies.

Incidentally, the atmosphere of free debate at the Congress has been imparted to the entire country. In many towns it has become a kind of tradition for people to gather after work in parks and squares to discuss what's worrying them. And not only discuss but debate from the most diverse viewpoints.

An explosion of social activities: The Soviet Union is experiencing an explosion of social activity, at all levels of society. Virtually every day, new unions, associations, societies and clubs of various hues, political, cultural, environmental, charitable and so on, are cropping up to rival the old public organizations that have been around already for decades. The artistic unions, those of the filmmakers, writers and theater worker, have had new life breathed into them as they inveigh against all sorts of bureaucratic hassles and restrictions.

In Moscow, Leningrad and elsewhere,

people have taken to picketing buildings of historical interest earmarked for demolition, and turning to the press, radio and television stations for support.

It is as if society has awoken from years of hibernation and realized (possibly for the first time) that life is in fact quite an interesting experience.

Meanwhile, acid comments have been made to the effect that with glasnost it's nonetheless more interesting to read than to live. And there might well be some truth in it. Glasnost has given back to the Soviet press the entitlement to write and speak the truth, the right to publish truly worthy articles, short stories and novels, whether the ideo-

also of numerous others would increase to such an extent that the country is now hard-put to supply enough paper to the newspapers so that limits don't have to be placed on subscriptions.

Glasnost has revealed the true extent of the bloody crimes committed by Stalin and his henchmen as they called upon the people to make every sacrifice in the name of a better future, and who exterminated in peacetime over 20 million Soviet citizens, according to the most conservative estimates. Glasnost has exploded the image of socialism that was inculcated for decades as a system consisting of two powerful entities - the "great leader" that issues the commands, and the masses

logical moguls like them or not.

Just a few years ago it was difficult to imagine that hundreds of thousands of people, millions even, would subscribe to dozens of publications each; that large queues would form outside newspaper kiosks, whatever the weather; that copies of *Moscow News* or *Ogonyok* would start changing hands on the black market in some parts of the country for three, five or even ten times the cover price; that the print runs not only of "progressive" publications such as these but

Left, potatoes seller. **<u>Above</u>**, the latest pop song.

that silently carry out his every directive. Glasnost has finally opened people's eyes to the obvious: to the fact that there is, and can be, no subject that is off-limits for the press, literature and the arts; to the fact that various views and opinions can be given on one and the same theme.

Glasnost has extended the vocabulary: now everyone can say and write words that previously seemed to have been forgotten forever, words such as "alternative", "pluralism", and even "faction" and "opposition". Glasnost has shown that you can regularly travel abroad, and not only on business or in a tourist group but also to visit friends and relatives, and still remain a Soviet citizen. It has turned out that the state won't come tumbling down if the exit restrictions are removed. It has turned out that the country can get by with a lot less zones closed to both its own people and to foreigners. It has turned out that those who were earlier considered dissidents, Alexander Solzhenitsyn, Josef Brodsky, Gennady Vladimov and others, are absolutely normal people, who perhaps only differ from everyone else by virtue of their outstanding talent. Millions have now had the chance to confirm this for themselves after reading their works in both the "fat" literary journals and in separate editions. Glasnost has become possibly the most typical feature of everyday life.

The shops are empty, the tables full: Today you can often hear foreigners who come to the USSR saying things like, "The shops are empty, to put it mildly, yet if you go visiting someone the table is always groaning with food." And this is how it really is. It is not easy to buy delicacies, but there are ways and means of obtaining them: via friends who work in shops, or at the market (although not many can afford this option; unlike in the West, market prices here are stratospheric) or by hunting round dozens of shops. Also, many items in short supply can be ordered through one's place of work. One way or another, guests, and not only foreign ones, are treated like kings: such hospitality is an outstanding feature of the Russian character. Not only that, what kind of special occasion can be allowed to pass without a glass of champagne or a shot of vodka....

Eating out: The better-off are nowadays spending more and more time with their families and friends in cooperative cafes and restaurants, which are on the increase in Moscow. There are already 60 or so, although some of them, say, "Kropotkinskaya 36" or the "Razgulyai", are so much in demand that it is by no means easy to get in. The prices in cooperative restaurants are higher than in the state-run establishments, but this is fully justified by better service and better food.

All told, there is a glaring shortage of eating establishments in the Soviet Union; even in Moscow most of them have the same old sign in their windows every evening: "Sorry, we're full". True, recent years have seen an increasing number of summer cafes, and joint ventures are springing up: in Moscow they're now building a chain of MacDonald fast-food joints, and Leningrad's popular "Chaika" is always jam-packed. The latter, however, caters mainly to foreigners, since it accepts payment only in convertible currency. Unfortunately, the rouble is as yet a long way from convertibility.

The leisure industry is unable to meet people's demands. There aren't enough cinemas, and few video establishments. The state of many theaters, especially in the provinces is pitiful. There's a reason for this. Under Brezhnev, for many years, social and cultural needs were placed far down the list of

priorities behind other sectors of the economy, and in its turn the absence of anything interesting or meaningful to do in one's spare time facilitated the spread of such social ills as alcohol and drug addiction. The cooperatives are to a degree easing the situation in this respect, but they have their own difficulties: increasing organized crime and especially the changeable nature of the legislation that governs the way they operate.

All types of cooperatives, in the manufacturing, construction, medical and service sectors, have experienced over the past two or three years all the "charms" that life has to offer. One minute they're being given the green light, the next they're being strung up in a noose of taxes. But there are good and bad cooperatives. The majority, of course, are in business not only for their own good but also for the good of the consumer; yet there are others that play on the shortages, selling kebabs made from frozen meat bought in the state shops at extortionate rates, or by offering ordinary blouses with popular Western designer labels stuck on them (and in the process, as you will readily understand, breaking the law). All this leads to public hostility. Things reached the stage when, for example, one of the demands made by the Kuzbass miners on strike in July of

housing problem is one of the most acute facing the country, even though construction goes on at a fast pace: from 1986 to 1988 alone, about 10 million new flats were built. Nonetheless, the housing queues are growing, and at the current time 14 million urban families, that is, almost one in five, is on the list. The rate of construction is set to grow, and this gives grounds for hope that the task — that of providing every Soviet family with a separate flat or house by the year 2000 — will be accomplished.

Varying housing conditions: One thing worth pointing out is that people in the USSR live in flats that are supplied for their use for an indefinite period by the state housing fund.

1989 was that catering sector cooperatives be closed down.

There are still many contradictions and the country has to heal itself from its temporary illnesses as it makes the transition from the command economy to a market economy.

Family life: Russians now spend more and more time at home, with their children, reading or watching TV. But not everyone can say today that his home is his castle. The

<u>Left</u>, a common apartment building in Moscow. <u>Above</u>, Babushkas in discussion of serious matters.

Moreover, no payments are made for the actual receipt of a flat; throughout the subsequent occupancy one only pays rent and bills for communal services on a monthly basis. An important fact: rent levels have remained unchanged for over 60 years and do not exceed 3 or 4 percent of the family budget.

Over recent years the amount of cooperative and private construction, with or without help from the state, has been rising and is expected to reach 50 percent by 1995. At present approximately 15 percent of housing (10 percent on a cooperative basis, 5 by private individuals) is built with the aid of state credits. Such credit can be for 70 to 80 percent of the overall value of the work, and can be paid off over 25 years.

In the Soviet Union, private homes are mainly to be found in the countryside and villages. On the one hand, the quality and dimensions of urban flats are standardized nationwide (for example, the area of a three-room flat in a new block is usually no more than 48 square meters); on the other, houses in the villages in, say, the Moscow region differ markedly from those in the Ukraine, which also bears witness to varying living standards. Near Moscow you will see mainly small, wooden huts with no modern conveniences. Go to the Ukraine, however, or to the

until recently thousands upon thousands of people, especially the young, have been deserting their native villages for the cities and, so to speak, for civilization; at the same time millions of city-dwellers have been doing the opposite - trying to get closer to the land and joining gardening and market-gardening societies and dacha cooperatives. We are still witnessing a boom in dachas, which has spread to the entire social spectrum. About 20 million urban families spend every weekend from April to October on their "plantations", which are not allowed to exceed 600 square meters. With no effort spared they set about tending their vegetables, fruits, flowers and berries, and build (frequently with

Soviet Baltic republics, and you will find well-appointed two-storey stone houses with areas of 100-120 square meters and usually a sauna and garage as well.

In general, it is the social backwardness of the countryside, where living standards lag behind those of the cities to a significant degree, that largely explains the low level of development and the inefficiency of our agriculture. This is now clear to all, including the government, which intends to step up the provision of social and cultural amenities there.

The dacha trend: Here's a strange paradox:

their own hands) small and relatively primitive dachas. In a country where construction materials are in chronically short supply, this is no mean feat. What they grow goes mainly for personal consumption, but sometimes also to the market. This is not something that can be termed "leisure" in the accepted sense of the word, but that is what it is called.

The old and the poor: If financial incomes have risen noticeably in the past then social and property stratification has become even more noticeable. Many economists consider stratification of society to be an absolutely normal phenomenon. Yet this process is leading to widespread discontent and indignation amongst millions of people who have to scrape by on 75 roubles a month or less. This means, unfortunately, that large families, the disabled and pensioners are suffering declining living standards against the background of rising inflation. There are 60 million pensioners alone in the country (the state foots the bill for looking after them). The maximum pension upon retirement from most professions and trades amounts to 120 roubles monthly. That's not a lot, to put it mildly. The majority of pensioners who retired in the 1960s and 70s on less than 50 roubles are, quite simply, living in poverty. In order somehow to improve their situation,

It is no exaggeration to say that care for the senior citizens is the most urgent of our social problems. The only thing that can possibly rival it is another national issue: that of the children.

The young: There are 83 million children in the USSR, almost one-third of the population. It would seem that the country gives to its children the best things that it can: well-equipped kindergartens and child care centers; sports centers and swimming pools; health resorts and theaters (there are over 160 dedicated children's theaters); music, arts and dance schools; books (one book in three published in the USSR is for children) and libraries. Virtually all of this, not to

the Supreme Soviet of the USSR decreed that as from October 1, 1989, the minimum pension shall be 70 roubles. This will at least do something to better the financial lot of some 20 million people.

This is only a small, even perhaps a symbolic step, but nonetheless highly important. Very soon a new Law on Pensions will enter into force and will, so it is hoped, considerably raise living standards for millions more pensioners.

<u>Left</u>, Maria Kalinina, Miss Moscow 1988. <u>Above</u>, Oktyabryatas – junior scouts.

mention health care and education, is supplied for children by the state either free of charge or at a nominal price. Yet for a long time eyes have been closed to many problems concerning the upkeep of the young in the vain hope that they would solve themselves.

The USSR is near the top of the world table for the mortality of children under 12 months old. Many children are brought up in special homes or boarding schools, after being abandoned or rejected by their parents. Juvenile delinquency is growing. And this is by no means all.

Today society has realized the full extent of the danger posed by such problems, and is rallying in defense of its children; care for children is increasingly becoming the domain of the public as a whole, on whose initiative the Soviet Children's Foundation (named after Lenin) was established in 1987. Financed by donations from public and state sector sponsors and hundreds of thousands of ordinary citizens, the Foundation does a great deal to assist orphans from childhood, including the organization of wide-ranging public awareness campaigns.

A 40 percent divorce rate: It seems that the majority of children's problems are derived primarily from their parents' disorganized

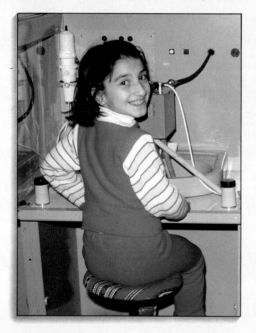

family lives, which in turn are determined by numerous social, moral and psychological factors. It has, unfortunately, become commonplace for marriages to break up, the Soviet divorce rate is 40 percent, which affects the lives not only of millions of adults but of children as well.

In earlier days, when separations were a far less frequent occurrence, the parties were unequivocally condemned for either lacking the desire or the ability to keep their family together. Nowadays, judging by public opinion polls, many people (to be precise, 37 percent) consider divorce to be a normal

phenomenon. Nonetheless, despite the soaring divorce rate, family life retains its position within society as one of the most precious things in life: 82 percent of people polled prefer to be married.

One of the saddest consequences of the divorce rate is the drop in the birth rate and the weakening of the family's role in raising children. Many people, fearing divorce, choose to have just one child, or even none at all. It is true that children suffer the most from divorces, and in the majority of cases remain to be raised by just one parent.

It is considered that one way to strengthen the family as an institution is to supply state and societal support for it from the outset. As a rule, young married couples and families experience financial and accommodation difficulties; the income of students and young workers is not great, so they tend to rely on parental assistance. True, there is now the opportunity to earn money by working in a cooperative or by taking more than one job, but not everyone can spare the time and effort to do this. The issue of accommodation is even more thorny for young couples. Few people want to live with their parents once they are married, yet nearly 50 percent of all young couples are forced to do precisely this. Moreover, their parents' flats are likely to be less than spacious. On top of all this, young couples usually lack experience of running a home and a family budget, of raising children, of the principles of hygiene and of health care for themselves and their children and much else besides.

How are such problems being tackled today? To help young families get off to a good start they are given interest-free loans of 1,500 roubles to improve their living conditions or to acquire household items. When the second child is born, 200 roubles of the loan are written off, and for the third child, 300. Young mothers receive a one-off payment of 50 roubles when their first child is born, and for the birth of the second and third, 100 roubles.

Young families are entitled to join cooperative housing construction organizations on favorable terms, and there are various other allowances also available. However, all of them are largely symbolic.

The system of education: "We all learned little by little, what we could and when we could." These words written by the great

Russian poet Alexander Pushkin (1799-1837) are relevant to this day. Despite the fact that over 100 million people study in Soviet educational establishments and that everyone has the right to not only secondary but also higher education free of charge, it must be said that there are many in the USSR who do not receive the education they should. Not only that, but the standards of professional training are significantly behind those of many countries.

It is unfortunate but true that many pupils have no desire to learn, and that when many students apply to go to a university or college (there are nearly 900 such establishments in the Soviet Union) the degree is more impor-

nomy suffers from a lack of top-class specialists. It seems knowledge has thus lost prestige, and the country has fallen behind in the sciences.

The system of education is now undergoing reform, the primary aim being to impart to it a more democratic form and content to motivate pupils and students to study not just for the sake of obtaining good marks.

Health care in the USSR: The health of society overall, depends largely on the good (or ill) health of its individual members, which in its turn is bound up with the state of the health service. The latter in the Soviet Union is no longer able to meet the requirements made of it. Today we don't conceal our dis-

tant to them than the knowledge they stand to gain. There is a reason for all this. It is no longer a secret that during the years of stagnation serious harm was inflicted on our education system. Young people were prevented from demonstrating the true extent of their abilities by perfunctory instruction and the drive for uniformity. Even though the country's higher education establishments turn out vast numbers of graduates, our eco-

Left, kids orphaned at the Leninakan earthquake in their new home in Yevpatoria, Ukraine. **Above**, weddings always draw a crowd.

satisfaction at the lack of up-to-date medical equipment in our hospitals and polyclinics, the shortage of medicines in our chemist shops, the dilapidated state of many of our hospitals.

The Soviet Union was the first country in the world to introduce free health care for all the people - this was back in the 1920s. More than one in three of all the doctors on the planet work in this country, in which there are about 25,000 hospitals with nearly 4 million beds. At the same time the mortality rate is higher than that of almost any developed country.

Just like the country as a whole, the health service is in crisis. There are many reasons for this, the main one being the fact that for two decades this vitally-important sector was far down the investment pecking order, priority being attached elsewhere.

This mistake (some call it crime) is now being put right, and medicine is now on the receiving end of additional funding. The entire health service is being overhauled. For example, from now on the pay of medical workers will be linked to the end results of treatment and preventive measures - a fall in the illness rate. They will cease to be remunerated purely on the basis of their number of "clients".

The joys of life: There is a Russian saying that: "A bad day's fishing is better than a good day at work." It could be added that: "Holidays always end too soon." Most workers in the Soviet Union have a yearly break of four weeks (the minimum is 15 working days). Where do they spend their holidays? This is a difficult question to answer since, quite naturally, different people have different tastes and opportunities. Nonetheless, it is possible to enumerate the main holiday trends. First of all, there are the dachas, which have already been mentioned. Secondly, there's the seaside, the Black and Baltic Seas, and the Sea of Azov. The Soviet Union, by the way, has over 14,000 rest homes, holiday hotels and resorts, which annually receive over 65 million visitors. Over a quarter of them (and in trade union resorts up to 80 percent) receive holiday vouchers that are completely or up to 70 percent subsidized at the expense of social security or state funds. Hundreds of thousands also receive such vouchers completely or partially paid for by their place of work.

Although the standards of service in the holiday resorts still leave something to be desired, for Russians the seaside is nevertheless the seaside.

Those who opt for organized holidays give the top place to what is called "tourism". Tourism in this sense includes everything: travel to different towns or along rivers, hunting and fishing, mountaineering, etc. The mass attraction of this kind of holiday (more than half the country's population goes in for it every year) is not only due to its accessibility. All tourism firms in the Soviet Union belong either to public organizations or the state. True, over the past couple of years increasing numbers of cooperatives have been organizing tours on a commercial basis at competitive rates.

Foreign travel is on the increase: in 1989 approximately two million Soviet citizens went on holiday to over 50 countries. This isn't much by world standards, but the important thing is that their number is growing, and has nearly doubled over the past two years. International tourism in the USSR is mainly handled by Intourist, which in effect has a monopoly on catering to foreign tourists. Plenty of problems have piled up in this respect.

To mention just one of them, the shortage of hotels, in such cities as Moscow and Leningrad. Although over 30 top-class hotels are now under construction in various cities, some of them as joint projects with foreign firms, it will take some time before there are sufficient hotel rooms available. Intourist offers more than 20 different types of tourism: group and individual travel, motor tours, special interest tours according to profession, skiing, cruises along the Volga, Dnieper and Don, visits for medical treatment, hunting and fishing, transit via the USSR, special tours for business people, tours to attend congresses, symposia and exhibitions, excursions for schoolchildren and young people, sea and river cruises, arts festivals and theater tours.

No joy without sport: For many people the joy of life means first and foremost sport. In summer football, volleyball and field and track events are most popular, and in winter, skiing and ice hockey. True, many prefer to root for their favorite team or sportsman from a seat in the stadium or, more frequently, the armchair in front of the TV. Nonetheless one might be surprised at the size of the exodus during winter weekends when skiers head out of town or to the nearest park to enjoy the frost and shake off the weariness of the working week. The kids

develop more quickly.

The Soviet Union is home to a multitude of different nationalities, nearly each of which has its own traditional games and pastimes fully conforming with the idea of sport. In the Central Asian and Transcaucasian republics, for example, various forms of wrestling and horseback racing are popular, while the northern peoples go racing in dog- or reindeer-hauled sleds or hold axe-throwing and archery competitions. The Russians have long enjoyed *gorodki,* a fairly straightforward version of skittles, in which chocks are set up in a square (the "town"), sometimes in a complex configuration, and then knocked out by throwing a heavy stick-like

play ice hockey in virtually every courtyard in the towns. Last but not least, there is no sport less popular than swimming, even in the depths of winter. Those hardy souls that go dipping in holes cut from the ice are termed "walruses", and their numbers are swelling. They can frequently be seen out with all the family, even babies. Experts reckon that the "walruses" are significantly less prone to illness, and that their children

Left, painter on Leningrad's Nevski Prospect. **Above**, windsurfing has become a fad throughout the USSR.

implement.

Nonetheless, the bulk of the population regards football and ice hockey as the kings of sport. Even if active participation is mainly the province of young men and girls, then the millions-strong army of supporters of these sports embraces all age groups and nationalities. Top footballers such as Oleg Blokhin and Alexander Zavarov, and hockey players such as Vyacheslav Fetisov and Sergei Makarov are household names. At times the streets of many towns are deserted when the national teams are in action, everyone is indoors watching them on the TV.

...and the TV: But people are not only glued to the box during major sporting occasions. Television is now a source of enjoyment for many, and has been transformed over the past couple of years thanks to glasnost. Such informational and musical programs as "Vzglyad" ("Viewpoint") and "Before and after Midnight" have an audience of nearly half the country, surpassing even serials. Most of all, these programs are controversial, topical and, quite simply, honest, and have in their own way become nationwide standard-bearers for glasnost.

At the moment, TV is winning the ratings battle with the cinemas and theaters, although the latter are far from empty.

they seem to give their preference to the cinema or the circus. On the subject of cinema and theater, it mustn't be omitted that today Soviet stage and silver screen buffs are becoming more and more familiar with the works of foreign artistes and companies, thanks to broadening cultural contacts. For the sake of justice it has to be added that the big crushes outside the cinemas usually take place when they're showing an American or Italian film, rather than a Soviet one.

Like anywhere else in the world many people in the USSR enjoy and take an interest in their work. Even more are fanatical readers. Lots of people are into stamp-collecting, and not only since perestroika, the

There is little chance of obtaining theater tickets in Moscow or Leningrad, Tbilisi or Kuibyshev. The reason for this is simple: people in the USSR love the stage - and not just the Bolshoi Ballet, which remains an object of national pride and even worship. The trouble is that tickets are extremely hard to come by. People go to the theater to see their favorite actors, to enjoy the work of the talented directors, and not least to absorb themselves in the thoughts and fantasies of the world's best playwrights, from Shakespeare to Dürrenmatt.

Children also enjoy the theater, although

young generation loves rock music in a big way. The older generations are interested in their health. And then there are those that are simply in love,...

Life in the USSR is varied and entertaining; no matter how hard one tries, one can never describe everything.

Therefore here is another Russian saying: "Better to see it once, than hear about it a thousand times..."

Above, road block at Nakhichevan. **Right**, mourning after Sakharov's death.

"Russia is a godless country"; that is a notion very often heard outside the USSR. There are also heart-rendering stories about believers being persecuted and churches in abandonment. These in no way reflect the reality in the USSR of today even though things are far from being smooth in the sphere of religion.

Freedom of conscience is the Soviet citizens' inalienable right, guaranteed by the Constitution. Article 52 reads in part: "Incitement of hostility or hatred on religious

Anyway, the figures prove the Soviet Union cannot be referred to as an entirely godless country.

Guaranteed rights: The right of believers are protected by the state, no matter what religion they profess. There are more than 20,000 active Orthodox, Roman Catholic and Lutheran churches as well as numerous synagogues, mosques, Buddhist datsans, chapels of Old Believers, Evangelical Christian Baptists, Seventh Day Adventists, molokans and other sects. Altogether there are some forty

grounds is prohibited". Since it is a private matter whether or not one professes any religion, no record of religious denomination is to be found in official documents and forms. Neither is this question asked during censuses, which is why no exact data on the number of believers is available. At the same time sociological surveys suggest that about 10 percent of urban dwellers are believers, and in the countryside they constitute up to 30 percent. It can be easily calculated therefore that there are approximately 50 million believers in the country, though it seems that their actual number is 20 or 30 million more.

different denominations. Any attempt to hamper religious rites runs counter to the law. Dismissal, refusal to employ or enroll on religious grounds are punishable with the full force of the law. Parents and guardians are free to educate their children or charges as they think fit as far as religion and morals are concerned; however, it is also inadmissible to force children into religion.

The past and the present: The USSR Constitution further states: "In the USSR, the church is separated from the state, and the school from the church." This means that the state does not interfere in the church's internal affairs. That is what the law says. In actual fact, for decades, beginning with the Stalin era, the law was simply ignored. Churches were closed down, or even destroyed as happened to the magnificent Christ the Savior Cathedral in Moscow which was barbarously blown up in 1931. The number of prisoners of conscience was growing, and their only crime was membership of an unauthorized religious sect. Numerous rulings were passed to ban the charitable activities of religious societies and priests. Today society admits its mistakes.

Perestroika and religion: Perestroika has notably corrected the relations between the church and the state and between believers

mocracy in a state governed by law.

Already churches have been reopened. 1988 alone saw 1,610 new religious societies registered, including 1,244 Russian Orthodox, 72 Georgian Orthodox, 71 Roman Catholic, 48 Muslim, and 36 Evangelical (Pentecostalists). More than 937 idle religious premises have been turned over to believers, including 788 to the Russian Orthodox church, 72 to the Georgian Orthodox church, 29 to the Roman Catholic church, and 26 to Muslims. 143 permits have been issued to build new religious premises. The premises of the Kiev-Pechory Lavra, the St. John's Convent of the Confession in Ryazan, the St. Nicholas-Vyazhischsky Monastery in

and non-believers, as required by democracy. The gap between words and deeds in what we call the freedom of conscience has been reduced. Life has dramatically changed and it is now widely understood that there exist direct and close ties between common human culture and worship. The state has revised its policy towards religion since freedom of conscience is an integral part of democracy in a state governed by law.

Preceding pages, village cemetery in Northern Russia. **Left**, Lenin's image displayed for Vorkuta miners. **Above**, Orthodox ceremonies are broadcast on TV now.

Novgorod, the Kapriyan Monastery in Moldavia and other monasteries have been turned over to the Russian Orthodox church.

The Russian Orthodox Church: The Russian Orthodox church is the biggest religious entity in the USSR. The supreme power in terms of doctrine, church government and church court is vested in the Local Council, which is periodically held with attendance of bishops, the clergy and laymen. The church is headed by the Patriarch of Moscow and All Russia, elected by the Local Council, who runs church affairs jointly with the Holy Synod. The Russian Orthodox church has more than

8,200 parishes and 74 dioceses.

There are about 7,000 Orthodox churches in the country, big and small, built of wood or stone. Most of them, especially the earlier ones, are true architectural monuments distinguished by their unique frescoes and icons. The Russian Orthodox church has 28 monasteries, of which the Trinity-St. Sergius Lavra in Zagorsk near Moscow is the biggest.

The spiritual and administrative center of the Moscow Patriarchate is the St. Daniel Monastery. It is the seat of the Patriarch and houses synodal institutions. In the monastery and around it are four active cathedrals and a conference hall for international meetings. The Patriarchate has its own "minis-

accredited to Moscow, and Muslim students who study in the capital. The majority of Soviet Muslims belong to the Sunnite branch, but there are also Shiites in the Caucasus, and Ismailites in the Pamirs. The Muslim affairs are run by four Boards, in Tashkent, Ufa, Makhachkala and Baku. Soviet Muslims take part in international Islamic gatherings and make hajji to Mecca.

Catholicism: The Catholic church has more than 1,150 churches in 12 Union republics, mainly in Lithuania where Catholics constitute the bulk of the religious population. Other Catholic areas are the Western Ukraine and Byelorussia, and parts of Latvia and Kazakhstan. There are 2 archdioceses, 4 dio-

tries", such as the department for foreign church relations, the publishing department and others.

Muslims in the USSR: Muslims live mainly in Central Asia and Kazakhstan, the Volga area, in the Urals, Siberia and in the Caucasus. There are several hundred major active places of worship and thousands of neighborhood and rural mosques. In the past few years dozens of new mosques have been opened and restored. There is a cathedral mosque in Moscow. On Fridays and religious holidays it is attended not only by Muscovite Muslims, but also by Muslim diplomats,

ceses, and about 640 parishes. Many Catholic churches are architectural monuments and are protected by the state. The local bodies of state authority render assistance in repairing and restoring churches. In 1988 the St. Kazimir Cathedral in Vilnius, the capital of Lithuania, and the Vilnius Main Cathedral, which for decades had housed museums, were turned over to the believers. In Klaipeda, Lithuania, the Regina Mundi Cathedral which formerly housed a philharmonic society has been restored to the Catholic community.

Jews: There are more than 1.8 million Jews

living in the Soviet Union. The current level of religious sentiment among them can be easily determined by the attendance of synagogues. In Novosibirsk, West Siberia, with a Jewish population of 11 thousand, about 200 people visit the synagogue on religious holidays. In Kuybyshev (the Volga region) about 3 percent of the city's Jewish population attend synagogues, and in Leningrad, about 1.5 percent. There are fewer believers among the urban population than in the rural areas and 98 percent of Soviet Jews live in cities. There are, however, three ethnic groups of Jews in this country, where the level of religious sentiment is notably higher than the country's average. These are the Georgian, Bukhara

of the Tora, and Tora calligraphers; it also has a kosher canteen.

Perestroika has not yet resolved all issues relating to the freedom of confession, though a lot has been done. Even today we can still hear the "illegal church" mentioned, meaning the Ukraine's Greeko-Catholic church, whose right to exist is questioned not by the state but by the Russian Orthodox church. Many zealous advocates of culture still prefer to use religious premises as concert halls, e.g. the Alexander Nevsky cathedral in Novosibirsk. In so doing they seem to forget that nowadays culture is unthinkable without restoring for good the church's long-standing significance.

and Gori Jews with a total population of 100,000. In Tbilisi there are as many Jews as in Kuybyshev, whereas ten times as many believers attend the synagogue on holidays. It can safely be said that about 20 percent of Transcaucasian and Bukhara Jews are believers.

All in all there are about 100 synagogues operating in the country. The Moscow Choral Synagogue runs a theological school, *yeshiva* which trains rabbis, cantors, readers

Left, Krasnoye selo. **Above**: left, 12th-century angel; and right, 20th-century monk.

A new religiosity: The attitude towards religion has changed drastically, a fact witnessed by the 1988 celebrations on the occasion of the Millennium of the Baptism of Rus, which became a major event of the year and almost a nationwide holiday. All the religious communities in the USSR support perestroika, not just paying lip-service to it but backing it by specific deeds, such as contributions to the construction of hospitals and children's homes. This is no wonder, since nowadays everyone is becoming increasingly aware that both believers and non-believers have a common goal, that of living a humane life.

Since it was ushered in by Sputnik, on October 4, 1957, the space age has seen several painful changes in the attitude of the Soviet people toward space exploration. The euphoria generated by the early successes diminished gradually, and today, you can often hear the demand to "close everything down" or (at least) to consider, and publicly discuss, how future programs to explore Mars will look against the singularly grim economic background.

Whatever else it may be, the space industry is certainly one of the more impressive showcases of modern science. Sputnik, the first man-made satellite, brought the huge (and, today, extremely profitable) mechanism of space exploration to life, and it is hardly surprising that even though more and more countries now partake in the space race, the Soviet Union is, after more than three decades, still a leader.

The USSR's star log carries records of outstanding achievements. Here are several "entries". The first man in space: On April 12, 1961, Yury Gagarin went up in the Vostok, and circled the globe in 108 minutes. He was followed by German Titov (a 24-hour flight in August, 1961) and the first woman cosmonaut Valentina Tereshkova (June 1963). The first space crew of three: Vladimir Komarov, Konstantin Feoktistov and Boris Yegorov (October 1964), and, of course, Aleksei Leonov and his unprecedented space walk in March 1965. Then came the first docking of two manned Soyuz craft (January 1969), and later the assembly of orbital complexes in outer space (April 1971). These are the main landmarks on the way to the strategic goals of the Soviet space program - the creation of perpetual orbital research complexes designed to aid the national economy.

The Mir orbital station has been in space for over four years, during which it has seen over 20 cosmonauts from the USSR, Syria, Bulgaria, Afghanistan and France. It was on the Mir that the standing world record for the longest space flight was set by Vladimir Titov and Musa Manarov - 367 days.

The Soviet space program makes wide use of both manned craft and remote-controlled vehicles. The two types of spacecraft complement each other. Over 2,000 cosmos satellites have been launched since the first of the series went up in 1967 to study the Sun and the farther stars, the Earth's surface and atmosphere, cosmic particles and the solar wind. These satellites do the work of communications experts, geologists, navigators and biologists. A certain number of them is deployed at a relatively small altitude of several hundred kilometers. Others, such as, for example, the Prognoz Solar Station, move hundreds of thousands of kilometers away from the Earth and return to communicate data about our Sun - and the enigmatic "solar kitchen" where Earth's climate is "cooked" - to our scientists.

Samples of lunar soil were brought back to our planet by the Lunokhods, remote-controlled "Moon buggies" that scoured the surface of the Earth's ancient companion. Automatic stations of the Mars and Venera (Venus) type reported the chemical composition of these planets' soil and atmosphere. Then, in March, 1986, two Vega stations penetrated deep into the core of that rare but recurrent space visitor, the Halley Comet. The Venus - Halley Comet project was remarkable not only in scientific terms: it proved that many countries (eight in this case) could work together and solve ultra-complex tasks in outer space.

Another obvious success of the Soviet space program was the December 1988 launch of the Buran shuttlecraft - the first flight was remote-controlled from take-off to landing.

The Energia/Buran tandem is clearly a novel word in space technology. (Energia is a kind of a super space-truck capable of lifting 100 tons - almost six times the capability of the French Ariane). The Buran can deliver up to 30 tons of payload into orbit, and then return with up to 20 tons.

Success and tragedy: It goes without saying that the way to space was never all roses and smiles. Because it is a way into the unknown,

Preceding pages, a walk outside Mir spaceship. **Right**, Sojuz blast off.

it will never be totally without risk; it will always be hard work, a job requiring extensive knowledge, impeccable health and, above all, courage.

Today, there are 65 cosmonauts in the USSR's "space club". All of them could tell a story or two - it's an open secret that "unplanned" (emergency) situations occur almost every trip.

There are also those who died on the space frontier: Vladimir Komarov (April, 1967, during the landing of his Soyuz-I); Georgy Dobrovolski, Vladislav Volkov and Viktor Patsayev (June, 1971, again during landing). Yury Gagarin, too, is no longer with us - he died in a plane crash during a training flight.

of secrecy was lifted, the Soviet space potential went on the market, another sign of perestroika. Generally speaking, the improvement of economic feedback from the space programs is vital, despite the fact that space exploration is the only kind of scientific research that yields a 300 percent profit. But that is not the limit, of course. Experts say that space-produced semi-conductors and medicines alone will fetch 20 billion US dollars by the year 2000. Time waits for no man. The children who were born in the spring of 1961 - Gagarin's year - have grown, and have children of their own now. Space exploration has grown; the roundabout fashion in which it has altered our notions of

These names, along with the name of Sergei Korolev (1906-1966), the designer of the world's first spacecraft, will probably always be remembered.

Glasnost reaches Baikonur: Perestroika and glasnost have left their mark on space exploration. Just a few years ago, who could have thought that foreign reporters would be allowed to visit Baikonur (that holy of holiest of the Soviet space program) as frequently as their colleagues from the USSR? There are no more omissions, no more "white spots" in official reports on the past and future of the space program. Even the space budget was finally made public. In addition, once the veil

creation has made it an important part of life.

The prospects: The immediate future will probably see large-capacity orbital superstations of the Mir-II category. A joint Soviet-American flight to Mars is a distinct possibility. In fact, if the appropriate agreement is signed in the next two years, the flight could take place sometime in 2010. Meanwhile, the USSR has designed the Marsokhod - an unmanned "Mars buggy". Martian soil will be brought back to Earth.

Above, cosmonauts on board the spaceship. **Right**, unmanned shuttle Buran to be taken off by Energia launcher.

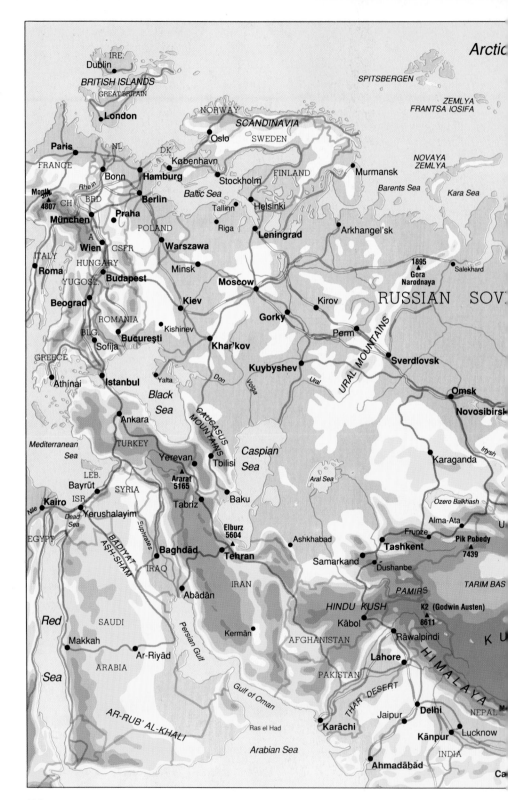

Arctic

IRE.
Dublin
BRITISH ISLANDS
GREAT BRITAIN
London

SPITSBERGEN

ZEMLYA
FRANTSA IOSIFA

NORWAY

SCANDINAVIA

Oslo   SWEDEN

Paris   NL   DK
FRANCE   København
        Bonn Hamburg
Monte Rhein   Stockholm
4807 CH BRD Berlin   Baltic Sea
München   Praha
        A   POLAND
ITALY Wien CSFR   Warszawa
HUNGARY
Roma   Minsk
YUGOSL. Budapest
Beograd   Kiev
    ROMANIA
    BLG.   Kishinev
        București
      Sofija
GREECE
  Athínai Istanbul   Yalta
        Black
        Sea
      Ankara
Mediterranean TURKEY
Sea   Yerevan
  LEB.   Ararat
Bayrūt SYRIA   5165
Kairo ISR   Tabriz
Nile Dead Yerushalayim
    Sea
EGYPT   Baghdād
        BADIYAT
        ASH-SHAM
        IRAQ
Red   Abādān
    SAUDI
Makkah   Kermān
        Ar-Riyād
    ARABIA
Sea
    AR-RUB' AL-KHALI
        Ras el Had

NOVAYA
ZEMLYA

Murmansk
    Barents Sea   Kara Sea

FINLAND   Murmansk

Tallinn Helsinki
Riga Leningrad   Arkhangel'sk

Moscow

Kirov

Gorky   1895
Perm   Gora
          Narodnaya   Salekhard

RUSSIAN SOV.

Khar'kov

Kuybyshev

Don Volga Ural URAL MOUNTAINS Sverdlovsk

Omsk

Novosibirsk

CAUCASUS MOUNTAINS

Tbilisi Caspian
    Sea   Karaganda Irtysh

Baku Aral Sea

Elburz   Ozero Balkhash
5604   Alma-Ata
    Ashkhabad   Frunze Pik Pobedy
Tehran   Samarkand Tashkent   7439
          Dushanbe

IRAN   TARIM BAS

    PAMIRS
HINDU KUSH   K2 (Godwin Austen)
  Kābol   8611
AFGHANISTAN   Rāwalpindi   K U

    Lahore   HIMALAYA

    PAKISTAN

Persian Gulf

Gulf of Oman   THAR DESERT

        Jaipur Delhi   NEPAL
Karāchi   Kānpur Lucknow

Arabian Sea   INDIA

    Ahmadābād   Ca

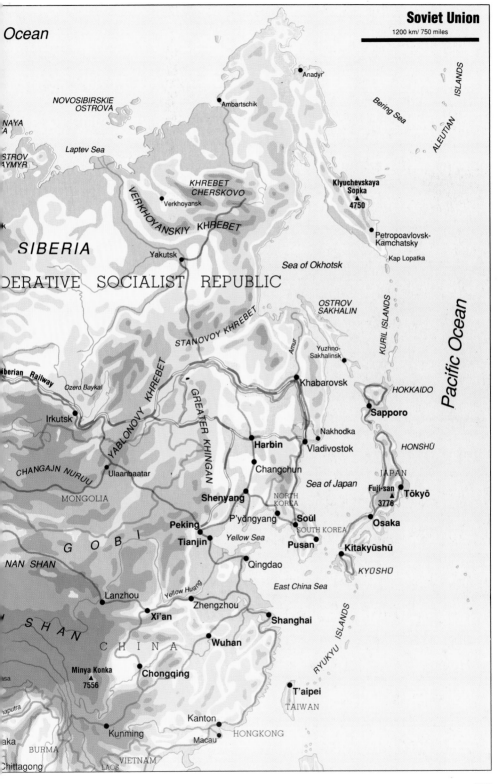

Ocean

NOVOSIBIRSKIE
OSTROVA

...NAYA
...A

...STROV
...AYMYR

Laptev Sea

Anadyr'

Ambartschik

Bering Sea

ALEUTIAN ISLANDS

KHREBET
CHERSKOVO

Verkhoyansk

VERKHOYANSKIY KHREBET

Klyuchevskaya
Sopka
▲
4750

...k

SIBERIA

Yakutsk

Sea of Okhotsk

Petropoavlovsk-
Kamchatsky

Kap Lopatka

...ERATIVE SOCIALIST REPUBLIC

OSTROV
SAKHALIN

STANOVOY KHREBET

Amur

Yuzhno-
Sakhalinsk

KURIL ISLANDS

Pacific Ocean

...berian Railway

Ozero Baykal

YABLONOVY KHREBET

GREATER KHINGAN

Khabarovsk

HOKKAIDO

Sapporo

Irkutsk

Nakhodka

HONSHŪ

CHANGAJN NURUU

Ulaanbaatar

Harbin

Vladivostok

Changchun

Sea of Japan

JAPAN

Fuji-san
▲
3776

Tōkyō

MONGOLIA

Shenyang

NORTH
KOREA

Osaka

GOBI

Peking

P'yŏngyang

Soŭl

Tianjin

Yellow Sea

SOUTH KOREA

Kitakyūshū

NAN SHAN

Pusan

Lanzhou

Qingdao

KYŪSHŪ

SHAN

Yellow Huang

East China Sea

Zhengzhou

Xi'an

Shanghai

CHINA

Wuhan

RYUKYU ISLANDS

Minya Konka
▲
7556

Chongqing

...sa

T'aipei

TAIWAN

Kanton

...aputra

Kunming

Macau

HONGKONG

...aka

BURMA

VIETNAM

...hittagong

LAOS

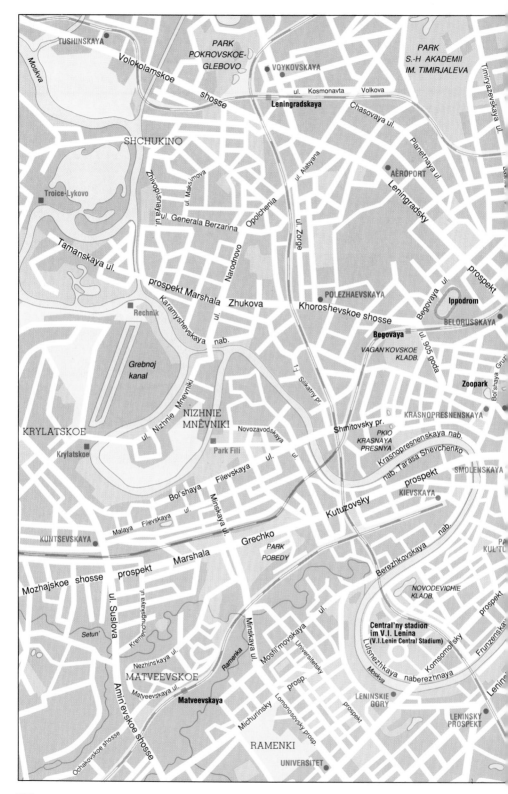

THE PRINCIPAL CITIES

Moscow

"Those who have been to Moscow know Russia" said one of Russia's poets. This could even be extended to mean those who have got to know Moscow can understand the Russian people. It is a fact that the Russian people, by nature, are made up of countless contradictions, which have, on the one hand, probably inspired society to great achievements and, on the other, plunged it into an abyss of great crisis.

Moscow as a city is also full of contrasts: contrasts in architecture, social life and in politics. As in each and every major city on this earth, Moscow cannot be described by words alone; it has to be visited and seen. Until very recently, Moscow, for some western visitors, was just the capital of the *"evil empire"*. Glasnost and perestroika have now somehow changed this view.

Foreigners who are for the first time in Moscow tend to be overwhelmed by very mixed feelings, ranging from shock and admiration to irritation and bewilderment. The first thing that strikes the visitor upon arrival in the capital of one of the superpowers, is the "unobtrusive service" that you will meet at **Sheremetyevo International Airport**. If you are not quick enough to get hold of one of the luggage trolleys, there is no reason to worry unduly: more often than not you will be met by "porters" waiting at the exit from the customs barrier who are only too willing to offer their services and who, for a "reasonable" fee in roubles and even more willingly in hard currency, will be only too delighted to whisk you off to any corner of the hospitable city. There is no reason to be too concerned by their "disinterested" assistance and fortunately you don't have to beware anymore of their seemingly lucrative offer to exchange money on the spot since the official tourist's exchange rate is similar to the former black market rate. They are not the Musco-

vites whose cordial good nature attracts millions of people to this ancient but ever young city.

More likely than not, the very first person you will meet when stepping onto Moscow soil will be a very polite and foreseeing translator-guide in the guise of a good looking girl, who, although not fully in command of any foreign language, is ever joyful and indefatigable. There could also be the earnest young man wearing something reminiscent of western fashions who is exceedingly efficient and knowledgeable. They will become "guardian angels" who will rid the visitor of any trouble associated with the notoriously "unobtrusive" services and will reveal the delights of Moscow.

Though the first impression may be that of a gray and monotonous city you will certainly be struck by the width of its streets, something uncommon in Europe. These streets are the pride of the Muscovites and are "roads into the future", as Joseph Stalin, the "Father of the People", used to call them. You will, no doubt, also be unpleasantly surprised by the poor quality of the road surface, but there are also the present "fathers of the city" and they tell relentlessly that this is due to the severe climate, although there might be other reasons as well. Alas, it is a characteristic feature of Russia as a whole. In the words of Winston Churchill, Russia has no roads, it has directions.

Approaching the center: On the way from the airport to the city you will see, at intervals, recently built housing complexes dashing past the bus or car windows; these for all their creator's magic ingenuity, are not terribly bewitching. And all the while there are the gilded cupolas of small Russian Orthodox churches looking like mushrooms which have grown up among these gray concrete monoliths. Unfortunately, this is not the only example of faceless monotony side by side with creative genius. On the main streets, one is immediately caught up in the unending flow of Muscovites and of visitors to the city. This shouldn't come as a great surprise since about two million tourists come to

Preceding pages, the Red Square reflections.
Left, reconstructed church on Comsomolsky Prospect.

Moscow everyday on top of Moscow's nine million inhabitants. It is very easy to distinguish those who live in Moscow from outsiders; above all by a hurried air, a seeming indifference to everything going on that is unconnected with his or her inner thoughts and, of course, by the very distinctive accent, although this will not immediately be fully appreciated by a foreigner.

Muscovites are very hospitable, although some will voice complaints at the hundreds of thousands of visitors raiding the shelves of the Moscow shops in search of foodstuffs and fashionable clothes. Sadly enough, this is the result of many decades of Brezhnevite policies according to which Moscow received priority supplies at the expense of the rest of the country.

Being tired of the hustle and bustle of the city at lunchtime, you have only to lose yourself in the intricate maze of the side streets off the Arbat to breath, for a moment, the air of the good old times, although the area has now lost its former grandeur. The grand old mansions, former estates of the Moscow aristocracy hug together with the modern residences of today's elite.

Trying **Pushkin Square** in the afternoon, or the **Old Arbat**, you will be surprised to come across familiar types: hippies, punks, *metallists* (heavy metal fans) and other attention seekers.

During an evening stroll you might also come upon Moscow's night dolls: late pedestrians, Hell's Angels tearing through the still night on their demon two-wheel vehicles; prostitutes pursuing their age old profession at hotel entrances; the homeless lured out of the Metro into the streets by the need for a breath of fresh air and a variety of "government employees" who are there to maintain order and to keep up the normal functioning of the metropolis. The rushing torrent of glasnost and democratization has given rise to a whole series of totally unfamiliar phenomena in Russian society.

Those who have already been to the Soviet Union will have inevitably noticed the drastic changes in the esthetic

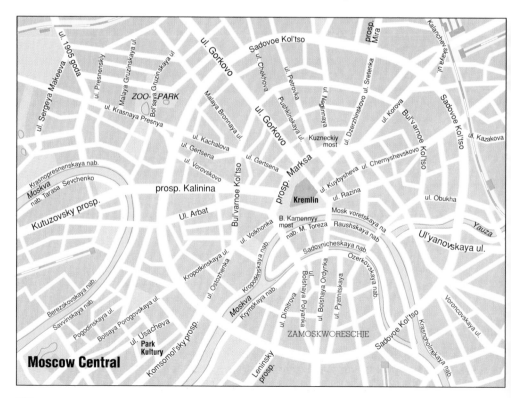

Moscow Central

look of Moscow. There are no more of those boastful slogans praising unfulfilled achievements which used to adorn every street corner. They have been replaced by slogans or graffiti in favor of a candidate or an unofficial movement. The former unanimity has changed into a powerful stream of protest and a multiplicity of opinions, which were once so ardently hustled down by the apparachiks. No doubt, the new system of economics has led to an increasingly stratified population.

This has immediately been reflected in the growth of certain kinds of crime such as the extortion of illegally earned money. Nevertheless, rumors that the Moscow mafia is negotiating with the Sicilian *Cosa Nostra* over dividing New York into spheres of influence have been largely exaggerated; rather they are an attempt to launch yet another *red threat* campaign.

Nevertheless, the face of the modern city is shaped by ordinary people: workers, students, self-employed citizens and employees, rather than by all-powerful mafiosi or by crowds of railway station pickpockets. Every one of them changes the face of their native town in their own way, and they are all doing one great thing: they are trying hard to raise their living standards to a qualitatively new level. Despite all its inconsistencies the city is bustling, alive, and surely will welcome the new century in a transformed and joyful mood.

A glimpse of Moscow's history: More likely than not the city got its name from the river running through the "seven hills". Muscovites like to remind you of these seven hills whereby they are associating the city with ancient Rome, although in fact there are more than seven hills. It is generally believed that the name Moskva came from the old Slavonic word *moksha* (wet), suggesting, that the terrain around the city was marshy. Early Slavonic settlements grew up there long before they appeared in ancient annals and scriptures. Nevertheless, the first reference to the city in the annals comes in 1147 when the Russian prince **Yuri Dolgoruky** (nick-

An ancient view.

named the Long Armed, because of either his physical constitution or his conquering spirit) is said to have thrown a lavish banquet-feast in a locality called Moskva. Around this time the first defenses appeared around the Kremlin, consisting of oak pales. At that time Moscow was part of the **Suzdal Knyazhestvo (Principality)** and served as a sort of battlement outpost to protect the **Velikoye Knyazhestvo (Great Principality)**. The new white stone walls which were built in 1367 which gave Moscow the name of **Byelokamennaya (White-Walled Moscow)**, were closely associated with the city's rising influence during the reign of Prince Ivan Kalita (nicknamed "the money bag") in the first half of the 14th century.

This period coincided with the Mongol-Tatar yoke which brought innumerable suffering and distress to the scattered and divided Slavic peoples. It can be said, however, that having a common enemy has helped greatly to unite all of the Russian lands under a common leadership.

The real growth of Moscow took place between the mid-15th to early 16th centuries during the reign of Ivan III, an enlightened and careful politician, who forged strong diplomatic ties with many of the European states. It was he, who invited to Russia prominent and renowned Italian architects: Pietro Antonio Solari, Marco Ruffo and Rudolfo Fiorovanti, whose combined creative genius styled the design of many buildings of the modern Kremlin.

The Kremlin: The Moscow Kremlin is frequently referred to as the "Eighth Wonder of the World" and with good reason. Today's red brick Kremlin walls were built between 1485-1495 under the guidance of the already mentioned architects Marco Ruffo and Antonio Solari. The roughly triangular wall is 2,230 meters or 1.4 miles long and at some point, 6 meter-wide (20 feet) and 20 meter-high (65 feet). There are four gates and 19 towers.

You walk into the Kremlin grounds through the **Kutafia Tower** and across

The Kremlin at night.

the **Troitsky (Trinity) Bridge**, in the Alexandrovsky Garden on the site of the former Neglinka River. On the orders of Catherine II, the river was channelled into a large stone pipe in the 18th century. This gate used to be the main entrance during regal occasions. It was also crossed by Napoleon's army.

Rumor has it that when the great French Emperor entered the Kremlin through the Spassky Gate he lost his tricorn hat. This has reinforced the Russian superstition that the Spassky Gate is a sacred place which shouldn't be crossed bareheaded.

In good old times the Kremlin was regarded as almost an unassailable fortress. It was surrounded by the Moskva River on the southeast and surrounded by a deep moat which linked the Neglinka and the Moskva Rivers. In the case of long siege the Arsenal (Sobakina) Tower had a hidden fresh water reservoir, a well and an underground passage to the Neglinka River. Since 1937 the five Kremlin Towers have been adorned by red ruby-glass stars 3.75 meters/12.3 feet in diameter. In former times they used to be decorated by a two-headed eagle: a symbol of the Czar and of Russian Aristocracy.

Once in the Kremlin you will undoubtedly be taken aback by the sight of a huge steel and glass structure placed in the center of the ancient capital. It is the Kremlin Palace of Congresses, built in 1961. The building replaced the former service quarters designed by Mikhail Possokhin who was also the architect of the modern Kalininsky Prospect.

On your left are the buildings of the former Arsenal built in 1701-1736 on the orders of Peter the Great. Their facade is adorned with Napoleonic military trophies, cannon barrels taken after the defeat of the French army in 1812. On your right at the foot of the Borovitsky Gate there is the **Armory** which is the oldest Kremlin museum. It houses not only samples of ancient armory, but also valuables of all Grand Princes from the Ruric family to the Romanovs, as well as monastic utensils and a rare collection of diamonds and jewelry in the

The Kremlin soldiers are proud of their marching skill.

USSR Diamond Fund.

By walking on, you reach the most ancient part of the Kremlin, the **Square of the Cathedrals**. The grandiose church in its center is the white-walled **Uspensky (Assumption) Cathedral**.

Contemporary with the Kremlin walls this was built by the renowned Aristotle Fiorovanti in imitation of the Uspensky Cathedral in the city of Vladimir. It was intended for the investitures, coronations and wedding ceremonies of the Grand Princes, Czars and Grand Bishops and also for announcing the most important state decrees (*ukasy*). The inside of the cathedral is adorned by exceptionally beautiful frescoes and icons including the famous 14th-century Trinity and the 11th- to 12th-century icon of the Vladimir Mother of God. Since the 15th century the cathedral was also the place where the Moscow Bishops and Patriarchs were laid to rest.

Closer to the river on the left stands the **Annunciation Cathedral** which was built at the same time as the Uspensky Cathedral by Pskovian masons as a private church for the Moscow Grand Princes. In 1572, during the reign of Ivan the Terrible, a separate entrance wing was built onto the side of the cathedral especially for the willful Czar. It should be mentioned that Ivan the Terrible was distinguished from early childhood by his "out of the ordinary" fantasies. He gave orders for a small wooden tower to be built on top of the Kremlin wall (the Czar Tower) beside the Spasskaya Tower. The young Czarevich enjoyed sitting in the tower and secretly watching the executions in Red Square. The Kremlin walls and towers guard many unsolved mysteries. Riddled with underground passages and a great number of monastic cells, they served both as a prison for those who were out of favor and as a place of refuge for those in want, for there was food and water in times of siege.

In its form and inner decor the Annunciation Cathedral is far superior to the other cathedrals built by Italian architects. Its iconostasis, which was inherited from the former Blagoveshensky Church, located on the same site, was painted by the great Russian artists Feofan Greek (Theophanes from Greece) and Andrei Rubliyov. The floor of the cathedral is covered with agate and jasper tiles, a gift from the Shah of Persia. At that time such luxury was not regarded as extremely shameful. The walls of the wing were decorated with the portraits of the Grand Russian Princes and, surprisingly enough, those of ancient sages - Aristotel, Plutarch and Virgil. It is likely that the Czars wanted to bring Moscow into line with European culture or to show themselves to be enlightened rulers.

Opposite the Annunciation Cathedral is the **Archangel Cathedral** named after Archangel Michael, which was built a hundred years later to the design of architect Alevisio Novi. The cathedral was a burial place for those Princes and Czars who reigned up to the time of Peter the Great. When the capital was transferred to St. Petersburg in 1712, the Grand Princes chose the Alexander Nevsky Lavra as a new burial place.

The tallest edifice in the Kremlin is the **Belfry** named after Ivan the Great, which was built by the Italian architect Bon Fryazin between 1505 and 1508. In 1600 it was heightened from 60 meters/ 195 feet to 81 meters/265 feet at the order of Czar Boris Godunov. For a long time the Belfry was the tallest building in Russia as, by the Czar's decree, it was strictly forbidden to erect anything higher. Between the Assumption and Annunciation Cathedrals there is a whole range of buildings. The youngest of them all is the Grand Kremlin Palace designed by a group of architects led by Konstantin Ton. It incorporated many secular and religious buildings. The oldest of them is the **Terem Palace** which used to be the residence of Czar Mikhail (1613-1645), the first Czar of the Romanov family. The new premises of the palace served as the Romanov's apartments during visits to Moscow.

The St. George and St. Vladimir Hall of the Kremlin palace were used for ceremonial receptions and signing ceremonies. In the hall of the Palace, which seats 3,000 people at one time, the sessions of the Supreme Soviet (the Soviet

Parliament) were held. From the St. Vladimir Hall you can go on to one of the Kremlin's oldest halls - the **Hall of Facets** so named because of the faceted white stone tiles which cover the facade overlooking the Palace Square.

The Granovitaya Palata was built between 1473 and 1491 by the Italian architects Marco Ruffo and Pietro Antonio Solari. The vaulted 500 square meter/5,381 square feet Chamber Hall was used for banquets and ceremonial occasions. However, this is off limits, access to this part of the Kremlin is forbidden. The Granovitaya Palata (Hall of facets) hides the small **Deposition of the Robe Church** built between 1484 and 1485 by the famous masons from the city of Pskov. Initially, it served as a private church for the Russian Patriarchs, but since 1653 it was requisitioned by the Czar's family. The church is next door to the **Czarina's Chambers** which used to be the reception rooms where the Czars received visitors in the 16th century. In 1681 they were united under one roof crowned by nine gilded cupolas.

You should not miss the eastern part of the Kremlin, which includes the government buildings; the main one was designed by the Russian architect Matvei Kazakov, at the end of the 18th century, for the Moscow department of the Senate. At present, it houses the **USSR Council of Ministers**.

After the October Revolution the top floor of the building was used as Lenin's living and working quarters. Now it is his **Apartment Museum**. The last building making up the Moscow Kremlin is that of the **Presidium of the Supreme Soviet** (the Soviet Parliament) opposite the former Senate and recognizable by the by the famous red flag flying over it.

The Red Square: Leaving the Kremlin you should not forget to touch the Kremlin Wall - a good omen which means that you will visit this hospitable city once again. Having been to the Kremlin, you will probably not be able to resist the temptation to have a look at the Red Square, which houses yet another of Moscow's shrines.

Taking a stroll across the Red Square.

If you walk along the **Alexandrovsky Garden** (at the foot of the Kremlin Wall) and turn right into Kremlin Avenue you will come to the main square of the USSR. As you walk through Alexandrovsky Garden, there is an unusual encrustation in the Kremlin Wall. This grotto, designed by Osip Bovet and styled after ancient man-made ruins, is a typical example of 19th-century landscape gardening. The centuries-old lime trees and emerald green lawns edged with wrought-iron fences attract thousands of tourists tired of the numerous sights of the city. The **Tomb of the Unknown Soldier** is here and the newly-weds in Moscow visit it as part of their wedding ceremony.

Further along the cobble pavement lies a large red-brick building decorated with miniature towers. This is the **History Museum** built between 1875 and 1881 by the architect Vladimir Sherwood, the son of a British engineer and a Russian noblewoman. The building represents the old Russian style of architecture and successfully provides

the final piece in the Kremlin ensemble. The Museum, which opened in 1883, houses a collection of rare materials and artifacts of Russian history, from ancient times to the present day.

The part of the Kremlin Wall between the Nikolskaya and Senatskaya Towers, at the right hand side of Red Square, is the **burial place of prominent statesmen, public figures and military leaders** who helped build the Soviet state. Maxim Gorky, Nadezilda Krupskaya, wife of Lenin, Yury Gagarin, the first man in space, Igor Kurchatov, the father of Soviet nuclear power, John Reed, the American journalist and many others are buried here (including some who soiled their name by their involvement in the Stalinist repression and the Brezhnevite "victorious march of developed socialism". In the center of the same side of Red Square, under the Kremlin Wall, lies the body of Lenin. The **Lenin Mausoleum** was designed by Aleksei Shchusev and took its present shape in 1929. It has now become the main platform of the Soviet government replacing the *Lobnoye Mesto* (the government platform in ancient Russia) and government leaders review the May 1st parade from here.

Red Square itself formed its present shape with the consolidation of the Russian state around Moscow. The moat, which had lost its military significance was filled in, providing space for a marketplace. Later in the 15th century by a decree of Ivan the Terrible, the wooden structures were brought down to exclude possible fires. The square became a shopping center with galleries for retail trade. In the mid-16th century, following great military-political victories over the Nagai and Kazan Khandoms (principalities), Ivan the Terrible ordered the building of the Pokrovsky Sobor (the Cathedral of the Veil - now known as St. Basil's Cathedral). Each of the nine cupolas covers a chapel named after the saint on whose feast-day the Russian armies won their battles. The central cathedral was completed by the great hall in the Barma Postnic, and this formidable Czar GUM was captivated by its beauty. Incidentally the cathedral was built in the mar-

The central hall in the GUM department store.

ketplace in contravention of a centuries-old tradition, yet another whim of the semi-mad Czar. The popular tradition has it that the Czar ordered the master mason and his apprentices to be blinded so that they could not build such a beautiful building anywhere else.

St. Basil Cathedral got its present name in 1588 when another chapel was added to it in honor of Basil the Blessed, whose grave and relics were worshipped in Russia at the time. In the 17th century Red Square turned into a public forum and a site of many popular uprisings. The Lobnoye Mesto (a raised circular platform in front of the St. Basil Cathedral) was used for public sermons and to read the Czar's *ukaz* (degrees). It was also used as a scaffold and as the site of horrible executions. In 1671, for instance, it witnessed the execution of Stepan Razin, the leader of a peasant uprising. In 1648 the execution of the Strelets, instigated to mutiny by Czarina Sifia, sister of Peter the Great, also took place here. One hundred years later, Yemelian Pugachev, another peasant

leader was also put to death on this site.

The square was called "Krasnaya" however, not because of its association with the blood spilt on it but because of its beauty. *Krasny* (red) meant beautiful in old Russian. In the mid-19th century the square was given a new lease of life.

Semi-demolished by Napoleon's army, Moscow had to be built anew. When Napoleon approached Moscow he stopped outside the city and waited for the Muscovites to bring him the keys to the gates. After a long and fruitless wait he entered the abandoned and devastated city. His planned triumphal entry was spoiled. Fires started soon afterwards. (No one can say for sure whether they were started deliberately or resulted from negligence). The troops, whose moral was low, found full wine cellars, and opened a pub in the Uspensky Cathedral. All this meant that Napoleon left Moscow with ill grace, not forgetting to thank the city for its "hospitality". Gunpowder charges were planted by his engineers in the arsenal and were intended to wipe Moscow

Pioneers swear solemn oath in Lenin Mausoleum.

from the face of the earth. But the will of providence, the rain and the heroic efforts of the Muscovites foiled the design. All the same, the city lay in ruins. Only about 2,500 out of 19,500 buildings survived.

The overall reconstruction plan was designed by Osip Bovet. He restored the Kremlin Wall and the towers and rebuilt the shopping galleries in the eastern part of the square. At the end of the 19th century these were replaced by newly built galleries. In 1893 Pomerantsev designed and built the Upper Shopping Galleries. Since 1955 they have been home to **GUM**, USSR's largest department store. In the 1890s the Middle Galleries were built behind the upper ones which are now occupied by public offices. About the same time the architect Chichagov built another tent-like red-brick building at the side of the History Museum. It used to house Gorodskaya Duma (the City Council). After Lenin's death in 1924 it became the **Lenin Museum**. With only slight modifications the Red Square ensemble remains intact to this day.

The master plan of the city: Historically Moscow was built as a circular settlement cut through by the main routes to Smolensk, Tver and Kaluga. Hence, the names of the main streets: **Tverskaya** (now **Gorky Street**), **Kaluzhskaya** (now **Leninsky Prospect**) and **Smolenskaya** (now **Kalininsky Prospect**). Many streets were called after churches and monasteries, for example Vozdvishenka and Roshdestvenka or according to different occupations and trades: Meshchanskaya (Petty bourgeois), Yamskaya (Coachman's), Zhivoderka (Slaughter-house), etc.

The **first ring** around the city is formed by the Kremlin Wall. The **second ring** was the former Kitai-Gorod Wall bordering the Kremlin on the northeast. This 2.5 km/1.5 miles long wall with 12 towers and several gates was built in the mid-16th century around the marketplace. Its name comes from the Mongolian "middle", i.e. a mid-fortress. The name was given to it by Elena Glinskaya, mother of Ivan the Terrible,

Dzerzhinsky, former Lubyanskaya Square in olden days.

146

after her native Kitai-Gorod in Podolia. Unfortunately, the walls of Kitai-Gorod have not been preserved to this day. Some remains can be seen in Sverdlov Square, near the Metropol Hotel, and there is another stretch at Kitaisky Avenue in Zaryadye.

The **third ring** was made up of the 9 km/5.6 miles long "White Town" walls. These ran along the route of today's Boulevard Ring, which was built at the end of the 18th and during the early 19th centuries. The walls of white stone (hence the name) were raised as early as the 16th century and served as a mighty fortress to defend the outskirts of Moscow. The walls were adorned with 10 gates and 17 blind towers.

The **next ring** used to be the Zemlyanoi Val (a rampart) built at the end of the 16th century around what is today the Sadovoye Koltso (Garden Ring). It was replaced by gardens at the end of the 18th century giving name to the whole area. Neither set of walls has been preserved to this day; the last of them was leveled in the 1930s during Stalin's reconstruction works.

The ancient streets of Kitai-Gorod: Opposite the Nikolskiye Gates is **October 25 Street** (the former Nikolskaya). This is one of Moscow's most animated streets. At the start of the street, on the right, is **GUM**, the department store. Most probably you will see long lines of people queuing up for those foods that are in short supply. You will rarely meet a Muscovite here, except, perhaps, late at night at closing time. Muscovites have a joke that the best shops have been built in the center to draw the visitors away from the rest of the city. Excellent proof is the huge department store in Komosolskaya (Comsomol) Square, which is better known as the Square of the Three Railway Stations (the Leningrad, Yaroslavl and Kazan Railway stations are all located around the square). Here, the procedure is simple - from the train into the department store and back to the train. The joke is fair but very sad because many Soviet visitors simply fail to notice the beauty of Moscow, all they come for is to shop.

In the 17th and 18th centuries, build-

ing number 7-9 in October 25 Street used to house the Slavonic-Greek-Latin Academy. It was the first higher educational establishment in Moscow. Many a student "gnawed at the granite of science" in this building, Mikhail Lomonossov, Russia's greatest scientist included.

On the same side of the street stands a magnificent "Russian Gothic" building with a sundial on its facade. It was built in 1814 as the printing house for the Synod, the highest church council in charge of religious affairs. It was here that the first Russian books were printed. Now it houses the **History and Archives Institute**. Number 17 is the **Slavyansky Bazar Restaurant**, the oldest in Moscow. It has been serving the best Russian food since 1873. Many Russian recipes have been lost and private cooperative restaurants are now trying to restore the former glory of Russian cuisine.

Turning right to **Kuibyshev Bystreet**, one can see the splendid **Bogyavlensky Sobor** (God-sent Church)

Cyrillic letters on tourist bus.

founded as far back as the 13th century by the Muscovite Prince Daniil Aleksandrovich. The present appearance dates back to the 17th century and is typical of Moscow Baroque. If you walk straight on you will reach **Kuibysheva Street** (the former Ilyinka). We can now note with satisfaction that the city authorities have yielded to the pressure of the electorate and started to return to the old street names. These were changed in the 1930s to commemorate the names of government officials. It is very probable that soon most streets will reassume their former names. This has already happened to the whole of the Brezhnev District and to Zhdanov Street.

Kuibyshev Street used to be the "City", or financial center of Moscow with its banks and Mercantile Exchange (now the USSR Chamber of Commerce and Industry), Joint-Stock Companies and a multiplicity of other public offices. It used to be a jolly commercial street with colorfully lit advertisements. These were later replaced by faceless gray name plates stating just the name of the office. Going down Vladimirov By-street there is the former Gostiny Dvor, an ancient shopping center famous for its facade, with its rhythmical alternation of pillars and arches. At present it is used by various offices as garages and warehouses. The very last street giving the final touch to the former Kitai-Gorod district is **Stepan Razin Street** (the former Varvarka). It cuts off the Zaryadie area from the rest of Kitai-Gorod. Zaryadie means "the area behind the marketplace".

The **Church of the Conception of St. Ann** is dwarfed by the huge 5400 room complex of the **Rossia Hotel**. The church was built at approximately the same time as the discovery of America by Christopher Columbus. Its unusual name stems from the old Russian custom of marking not only the birth of the Virgin Mary, but her conception as well. There is also part of the Kitai-Gorod wall alongside the church. To the right towards the **Vassillievsky Slope** is the **Moskvoretsky Bridge**, which was used by the German teenager Mathias Rust

Trees prepared to survive winter temperatures at Moscow University.

as a landing strip. Here too, is the Old English Club, which in the 16th century was the residence of British merchants and diplomats. Next door is an impressive ensemble in **Varvarka Street**. It is the **Znamensky (Omen) Monastery** with its tall, five-cupola cathedral built in the 17th century. Since some time it houses the **All-Russian Society for the Preservation of Historical and Cultural monuments**.

Very close to it stands the **Church of Varvara the Martyr** dating from the 18th to 19th centuries. Next to it are the 16th- to 17th-century rooms which used to belong to the boyarin (nobleman) Romanov family whose heirs later became the famous Russian Emperors. The building is now a museum displaying the splendid interiors of a Russian nobleman's home. Walking towards **Nogin Square** (formerly Varvarka Square) you may stroll into the **Illyinsky Boulevard** laid down in 1882. To the left there are the short gray buildings of the Central and Moscow Committees of the CPSU, the Communist Party of the Soviet Union.

Further down Solyanka Street is the former marketplace, notorious in the 19th century for its slums, brothels and scores of thieves and other criminals. Popular tradition has it that the Khitrov pickpockets were smart enough that they once stole a bronze cannon from the grounds of the Kremlin. To escape public disgrace, the Governor-General ordered his men to find and return the cannon at all costs. Facing such a predicament, the police had to negotiate with the criminal chieftains. The following morning the stolen cannon was returned to its place and the honor of the uniform was saved. In a short while, however, it was found out that the returned cannon had itself been stolen that night from the opposite side of the Kremlin wall.

Such amusing stories are myriad in this old corner of Moscow. With time and inclination, you can stroll along Solyanka Street to the Yauza River Embankment and climb up the Yauza Boulevard (which is the starting point

In all its modernity there are still some old wooden structures in the city.

of the Moscow Boulevard Ring).

Walking along the Boulevard Ring: Here you see many a splendid mansion, once the property of Moscow's former nobility. Number 14a in Solyanka Street is the former mansion of the Naryshkins, which was later refurbished as the **Obstetrical Institute**. Number 14 used to house the Trustee's Council. Now it is the **Academy of Medical Scientists**. Next door in Zabelina number 4 is the **Ivanovsky Monastery** (1860-1879). It used to be a prison for the most dangerous female criminals and dissenters. Solyanka 12 displays the Ceremonial Gates of the Imperial Education House, a charitable institution for homeless children and foundlings. Now it is the **Military Academy**.

In Kulishki there is the **Church of All Saints**. This used to be a forested area along the Vladimirskaya Road which later became Solyanka Street. **Illyinsky Gate Square** ends at the monument unveiled in 1887 to Grenadiers who fell in the battle of Plevna during the Russian-Turkish War. The square contin-

ues with one block of the **Polytechnic Museum** which was built in 1874-1907. The museum boasts more than 40,000 exhibits which trace the development of Russian technology and science.

The **Church of St. John the Baptist**, a former Baptist church built in 1825 is to the left (Novaya Square 12). It now houses yet another museum, the **Museum of the History and Reconstruction of Moscow**.

In the time of Czar Ivan the Terrible, the area around Bogdan Khmelnitsky Street, which flows into Chernishevsky Street, was built up with foreign embassies. The Lithuanian embassy was near Chisto Prudni (the clear ponds), while further beyond the earth rampart, in today's Baumanskaya Street, was the German mission. By the end of the 17th century most of the land belonging to the Germans became the property of Moscow boyars.

The district grew beautiful with the palaces of the old Russian boyar families, the Dolgorukiy (Kolpachny Lane 1), the Lopoukhin (Starosdasky 5) and

Do you want to change your flat? Are you looking for a bargain?

the Botkin (Petroverigsky Lane 4). Time has spared the glorious **Yelochov Church** at the crossroads of the former Basmanniy Streets, the Spartakovskaya of today. Inside the church you can see a superb choir and afterwards enjoy food at the **"Razgulay"** cooperative restaurant which serves old Russian dishes.

Walking along **Chistoprudny Boulevard** one will reach Kirov Street on the right of the metro station of the same name. The Grand Prince Menshikov's name was immortalized by the **Archangel Gabriel Church** which dominates the neighborhood. It was built early in the 18th century and is also known as Menshikov Tower.

In the 16th and 17th century this part of the town was owned by the English and Polish trading missions. The tradition must have been so strong that even now this district is known for the offices of foreign firms.

Today's **Armyansky (Armenian) Lane** once hosted an Armenian mission which can be traced in the former Lazarev Institute of Oriental Languages, founded in 1916 by the rich Armenian family of Lazaryan. The building has been preserved to this day and is now used by the mission of the Armenian Soviet Constituent Republic. Every Soviet constituent republic has its plenipotentiary mission in Moscow.

Markhlevskogo and Lubyanka Malaya streets used to host the French mission. Early in the 19th century the business-like French opened fashion and jewelry shops there. The Catholic church of **St. Ludovic** is still there in Lubyanka Malaya 12.

Kirov Street: The heavy and impressive **Yushkov House**, built late in the 18th century by the Russian architect Vasily Bazhenov, borders **Kirov Gate Square** (Kirov Street 21) on one corner. For many years this building hosted an art school whose graduates included many of the great names of Russian art. It overlooks a mansion at Kirov Street 35, which during the years of World War II housed the headquarters of the Supreme Commander-in-Chief and Stalin's office. Part of the General Head-

People can hire comfortable Chaika cars for wedding ceremonies.

quarters and communication facilities was hidden underground in passages off the Kirov metro station.

While walking down Kirov Street towards Dzerzhinsky Square (formerly Lubyanka) it is difficult to miss a fanciful house styled as a Chinese pagoda; this is the **tea shop** once owned by Perlov, a merchant who imported tea from China. The shop still keeps the tradition alive though with tea from Soviet Georgia, which is more like sawdust than the tasty gift from the Orient. The shop, however, is the last to be blamed for it.

Kirov Street opens into Dzerzhinsky Square where you will find the former Trading House of Kuznetsov, the owner of the biggest porcelain factories in pre-revolutionary Russia. In Soviet times it has to some extent been reconstructed. Now named Dom Farfora (Porcelain House) it still trades porcelain. The Kirov Street hosts dozens of shops, cafés and restaurants which makes it one of Moscow's busiest areas.

Dzerzhinsky Square: This wide square, from which several streets radiate, bears the name of the closest comrade-in-arms of Lenin, Felix Dzerzhinsky. The present KGB headquarters stands on the site of the former gloomy dungeon which was the prison of the Imperial Secret Police. The prison was abolished after the death of Catherine II, on the special orders of her son Emperor Paul I.

The **Polytechnic Museum** faces a huge modern building. This is **"Detsky Mir"** (Children's World) which stands on the site of the former Moscow foundry (Pushechny Dvor) of the 15th to 18th centuries. It was there that, in the 1580s, Andrei Chokhov cast the bronze Czar Cannon now on display in the Kremlin.

Sretenka and Rozhdestvenka: Dzerzhinsky Street runs into Sretenka Street and further into **Prospect Mira** (Peace Avenue), the former First Meshanskaya Street. In the past this was the main route northwards to Vladimir and Zagorsk. In the 17th century, Sretenka, which owed its name to the Sretensky monastery, was chosen by the richest Russian boyars, the Pozharskys and the Khovanskys, for their estates. Rozhdest-venka bears the name of the Rozhdestvensky convent, built as early as 1380 on the orders of the stepdaughter of Ivan Kalita. Next to the convent there is the Stroganov School of Design, housed in the building which used to belong to Prince Vorontsov till 1890.

Neglinka: Going down Neglinka Street, which runs along the bed of the river by the same name (now channeled deep underground) you come to the main **shopping center**. Since the last century this part of Moscow has been the largest shopping district, once noted for its French fashion stores. Petrovsky Passage, the first lane off Neglinka, was built by the end of the 19th century. Early this century the first Russian department store came into being, right behind the **Maly Drama Theatre**; then it was known as *Murr and Merilize*, today it is the **Central Department Store (TsUM)**.

Nearby is the oldest public baths in Moscow, the **Sandunov Baths**, which were built in the 18th century by the actor S. Sandunov. Every social stratum in Moscow favored their own baths. The Sandunov bathhouse was famous for its lavish suites with marble pools and for its after-bath tea ceremony, served on silver plates. The Russians, contrary to the western Europeans, always took hot steam baths using a switch of green birch or oak twigs for massage. Taking a bath in Russia was a form of social intercourse accompanied by the consumption of *Kvas*, a home-brewed beer, or something even stronger, rather than just a mere hygienic procedure. This tradition is still very alive among Muscovites, the only difference being that tea is no longer served on silver plates and there is a long queue for a mug of *kvas* or a bottle of beer.

Neglinka street ends on **Trubnaya Square** (Tube Square), which owes its name to the pipe in the defensive wall of the *Beliy* (White) Town, where the Moscow Hermitage was later located. Unlike the Hermitage in Leningrad, or the Museum of Fine Arts, this was a museum of another kind, a five-star Moscow restaurant, a Palace of the Gluttons, in Moscow jargon. It was opened by

The Bolshoi Theater, the first address for ballet lovers the world over.

three Frenchmen, Olivier, Marius and a chef named Duget, on the waste ground near Tsvetnoy (Flowers) Boulevard. Today we would probably term it a joint venture. Its status, however, brought in good money for the owners.

In the 19th century, **Tsvetnoy Boulevard** gave shelter to the homeless and the so-called Lilies of the Street. The Boulevard ended in **Sukharev Square** which was named after the Sukharev Tower built on the order of Peter the Great in memory of the only Strelets army officer loyal to him during the Strelets rebellion. At that time the tower supplied drinking water to the city. In the 1930s the tower was pulled down as part of the reconstruction works involved in creating Kolkhosnaya (Collective farm) Square.

The square was also known for the officially permitted market for stolen goods which took place once a week. That permission was given by Governor Rostopchin after the Great Fire of 1812 when the Moscow rich came back to their raided homes and tried to trace their stolen possessions. Here, too, is the building of the former Sheremetyev Public Hospital, today named after Doctor Sklifasovsky.

Sverdlov Square: Two streets, Neglinka and Petrovka (named after the Vysoko-Petrovsky monastery built on the orders of Prince Ivan Kalita) meet in Teatralnaya (Theater) Square, known as **Sverdlov Square** today. Here you will find the word-famous **Bolshoi Theater**. The former Grand Imperial Theater was built in 1825, then restored and considerably remodeled after a fire to the design of architect Osip Bovet. The theater, however, takes its pride from the company, rather than from its walls. The theater enjoys such popularity among the Soviet people that it is a problem to get a ticket despite a very low price.

The Bolshoi's neighbors are the **Maly Theater**, the oldest drama theater in Moscow, and the **Central Children's Theater**, opened in 1921 as the first professional drama theater for children.

On the other side of Theater Square is the grandiose **Hotel Metropol**, which

To telephone within the city costs only 2 kopecks.

154

was built in 1899-1905 to the modernist design of the Scottish architect William Valkot and the Russian architect Leo Kekushev. Mosaic panels on the facade were designed and executed in part by the Russian artist Mikhail Vrubel.

The nearby area is taken up by the **Moskva Hotel**, which was built in two stages, first in 1935 and later in 1977, on the site of Okhotny Ryad (Hunter's Row); this was the name of that part of the modern Marx Avenue which stretches from Neglinka to Gorky Streets. It was once a big market place where hunters used to trade their quarry. All the small shops selling meat and fish, as well as the greengrocer's shops on the ground floor, enjoyed a single roof and faced a big square - Monetny Dvor (Money Yard). The place was the filthiest in Moscow and all those booths and shops were cleared after the Revolution. Time has spared two remodeled mansions owned by Prince Golytsin and his sworn enemy Troekurov.

The corner of **Pushkinskaya Street** (formerly Bolshaya Dmitrovka) is marked by a greenish building with a colonnade, the Trade Union House. Before the October Revolution the building (architect Matvei Kazakov) belonged to the Aristocratic Club and was the biggest and most beautiful house in Moscow. The Hall of Columns was the scene of social gatherings, receptions and balls which brought together all the Russian aristocracy. Russian poets, such as Pushkin and Lermontov, as well as Leo Tolstoy, all enjoyed parties there.

Moscow had several clubs for different social strata. There was the Tradesman's Club (today it is the Nemirovich-Danchenko and Stanislavsky Ballet and Opera Theater), the English Club (Museum of the Revolution) and the German Club, the so-called "Schuster Club" (the Central House of Artists). At the beginning of Gorky Street is the Hotel National. Next is the former first US Embassy in the USSR; which was housed here from 1934 to 1954. Today the building belongs to Intourist, the Soviet travel agency.

Confidential talk.

At the corner of Herzen Street (Bolshaya Nikitskaya) is the old home of the Moscow University built in 1776-1793 by Matvei Kasakov and restored by Domenico Gilardi after the Great Fire of 1812. Originally the building belonged to the Pashkov family and was bought to house the university in 1833. The main attraction in the square is the former Manege, an architectural monument built, to celebrate Russia's victory over Napoleonic troops in the 1812 Patriotic War. The spacious hall was used for horse riding, military parades, exhibitions and concerts. Today the **Manege** welcomes thousands of people, rather than horses, lining up for exhibitions and all kinds of contests.

Gorky Street: At long last we find ourselves in Moscow's Broadway, Gorky Street (formerly Tverskaya Street). It became the town's main avenue in the early 1800s, linking, figuratively speaking, St. Petersburg, the capital at the time, with Moscow. Members of the Czar's entourage, shuttling between the two capitals, were a customary sight

here. Tverskaya Street boasted triumphal arches in Tver Gate Square (now **Pushkin Square**) and in the square by the **Byelorussky Station**, which was erected somewhat after Bove's original design. When the square was enlarged in the 1930s, Bove's arch was relocated to Kutuzovsky Avenue, where it graces one of the town's privileged districts to this day.

The most incredible things were done to Gorky Street in the 1930s: the street was straightened, evened out and widened. Several edifices were moved deeper into the block. The former residence of the Moscow Governor General, which housed the Moscow Council of Deputies after the Revolution, was moved back and gained two additional storeys in the process.

The monument to Pushkin was moved from one side of the boulevard to the other, into the small square in front of the modern-looking Rossiya Movie Theater. The movie-house was built in place of the majestic Strastnoi Monastery. Gorky Street 14, a building just a few steps off the boulevard, housed one of Moscow's largest food stores. The building was bought in 1898 by a big wheeler-dealer, Yeliseev, who owned a chain of food stores. The "supermarket" on the building's ground floor amazed even the finicky Muscovites, certainly no mean feat. The only people it amazes today are foreigners, who are not used to seeing such an abundance of empty space on the shop's shelves.

This is another instance of the paradoxical nature of socialism (as the Russians frequently joke): there is maybe nothing to buy in the stores, but every refrigerator is stuffed with food.

On the way to Mayakovsky Square, notice how the buildings become more and more similar in their pomposity. In every dictatorial era the architecture is strangely similar, be it in Moscow, Berlin or Rome, monumental lines and colors ranging from light gray to darker shades. The square has a batch of memorable places. For one there is the **Tchaikovsky Concert Hall** (built in 1940), the traditional setting for numerous international music contests. Next

Something goes wrong in the Kremlin machinery and needs to be replaced.

door, in what used to be the circus, is the **Satire Theater**, which Muscovites dearly love, and the **Peking Hotel** with its Chinese restaurant.

From the square in front of the Byelorussky Station (from which the trains go to Byelorussia and Western Europe), a highway leads to Sheremetievo 2, the airport at which most foreigners land. (A few statistics: Moscow has 7 railway stations and 5 airports which link the city with all the regions of the Soviet Union and with foreign countries; 132 metro stations (the subway lines are 213 km/132 miles long) and two river ports, the North and the South, accessible from any world seaport through the Volga and the Moscow Canal.)

Herzen Street: Running side by side with Gorky Street is Herzen Street. This is the old road to Tver (now Kalinin). In the 16th century, Ivan the Terrible had his guards stationed here in Opriechni Dvor. This street too was favored by Moscow's aristocrats. Not far away, in the vicinity of today's Nezhdanova Street (once known as Swedish Cul-de-sac) was an 18th century Swedish townhouse. Also nearby is the 18th-century English Church (Stankevicha Street 8). The **TASS** (Telegraph Agency of the Soviet Union) building stands in the square of the Nikitskie Gates. In front of it, where Kachalova Street merges with the square, is the **Cathedral of the Great Ascension** where Alexander Pushkin was married. To the right, at Kachalova Street 6, there is a peculiar mansion built in 1902 by the Russian architect Fyodor Shekhtel.

Maxim Gorky, the writer, lived here in the 1930s. After his death a museum was opened in the house. Going up the block from Alekseya Tolstogo Street, there are several excellent palace-like structures, many of which are still owned by foreign embassies.

Beyond, between the streets of Malaya Bronnaya and Pionerskaya, lie the **Patriarshiye Prudy**, the Patriarch's Ponds (now Pioneer Ponds). The writer Mikhail Bulgakov used the pond as a setting for his famous "Master and Margarita". Close by, there is a coop-

Waterworks dedicated to Friendship of the Soviet Peoples at the All Union Exhibition.

erative café by the same name. In the 19th century, this neighborhood, Bronnaya Sloboda, was the place where students lived - Moscow's Quartier Latin.

The Novodevichi Convent: Going south from the central square by the Kremlin we find two streets continuing southwest where Manezhnaya Street ends: **Volkhonka Street** and **Kropotkinskaya**, the last named after the famous anarchist revolutionary, Pyotr Kropotkin. They both point to the Novodevichi Convent which was built early in the 16th century on a hill on the bank of the Moskva River, complete with an earthen mound to guard the approaches to Moscow. The Novodevichi Convent is one of Moscow's most beautiful and historically interesting ensembles. There is a cemetery in which many people of historical and cultural fame are buried.

In the square where the street crosses Gogolevsky Boulevard, Moscow's largest cathedral, the majestic Cathedral of Christ the Saviour once stood. In 1931 it was decided to build in its place an equally impressive monumental structure, the Palace of Soviets, with a 50 meter (150 feet) tall statue of Lenin on top. The cathedral was duly torn down, but the palace was never built. The war and unstable ground killed the grandiose project, a vandalous scheme if ever there was one. Today the lot is occupied by the Moskva public swimming pool.

Moscow's temples of art: The **Pushkin Museum of Fine Arts** is situated on the opposite side of this enormous swimming pool. It was built in 1912 to imitate the Dresden Albertinum Museum. The museum was opened on the initiative of the Moscow University professor Ivan Tsvetaev (father of poetess Marina Tsvetaeva). At the very outset it was to be an exhibition of replicas of world sculptural masterpieces.

It can now boast of a brilliant collection of paintings, sculpture, and works of architecture belonging to various foreign schools and trends: Ancient Greece and Egypt, European classicism, impressionism and late 20th century neorealism.

Shopping means queueing.

158

There are works by Frans Snyders and Pieter Paul Rubens, Rembrandt, John Constable, Claude Monet, Vincent van Gogh, Pablo Picasso, Henri Rousseau and many others. Leading museums of the world frequently compete to borrow them for their own exhibitions.

It is not too easy to buy a ticket because it is normally packed with excited crowds of Muscovites and tourists. Sometimes this means queuing for hours on end before getting a chance to see these creations of human genius. But Muscovites are known for their love for the arts and their patience.

As to the Pushkin Museum's European and Classic art treasures, Moscow may only be surpassed by those of Leningrad. As to Russian and modern art, Moscow is the uncontested leader.

Moscow's art treasures have been kept by the two largest museums: the Pushkin Museum and the **Tretyakov Gallery**. The Tretyakov, in Lavrushinsky Pereulok 10, was named after his founder, a wealthy industrialist and patron of the arts. In 1850 he bought his first paintings and started a collection intending to open in Moscow a museum of arts to the public at large. In 1892 he gave to the city nearly 3,500 pieces of art and the building for the gallery. Today its collection has over 47,000 paintings, many of which have never been displayed because of lack of space. The Tretyakov Gallery is mainly a museum of Russian art.

There are several sections: old Russian art, Russian paintings of the 18th century, art of the first and second half of the 19th century, art of the end of the 19th and the early 20th century and modern art.

Old Russian art is represented by inlaid pictures, bas-reliefs and icons as well as other samples of church decoration. The 12th century icon of the Mother of God from Vladimir is the oldest of them all and perhaps the most unique.

It began its life in Byzantium, from where it was brought to Kiev and later to Vladimir. For many years it has then been glorifying the Assumption Cathedral of the Moscow Kremlin.

Modern art is represented by such names as Karl Brullov, Aleksandr Ivanov, Ivan Aivazovsky, Vasily Surikov, Ilya Repin, Mikhail Vrubel, Martiros Sarian, Aleksandr Deineke and many other well-known artists.

The residence of the Patriarch: Continuing straight ahead, Komsomolsky Avenue leads to Khamovniki and ends where Vernadskogo Avenue begins. The latter leads to one of the capital's plusher districts, **Yugo-Zapad**.

A brief word about another place in Moscow. It starts with the **Bolshoi Kamenny Most** (Great Stone Bridge) which was considered to be one of the world's wonders in its days. The bridge was built by the *starets* (holy man) Filaret in 1687-1690. The dry shelter of the wooden arches under the bridge provided a home for thieves and robbers. Here the road to the southern part of the town used to begin. It went by the **Donskoi Monastery** and the **Svyato-Danilov Monastery** to Kaluga and Tula. Both monasteries, by the way, were recently returned to the Orthodox

Church; the Svyato-Danilov became the Patriarch's residence.

Zamoskvorechye: Between the Kammeny and the Krasnokholmsky bridges is another ancient quarter of the city, Zamoskvorechye (meaning "beyond the Moskva River"). In the 17th century, it was a place where artisans lived, hence many of the local names: Kadashevskaya Street (barrel makers), Novokuznetskaya Street (blacksmiths) and so on. In the 19th century the district was taken over by rich merchants who built many fine mansions and abundant churches. It was here that Pavel Tretiakov, the wealthy tradesman, founded his art gallery in 1892.

Today the masterpieces from the Tretiakov Gallery are on exhibit in the new Exhibition Center in Krumsky Val 10, in front of Gorky Park.

Gorky Park surrounds *Neskuchny* (Never Dull) Garden, an old park just behind the 1st City Hospital on the slopes going down to the Moskva River. The park was founded by Demidov, the millionaire industrialist, in the middle of the 18th century. It got its name because of the magnificent collection of fairy-tale plants from overseas which decorated the fantastic paths. Today the main mansion houses the Presidium of the USSR Academy of Sciences. Leninsky Avenue is known as the Avenue of Soviet science because of the 30 plus research centers situated along it.

Kalininsky Avenue: This avenue starts from the Manege and under its former name of Vozdvizhenka Street it led, during the 16th century, to the Krestovozdvizhenzky Monastery. It became a central street as late as in the 19th century when it surpassed Frunze Street in importance. The first building on the right corner is the reception building of the Presidium of the USSR Supreme Soviet. On the left, the huge edifice is the nation's largest library, named after Lenin. The library, which has over 30 million books, was founded long before the Revolution in the so-called Rumiantsev Museum in the Mansion of Pashkov the wealthy landowner, high up on Vagankovo Hill.

Kalinin Prospect at night.

Just where the avenue takes off, the Romanov, Naryshkin and the Shermetiev families had their residences in the 18th century. Next door the quaint pseudo-Moresque house now belongs to the Union of Soviet Friendship Societies. The house used to belong to the Morozovs, a family of former Moscow millionaires.

The Old Arbat: Branching off from Kalininsky Avenue begins one of Moscow's best known streets: the Old Arbat. It derives its name from the Arabic *rabat* meaning suburb. The Arbat, which is over five centuries old, was the starting point of the ancient road from the walls of the White City to Smolensk. In the mid-18th century the neighborhood was populated by the aristocracy. It is not for nothing that Alexander Herzen, the Russian writer and revolutionary, called it **Moscow's St. Germaine des Pres**. After it was turned into a pedestrian-only district several years ago, the Arbat became a favorite destination for tourists. As a rule, Muscovites are only represented here by the artists and buskers.

Satirical and political cartoonists who can't get access to official art galleries display their work here. The numerous small shops, coffee shops and grill bars aim to please everyone's palate and attract throngs of visitors: in the Soviet Union one learns to combine the pleasant with the useful.

Arbat Street ends in Smolenskaya Square where the Foreign Ministry Tower stands. There are seven such towers in Moscow, all built roughly in the same period - in the late 1940s and early 1950s. They cannot, of course, be called faceless. Standing next to modern structures, they are reminders of their era, the era of Stalinist despotism, of socialist empire-building.

The symbols of today, however, are not so much architectural trademarks; they are joint ventures, cooperatives and meetings, demonstrations, that at times, border on open confrontation with the government; they are crowds of young people flooding the churches in the quest for new ideals. The principal symbol of today is genuine freedom of

speech, freedom of assembly and freedom of conscience. In this respect Moscow is full with sights and an atmosphere that fits our time and day.

Museum estates
in the environs of Moscow

The Kuskovo Museum of Ceramics and Estate: (Yunost Street 2, Zhdanovskaya Metro Station. Open, except Mon. and Tues., 11 a.m. to 7 p.m.). The Kuskovo Estate was the summer residence of the aristocratic Sheremetiev family. The house was built in 1715 by Boris Sheremetiev, Peter the Great's field marshal. Today it stands unaltered after reconstruction in the mid-18th century when Pyotr, Sheremetiev's son, had it transformed into a pleasure palace. The several buildings that survive to date include the **Central Palace**, the **Danish House**, the **Hermitage**, the **Grotto** and the **Conservatoire**. In 1938, the ceramics museum was opened in the grounds. Today, the museum has over 18,000 pieces of ceramics dating from the 17th century to modern times.

The Ostankino Palace Museum of Serf Art: (Pervaya Ostankinskaya Street 5, VDNKh Metro Station. Open, except Tues. and Wed., 10 a.m. to 5 p.m. in summer and 10 a.m. to 3 p.m. in winter). The Ostankino Estate also belonged to the Sheremetievs. It was built at the same time as the Kuskovo Estate by Pyotr Sheremetiev's son. It was designed as an out-of-town residence for solemn receptions and gala functions, and purposely situated in the immediate vicinity of the Czar's Alekseevskoye residence.

Built in 1798, the adjoining theater had a company of professional serf actors, who were known far and wide for their ability. The rooms and furniture of the palace have survived in immaculate condition.

The Kolomenskoye Museum and Reserve: (Proletarsky Prospekt 31, Kolomenskoye Metro Station. Open, except Tues., 11 a.m. to 5 p.m.). Kolomenskoye dates back to the 14th century.

It was visited by the victorious Grand Prince Dmitry Donskoy on his way back from the Kulikovo battle. In the 16th century, after the foundation of the state of Russia, Kolomenskoye became the summer residence of the royal family. The most interesting buildings that have survived include the **Ascension Church** (1532), the **Church of the Icon of the Kazan Virgin** (17th century) and the house of Peter the Great, in which he lived while the Russian fleet was being built in Archangel on the Northern Dvina. The first Russian emperor passed his childhood days in Kolomenskoye. In one of the buildings there is a museum of clockwork, keys and locks of the 16th to 19th centuries.

The Abramtsevo Museum Estate: (72 km/45 miles by car along Yaroslavskoye Shosse. Open, except Mon. and Tues., 11 a.m. to 5.30 p.m.). One of the great cultural centers of 19th century Russia. Owned first by the famous Russian writer and thinker Sergei Aksakov, it evokes the memory of his closest friends, Gogol, Turgenev, Belinsky and many others. In 1870 the estate was purchased by the wealthy industrialist and patron of the arts, Savva Mamontov, who loved talented people. He was patron to Fyodor Shalyapin, Mikhail Vrubel and Apollinary Vasnetsov. Several other artists also worked here including Repin, Korovin and Polenov. Their works are on display in the museum which was opened here after the Revolution.

The Novoierusalim Museum Reserve: (58 km/36 miles by car along Volokolamskoye Shosse. Open, except Mon., 10 a.m. to 6 p.m.).

The monastery in Novoierusalim (New Jerusalem) was built in the 17th to 19th centuries on the banks of the Istra River. It was founded by Patriarch Nikon in 1656. Destroyed during the war, it was restored and reused as a museum of applied arts. It has a collection of 18th to 19th century art and 16th to 17th century weapons. In the park there is an ethnographic museum of 17th-century timber buildings.

Soviets love the cinema and many of their movies are masterpieces.

MOSCOW

The airport: Moscow International Airport, Sheremetevo 2, is the main entry point to the USSR. The airport has great difficulty in handling the quickly growing number of passengers who want to visit the Soviet Union and at the same time the growing number of those who want to emigrate. Tourists have to expect waiting times of an hour or more to pass through passport and customs control. However, Aeroflot and Lufthansa recently started a joint venture to modernize the airport and changes can soon be expected. In 1989 construction started for the new Sherhotel for transit passengers. In the main arrival hall there is an exchange office and an Intourist counter.

Travel Essentials: Airport Sheremetevo 2, Information, Tel. 155-5005; Airport Intourist Bureau, Tel. 156-9435; Aeroflot International Enquiries, Tel. 245-0002; Railways Information, Tel. 266-900; International Shipping Lines (Booking Office), Tel. 291-9331; Intourist Head Office, prosp. Marksa 16, Tel. 203-6962.

From the airport to town: The only convenient way to reach Moscow from the airport is by taxi, by a reserved hotel car for business travelers or by reserved bus for tourists arriving in groups. The official taxi fare, based on a rate of 20 kopecks per km plus 20 kopecks service, varies between 15 and 25 roubles. Foreign travelers, however, will most probably be asked to pay in hard currency. Taxi, Tel. 927-0000.

Public transport: If you want to make the acquaintance of Moscow's public transport system at once, there is an overcrowded bus, route 551, which will bring you (for five kopecks) to the nearest Metro station (Rechnoy Vokzal).

All public transport in Moscow costs five kopecks (except for buses running the routes 300 to 499) regardless of distance and direction. The Metro is the most convenient and fastest way to move around in Moscow.

Railway stations: Most Moscow railway stations are in the vicinity of the Garden Ring (Sadovoe Kol'tso), i.e. relatively close to the city center, and all have metro stations nearby. **Byelorussky** and **Kievsky** are the terminals for trains from Western and Eastern Europe and **Yaroslavsky** Terminal

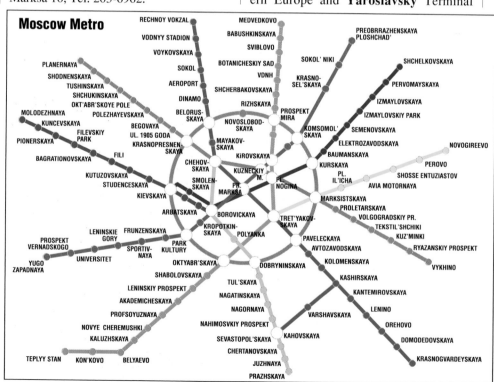

Moscow Metro

(neighboring two others, **Leningradsky** and **Kazansky**) is the station for long distance trains from the east.

ACCOMMODATIONS

Savoy (de luxe), ul. Rozhdestvenka 3, Tel. 928-0768; **Metropol** (de luxe), prosp. Marksa 1 (newly opened after reconstruction).

Business class hotels: Intourist, ul. Gorkovo 3-5, Tel. 203-4008; **Kosmos**, prosp. Mira 150, Tel. 217-0785; **Mezhdunarodnaya**, Krasnopresnenskaya nab. 12, Tel. 253-2378; **National**, prosp. Marksa 14/1, Tel. 203-6539.

Other Intourist hotels: Akademicheskaya 1, Leninsky prosp. 1 and **Akademicheskaya 2**, ul. Donskaya 1, Tel. 238-2550; **Aeroflot**, Leningradsky prosp. 37, Tel. 155-5624; **Altai**, ul. Botanicheskaya 41, Tel. 488-6829; **Belgrade 1 and 2**, Smolenskaya pl. 5, Tel. 248-6734, 248-1643; **Budapest**, Petrovskie Linii 2/18; Tel. 924-8820; **Kievskaya**, ul. Kievskaya 2, Tel. 240-1444; **Leningradskaya**, ul. Kalanchyovskaya 21/40, Tel. 975-3008; **Minsk**, ul. Gorkovo 22, Tel. 299-1300; **Mir**, B.Devyatinsky per. 9, Tel. 252-9519; **Moskva**, prosp. Marksa 7, Tel. 292-1100; **Mozhayskaya**, Mozhayskoe shosse 165, Tel. 446-1754; **Ostankino**, ul. Botanicheskaya 29, Tel. 219-2880; **Pekin**, B.Sadovaya ul. 5, Tel. 209-3400; **Rossiya**, ul. Razina 6, Tel. 298-5531; **Salyut**, Leninsky prosp. 158, Tel. 438-6565; **Sovetskaya**, Leningradsky prosp. 32, Tel. 250-7255; **Ukraina**, Kutuzovsky prosp. 2/1, Tel. 243-3030.

Youth hostels: Molodyozhnaya, Dmitrovskoe shosse 27, Tel. 210-4565; **Orlyonok**, ul. Kosygina 15, Tel. 939-8844; **Sputnik**, Leninsky prosp. 38, Tel. 938-7106; **Yunost'**, Khamovnichesky val 34, Tel. 242-1980.

EATING OUT

Restaurants: Aragvi (Georgian cuisine), ul. Gorkovo 6, Tel. 229-3762; **Arbat**, prosp. Kalinina 26, Tel. 291-1445; **Arlekino** (Italian cuisine), ul. Druzhinnikovskaya 15, Tel. 205-7088; **Baku** (Azerbaijan cuisine), ul. Gorkovo 24, Tel. 299-8506; **Bombay** (Indian cuisine), Rublyovskoe shosse 91, Tel.

141-5502; **Delhi** (Indian cuisine), ul. Krasnaya Presnya 23b, Tel. 255-0492; **Havana** (Cuban cuisine), Leninsky prosp. 88, Tel. 138-0091; **Hermitage**, Karetny Ryad 3, Tel. 299-1160; **Kropotkinskaya 36** (Moscow's first coop restaurant), ul. Kropotkinskaya 36, Tel. 201-7500; **Lasagne** (Italian cuisine), ul. Pyatnitskaya 40, Tel. 231-1085; **Mei-hua** (Chinese cuisine), ul. Rusakovskaya 2/1, Tel. 264-9574; **Pkhenyan** (Korean cuisine), ul. Sretenka 23/25; **Praga** (Czech cuisine), Arbat 2, Tel. 290-6171; **Riviera** (French cuisine), Krasnopresnenskaya nab., on board the "Alexander Blok", closed in winter time; **Slavyansky Bazar** (Slavonic cuisine), ul. 25 Oktyabrya 13, Tel. 921-1872; **Sofia** (Bulgarian cuisine), ul. Gorkovo 32/1, Tel. 251-4950; **Tren-Mos** (American cuisine, credit cards only), Komsomolsky prosp. 21, Tel. 245-1216; **U Yuzefa** (Jewish cuisine), ul. Dubininskaya 11, Tel. 238-4646; **U Pirosmani** (Georgian cuisine), Novodevichy proezd 4, Tel. 247-1926; **Uzbekistan** (Central Asian cuisine), ul. Neglinnaya 29, Tel. 924-6053.

Cafés & Bars: DAB (Beer pub), Hotel Belgrad 2; **Löwenbrau** (Beer pub), Intourist Hotel; **Pokrovka** (Byelorussian Café), ul. Chernyshevskovo 4; **Vstrecha**, ul. Gilyarovskovo 3; **Yakimanka**, ul. B.Polyanka 2/10; **Zaliv Kha Long** (Vietnamese Café), ul. Krylatskaya 2.

MUSEUMS

Art, Architecture, Literature and Musical Museums: Pushkin Fine Arts Museum, ul. Volkhonka 12. Pushkin Museum had been founded by the father of the famous Russian poetess Marina Tsvetaeva (1982-1941), prof. Tsvetaev, as a museum and educational institution for professional artists and public. Now the museum is known not only by its own rich collections, but also by regular temporary expositions of extracts from the most well-known art depositories of the world.

Among the masterpieces of Pushkin museum are works by Rembrandt, Boticelli, Lucas Cranach the Elder, Goya and Michelangelo. The second half of the 19th century and the beginning of the 20th century are represented in particular with works by Auguste Renoir, Edgar Degas, Auguste

Rodin, Vincent van Gogh, Paul Gaugin, Fernand Leger, Henri Matisse and Pablo Picasso.

The Ground floor (see plan on the next page). Halls 1 and 2: Ancient Art - Egypt and Middle East. Hall 3: Icons. Byzantinian schools of the 14th century. Halls 4 and 5: Italian Art - paintings of 8th-16th centuries. Halls 6, 8, 9 and 10: Collection of Dutch, Flemish and German painting of 15th-17th centuries. Large Hall 7: Ancient Greek and Roman art. Statues, reliefs etc. A lot of copies. Hall 13: Paintings of France, 17th-18th centuries. Hall 14: Used for temporary expositions if they are not too large. If it happens, neighbouring halls are also used.

The First Floor: Hall 16: Ancient Greece, 5th century BC. The nummeration of halls does not correspond to a chronological order, therefore the following route is recommended. Halls 29, 28 and 27: Art of Italian Renaissance. Hall 26: Medieval Art. Hall 25: Copies of some of the world's best known sculptures. Hall 24: Ancient Greece, 1st-4th century BC. Halls 23-17: Collection of European paintings of the 19th century to the beginning of the 20th century.

New Gallery of Pushkin Museum, ul Marshala Shaposhnikova 4;

Tretyakov Gallery, Lavrushensky per. 10. Tretyakov gallery, founded by a merchant and patron of the arts Tretyakov, a portrait of whom can be seen among the exposition of this museum, disposes one of the richest collections of Russian painting.

The collection of icons from Tretyakov Gallery (Tretyakovka, as muscovites call it) is counted by appreciators as one of the most precious in the world. Here are icons of Byzantine, Kiev, Novgorod, pskov and Vladimir-Suzdal schools of icon painting, since the very beginning of the 12th century until late 17th century.

Among the works of art of the 18th-19th centuries worth mentioning are masterpieces by Dmitry Levitsky, Alexander Ivanov, Karl Brullov, Alexei Venetsianov, Ilya Repin, Vasily Polenov and Victor Vasnetsov.

The early 20th century is represented by Valentin serov, Konstantin Korovin, Mikhail Vrubel, Vasily Borisov-Musatov and others.

Other Museums of Art, Architecture, Literature and Music are **New Tretyakov Gal-**lery and the **Central Painter's House**, Krymsky Val 10/14; **Andrej Rublyov Museum**, Andronikov Monastery, pl. Primakova 10; **Chekhov House-Museum**, Sadovo-Kudrinskaya ul. 6; **Dostoevsky Museum-Flat**, ul. Dostoevskovo 2; **Folk Arts Museum**, ul. Stanislavskovo 7; **Glinka Musical Museum**, ul. Fadeeva 4; **Lermontov House-Museum**, ul. Malaya Molchanovka 2; **Literature Museum**, ul. Petrovka 28; **Museum of Oriental Art**, Suvorovsky bul'var 12a; **Manege Exhibition Hall**, pl. 50-letiya Oktyabrya 1; **Shchusev Architectural Museum**, prosp. Kalinina 5.

History Museums: Museum of History and Reconstruction of Moscow, Novaya pl. 12; **Decembrists Museum**, ul. Karla Marksa 23; **Museum of the Revolution**, ul. Gorkovo 21; **Lenin Museum**, pl. Revolyutsii; **Pokrovsky Sobor Museum**, Krasnaya pl. (Red Square); **Museum of the Armed Forces**, ul. Sovetskoy Armii 2.

Scientific Museums: Polytechnical Museum, Novaya pl. 3/4; **Sergey Korolyov House-Museum**, 2/28 6oy Ostankinsky per.; **Frunze Museum of Aviation**, Krasnoarmeyskaya ul. 4.

PERFORMANCES

Bolshoi Theater, pl. Sverdlova, Tel. 292-6743; **Kremlin Palace of Congresses**, Kremlin, Borovitskie Vorota (gate); booking office, prosp. Kalinina 1, Tel. 926-7901; **Stanislavsky and Nemirovich-Danchenko Opera and Ballet Theater**, Pushkinskaya ul. 17, Tel. 229-8388; **Maly Theater**, pl. Sverdlova 1/6; **MKkAT**, Staraya Stsena (old stage), proezd Khudozhestvennovo Theater 3, Tel. 229-8760; **MKhAT**, Novaya Stsena (new stage), Tverskoy bul'var 22, Tel. 203-6222; **Mossovet Theater**, B.Sadovaya ul. 16, Tel. 299-2035; **Mayakovsky Theater**, ul. Gertsena 19, Tel. 290-6241; **Sovremennik Theater**, Chistoprudny bul'var 19a, Tel. 921-1790; **Taganka Theater**, ul. Chkalova 76, Tel. 271-2826; **Vakhtangov Theater**, Arbat 26, Tel. 241-0728; **Obraztsov Puppet Theater**, Sadovo-Samotechnaya ul. 3; **Circus**, prosp. Vernadskovo 7.

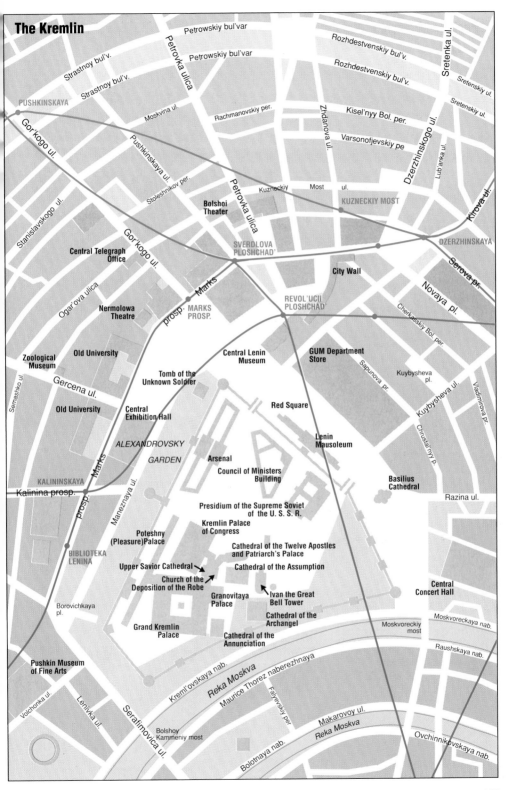

The Kremlin

Strastnoy bul'v.
Petrowskiy bul'var
Petrowskiy bul'var
Rozhdestvenskiy bul'v.
Rozhdestvenskiy bul'v.
Sretenka ul.

Strastnoy bul'v.
Petrovka ulica
Sretenskiy ul.

PUSHKINSKAYA
Sretenskiy ul.

Moskvina ul.
Rachmanovskiy per.
Kisel'nyy Bol. per.
Dzerzhinskogo ul.

Gor'kogo ul.
Pushkinskaya ul.
Zhdanova ul.
Varsonofjevskiy pe
Lub'anka ul.

Stanislavskogo ul.
Stoleshnikov per.
Kuzneckiy
Most
ul.
Kirova ul.

KUZNECKIY MOST

**Bolshoi
Theater**
Petrovka ulica

Gor'kogo ul.
**SVERDLOVA
PLOSHCHAD'**
DZERZHINSKAYA

**Central Telegraph
Office**
Serova pr.

Ogar'ova ulica
Marks
City Wall
Novaya pl.

prosp.
**MARKS
PROSP.**
**REVOL'UCII
PLOSHCHAD'**
Cherkasskiy Bol. per

**Nermolowa
Theatre**

Gercena ul.
**Zoological
Museum**
Old University
**Central Lenin
Museum**
**GUM Department
Store**
Kuybysheva
pl.
Sapunova pr.
Kuybysheva ul.
Vladimirova pr.

Semashko ul.
**Tomb of the
Unknown Soldier**
Red Square
Chrustalnyy p.

Old University
**Central
Exhibition Hall**
**Lenin
Mausoleum**

ALEXANDROVSKY
Arsenal

GARDEN
**Council of Ministers
Building**
**Basilius
Cathedral**

KALININSKAYA
Marks
Razina ul.

Kalinina prosp.
prosp.
Maneznaya ul.
**Presidium of the Supreme Soviet
of the U. S. S. R.**

**Kremlin Palace
of Congress**

**BIBLIOTEKA
LENINA**
**Poteshny
(Pleasure)Palace**
**Cathedral of the Twelve Apostles
and Patriarch's Palace**

Upper Savior Cathedral
Cathedral of the Assumption
**Central
Concert Hall**

Borovichkaya
pl.
**Church of the
Deposition of the Robe**
**Granovitaya
Palace**
**Ivan the Great
Bell Tower**

**Cathedral of the
Archangel**
Moskvoreckaya nab.

Moskvoreckiy
most

**Grand Kremlin
Palace**
**Cathedral of the
Annunciation**
Raushskaya nab.

**Pushkin Museum
of Fine Arts**

Volchonka ul.
Lenivka ul.
Kreml'ovskaya nab.
Reka Moskva
Maurice Thorez naberezhnaya
Falyevskiy per

Seratimovica ul.
Makarovoy ul.
Bolshoy
Kammeniy most
Reka Moskva
Ovchinnikovskaya nab.

Bolotnaya nab.

167

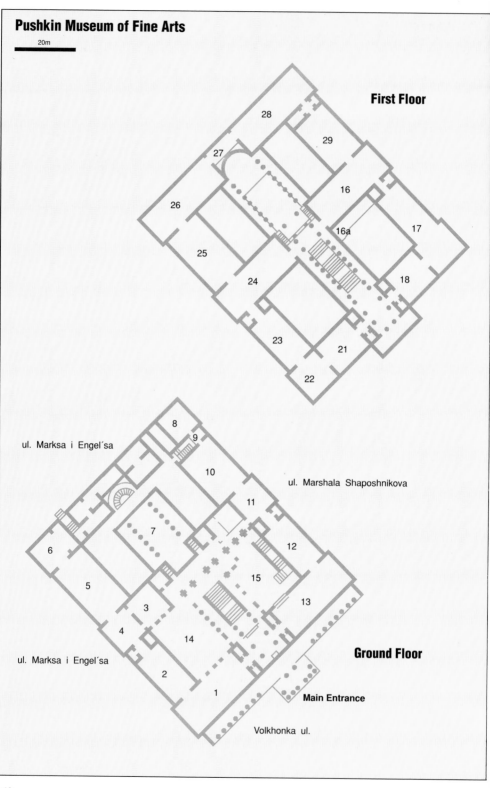

Pushkin Museum of Fine Arts

20m

First Floor

28
29
27
16
26
16a
17
25
24
18
23
21
22

ul. Marksa i Engel´sa

8
9
10
ul. Marshala Shaposhnikova
11
7
12
6
15
5
13
3
4
14
ul. Marksa i Engel´sa
2
Ground Floor
1
Main Entrance

Volkhonka ul.

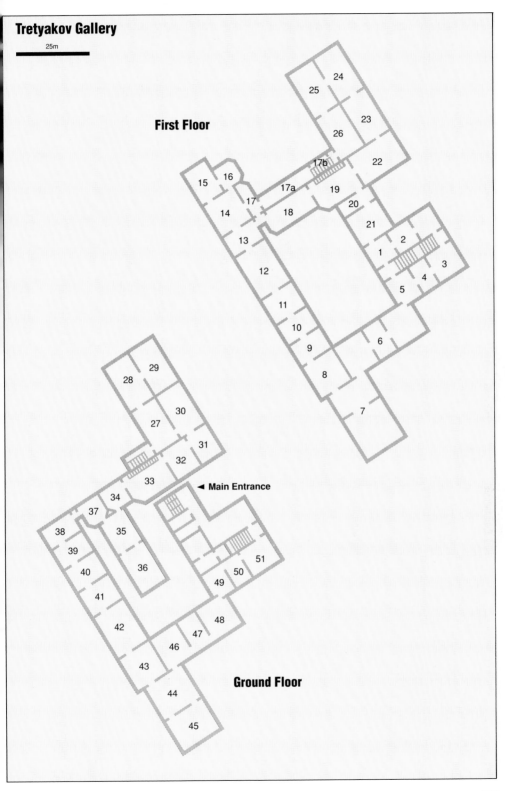

Tretyakov Gallery

25m

First Floor

◄ **Main Entrance**

Ground Floor

THE GOLDEN RING OF RUSSIA

For six centuries, the place was known as Sergiy's Town - **Sergiyev Posad**. For the past six decades, it's been known as Zagorsk ("place beyond the mountains"). But, as usual, things are not what they seem, and it would be highly naive to think that the town's new name has something to do with mountains. No, the town which bore the name of the venerable Sergiy of Radonezh - the man who founded the Troitse-Sergiyevsky (Trinity-St. Sergius) Monastery here in the middle of the 14th century, the man who blessed Prince Dmitry Donskoi on the eve of the battle at Kulikovo (1380), the man who, according to Dmitry Likhachev, was admired as "the spiritual leader of the Russian people" - that town was renamed, absolutely out of the blue one fine morning in 1930, in honor of an obscure secretary of the Moscow Party Committee, Vladimir Zagorsky who had probably never even set foot there. That same year, the lavra (that honorary title which means, in Greek, "main monastery", was bestowed upon the Trinity-St. Sergius in 1744) lost two of its greatest treasures: the Trinity, Andrei Rublyov's masterpiece, painted by Russia's greatest artist of the Middle Ages "in honor of Sergiy" (transferred to Moscow's Tretiakov Art Gallery), and the world's largest bells from the Trinity Belfry (which was destroyed).

Today, demands to give Zagorsk its original name back are heard more and more often in Moscow's literary and scientific quarters. But a plebiscite conducted by municipal authorities seems to have yielded a negative answer.

Of course, there is a reason for the fact that we decided to start our tour of the Golden Ring - one of the most popular routes among Soviet and foreign lovers of old Russian architecture - with Zagorsk. Yes, there is a reason: the situation around Zagorsk shows how the Soviet people are rediscovering an interest - no, interest is too mild a word - a spiritual yearning for the nation's cultural roots and origins. The Russian people are only now beginning to realize that without respect for the history and the roots of their culture, there is, figuratively speaking, neither present nor future. Hence the rejection of that which has been foisted upon them, place names included; hence the desire to get past the superficial and back to the origins.

As a matter of fact, a ring is what the zig-zags of the route resemble least of all. But whatever it is geometrically, the northeastern territory of ancient Muscovy, where whole towns are museums, is certainly solid gold as far as history and culture are concerned.

The 719 km-long (415 miles) route starts and ends in Moscow, passing through several towns of Ancient Rus - Pereyaslavl-Zalessky, Rostov Veliky, Yaroslavl, Kostroma, Suzdal, Vladimir and Zagorsk, which we have already mentioned. Zagorsk is the most convenient place to start: it lies a mere 70 km/ 44 miles to the north of Moscow along the Yaroslavl Highway. By so doing, however, we disrupt the order of historical succession - there are older towns. Take, for example, the town of Pereyaslavl-Zalessky, the birthplace of the famed Russian prince Alexander Nevsky, who defeated an army of German knights on Lake Chudskoye in 1242. But we will return to Pereyaslavl later.

Zagorsk: The matchless architecture of the **Trinity-St. Sergius**, one of the oldest seats of the Orthodox church, and the vast collections of ancient Russian painting and precious-metal articles are an unfailing tourist attraction. The monastery is a kind of Mecca for Orthodox pilgrims, who come here, to the whitestone Trinity Cathedral, to honor the remains of the venerable Sergiy of Radonezh, exalted as "protector of the Russian land" early in the 15th century. The monastery is a fortress known for its heroic resistance (16 months under siege!) during the Polish-Lithuanian invasion 370 years ago. The monastery is a museum of national importance; as such, it is protected by the state. It is also a major religious center: the faithful flock to its churches by the thousand. The monastery runs a clerical school (seminary); to become a student, you have to come out ahead of what can only be called a formidable competition.

The architectural highlights of the Trinity-St. Sergius include the dome and roof of the Trinity Cathedral, their gold plates and inside the cathedral, an iconostasis adorned by the works of Andrei Rublyov.

The five-domed **Assumption Cathedral** (formally the main church in the monastery) is the architectural center of the ensemble. It was founded by Ivan the Terrible's men in 1559. The simple rectangular tomb near the northwestern corner of the cathedral contains the remains of Czar Boris Godunov and his family. Along the south wall of the fortress, there is the refectory and the **Sergius Church** (late 17th century). The huge expanse of the refectory boasts a vaulted ceiling that has no internal supports - a testimonial to the technical accomplishments of Russian builders.

Until recently, the handsome **Metropolitan's Quarters** housed the residence of the Patriarch of the Orthodox Church. The building has a two-storied main facade, but from the northern side, you see another ground floor; cut into the slope in the 16th century, it is the oldest part of the building.

The jewel of the architectural ensemble is the **tall, five-level steeple**, easily the most beautiful in Russia. It was built by Dmitry Ukhtomsky in the middle of the 18th century. Zagorsk cannot be imagined without it (a fact acknowledged by movie people, both in the USSR and abroad, who use it as a kind of permanent set). Leaving Zagorsk, its remarkable silhouette remains in sight for some time, before finally vanishing behind the horizon.

Pereyaslavl-Zalessky: An hour's drive to the northeast, on the banks of Lake Plescheevo, which resembles a crystal dish more than anything else, there stands the town of Pereyaslavl-Zalessky, also known as "town-on-the-waters". It was founded, together with Moscow, by Prince Yury Dolgoruky in the 12th century. Pereyaslavl is the birthplace of the Russian navy. It was also here that Peter

The Kremlin of Rostov the Great.

Видъ Кремля Города ростова Великаго, Ярос Губ.

the Great built his *poteshnaya* (amusement) flotilla at the end of the 17th-century, thereby writing the first page in the history of Russian shipbuilding and seafaring.

Now for a brief account of the town's architectural attractions. Let us start with the heart of Pereyaslavl, the Red Square and the whitestone **Spaso Preobrazhensky Cathedral**, the oldest in the whole of northeastern Russia, Moscow included (1152-1157). To the south of the cathedral stands the **Church of Peter the Metropolitan** with its faceted, hipped roof (1585). Finally, there's the pride of Pereyaslavl, the **Goritsky Monastery**, founded in 1337-1340 during the reign of Ivan Kalita and two more monasteries - **Danilov** and **Nikitsky**. The gate of the Goritsky Monastery voluptuously decorated with a whimsical ornament, is certainly something for the museum-goer. The monastery, by the way, has been a museum since 1919.

The road leads on to **Rostov Veliky** (Rostov the Great) which is but an hour away. The town has been dubbed "a symphony in stone", "Russia's Eternal City" and "the earthly wonder worthy of the next world". It has a fairy-tale quality as it stands against the background of the mid-Russian landscape behind the vast expanse of Lake Nero.

Rostov, like its ancient rival, Novgorod, has been called "the Great" for many centuries now. By the end of the first millennium, it was already the oldest, wealthiest and most populous center of Russian statehood.

Today, Rostov is famous for its **Kremlin** (18th century), the former residence of the metropolitan, resplendent with the gleam of the gold and silver of its towers, cupolas, cornices and lace crosses. In August 1953, a tornado tore the churches of Rostov apart, and we must be thankful to the restorers and their ancient skills, without whom we could no more enjoy their magnificence.

It is utterly impossible to describe the treasures of the Kremlin in a few short lines. In any case, it is certainly much better to see, than to read about them. There is the **Spas-na-Senyakh Church**

(1675), the **Assumption Cathedral** (16th century), the **Odigitry Church** (1693), the famous icons (15th to 18th centuries) the collection of portraits as well as china (18th to 19th centuries), and the Rostov enamels.

Enamels are the trademark of Rostov the Great and, as such, deserve attention. This ancient art was developed in Rostov at the end of the 18th century. It is based on the unique properties of an enamel surface, to which flammable paints are applied. The works of the Rostov enamel masters are known all over the world. For Russians they are nearly impossible to come by, except in the hard-currency Berioska stores.

Yaroslavl: Moving on to Yaroslavl (60 km/37 miles away from Moscow), you reach one of Russia's largest regional centers (over 600,000 inhabitants). Yaroslavl is some ten centuries old. In 1010 Yaroslav the Wise founded a fort on the Volga bank. Legend has it that the prince came upon a bear in those deserted parts and killed it with an axe. The bear then became the local totem and was even included in the region's coat of arms. Today, the mascot greets us as we enter Yaroslavl. From time immemorial, Yaroslavl was considered one of the most beautiful towns in Russia. The abundance of frescoes and ceramic ornaments in its churches earned it the title of the "**Florence of Russia**".

A breathtaking vista of white (the walls and towers of the **Spassky Monastery**), and gold (the domes of its 16th-century cathedral) opens to the traveler coming from Moscow. It is literally impossible to tear your gaze away from the tall **Bogoyavlenskaya Church**, whose ceramic-tiled walls give it the appearance of being studded with jewels. In the central square of the city, there is the masterpiece of local architecture - the **Cathedral of Elijah the Prophet**, which was built under orders from the town's merchants in 1647-1650. Its walls and vaults are a vast museum of old Russian paintings.

And one more thing. It was Yaroslavl that preserved for Russia its greatest literary masterpiece, *Slovo o polku Igor-*

At the outdoor museum in Suzdal.

eve, written in the 12th century. The only surviving copy was found in the Spaso-Preobrazhensky Monastery.

Yaroslavl is also the birthplace of the Russian national theater. Fyodor Volkov, the father of the Russian theater, started his career here in the 18th century; the local theater bears his name to this day. Here the circle around the Golden Ring has to be interrupted to go via Moscow, to Vladimir and Suzdal, thereby passing through the beautiful mid-Russian landscape which makes time pass quickly for the traveler.

Not so for the people who live in the ancient Russian towns along the way: forced to embark on weekly bus or electric-train voyages to Moscow by the emptiness of food-store shelves (there's been no sausage for years), they are probably sick of the landscape. The grandeur of nature and the magnificence of ancient towns are just as much a part of their daily life as alas, the all-pervading deficit, the provincial, bleak look of the streets, and the impotent service industry. People live on, of course, taking pride in their native parts and enjoying the brighter sides of life; they try to convince themselves and others that man does not live by bread alone.

Vladimir: The city lies 166 km (100 miles) to the east of Moscow. It is another pearl of ancient Russian culture. Founded on the banks of the Kliazma by Prince Vladimir Monomakh in 1208, it played a key role in the formation of the Russian state. In the middle of the 12th century, the city became the capital of the Vladimir-Suzdal Principate. In 1288 Vladimir was besieged and looted by the Mongol hordes. Early in the 17th century, it fell to the invading Poles and Lithuanians.

Vladimir's whitestone structures (12th century) are known all over the world. Of these, the foremost is the **Assumption Cathedral**, with its striking decor, perfect architectural forms, and frescoes by Andrei Rublyov and Daniil Chyorny. But the most beautiful church in the city is the **Dmitrievsky Cathedral** with splendid carvings of plants, birds, animals and hunting scenes on its facade.

The third architectural marvel in Vladimir, the **Golden Gate**, is a rare specimen of military architecture, a symbolic blend of impregnability and hospitality, it was built as a replica of the Golden Gate in Kiev.

Another place to see is the Assumption Cathedral in the **Knyaginin Monastery** (16th century) located in the northwestern part of the city. Frescoes by 17th-century painters are the pride of the cathedral. It is these masterpieces of ancient Russian architecture that are the image of Vladimir. The historical center of the city has over 700 less valuable buildings dating to the 19th and the early 20th centuries.

Suzdal: The last town left in the Golden Ring is Suzdal, the capital of Yury Dolgoruky's Rostov-Suzdal Principate. A short 30 kilometers (18 miles) from Vladimir, standing on the Poklonnaya (Bowing) Hill, lost among the never-ending fields, it suddenly comes into view, and the traveler takes in the jagged cornices of its belfries, hipped roofs and cupolas.

It is almost a sin to hurry along its streets, for there are so few of them. You should take a rest on the steep bank of the Kamenka River, and submit yourself to the spell of its quiet beauty, for it is a spell the soul never forgets. Equally memorable are the orange-red walls of the **Spaso-Yefimiev Monastery**, the foam-white walls of the **Pokrovsky**, the lacework of the gates leading to the **Monastery of the Deposition of the Virgin's Robe**, the architectural finesse of the churches, and the indented silhouettes of the belfries.

When Kiev fell to Lithuania, Suzdal was elevated as the Orthodox capital of medieval Rus. The Grand Princes and the Czars spared no expense when it came to building "the sacred cloisters". The townsfolk built their churches outside the city walls; there are so many for such a small town that it's difficult to name them all. But it's equally difficult not to admire the whitestone **Cathedral of the Nativity of the Virgin** (1225) with its dark-blue, gold-spotted cupolas, or to remain indifferent to the Golden Gates, which stand without equal among the creations of medieval Rus. And, of course, there is the **Museum of Russian Carpentry** with its two magnificent wooden churches, built with nothing but an axe and a chisel - the **Preobrazhenskaya** and the **Nikolskaya** - brought to the museum from faraway corners of the Suzdal region.

Suzdal, by the way, is one of the best tourist centers in the USSR in terms of service. You will find an abundance of restaurants (unlike in Yaroslavl and Vladimir), where you will be served traditional Suzdal dishes - meat as the merchants used to cook it, mushroom soup, and *medovukha*, the traditional Russian beverage made of honey. There are several hotels here, including the wooden *izba's* (peasant cottages) in the territory of the Pokrovsky Monastery, complete with wooden furniture in the style of ancient Rus. A well-equipped beach, boating, troika and horseback riding make it perfect for resting relaxation. Suzdal is the ideal place to end a tour of the Golden Ring, Russian history's "chronicle in stone".

Left, coat of arms above, of Jaroslavl, below of Vladmir. **Right**, Mother of God icon from Yaroslavl.

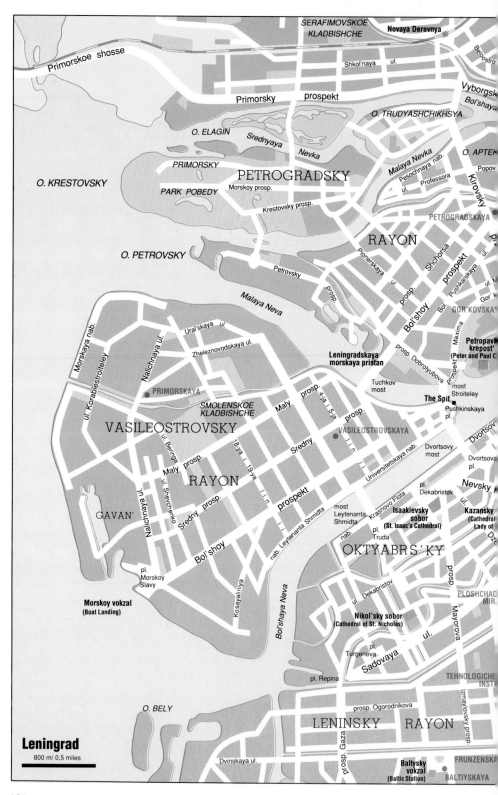

SERAFIMOVSKOE
KLADBISHCHE   Novaya Derevnya

Primorskoe shosse   Shkol'naya   ul.   Belostro

Primorsky   prospekt   Vyborgsk
                                                                       Bol'shaya
                                    O. TRUDYASHCHIKHSYA

O. ELAGIN   Srednyaya   Malaya Nevka   O. APTEK
                          Nevka   Pesochnaya nab.
PRIMORSKY   Professora   Popov
O. KRESTOVSKY   PETROGRADSKY   Malaya Nevka   ul.   Kirovsky
PARK POBEDY   Morskoy prosp.   PETROGRADSKAYA

              Krestovsky prosp.   RAYON

O. PETROVSKY   Pionerskaya   Shchorsa   prospekt
                      Petrovsky   ul.   prosp.   Pushkarskaya
                                 prosp.   Gor'k

                 Malaya Neva   Bol'shoy   Bol'   GOR'KOVSKA'

              Ural'skaya   ul/   Maxima
       Nalichnaya ul.   Zheleznovodskaya ul.   prosp. Dobrolyubova   Petropavl
Morskaya nab.   Leningradskaya   krepost'
                                                 morskaya pristan   (Peter and Paul C

ul. Korablestroiteley   Tuchkov   most
                      PRIMORSKAYA   most   Stroiteley
                                                                    The Spit
              SMOLENSKOE   Maly   prosp. 4-ja   Pushkinskaya
              KLADBISHCHE   5-ja   pl.

VASILEOSTROVSKY   18-ja   Sredny   prosp.   VASILEOSTROVSKAYA   Dvortsov

              Maly   prosp.   19-ja   Universitetskaya nab.   Dvortsovy
       ul. Beringa   Dvortsovy   most
RAYON   ul. Shevchenko   most   pl.

GAVAN'   Nalichnaya ul.   Sredny   prosp.   prospekt   pl.   Nevsky
                                                              Dekabristov
                                    most   Krasnovo Flota
                              Leytenanta   Isaakievsky   Kazansky
                              Shmidta   sobor   (Cathedral
              Bol'shoy   nab.   (St. Isaac's Cathedral) Lady of
                              nab. Leytenanta Shmidta pl.
       pl.   Truda
       Morskoy   OKTYABRS'KY
       Slavy
Morskoy vokzal   PLOSHCHAD
(Boat Landing)   Kosayalinya   Nikol'sky sobor   MIR.
                                        (Cathedral of St. Nicholas)   prosp.   Mayorova

              Bol'shaya Neva   ul. Dekabristov
                                        pl.
                                        Turgeneva   Sadovaya   ul.
                                                              TEHNOLOGICHE
                              pl. Repina   INST

O. BELY   prosp. Ogorodnikova
                                                         Izmaylovsky prosp.
              LENINSKY   RAYON

Leningrad   FRUNZENSKA
              Dvinskaya ul.   Baltysky
800 m/ 0,5 miles   vokzal
                                        (Baltic Station)   BALTIYSKAYA

184

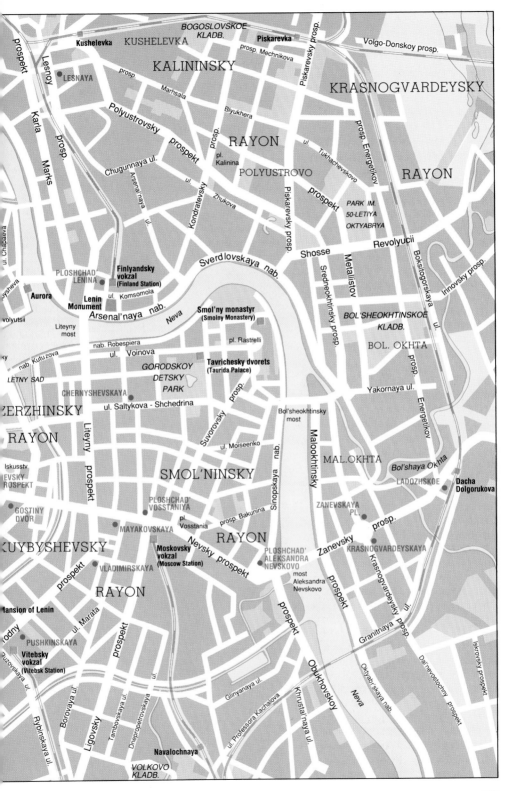

BOGOSLOVSKOE
KLADB.
Kushelevka   KUSHELEVKA   Piskarevka
prosp. Mechnikova
Volgo-Donskoy prosp.
Lesnoy
prospekt
LESNAYA
KALININSKY   KRASNOGVARDEYSKY
prosp.
Marhsala
Karla
Blyukhera
Polyustrovsky   prospekt
Marks
prosp.
RAYON
pl.
Kalinina
RAYON
Chugunnaya ul.   POLYUSTROVO
ul. Tukhachevskovo
Arsenalnaya ul.
Kondratevsky prosp.
Zhukova
prosp. Energetikov
PARK IM.
50-LETIYA
OKTYABRYA
Piskarevsky prosp.
prospekt
Revolyucii
ul. Chdpaeva
Sverdlovskaya nab.
Shosse
Metallistov
Boksllogorskaya ul.
Irinovsky prosp.
ysheva
PLOSHCHAD'
LENINA
Finlyandsky
vokzal
(Finland Station)
Sredneokhtinsky prosp.
volyutsii
Aurora   Lenin
Monument
ul. Komsomola
Smol'ny monastyr
(Smolny Monastery)
BOL'SHEOKHTINSKOE
KLADB.
Arsenal'naya nab.   Neva
BOL. OKHTA
Liteyny
most
Voinova
pl. Rastrelli
prosp.
ky
nab. Kutuzova
nab. Robespiera
ul. Voinova
Tavrichesky dvorets
(Taurida Palace)
Yakornaya ul.
LETNY SAD
GORODSKOY
DETSKY
PARK
Energetikov
CHERNYSHEVSKAYA
Bol'sheokhtinsky
most
ERZHINSKY
ul. Saltykova - Shchedrina
Suvorovsky prosp.
Malookhtinsky prosp.
MAL.OKHTA
Bol'shaya Okhta
RAYON
Liteyny prospekt
ul. Moiseenko
nab.
LADOZHSKOE
Dacha
Dolgorukova
Iskusstv
EVSKY
ROSPEKT
SMOL'NINSKY
Sinopskaya nab.
ZANEVSKAYA
PL.
GOSTINY
DVOR
PLOSHCHAD'
VOSSTANIYA
prosp.
KRASNOGVARDEYSKAYA
MAYAKOVSKAYA
pl.
Vosstania
prosp. Bakunina
RAYON
Zanevsky   prosp.
KUYBYSHEVSKY
prospekt
VLADIMIRSKAYA
Moskovsky
vokzal
(Moscow Station)
Nevsky prospekt
PLOSHCHAD'
ALEKSANDRA
NEVSKOVO
most
Aleksandra
Nevskovo
Krasnogvardeysky prosp.
ul.
RAYON
Mansion of Lenin
prospekt
ul. Marata
Granitnaya ul.
Oktyabr'skaya nab
Dalnevostochny prospekt
Iskrovsky prospekt
rodny
PUSHKINSKAYA
prospekt
Vitebsky
vokzal
(Vitebsk Station)
uzovskaya ul.
Borovaya ul.
Tambovskaya ul.
Dnepropetrovskaya
Ligovsky prospekt
Obukhovsky   prospekt
Glinyanaya ul.
Khrustal'naya ul.
Neva
ul. Professora Kachalova
Rybinskaya ul.
Navalochnaya
VOLKOVO
KLADB.

Leningrad

It is not the way of the human race to cherish its capital cities. Yet people rarely denigrate their capitals, either. But, as in many other things, Soviet people are an exception.

As most people will tell you, Moscow, that mother city of Russia and the country's first capital, still remains what it has been for centuries - a huge, sprawling village. Migration to Moscow has reached such proportions that only a small number of Muscovites have parents who were born there. It was only in late 1989 that Moscow got its first Moscow-born party leader, for the first time in Soviet history. Adding insult to injury, Moscow was subjected to such sweeping, and totally disorderly, reconstruction that today, there's hardly an old wall left standing.

Leningrad is different. This city, situated to the north-northwest of Moscow (just a night away in a railway sleeping-car), retains its ancient walls. Conceived by Peter the Great as a model for all the cities of the empire to emulate, yet not without a unique touch of Russianness, the city was always valued as an architectural ensemble.

Leningrad, the country's second city in terms of size and importance, is still young. It was founded by the great Czar and reformer in 1703, on lands wrested out of the hands of the Swedes. The city is built on the spot where the Neva surrenders its deep waters to the Gulf of Finland. Killing two birds with one stone, Peter opened the way to the sea (his greatest dream), which was absolutely imperative if Russia was to develop. He also moved the capital from Moscow to this new frontier town, establishing the center of his realm in such an eccentric position that his successors had no choice but to add several hundred kilometers of territory to the north and to the west in order to protect it.

A city built in the swamps: Despite the marshy land, the scarcity of construction materials and manpower, despite the tremendous strain of the endless Northern War, the city grew at such a lively pace that Peter proclaimed it the new capital, moving all organizations of state there in 1712. After that, construction proceeded ever quicker: by the end of the 18th century; St. Petersburg had over 200,000 inhabitants and, by the end of the 19th, over a million.

St. Petersburg remained the nation's capital for more than two centuries (Lenin re-established Moscow as the national capital in 1913). After Lenin's death, the city on the Neva was named Leningrad in his honor.

As Stalin started his systematic destruction and reconstruction of old Moscow in the 1930s. Leningrad - miraculously - survived. Yet it was destined to suffer as Moscow never had. Its tragedy was all the more terrible since it had developed from within. Stalin had no love for that city, to say the least. Not without reason, he considered Leningrad too westernized and intellectual, too strong in its revolutionary tradition, too rebellious and independent of the country's totalitarian center. The "Father

Preceding pages: the curtain is lifting on Nevski Prospect; a monumental city. Below, the Peter and Paul Fortress is of the same age as the city itself.

of All Peoples" and his clique, who reigned in Moscow, went out of their way to drag the former capital through the mud.

A blockade unequaled in history: These atrocities assumed many different forms, but all of them pale before the tragedy that befell Leningrad in the years of World War II. For 900 days, Leningrad was besieged by Hitler's army; at times, the daily bread ration fell to 125 grams (under 4 ounces). Hunger and cold killed a million people. At the **Piskarevskoye Memorial Cemetery** alone, 600,000 victims lie buried.

A true history of the blockade is yet to be written. As it is, one cannot help wondering why Leningrad was kept without food even when the tie with the "mainland" was re-established on the "Road of Life" over the frozen surface of Lake Ladoga. It is highly probable that in his thoughts, the tyrant had time and again surrendered the city to the enemy in his desire to settle all scores, and the devil take those who got left behind!

But Stalin was proved wrong. The war inspired the people of Leningrad, and raised the nation's esteem for their city. It is here, incidentally, that the roots of yet another campaign of terror lie, including the so-called "Leningrad case" of the late 1940s and early 1950s. Everybody who was anybody in the Leningrad power structure, even those who had worked in Leningrad but had moved to other towns by that time, were systematically rooted out and killed.

To this day, the two capitals - and, of course, the patriotically-minded people of Moscow and Leningrad - continue their endless debate: which is the better city? Yet the differences are there and will apparently be there for a long time to come, because they are reproduced in Leningrad's every new generation. If we remember that the town had been conceived as "a window into Europe" (as Alexander Pushkin, the Russian poet, put it), we shall understand the pain with which the people of Leningrad now watch their great city being reduced to the level of a common provincial center.

Monument to Peter the Great.

The municipal budget lags hopelessly behind the city's needs. Housing and municipal communications fall into decay. Too many people still live in "communal" apartments (where the kitchen and the bathroom are shared by two or more families). Yet, provincialism remains a long way off, kept at bay by pride in the face of ever-multiplying difficulties. The people of Leningrad are much more patriotic about their city than the people of Moscow could ever be. They are more knowledgeable about the history of their town. And even a Muscovite will tell you that they are "more cultured" in Leningrad, that they are better educated, particularly in humanitarian subjects, that they have superior manners and are more polite and respectful than Muscovites are. They are more reserved. They dress smartly.

The average level of education of industrial workers is much higher in Leningrad. The number of office workers is much smaller, yet the share of intellectuals among the population is greater than in Moscow. Leningrad does not have as many rich people as Moscow, but then again, it does not have any professional paupers, either. The crime rate is lower in Leningrad and even traffic violations occur much less frequently here.

The greatest worry of the people of Leningrad is the gradual decay of the town they live in. As a playwright once said, "I always thought of the avenues and squares as the magical decoration of a stage occupied by characters from an altogether different play. Now, even the decoration seems ready to fall apart from old age."

Some take part in "save-our-town" protests, others recognize their plight as unavoidable in a rigidly centralized state, where everything not of the capital is automatically considered second-rate. Still others console themselves that Leningrad is not the capital: if it were, half the buildings in the historical center would have been torn down long ago to create space for new ministries, office buildings and residential areas for the elite; as it is, new construction is prohib-

Cruiser Aurora which signed for the Bolshevik Revolution in 1917.

ited in the central part of Leningrad.

The people of Leningrad also worry about the dike, whose huge, nearly blind walls are being erected on the city's outskirts, purportedly to guard it against floods, but actually fraught with frying-pan-to-fire problems: some experts do think that once the dike disturbs the natural circulation of water between the river and the sea, the delta of the Neva and even the Gulf of Finland itself will turn into a hopeless, stagnant bog.

Leningrad is situated on the 60th parallel - the same as Oslo, the southernmost tip of Greenland, Whitehorse in Canada, the Liama Volcano in Alaska, the St. Matthew Island in the Bering Sea, Magadan of tragic Gulag fame in the Far East, and Oleminsk in Siberia. With 5 million inhabitants, it is the world's largest city in the Arctic Region.

The White Nights of Leningrad: The Baltic gives Leningrad its humid sea climate with somewhat cold winters (the average temperature in January is -8°C/18°F) and cool summers (average July temperature is 16°C/61°F). The number of sunny days is relatively small, rain is a normal occurrence, and if there is no wind, there is fog.

Leningrad is famous for its so-called "White Nights" (June-July). The sun never seems to set, and it is possible to read at night without a lamp. On a white night, most people prefer strolling in the streets and embankments to reading.

Leningrad is situated in the delta of the Neva on 12 large islands, which, in turn, are divided into almost a hundred small islets by canals and rivulets. The city has more bridges than there are days in a year. The Neva is a surprisingly large-watered and wide river for its length (over 500 meters/1650 feet in downtown Leningrad and just over 70 km/44 miles in length). It originates in Lake Ladoga, which, by the way, is the largest in Europe.

The center of the town: The best way to make your acquaintance with Leningrad is to see its central square, the **Dvortsovaya (Palace) Square.** The name comes from the Winter Palace, the former official residence of Russian em-

Bank of the Neva near the Peter and Paul fortress.

perors. The baroque palace was built in 1754-62 by the great son of a Florentine sculptor, Bartolomeo Rastrelli. The length of the roof cornice is almost two kilometers, it is adorned with 176 sculptures, positioned alternately with vases.

The Hermitage: The Winter Palace is flanked by the **New Hermitage**, its frontal balcony resting on ten figures of Atlas (1842-51, architect Leo von Klenze). Then comes the **Hermitage Theater** (1783-87, architect Giacomo Quarenghi). A covered arch over the Winter Ditch links that building to the **Old Hermitage** (1773-84, architect Jean-Baptiste Vallin de la Mothe). Together, the five structures make up one of the world's foremost museums of art - the Hermitage.

The Winter Palace is one of the largest among all known buildings of its kind: it stands on nine hectares, and the overall area of its rooms totals 46,000 square meters/495,000 square feet. It has 1,057 rooms, some 1,945 windows and 117 staircases. Each of its rooms is a work of art. Mighty and imposing, the building seems to grow out of the ground, holding the viewer's attention for a long time.

The Hermitage is hardly the secluded place its name implies. But the name that Catherine had given the palace has stuck, and is now applied not only to the private collection of the empress, but to the entire museum, which has several buildings and over two million items, of which only a fraction is on display.

First and foremost, there are the famous paintings that penniless French, Italian, Austrian and German courtiers sold from their collections. Then there's the less-famous yet incredibly rich "Russian collection" (a part of which is on display in the Menshikov Palace). Many rooms are given to priceless archaeological findings, antiques from the Orient, Greece and Rome. Then, there's the famous "mintz-cabinet". Particularly valuable items are stored in the Hermitage's "Golden Storeroom".

To make a long story short, the Hermitage is a double-edged masterpiece of world significance: it is both an architectural marvel with luxurious interiors,

and a treasury of world culture, where works of art are gathered by the hundred thousand. It was calculated that even a passing acquaintance with all of them would take several weeks, if not months.

People are always lining up for something they want in any city in the USSR. Deficit rules the land, and few foreigners are surprised to see a long line in a shop or a food store nowadays. But a museum? Yet there it is - a line of several thousand people willing to wait for untold hours to see the Hermitage; on weekends, people stand round the clock, jealously guarding their turn and organizing makeshift roll-calls. It is all the more surprising considering that most of these people come from the provinces, on a two- or three-day trade-union group tour of Leningrad.

There is the joke about the tourist who is there not to admire the sights, but simply to register his presence. Reaching some rock of historic fame, he doesn't even bother to lift his eyes, but ticks off the appropriate spot on his tourist map, and turns back, ever the incurious. Every day in the Hermitage, you can glimpse groups of exhausted, fussy provincials questioning one another, "We have an hour. Now quick, what are we supposed to be looking for?"

Deplorably, the few short minutes spared for the treasure that is the Hermitage symbolizes the absence of internal freedom. The typical Soviet citizen has neither the time nor the opportunity not to be "like everyone else", to avoid standing in line, to stand apart from the crowd - in other words, to attain and retain individuality of self. Helpless before the instinct of the herd, obsessed by the mania of imitation, people are not infrequently spiritual paupers, try as they might to storm the Hermitage or Moscow's Tretiakov Gallery (which has lines of equal notoriety).

One of Europe's greatest architectural ensembles: Forming a semi-circle opposite the Winter Palace is the building that used to house the **General Staff** (the military authority of the Russian Empire). Its construction was begun in 1819, in accordance with the designs of another famous Italian, Carlo Rossi, and

Main staircase in the Hermitage.

finished in 1829. There is an arch of formidable dimensions in the center of the building; it connects the square with Nevsky Prospekt. The arch is crowned with a triumphal chariot drawn by six horses.

The **Alexander Column**, with - as one guidebook claims - "a life-sized angel" on top, stands in the center of the square. Over 50 meters (165 feet) high, the monument was designed by Auguste Montferrant and erected in 1834 in honor of Russia's victories over Napoleon, which is why the angel's face resembles that of Emperor Alexander I (1801-25). The column weighs over 600 tons; the granite monolith, which had been cut out of a rock face some 300 km (186 miles) away, to the north of the city, stands on the pedestal without any props, owing to its weight and the accuracy of Montferrant's calculations.

The last, and plainest, addition to the square, the **Guards Corps building**, was constructed in 1848 and designed by Alexander Bruillov. Leningrad's central square has seen it all: military parades and mass gatherings, peaceful bread-marchers shot down by government troops in January 1905; the armed uprising of November 1917; more parades and mass gatherings, by then strictly regulated, formalized, timed to coincide with national holidays on May 1 and November 7, and proceeding under the watchful eye of army units, the police, and the KGB. But some things have changed with perestroika. Now the square no longer frowns on juvenile skateboard wizards; hosts international rock concerts, sponsored by organizations like Scandinavia's "Next Stop Soviet!", and even tolerates unsanctioned gatherings of Leningrad's police-force, out for better working conditions and decent apartments!

The Palace Square is open on the fourth side. 30 meters (100 feet) or so in that direction, stands the **Admiralty**, built by a Russian architect, Andreian Zakharov in 1823 (though construction actually started in 1806). In the year when the city was founded, the first Russian shipyard on the Baltic started work here. To this day, the Admiralty has not relinquished its bonds with the sea: it has housed, for many a decade, a school for naval officers. The Admiralty building, adorned with a golden sailing ship atop a spire - the symbol of the city - is stretched out along the Neva for nearly half a kilometer; unfortunately, the view from the river is blocked by apartment houses erected at the turn of the century.

The Admiralty is the only building between the Palace Square and the **Decembrists' Square** (formerly Senate Square), whose main attraction is the monument to the founder of the city, the great reformer, Peter the Great. The monument was ordered by Catherine II from the French sculptor, Etienne Falconet, in 1782 (Falconet's 18 year-old apprentice, Marie Anne Collot, helped with Peter's head). This sculpture, certainly the most famous in the country, inspired the great Pushkin's poem, "The Bronze Horseman" (some of the poet's more prosaic and enterprising compatriots planted cabbage and potatoes in the square during the war).

Left, the construction of the Alexander Column in 1832. **Right**, St. Isaac cathedral.

The monument is flanked by Carlo Rossi's two buildings of the **Senate** and the **Synod** (a kind of ministry of Orthodox church affairs), which are linked into a single whole by an arch. Rossi's masterpiece, built in 1834 (construction started in 1829), is certainly worthy of the great monument to the great Czar.

Behind the Bronze Horseman, rises the majestic **St. Isaac's Cathedral**, created by Montferrant in 1818-1858. Americans will see a resemblance to the Capitol, and Europeans - to St. Peter's in its domed structure (one of the highest in the world - over 100 meters or 328 feet, the height of a 30-storey house). Inside the cathedral is enough place for 14,000 people.

The other side of the square is formed by the **Maryinsky Palace**, built for the daughter of Nicholas I by architect Andrei Shtakenshneider in 1844-53. Thirty years after it was finished, it was turned over to the State Council (it is today's municipal council).

The equestrian **monument to Nicholas I**, designed by Pyotr Klodt for this square in 1859, is recognized as a true masterpiece. The huge equestrian statue rests on only two points of support. The square has several other famous edifices, including the huge **Astoria Hotel**, a modernist structure which was built in 1912 by the Swedish architect, Fyodor Lidval, it is now being renovated in a joint venture with a Finnish firm.

No description of the St. Isaac's Square could ever be complete without an account of the events surrounding the **Angleterre Hotel**, a modest building to the left of the Astoria. Some years ago, the authorities decided to have it torn down and built anew. But these plans - to everyone's surprise - met fierce resistance. Unwillingness to lose a monument of the past (Sergei Yesenin, the poet, committed suicide there in 1925), indignation at the arbitrary, hushed-up decision of the municipal authorities, who did not even bother to inform the people of their plans, made them demonstrate. Thousands of young people stood guard round the building around the clock for two weeks, formed pick-

The Admiralty building.

ets, signed petitions, organized manifestations, blocked the path of the bulldozers with their bodies, and generally defied the will of the city fathers. The young people lost - the building was torn down. But it changed the atmosphere in the city, generating a social upsurge and creating hope for common people, while the authorities realized that old methods would no longer work.

The **Blue Bridge**, the widest in the city (its width, over 100 meters or 328 feet, is several times greater than its length), is also a part of the St. Isaac's Square. You can cross the bridge to the **Moika River** and return along the embankment to the Palace Square, continuing in that direction along **Khalturina Street**, which runs parallel to the Palace Embankment of the Neva.

Khalturina Street ends in **Marsovo Polie (Field of Mars)**, the traditional site (for over two centuries) of parades and military displays. Since 1957, there has been a revolutionary pantheon and an **eternal flame** in its center.

In the northern part of the field, next to Kirov Bridge, Russia's first monument to a person who was not a czar was erected in 1801. Mikhail Kozlovsky cast the Generalissimo Alexander Suvorov as Mars (Suvorov did not lose a single battle throughout his long military career). During the blockade, this was probably the only monument that had not been taken down: it was to inspire the defenders of Leningrad.

To the east of the field, lies the **Summer Garden**, which has about the same area as the Field of Mars and is regarded by all as the finest park ensemble Leningrad has. Founded in 1704, it has no less than 3,000 limes, most of which were planted early in the last century, several dozen excellent marble statues, and, of course, the first palace of Peter the Great (known as the **Summer Palace**), which was built in 1710-14 by Domenico Trezzini. The **grille** that separates the Summer Garden and the Neva is matchless in its harmony and beauty; designed by Yury Felten in 1784, it has become a symbol of the city. The Summer Garden also boasts a

Ballet in Leningrad.

magnificent vase of dark-red porphyry, a gift from the King of Sweden to Nicholas I. And, of course, there is the statue of the famous Russian fable writer, Ivan Krylov, depicted by Pyotr Klodt among his several characters (1855), a statue which is very popular with the garden's numerous visitors.

To the south lies the gloomy, imposing, dark-red **Mikhailovsky Castle**, built in 1800 for Paul I. Trusting no one, the emperor had the castle isolated from the city: it was surrounded by moats and protected with cannons. In the end, this did not help: a mere 40 days after he moved there, Paul was assassinated by members of his court in the castle's bedchamber. Later the castle housed the **Military Engineer's School**, of which Fyodor Dostoyevsky was a graduate. Today, there are plans to evict the assorted departments that have gained footholds in the once beautiful castle and to turn it into a museum. Looking closely, you will see that none of the four facades is identical.

Voinov Street takes us to the east of the Summer Garden. It has two famous sights at its opposite end. One is the Tauride Palace, built in the 1780s by Ivan Starov for Prince Potemkin, lover and favorite of Catherine the Great. The State Duma (parliament) met here from 1906 to 1917, in the early 1970s, the palace was used by the first secretary of the Leningrad party committee, Grigory Romanov (nicknamed "the Czar"), for his daughter's wedding. This cynical gesture caused the people of Leningrad to joke, not without bitterness, that history has gone backwards and given them another Romanov.

Smolny (a Russian adjective derived from *smola*, tar) lies further to the east. In the old days, they used to make all of the city's tar here until Bartolomeo Rastrelli built a five-domed baroque cathedral here in 1769 (construction was started in 1748). An institution for the daughters of the nobility - a classic building after Quarenghi's design - was added in 1808. In the summer of 1917, the institution was closed, and the Council of Workers' and Soldiers'

Smolny Monastery and Church.

Deputies, then headed by Leon Trotsky, moved there from the Tauride Palace. It is from here that Lenin presided over the armed uprising and it was here that Soviet power was proclaimed and that the Soviet government had its seat before moving to Moscow in March 1918. Today, the Smolny houses the regional and city party committees of Leningrad.

Along Nevsky Prospekt: A glance at the map will show that Nevsky Prospekt, ties, in the manner of a bowstring, the two ends of a bend in the Neva. Nevsky starts near the Admiralty. It has two sections, both of which are quite straight, as indeed are all the streets in the city. The first section is 3 km (1.9 miles) long. It ends at **Ploschad Vosstania** (Square of the Uprising), near the **Moscow Railway Station**. This is the real Nevsky, rightly considered Leningrad's center of commerce and culture. The next two kilometers, (1.2 miles) ending at the **Alexander Nevsky Lavra**, are inferior in many ways, though the name of the avenue is the same.

The first thing you notice here is that there are practically no houses less than 70 years old; in fact, most were already standing by the middle of the last century. Strange as it may seem, the various architectural styles, ranging from classic to modernist does not create an impression of eclecticism; rather, Nevsky - as indeed all of Leningrad - emanates harmony and the feeling of belonging to a community.

From morning till night the street is filled with throngs of merrymakers out to see and be seen. Numbers 7-9, built in 1912, is the Bank of Commerce. Inspired by the Italian Renaissance, architect Marian Peretiakovich copied - not without a measure of success - Venice's Palace of the Doges.

To the left, Number 14 (a recent addition; the building is only half-a-century old) bears the inscription restored some 20 years ago: "Citizens! This side most dangerous during artillery bombardment!" It was put up during the final stages of the Nazi blockade. Number 18 was occupied, throughout the last century, by the Wolf & Beranger confec-

tionery company, a place frequented by nearly all the celebrities in St. Petersburg, including Pushkin, the poet, who lived around the corner on the Moika. It was from here that he went to his fatal duel. Today the building houses a café named **Literaturnoye** (a bid to recapture some of the old glory). On the right-hand corner of the Moika crossing, is the palace built for Count Stroganoff (who gave his name to the celebrated Beef Stroganoff) by Rastrelli in 1764. His buildings are easily recognized by his favorite color - green, just as Rossi's creations are all a tell-tale yellow.

A little further along, on the right-hand side, stands the "jewel of Nevsky" - the monumental **Kazan Cathedral**, built in 1801-11 by Alexander Voronikhin, the architect who started out as a serf of Count Stroganoff. Since the altar of any Orthodox church must look to the west, the cathedral could not face Nevsky; ingeniously, the architect therefore gave the side facade of the cathedral a splendid appearance with a semi-circle of 94 columns. In the square in front of the colonnade, there are two monuments to the commanders-in-chief of the army that defeated Napoleon in 1812 - General **Barclay de Tolly** and Field Marshal **Mikhail Kutuzov** (whose grave is inside the cathedral). Unfortunately, the interior of the cathedral has been (for many years) desecrated by a rather vulgar Museum of Religion and Atheism. In the past eight years, the square near the Kazan Cathedral has become a favorite meeting-place for assorted youth groups known in the country as "informals".

Opposite the cathedral there is a tall building with a globe on top. It was built in 1902-1904 for the Singer Sewing Machine Co.

The globe, supported by Atlas, was its trademark. In 1902-1904 it became the **"House of Books"**: the first two floors were given to a large bookstore, and the upper floors to various publishers.

Near this spot, Nevsky crosses the **Griboyedov Canal**. Several hundred meters away, the majestic **Church of the Resurrection**, built in the Russian

style at the end of the last century rises to a height of nearly 90 meters/295 feet. It is also known as the **Church-on-Blood**, because it stands on the spot where Emperor Alexander II was assassinated by terrorists in 1881. Nearby, a little closer to Nevsky, is the **Chaika**, a popular hard currency restaurant run by a Soviet-West German company; among certain Leningrad party functionaries it is known as "an oasis of western decadence in the center of the cradle of the proletarian revolution".

The next street to cross Nevsky on the left leads you past the **Europeiskaya Hotel** to the **Square of the Arts**. The name is quite appropriate, as can be seen: in the center of the square is a **monument to Alexander Pushkin** (a fairly recent addition designed in 1937 by Mikhail Anikushin); in the background, is the **Russian Museum**, formerly the Mikhailovsky Palace built by Carlo Rossi in the 1820s). The square also has the **Philharmonic** (formerly the Gentry Assembly), the **Maly Theater of Opera and Ballet**, the **Operetta Theater**, the **Komissarzhevskaya Drama Theater**, the **Museum of Ethnography** and the **museum-apartment of the artist Isaac Brodsky** (until recently it was the only place where the works of "the bourgeois avant-guardist" Marc Chagall, were openly displayed).

Further along Nevsky there are several interesting buildings to the right. The dark-red building with the tall clock tower housed the city Duma (parliament) until 1917. The next block is totally taken up by the two-storied arcades of the **Gostiny Dvor**, the city's largest department store, where thousands of customers have been coming for three centuries now.

The second side of Gostiny Dvor faces **Sadovaya (Garden) Street**; beyond this crossroads, on the same side of the avenue, is the country's second largest public library (over 25 million books).

The square beyond the library is nearly all Carlo Rossi's creation. The Aleksandrinsky Theater (today it is the **Pushkin Drama Theater**). It is easily recognized by Apollo's chariot which sits on top (similar to the Bolshoi in

The splendor of Orthodox architecture.

Moscow). Behind the theater there's Rossi Street which only has two buildings but is nevertheless unique in its integrity and harmony. In the center of the square, there is an imposing monument to Catherine II showing her surrounded by her lieutenants (sculptor Mikhail Mekeshin).

On the left-hand side of Nevsky, opposite the monument to Catherine II, is a building with huge windows and allegorical figures. The building is a happy illustration of the ancient demand, Bread and Circuses! The lower floor has housed, for nearly a century now, Leningrad's foremost supermarket, and there is also the **Comedy Theater** which is located on the floor above.

Beyond the square what remains of Nevsky, before you reach the **Fontanka River**, is taken up by the **Anichkov Palace (now Pioneer Palace)**, whose various parts were built by Rossi, Rastrelli, Mikhail Zemtsov and others. The next highlight on the prospect is the Anichkov Bridge across the Fontanka. The **four equestrian groups** by Pyotr Klodt on the four corner depict the taming of a wild stallion.

Most of the buildings beyond the Fontanka are apartment houses, built by speculators in the second half of the last century. Nearly all the ground floors of these buildings are given over to shops, restaurants and movie theaters.

Vasilyevsky Island: Crossing the Neva via the Palace Bridge (near the Winter Palace), you reach a square that is considered the pearl of the Neva panorama: **The Spit**. Its flawless architectural ensemble is made up, on three sides, by the arms of the Neva, and, on the fourth, by the building of the Stock Exchange, designed by Thomas de Thamon (1805-10) as a Greek temple with 44 Doric columns. Today, the building houses the **Naval Museum**.

Until the middle of the 19th century, there was a port here: to this day, there are two beacons in the form of **rostral columns** (from "rostrum" the curved end of a ship's prow). At the foot of the columns, there are four allegorical figures representing the Volga, the Dnieper, the Neva and the Uolkhov.

Leningrad's passenger seaport is still on Vasilievsky Island, but on its other side, where it faces the sea to the west.

The Stock Exchange building is flanked on either side by edifices much too formidable for their purpose (the customs building and bonded warehouse). Today, these buildings house research establishments, notably the Pushkin House (**Institute of Russian Literature**), where every manuscript ever written by the poet is stored.

University Embankment runs along the Neva to the left. The tower-topped house at the very beginning of the embankment is the first museum that was built in Russia, the **Kunstkammer**, founded by Peter the Great. Today, it houses a **museum of anthropology and ethnography**.

The classic building behind is the **Leningrad Scientific Center of the USSR Academy of Sciences**. Recently a monument to Mikhail Lomonossov, father of Russian science and founder of the Academy of Sciences (1725), was erected in the square behind it. Alongside, the building intended for Peter the Great's 12 collegiums (ministries) presents its narrow, white-red side to the river. In 1819, the building was turned over to the city university, and has remained in its possession ever since.

The university also owns the houses located further along the quay. Number 15, on the corner, is the **Menshikov Palace**, which did (as, indeed, did the whole of Vasilievsky Island) belong to Prince Alexander Menshikov. Menshikov was Peter the Great's fortune-hunting crony, who sold meat pies in the street as a boy. This is the oldest palace in the city (1710-14). Unfortunately, it fell into the hands of the military, who managed, in just over two centuries, to transform the place into a veritable pigsty. It was restored a few years ago and turned into a museum affiliated to the Hermitage.

Where St. Petersburg originated: In the center of the city, where the Neva is widest, there rise the bastions of **Petropavlovskaya, Peter and Paul Fortress**. The fortress is of the same age as the city itself; the day the first stone was laid in its foundation - May 16, 1703 - is regarded as the birthday of St. Petersburg. Three years later, the earthen mounds of the fortress were replaced by stone walls, 700 meters (2,370 feet) of which (facing the Neva) were dressed in granite in the second half of the 17th century.

In 1790, the bastions of the fortress were decorated with round sentry-boxes suspended from stone corbels. Nowadays, the narrow strip of no-man's-land between the river and the foot of the castle wall is used by local hotheads as a beach, even though there's no place to change - and there are no lifeguards.

The fortress has never been used as a fortress for the simple reason that no enemy has ever penetrated the city's defenses. It was destined to serve a more shameful purpose - that of Russia's main political prison (1718-1919) as the ample exposition of the museum located within its walls testifies.

The golden steeple of the **Peter and Paul Cathedral** flies high over the fortress and over the entire city. The cathedral was built in 1712-33 by Domenico Trezzini. The belfry is remarkable for its height - 121.8 meters (400 feet) - as is the mellifluous chime of its clock.

The internal design of the cathedral is solemn and, to a surprising degree, unchurchlike. It's light and airy; the columns, pilasters and other architectural details are painted to resemble marble; the ceiling is brightly colored; most stucco mouldings are glided. The decor of the cathedral is made complete by its crystal chandeliers with bronze and colored-glass fragments. The iconostasis, carved out of oak and gilded, resembles a triumphal arch.

The cathedral contains the sarcophagi and remnants of all the Russian emperors who reigned from Peter the Great to Alexander III as well as the tombs of the other members of the royal family. In front of the cathedral, in the central square, there is another building of interest. Made unique by its pediment, central arches and corner towers, the **Mint**, which dates to 1724, is today the largest in the world. It is here that nearly

The facade of Yekaterininsky Palace.

every coin in the country is minted, to say nothing of orders, medals and assorted memorabilia.

Their eyes fixed on the ground, children can often be seen prowling near the blind walls, searching in the naive belief that the odd coin or some other form of loot from the Mint be found underfoot.

The environs of Leningrad: It is impossible to understand Leningrad completely without seeing the pearls of its environs - Pushkin, Petrodvorets, and Pavlovsk. All three are former summer residences of the Czars.

Unlike Leningrad itself, they fell into Nazi hands during the war and were all but destroyed during the German retreat. Palaces were turned into ruins, and thousands of priceless museum items disappeared. It took superhuman efforts to restore the past splendor of these places. It also took money, professionalism, and time.

The best way to cover the 15 or so kilometers (9 miles) separating Leningrad and **Petrodvorets** is to take a hydrofoil trip over the waters of the Gulf of Finland, on whose terraced shores Peter the Great founded the town in 1709. The first and lowest terrace was chosen as the site for the Lower Park, directly on the seashore. The second terrace hangs over the first; the face of the cliff is 18 meters (60 feet) high. It is here that the town itself stands. At the very edge, there's the Upper Park and the jewel of Petrodvorets, Rastrelli's famed **Grand Palace**.

Still farther inland, rising 100 meters (328 feet) above the sea, is the third terrace. Its subsoil waters fuel the fountains of the **Grand Cascade**. "Plunging cascades, fountains reaching to the skies, fine drops of spray everywhere, the deafening roar of water and the glitter of the golden statues tear an involuntary cry of amazement and rapture from your lips as you stand enchanted by this magical, miraculous sight." This colorful description, made by a foreign visitor a century and a half ago, still holds true today.

The town of **Pushkin** lies 14 km (8.5 miles) to the southwest of Leningrad. It was known as Tsarskoye Selo (the

Czar's village) until 1918; it was here that the royal family spent most of the year. In the center of the huge park, there's the famous baroque **Yekaterininsky Palace**; the architect, predictably, is Rastrelli. The palace inspires awe both with its size (its facade is over 300 meter/984 feet long) and its voluptuous architectural decor.

The palace is also known for its luxurious, fairy-tale interior. As examples, consider the size of the **Grand Throne Room** with its 800 square meters (8600 square feet) of space, and the riches of the **Amber Room**, which disappeared during the Germans occupation.

In the beginning of the 19th century, there was a lyceum in the right wing of the palace. The poet Pushkin, after whom the town was renamed, studied there for six years.

Pavlovsk is located on the same railway line (Russia's first, built in 1837) barely three kilometers away from Pushkin. These lands were given by Catherine II to her son and heir, Paul I, who had a palace built there by Charles

The Petrodvorets after the Nazis left.

Cameron and Vikenty Brenna. Fortunately all the furnishings and fragments of the interior of the palace, which combines elegance and simplicity, were evacuated before the Germans came; today, it is the most authentic palace museum in the vicinity of Leningrad. Many are also attracted to Pavlovsk by the vast park, a place which never fails to amaze with its cornucopia of landscapes, ponds, rivulets, picturesque sculptures and toylike pavilions.

Leningrad's future: According to Leningrad's municipal authorities, a mere 0.4 percent of the city's population survives from before the war. Leningrad is a youthful city and a city that lives on. The old walls still stand; people still live within them.

As the Hotel Angleterre conflict proved, it was not for nothing that the independent youth associations showed great courage and resolve. In the several days they spent defending the Angleterre, those youngsters changed so much that they are totally different now. Thousands of their fellow citizens have changed as well. There are many examples of their changed attitudes; the most famous is the fact that the people of Leningrad refused to re-elect all five top municipal party and state officials several months after the incident.

Churches have been demolished in other cities than Moscow, and in other times than the 1920s and 1930s. The Znamensky Cathedral in Leningrad was blown up after the war; several years later, the church in Sennaya Square (Peace Square today) was torn down. In those days, the attitude towards such vandalism was altogether different: people just didn't pay attention, let alone interfere. But the present has changed the people of Leningrad, just as it has changed the entire nation. Yet, despite the change they retain, unmistakably, the Leningrad spirit, with its intellectual flair, tolerance, respect fur culture and faith in sacred places.

For most of them, Leningrad is a sacred place, unique in its glorious history and facing hopefully, an equally glorious future.

Waterworks in front of the Petrodvorets now.

LENINGRAD

ACCOMMODATIONS

From Leningrad International Airport, Pulkovo 2, you will get to the city best by bus or taxi. The airport is just 10 minutes by bus from the domestic airport Pulkovo 1. Bus tickets are 5 and 10 kopecks. The taxi fare to the city can vary between 3 and 15 roubles depending on the distance and the category of car (municipal or cooperatives).

The most convenient local transport is Leningrad's Metro. Construction started before the war and was completed in 1955. All Intourist hotels and most others have Metro stations marked "M" nearby.

Travel Essentials: Aeroflot Information, Tel. 29-390 21; International Department, Tel. 314-6943. The Central Aeroflot agency is situated on Nevsky prosp. 7-9. Reservation for domestic flights can be made at Aprel'skaya ul. 5; Railway Terminal Information, Tel. 168-0111; Taxi, Tel. 312-0022; Central post-office, ul. Soyuza Svyazi, 9, Tel. 312-8302; Intourist Office, Isaakievskaya pl.11; Sputnik Office, ul. Chapygina 4, Tel. 234-0249.

Astoria (Intourist), ul. Gertsena 39, Tel. 219-1100; **Evropeyskaya**, ul. Brodskovo 1/7, Tel. 210-3295; **Kareliya** (Intourist), ul. Tukhachevskovo 27/2, Tel. 226-5701; **Leningrad** (Intourist), Vyborgskaya nab. 5/2, Tel. 542-9031; **Moskva** (Intourist), pl. Aleksandra Nevskovo 2, Tel. 274-2051; **Pribaltiyskaya**' (Intourist), ul. Korablestroiteley 14, Tel. 356-5112; **Pulkovskaya** (Intourist), ul. Pobedy 1; Tel. 264-5100; **Baltiyskaya**, Nevsky prosp. 57, Tel. 277-7731; **Gavan**, Sredny prosp. 88, Tel. 35-68504; **Kievskaya**, Dnepropetrovskaya ul. 49, Tel. 166-0456; **Ladoga**, prosp. Shaumyana 26, Tel. 528-5628; **Mir**, ul. Gastello 17, Tel. 293-0092; **Neva**, ul. Chaikovskovo 17, Tel. 278-0504; **Oktyabrskaya**, Ligovsky prosp. 10, Tel. 315-5362; **Rossia**, pl. Chernyshevskovo 11, Tel. 296-7349; **Sovetskaya**, Lermontovsky prosp. 43/1, Tel. 259-2552; **Sputnik**, prosp. Toreza 34, Tel. 552-8330; **Tourist**, ul. Sevastyanova 3, Tel. 297-8252; **Vyborgskaya**, Torzhkovskaya ul. 3, Tel. 246-9141; **Olgino Motel and Campingsite** (Intourist), Primorskoe shosse 5 (18th km), Tel. 238-3551.

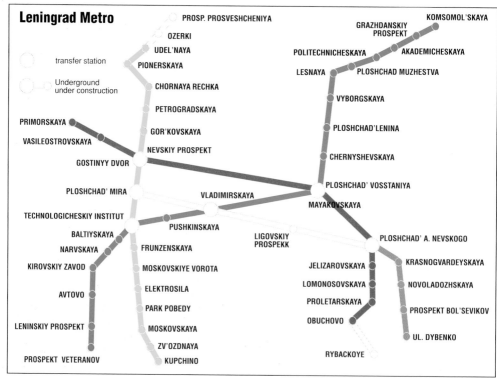

Leningrad Metro

transfer station

Underground under construction

PROSP. PROSVESHCHENIYA
OZERKI
UDEL'NAYA
PIONERSKAYA
CHORNAYA RECHKA
PETROGRADSKAYA
GOR'KOVSKAYA
NEVSKIY PROSPEKT

GRAZHDANSKIY PROSPEKT
KOMSOMOL'SKAYA
POLITECHNICHESKAYA
AKADEMICHESKAYA
LESNAYA
PLOSHCHAD MUZHESTVA
VYBORGSKAYA
PLOSHCHAD'LENINA
CHERNYSHEVSKAYA

PRIMORSKAYA
VASILEOSTROVSKAYA
GOSTINYY DVOR
PLOSHCHAD' MIRA
VLADIMIRSKAYA
TECHNOLOGICHESKIY INSTITUT
PUSHKINSKAYA
BALTIYSKAYA
NARVSKAYA
FRUNZENSKAYA
KIROVSKIY ZAVOD
MOSKOVSKIYE VOROTA
AVTOVO
ELEKTROSILA
PARK POBEDY
LENINSKIY PROSPEKT
MOSKOVSKAYA
ZV'OZDNAYA
PROSPEKT VETERANOV
KUPCHINO

PLOSHCHAD' VOSSTANIYA
MAYAKOVSKAYA
LIGOVSKIY PROSPEKK
PLOSHCHAD' A. NEVSKOGO
JELIZAROVSKAYA
KRASNOGVARDEYSKAYA
LOMONOSOVSKAYA
NOVOLADOZHSKAYA
PROLETARSKAYA
OBUCHOVO
PROSPEKT BOL'SEVIKOV
UL. DYBENKO
RYBACKOYE

Fontanka, nab. Fontanki, where the river is crossed at ul. Dzerzhinskovo, Tel. 310-2547; **Trojka**, ul. Zagorodnaya 27, Tel. 113-5343;

Other restaurants: Admiralteysky, ul. Gertsena 27, Tel. 315-5661; **Aragvi** (Georgian cuisine), ul. Tukhachevskovo 41, Tel. 225-0336; **Austeria**, Peter & Paul Fortress, Ioannovsky Ravelin, Tel. 238-4262; **Baku** (Azerbaijan cuisine), ul. Sadovaya 12, Tel. 311-2751; **Belaya Loshad** (White Horse Beer Restaurant), Chkalovsky prosp. 16, Tel. 235-1113; **Bukhara** (Uzbek cuisine), prosp. Nepokoryonnykh 74, Tel. 538-4553; **Demyanova Ukha**, prosp. Gorkovo 53, Tel. 232-8090; **Kavkazsky** (Caucasian cuisine), Nevsky prosp. 25, Tel. 214-6663; **Metropol**, ul. Sadovaya 22, Tel. 310-2281; **Neva**, Nevsky prosp. 46, Tel. 210-3466; **Nevsky**, Nevsky prosp. 71, Tel. 311-3093; **Okean**, Primorsky prosp. 15, Tel. 239-6984.

Cafés and Bars: Intourist, Kronstadt, Kommunisticheskaya ul. 1; **Korchma** (wine), prosp. Engelsa 83; **Leningrad** (dairy dishes), Nevsky prosp. 96; **Literaturnoe Café**, Nevsky prosp. 18, Tel. 312-8536; **Pogrebok**, ul. Gogolya 7, Tel. 315-5371; **Rakushka** (cockle-shell), prosp. Maklina 44; **Shokoladnitsa**, Moskovsky prosp. 200.

Pizzerias: Budapeshtskaya ul. 71; Moskovsky prosp. 73; Nevsky prosp. 44; ul. Rubinshtejna 30; 5aya Sovetskaya ul. 18.

Beer Pubs: Akvarium, Budapeshtskaya ul. 44, korp. 1; **Gavan**, Srednegavansky prosp. 9; **Medved**, Potemkinskaya ul. 7; **Petropol**, Sredny prosp. 18; **Staraya Zastava** (old out-post), pl. Mira 7.

Leningrad itself is a huge museum of 18th and 19th century architecture and sculpture.

Museums of Art and Literature: The **Hermitage** in the Winter Palace on Dvortsovaya pl. (Palace Sq., the entrance is on Dvortsovaya nab. 34). A lot of people come to Leningrad with only one purpose - to visit Hermitage Museum. No wonder that long lines to the booking office are quite common here. The first exposition of paintings from Hermitage collection was opened to the elite of Russian society in the late 18th century by Catherine the Great. In the 19th century, the circle of people allowed to view the growing art collections situated, during that period, in the houses known as New, Old (or Large) and Small Hermitage, steadily widened. The Winter Palace remained the residence of the Russian czars until the 1917 Revolution.

To tour the whole of the Hermitage thoroughly or even half of it in one day is impossible. Therefore, the best way for those who have a special interest in the art of a particular period is to concentrate on the exhibits of that period and have a quick look at the other departments (see plan on the next page).

On the ground floor of the Winter Palace are the following departments: Halls 11 till 33: Works of art, household utensils of primitive people. Halls 34 till 65: Objects of art of ancient cultures excavated from Soviet Central Asia. Halls 80 till 97: Eastern antiquities - Egypt, Mesopotamia, Assyria and Shumer. The antique art department is situated on the ground floor of the Small and Large Hermitage (halls 100-131).

On the 1st floor of the Winter Palace, the side looking to Dvortsovaya square is devoted to Western European art. The same exposition occupies the 1st floor of the Small and Large Hermitage.

The other rooms of the 1st floor of the Winter Palace (halls 167 till 199) exhibit objects of Russian art and culture. The opposite (embankment) side of the 2nd floor of the Winter Palace is a place of numismatic collections.

The areas between the embankment and square sides (halls 351-397) contain the exposition devoted to medieval and new Oriental art.

Russian Museum in Mikhailovsky Palace, Inzhenernaya ul. 4/2. Mikhailovsky Palace in Leningrad was opened to the public as the museum of Russian art by the order of the last Russian czar, Nicolas II. At that time, the museum contained an exposition depicting the life of more than a hundred of the ethnic groups populating Russia. However, the ethnographic branch later separated and became the Museum of Ethnography of Peoples of the USSR (situated in the right wing of Mikhailovsky Palace).

The Russian Museum itself occupies the central building of the palace, the left wing

(Fligel' Rossi) and the premises from the left side of Fligel' Rossi, the so-called Benois Building.

The masterpieces of Russian art from the 12th to the 18th centuries are placed on the 1st floor of the Mikhailovsky Palace. On the ground floor of the palace, collections of the 19th-century paintings and decorative and applied art are installed. The same exposition occupies the ground floor of Fligel' Rossi. The ground floor of Fligel' Rossi is connected to Bernois Building where Russian art of the 19th to early 20th centuries and art of the Soviet period are exhibited on both its floors. The 1st floor of Fligel' Rossi is occupied by temporary exhibitions.

Besides these, there are many more Museums of Art and Literature: the **Museum of the Academy of Arts**, Universitetskaya nab. 17; **Brodsky Museum-Flat**, pl. Iskusstv 3; **City Sculpture Museum**, pl. Aleksandra Nevskovo 1; **Necropolis of Alexander Nevsky Lavra**, ul. Rasstannaya 30; **Literatorskie Mostki Necropolis** (this museum also takes care of all the old sculptures around the city); **Menshikov Palace-Museum**, Universitetskaya nab. 15; **Dostoevsky Museum-Flat**, Kuznechny per. 5/2; **Pushkin Museum**, nab. Mojki 12 (Pushkin's Flat) & ul. Komsomolskaya 2, Pushkin town (Liceum); **Repin Museum-Estate**, Primorskoe shosse 411, Repino town; **Russian Literature Museum**, nab. Makarova 4; **Museum of Theater**, pl. Ostrovskovo 6.

Among **Museums of History** there is a group of museums in Peter and Paul Fortress, the **Museum of History and Regional Studies**, Komsomolskaya ul. 22, Pushkin town, and a variety of revolutionary museums: **Aurora Cruiser**; **Lenin Flats**; **Lenin's Museum**, ul. Khalturina 5/1; **Lenin's Hut**, next to Razliv Lake etc.; there are also the **Museum of the History of Artillery and Communications**, Lenin Park and the **Naval Museum**, Pushkinskaya pl. 4.

Scientific Museums include the **Museum of Anthropology & Ethnography** (Kunstkammer), Universitetskaya nab. 3; the **Museum of Arctic and Antarctic**, ul. Marata 24a; the **Meteorological Museum**, ul. Belinskovo 6/46; the **Popov Museum-Flat**, ul. Professora Popova 5 and others.

PERFORMANCES

Kirov Academic Theater of Opera and Ballet, Teatral'naya pl. 1, Tel. 216-1211; **Gorky Academic Bolshoy Drama Theater**, nab. Fontanki 65, Tel. 310-0401; **Pushkin Academic Drama Theater**, pl. Ostrovskovo 2, Tel. 311-1212; **Lensovet Academic Theater**, Vladimirsky prosp. 12, Tel. 312-2758; **Academic Comedy Theater**, Nevsky prosp. 56, Tel. 314-2638; **Bolshoy Puppet Theater**, ul. Nekrasova 10, Tel. 272-8808; **Shostakovich Philharmonic Society**, ul. Brodskovo 2 and on Nevsky prosp. 30; **Glinka Academic Choir**, nab. Mojki 20; **Oktyabrsky Concert Hall**, Ligovsky prosp. 6; **Circus**, nab. Fontanki 3; **Intourist Cultural Center**, prosp. Obukhovskoy Oborony 32. **Intourist Theater** Booking Office, ul. Dumskaya 2, Tel. 314-5685.

SPORTS

Kirov Stadium, **Primorsky Park Pobedy**; **Lenin Stadium**, **Petrovsky Ostrov** (island); **Yubileyny Palace** of Sports, prosp. Dobrolyubova 18; **Winter Stadium**, Manezhnaya pl. 6; **SKA** Swimming Pool, Litovskaya ul. 3; **Spartak** Swimming Pool, Konstantinovsky prosp. 19; **Chigorin** Chess Club, ul. Zhelyabova 25; **Cycletrack**, prosp. Engelsa 81; **Yacht Club**, Petrovskaya kosa 7; **Tennis Courts**, nab. Fontanki 33.

SHOPPING

Beriozka (hard currency shops): In the Intourist hotels, at Pulkovo 2 Airport and at ul. Gertsena 26; Gostiny Dvor Department Store, Nevsky prosp. 35; Dom Leningradskoy Torgovli Department Store, ul. Zhelyabova 21-23; Dom Knigi (house of books), Nevsky prosp. 28; Beriozka (jewelry), Nevsky prosp. 7-9; Heritage Art Salon, junction of Nevsky prosp. and pl. Vosstania; Kuznechny Market, Kuznechny per. 3; Torzhkovsky Market, Torzhkovskaya ul. 20; Vasileostrovsky Market, VO, Bolshoi prosp. 18.

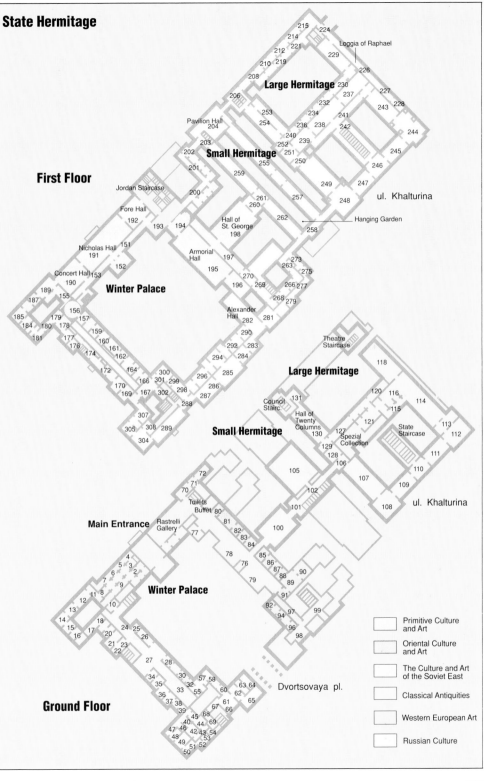

State Hermitage

First Floor

Ground Floor

Large Hermitage

215 224
214
212 221
210 219
208
Loggia of Raphael
229
226
Large Hermitage 230
206
237
227
253
254 232
236 238
240 239
252
251
255 250
259
234 241
242
243 228
244
245
246
Pavilion Hall
204
203
202
201
200
Jordan Staircase
Fore Hall
192
193 194
Small Hermitage
249 247
248
261
260
257
262
258
ul. Khalturina
Hanging Garden

Nicholas Hall 151
191
152
Concert Hall 153
190
189
187
155
156
185 179 157
184 180 178
181 177
176 160
174 161
172 164 162
170 166 301 299
169 167 302 298
307
305 308 289
304
Hall of
St. George
198
Armorial
Hall 197
195
196 269 268 279
Winter Palace
Alexander
Hall 282 281
290
292 283
294 284
296 285
286
287
288
273
263 275
270
266 277
268
300
301 299
302 298

Large Hermitage
Theatre
Staircase
118
120 116
115 114
121
113
112
State
Staircase
111
110
109
108
ul. Khalturina

Council
Stairc.
Hall of
Twenty
Columns
130
Small Hermitage
131
127 Spezial
Collection
129
128
106
105
102
101
100
107
108

72
71
70
Toilets
Buffet 80
81
82
83
84
78
76
79
85
86
87
88
89
90
91
92 97 99
94
96
98

Main Entrance Rastrelli
Gallery
77

Winter Palace

4
5 3
6
7 2
9
8
11
12 10
13
14 18
15 17
16
24 25
20 26
21 23
22
27 28
34 30 57 58
35 32
33 55
36 37 38
39
40 45 68
44 69
42 43 54
47 46
48
49 51 53
50 52
60
62
61
66
63 64
65
67

Dvortsovaya pl.

Primitive Culture
and Art

Oriental Culture
and Art

The Culture and Art
of the Soviet East

Classical Antiquities

Western European Art

Russian Culture

Russian Museum

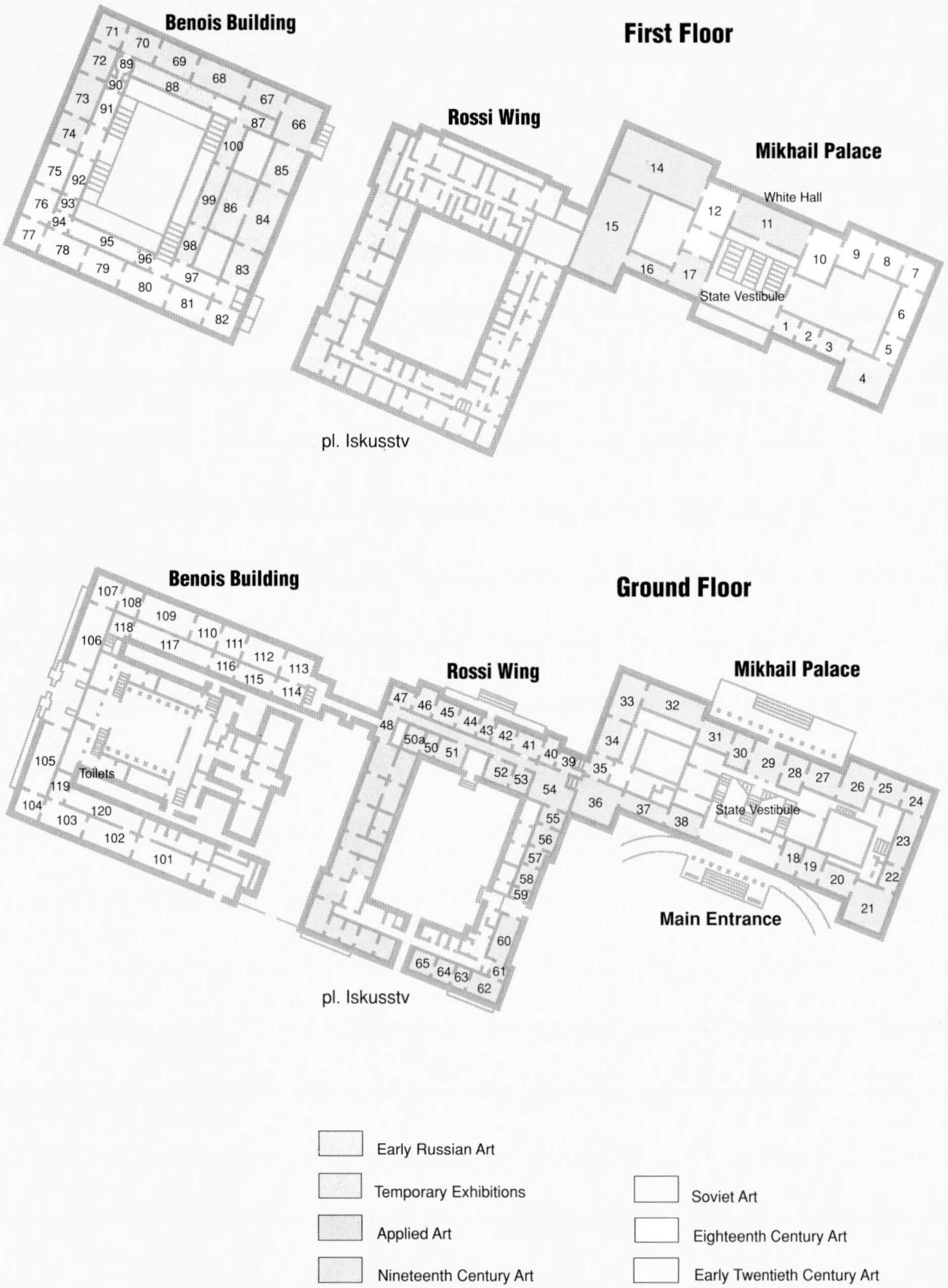

Benois Building

First Floor

71 70
72 89 69
90 88 68
73 91 67
74 87 66
100 85
75 92
99 86 84
76 93 94
95 98
77 78 96
79 97 83
80 81
82

Rossi Wing

14

Mikhail Palace

White Hall

12
11

15

16 17 10 9 8 7

State Vestibule

1 6
2 3 5
4

pl. Iskusstv

Benois Building

Ground Floor

107
108 109
118 110
106 117 111
116 112 113
115 114

Rossi Wing

47 46 45
48 44 43 42 41
50a 50 51 40 39
52 53 54
55
56
57
58
59

60

65 64 63 61
62

105
Toilets
119
104 103 120
102
101

Mikhail Palace

33 32
34 31
30
35 29 28 27 26 25 24
36 37 38
State Vestibule
23
18 19 22
20 21

Main Entrance

pl. Iskusstv

Early Russian Art	
Temporary Exhibitions	Soviet Art
Applied Art	Eighteenth Century Art
Nineteenth Century Art	Early Twentieth Century Art

Kiev

"Kiy's great city", named after the eldest of the three brothers who, as legend has it, founded Kiev late in the 5th century AD, has seen it all: Christian unification with Byzantinum in 988, the Mongol invasion in 1240. Polish and Lithuanian conquerors (1363-1653), unification with Russia in 1654 and, finally, the vandalism of the plundering Nazi, "priests of the new world" (1941-1943). Then, in our age of "the most humane social system", the city was put within an inch of its life by the Chernobyl tragedy, the latest of the numerous black pages in the town's history. The disaster came in the spring of 1987 as the terrible anticlimax of the policy which lacked both responsibility and principle, even though it was ostensibly oriented towards public welfare. Chernobyl became a kind of a new frame of historical reference for Kiev and, probably, for the entire nation. They say that natural calamities and wars purify a nation's morals. The terrible effects of the tragedy made many people, in Kiev and in other towns, take another look at themselves, at the past and the present. Suddenly, people started paying attention to forgotten spiritual and cultural values, ecology, moral salvation and respect for each other. Kiev is cleaner, and not merely because the streets are watered twice a day now; once the people were shown the frailty of human existence, they changed. It goes without saying that it is the people who give any city its image.

Who are the people of Kiev, the inhabitants of the capital of the Ukraine, the republic with the second largest population in the USSR? Most of them are Ukrainians. They are bilingual and Russian is more often than not spoken even in their homes. In terms of outward appearance, they are the same as the people of Moscow or Leningrad, except that in Kiev which is the southernmost of the three, the women are darker, and

Preceding pages, carnival in Kiev. **Below**, view of the Kievo-Pecherskaya Lavra across the Dnieper.

the men wear mustaches. Beards, by the way, were never worn in the Ukraine. It must be their "southern" origin that gives the local dwellers their cheerful, amiable manner.

Their hospitality surrounds the visitor from the first moments in Kiev. The town is pretty in any season. It has mild winters (it is on the same latitude as Frankfurt and Prague) and warm, sunny summers. Then the city becomes a sea of green, and the visitors' delight.

The Golden Gate of Kiev: It is customary to start the tour of the town from its central - and oldest - part. Let's observe the tradition and start from the **Verkhny (Upper) Town**. Unfortunately, the walls of the ancient fortress of the *Polyans* (an eastern Slav tribe) did not survive. Of the few remaining specimens of fortification that got down to us from the times of Yaroslav the Wise (1019-1054), the **Golden Gate** is the most remarkable. It has seen many guests, invited or otherwise, in its long history. They say that Batu Khan himself entered the captured city through this gate. Today, its former glory fully restored, the gate once more hails the traveler with the glitter of the gilded cupolas of the gate church. Today, there is an exhibition of Ancient Russian defensive fortification there. A little further up Vladimirskaya Street, there stands another of the wise prince's creations, the **St. Sophia's Cathedral**. The majestic 19-domed cathedral was named for its Constantinople counterpart (*Sophia* means God's wisdom in Greek). Its construction was started in 1037 on the site of the decisive battle of the Pecheneg war; for many centuries since, it served Ancient Rus as the center of religious and political life. It was in this cathedral that great princes were anointed; it was here that foreign ambassadors were received. In a side altar, the remains of the prince lie under a marble tombstone.

A symbol of unification: In the square before the cathedral, there is the monument (1888) to the great Cossack leader, wise politician and military man, Bogdan Khmelnitsky, who stood at the

helm of the Ukrainian people's liberation struggle against the Polish overlords in 1648. In 1654, this square saw the people of Kiev meet the Russian embassy which presided over the unification of the two nations as the Ukrainians gave the oath of eternal allegiance to Russia. Our contemporary also chose to commemorate this happy event, albeit in too symbolic a form: a **giant arc** that unites the two fraternal peoples in concrete. A nice view of this sample of monumentalism can be had from **Vladimir's Hill**.

Closer to the Dnieper, in the oldest part or the town - **"the settlement of Vladimir"**, the man who baptized pagan Russia with fire and sword in 988 - there stands what remains of the 10th century **Desyatinnaya Church**, the first Christian church in Russia to be made of stone. The church was burned in the black year of 1240, when the innumerable armies of Batu Khan conquered the city and burned it to the ground. There is another highlight left to be seen in the old town - Rastrelli's **Andreevskaya Church**. Rastrelli, the accomplished architect of St. Petersburg fame, did some building in Kiev, too. The single-domed cathedral with its five lesser cupolas seems to hover over the city. Historians say that it was here that the legendary Kiy founded his settlement.

From the observation platform, one gets a magnificent view of **Podol**, another old part of the city, and of the left bank. The left bank, by the way, is less steep, which is why it was settled much later than the right. The first chain bridge over the Dnieper was built between 1848 and 1853; at that time, it was the largest in the empire. Today, there are six bridges. New residential areas have appeared on the left bank in Berezniaki, Darnitsa and Rusanovka. **Gidropark**, overflowing with every shade of green, is loved by the locals for its sandy beaches, bars, restaurants and, of course, its yacht club.

The Montmartre of Kiev: It is at the right bank, where the city's origins lie. Andreevskaya Church stands at the beginning of one of the oldest streets in Kiev

Kievan woman during festival.

- Andreevsky spusk (descent). In ancient times, the street linked the administrative part of the Upper City with Podol, the quarter of merchants and artisans. Andreevsky descent is very young in spirit, a street akin to Moscow's Arbat or the Montmartre in Paris. It is a traditional place for outdoor fetes (although walking is pleasant only when you go downhill; the steep slope makes the return trip tiring), film festivals and the like. On holidays, the street dresses up in the most fantastic decorations and fills with folk heroes, street dancers (*skomorokhi*), young painters and jewelers who air their creations for the benefit of the holiday-makers. Here, in No. 13, was the home of the brilliant Russian writer, Mikhail Bulgakov (1891-1940), the author of several outstanding works.

At the square of the River Terminal one can take a boat tour across the waters of the Dnieper, or if the weather isn't too good, there is a cable-car that goes back up (the funicular dates to 1905). Disembarking in Kalinin Square, one

Monument of Reunification.

can go down to the Kreschiatik, or stroll along Vladimirskaya Street. This should give some idea of modern architecture's attractions and besides, one experiences the hustle and bustle of a megacity, its rhythm and the mood of its people. The massive gray structure in the beginning of Vladimirskaya Street, isolated behind the "triumphal arch", is a symbol of Stalin's "triumphal progress of socialism". As can be guessed, it is the building of the municipal party headquarters. Such mementos of the 30s abound in any Soviet city. The bigger the city, the more formidable the symbol of the CPSU's "power" and "staunchness". Straight ahead, the Sofia fills the square with an atmosphere of its own, a blend of grandeur and simplicity. Vladimirskaya Street crosses Sverdlov Street. The Golden Gate is uphill to the right. A little farther down that street, there stands the **kenasa**, formerly a church of the Karaim monks, and now the Actor's House. At the crossroads of Vladimirskaya Street. and Lenin Street, we find the **Opera and Ballet Theater**

which bears the name of the great Taras Shevchenko (1814-1861). The stage of this theater has seen Fyodor Shaliapin, Ivan Kozlovsky, Titta Ruffo, and the great primas - Maya Plisetskaya and Galina Ulanova. The theater, by the way, was founded in 1863 as a "Russian opera". Talking about theater, we might as well mention that the tradition of Ukrainian song and dance has deep historical roots. Way back in 1036, Yaroslav the Wise's granddaughter Anna had a convent open a school for girls, where singing was studied quite seriously. Today's Kiev has some 15 professional and 10 amateur folk theaters. Besides drama theaters, there is an operetta, and a puppet theater (which, by the by, occupies the former synagogue). But let us return to the past century once more. A little further up Shevchenko Boulevard, we suddenly find ourselves face-to-face with the 19th-century **St. Vladimir Cathedral**. The architectural effect it produces is enthralling. Here, in the midst of a great modern megacity, its forms evoke the presence of distant Byzantinum. The cathedral is functional. Enter the rounded vaults of the Ukraine's number one church - it is cool here, and everything speaks of perpetuity and mystery. Painted by the great Russian masters, Viktor Vasnetsov, Milhail Vrubel and Mikhail Nesterov, with folklore scenes, the cathedral reconciles the landmarks of the past and the present. Down the street, at the corner of Shevchenko Boulevard, you often see crowds of young people.

The "red" university: There, in the small square before the university, known far and wide for its freedom of thought and democratic leanings since the 19th century, student rallies and manifestations of the democratic front *Rukh* are held. They will tell you in Kiev that Nicholas II ordered the rebellious university painted red, an unusual color for such an institution. One way or the other, it certainly lives up to its revolutionary color today.

Straight ahead down Shevchenko Boulevard, we find the Bessarabskaya

Left, youngsters eager to pose before camera. Right, orderly at a rally in Kiev.

Square and its main attraction - the **Bessarabsky Market** built early in this century in the style of Ukrainian Modern. Here, one can find a cornucopia of everything vegetarian that grows in the Ukraine - and in many other places, as well. There are souvenirs and folk crafts, too. It is here that the main street of contemporary Kiev starts (or, more accurately, ends).

Kreschiatik (derivative of the Old Russian word for Baptism) probably owns its name to the memorable Baptism in the 10th century, when there was a gorge with crossing rivulets in its place. The street wasn't so wide in the past. It was 30-40 meters (100-130 feet) wide before World War II. After Kiev was almost totally destroyed (it compares with Dresden in terms of damage incurred), it was rebuilt anew in the 50s and the 60s.

In the early 60s, the Kreschatik Restaurant, which has the metro entrance in its ground floor, was built. In those same years, the city got its first subway line. Notice how deep down some stations are. There's a reason: the proximity of the huge river and the uneven terrain tend to aggravate construction problems. Be that as it may, the metro continues to be the fastest and cheapest form of public transport. On top of Kreschatik hill, the 16-storied **Moskva Hotel** was built in the mid-60s. Behind it, there is another historical area of Kiev - Pechersk (we will return there later). The hotel faces the **Oktiabrsky Palace of Culture**. Concerts of folk, classical and pop music are given there. On the other side of the street, near the metro station Kreschiatik, there is a kind of a supermarket, which differs from its Western analogs by the dismay it causes to the local population, let alone foreigners, who come here in search of something to buy.

There's also the sadly famous Central Post Office next door. When a portal of that building collapsed in 1989, it killed 11 people. A graphic illustration of the plan-report system of construction (or destruction, take your pick).

Leninskogo Komsomola Square: In its center, there is a huge white building -

the museum of the leader of the world proletariat, Vladimir Lenin. Looking at the building, one cannot help thinking that such a pompous structure would have hardly been approved by that modest man. As it is, it is not difficult to see that all the architectural experiments in this street suffer from megalomania.

We end our tour of Kiev's widest (up to 100 meters/320 feet) and, at the same time, shortest (1.5 km/4,920 feet), street near the **Dnipro Hotel**. Here, Intourist is ready to receive visitors with open arms. From the hotel, Kirov Street takes you into **Pechersk**. That old part of the town derives its name from the ancient monastery on the bank of the Slavutich (from *Slava*, as the Dnieper was called in the old days). The mighty river has served the city since time immemorial, uniting it with Byzantinum in the south and the Baltic in the north. Today, it has been transformed into a veritable cascade or artificial reservoirs, of which the largest is called Kiev Sea.

Home of Dynamo Kiev: The main street of Pechersk, Kirov Street, starts at the

Wall newspapers are one of the main sources of information.

old Dynamo Stadium, the home of Kiev's most popular football team, which has, on many occasions, won the national title, the UEFA Supercup and other assorted trophies. The team gave our football Oleg Blokhin, Alexander Zavarov and Igor Belanov. There is another administrative monstrosity on the other side of the street - the gray-colored, arched building of the **Ukrainian Council of Ministers**. It faces the **Mariinsky Palace**, designed by the famed Rastrelli.

The palace was built by Ivan Michurin in the middle of a park in 1755, originally for Empress Yelizaveta, the daughter of Peter the Great. The name comes from the wife of Alexander II, Maria, who had the palace rebuilt after a fire in 1819. Its left wing borders on the house with the glass dome, the Supreme Soviet of the Ukraine. We should point out that the architecture of both Kiev's, ancient and modern, is quite different from that of the nation's younger capitals. The medieval churches have finned outlines; there's nothing flowing or rounded about them. The modern structures look brighter and more spacious. The finicky eye of the connoisseur is certain to find pleasure in the **State Bank** (9 Oktyabrskoi Revolutsii Street) built at the turn of the century in the style of Italian Renaissance, and, of course, in the former **Church of St. Nikolas** (75 Krasnoarmeiskaya Street), today the House of Organ Music.

The caves of the ancients: Another holy place of the ancients, the **Kievo-Pecherskaya Lavra**, is perched on the steep bank or the Dnieper. It was founded in 1051 and expanded over the centuries. Yaroslav the Wise who respected religion extremely spent enormous sums on churches - with good reason, as we can see today. For many centuries, the monastery served as a haven for scientists and enlighteners. From the utilitarian point of view, the monastery was a valuable fortress, which repeatedly saved the city during enemy invasions. It was rebuilt in a big way in the times of Peter the Great, who added a stone wall and assorted fortifications that were to help him against the Swedes. Peter spared no

effort in his desire to transform the old part of Kiev into an impenetrable fortress. The oldest part of the monastery, the Lower Lavra, is a series of caves. Apparently, the name "Pechersk" is derived from *peschera* which means cave. The subterranean galleries of the **Nearer Caves** stretch for over 1.5 km/4,920 feet, uniting cells, crypts and three underground churches. The monks found it advantageous to serve God without leaving their underground sanctuary. The walls of the caves bear inscriptions in Ancient Russian, Polish and Armenian. The **Farther Caves** are linked to the Nearer Caves with a sheltered gallery; their length is 300 meters/985 feet. They say that in the old days, there was a secret passageway, which the monks used to leave the monastery secretly.

Next to the Lavra, in the territory of the ancient village of **Berestovo**, there lie, in the stone 12th-century **Spas Church**, the remains of Yury Dolgorukiy, the son of Kiev's Vladimir Monomakh and founder of Moscow. The monument was erected by the grateful people of Moscow to commemorate the city's 800th anniversary .

The monastery, naturally, has a steeple (96.5 meter/316 feet high) with, incredibly, a clock that still runs. The oldest buildings in the monastery are the **Troitskaya Gate Church** (12th century) and the **Assumption Cathedral** now in ruins. Most buildings in the Lavra date to the 18th century. They were built by Stepan Kovnir, a serf architect. To commemorate the millennium of Christianity on Russian soil, part of the monastery - the Nearer Caves and the Farther Caves - were returned to the Russian Orthodox Church. The monastery has been reopened. There is also a clerical school here now. Happily, another one of the Christian shrines has found its way back into the hands of its original masters.

Kiev is ancient, yet eternally young. Having emerged intact from every conceivable cataclysm, including the Chernobyl tragedy, Kiev continues to be very much alive and beautiful as always - something that everyone who's ever been here will agree with.

KIEV

You can reach the city from Kiev International Airport, Borispol, by bus and taxi. Until the projected Ukrainian national currency is established, the prices are in roubles: bus 80 kopecks to pl. Peremogy. The taxi is about 10 roubles to almost any part of the city. The railway station is situated close to the center of the city; people are always queuing for municipal taxis; cooperative-taxis are easier to come by but they are slightly more expensive. The Kiev Metro (the nearest Metro to the railway station is in the vicinity of the local train station) consists of 3 lines. The oldest line connects the districts on the left bank of the Dnipro (Ukrainian name of the Dnieper) with the former western suburbs Nivki and Svyatoshino. The second line runs from north to the southwest and the third line (still under construction) will link old aristocratic Pechersk with the Syrets district). Metro fares, like the bus and tram fares are purely symbolic; 5 kopecks regardless of distance and direction.

Travel Essentials: Borispol Airport Information, Tel. 295-6701; Aeroflot booking office is on prosp. Peremogy next to pl. Peremogy, Tel. 274-5152; Railways Information, Tel. 005; River Station Information, Tel. 416-1268; Central post-office, pl. Zhovtnevoji Revolyutsiji; Taxi, Tel. 058, 082; International telephone connections, Tel. 074 (from hotels) otherwise 079; Intourist Office, vul. Lenina 26; Sputnik Office, Tel. 212-2416.

ACCOMMODATIONS

Bratislava (Intourist), vul. Andriya Malyshko, Tel. 559-6920; **Dnipro** (Intourist), pl. Lenins'kogo Komsomola, Khreshchatyk 1/2, Tel. 22 98-287; **Lybid** (Intourist), pl. Peremogy, Tel. 274-0063; **Rus**(Intourist), vul. Gospital'na 4, Tel. 220-5233. **Golosiivs'ka**, prosp. 40-richya Zhovtnya 93, Tel. 261-4268; **Druzhba**, bul'var Druzhby Narodiv 5, Tel. 268-3406; **Kyiv**, vul. Kirova 26/1, Tel. 293-0155; **Leningrads'ka I korp.** - bul'var Tarasa Shevchenko 4, Tel. 225-7101, **2 korp.** - vul. Lenina 3, Tel. 221-7080, **3 korp.** - vul. Volodymirs'ka 36, Tel. 224-4226; **Myr**

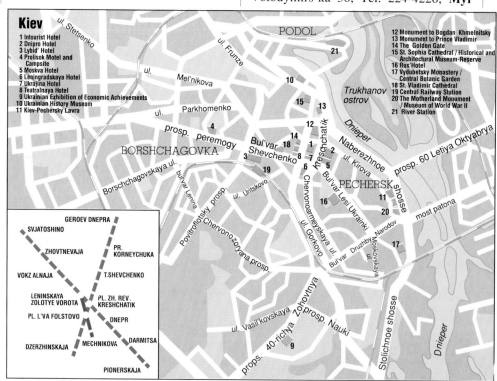

Kiev

1 Intourist Hotel
2 Dnipro Hotel
3 Lybid' Hotel
4 Prolisok Motel and Campsite
5 Moskva Hotel
6 Leningradskaya Hotel
7 Ukrajina Hotel
8 Teatralnaya Hotel
9 Ukrainian Exhibition of Economic Achievements
10 Ukrainian History Museum
11 Kiev-Pechersky Lavra

12 Monument to Bogdan Khmelnitsky
13 Monument to Prince Vladimir
14 The Golden Gate
15 St. Sophia Cathedral / Historical and Architectural Museum-Reserve
16 Rus'Hotel
17 Vydubetsky Monastery / Central Botanic Garden
18 St. Vladimir Cathedral
19 Central Railway Station
20 The Motherland Monument / Museum of World War II
21 River Station

PODOL

Trukhanov ostrov

BORSHCHAGOVKA

prosp. peremogy

Bul'var Shevchenko

Mel'nikova

Parkhomenko

Kreshchatik

Dnieper

Naberezhnoe

PECHERSK

prosp. 60 Letiya Oktyabrya

Borshchagovskaya ul.

bul'var Lenina prosp.

ul. Uritskovo

Chervonoarmeyskaya ul.

Bul'var Lesi Ukraïnki

most patona

GEROEV DNEPRA

SVJATOSHINO

ZHOVTNEVAJA

VOKZ ALNAJA

LENINSKAYA
ZOLOTYE VOROTA

PL. L'VA FOLSTOVO

DZERZHINSKAJA

PR. KORNEYCHUKA

T.SHEVCHENKO

PL. ZH. REV. KRESHCHATIK

DNEPR

MECHNIKOVA

PIONERSKAYA

DARMITSA

Povitroflotsky Chervonozoryana prosp.

ul. Gorkovo

Druzhby Narodov ul.

Moskovskaya ul.

ul. Vasil'kovskaya

40-richya Zhovtnya prosp.

prosp. Nauki

Stolichnoe shosse

Dnieper

(Sputnik), prosp. 40-richya Zhovtnya 70, Tel. 268-5600; **Moskva**, vul. Zhovtnevoji Revolyutsiji 4, Tel. 228-2804; **Slavutych**, vul. Entuziastiv 1, Tel. 555-7926/0911; **Teatral'na**, vul. Golosiivs'ka 7, Tel. 265-8988; **Ukrajina**, bul'var Tarasa Shevchenko 5, Tel. 221-7584/335; **Prolisok Motel & Campingsite** (Intourist), Svyatoshino, 5a proseka, Tel. 444-0093.

EATING OUT

Restaurants & coop-Restaurants: Dynamo, vul. Kirova 3, Tel. 229-4038; **Dubky**, vul. Stetsenko 1, Tel. 440-5188; **Krakiv**, prosp. Peremogy 23, Tel. 274-1908; **Kureni**, Parkova doroga (Park Way) 19, Tel. 293-4062; **Leipzig**, vul. Volodymirs'ka 39/24, Tel. 229-5616; **Lisova Pisnya**, Mins'ky prosp. 4, Tel. 431-2378; **Maxim**, vul. Lenina 21, Tel. 224-1272; **Metro**, Khreshchatyk 19a, Tel. 229-4056; **Mlyn** (mill), Gidropark, Tel. 517-0833; **Praga**, Ukrainian Exhibition of Economic Achievements, Tel. 261-7503; **Salyut**, vul. Sichnevogo Povstannya 11a, Tel. 290-5119; **Stolychny**, Khreshchatyk 5, Tel. 229-8188; **Vitryak** (windmill), prosp. Akademika Glushkova 11, Tel. 266-7138; **Zoloti Vorota** (Golden Gate), L'vivs'ka pl. 8, Tel. 212-5504.

Cafés, cooperative-cafés, Bars: There are many cafés along Kreshchatic and adjacent lanes and also: **Albena**, vul. Komandarma Kameneva 2, Tel. 295-8161; **Florentsia**, prosp. Pavla Tychiny 7; **Kavyarnya**, Mykil's'ko-Slobods'ka vul. 4; **L'vivs'ka Brama**, vul. Vorovs'kogo 1/37; **Ukrajins'ki Stravy** (Ukrainian dishes), vul. Budivel'nykiv 32/2; **Shokoladny Bar**, vul. Saksagans'kogo 129.

Beer Pubs: vul. Igorevs'ka 5; Rusanivs'ka nab. 10; Vasyl'kivs'ka vul. 11/11; Voloshs'ka vul. 49.

MUSEUMS & EXHIBITIONS

Museum of History of Kiev, vul. Chekistiv 8; **Ukrainian History Museum**, vul. Volodymirs'ka 2; **Museum of Regional Studies**, vul. Lenina 15; **Shevchenko House-Museum**, per. Shevchenko 8; **Museum of Ukrainian Fine Arts**, vul. Kirova 6; **Lenin Museum**, pl. Lenins'kogo Komsomola; **Museum of Western and Eastern**

Art, vul. Repina 15; **Museum of Historic Jewelry**, Kyevo-Pechers'ka Lavra; **Museum of Veterinary Science**, vul. Volyns'ka 12; **Exhibition of Modern Ukrainian Painting**, vul. Lenina 3b; **Ukrainian Exhibition of Economic Achievements**, prosp. Akademika Glushkova 1; **Exhibition of China and Ceramics**, Kreshchatyk 34.

PERFORMANCES

Shevchenko Academic Theater of Opera and Ballet, the corner of vul. Lenina and vul. Volodymirs'ka, Tel. 228-3920; **Franko Ukrainian Drama Theater**, pl. Ivana Franko 3, Tel. 229-5991; **Lesya Ukrainka Russian Drama Theater**, vul. Lenina 5, Tel. 224-9063; **Philharmonic Society**, pl. Lenins'kogo Komsomola; **October Palace of Culture**, ul. Zhovtnevoji Revolyutsiji 1, Tel. 228-7492; **Ukrajina Palace of Culture**, vul. Chervonoarmijs'ka 103, Tel. 268-9050; **Circus** (since 1989 in repair), pl. Peremogy.

SPORTS

Central Stadium, vul. Chervonoarmiys'ka 55, next to the Hotel Rus; Dynamo Stadium and Swimming Pool, vul. Kirova 3; Palace of Sports, Sportyvna pl., next to the Hotel Rus; Hippodrome, prosp. Akademika Glushkova 10.

SHOPPING

Kashtan (hard currency shops), bul'var Lesi Ukrajinki 24/26 and vul. Sichnevogo Povstannya 21; Central Department Store, vul. Lenina 2; Ukrajina Department Store, pl. Peremogy; Inozemna Knyga (foreign books); Bessarabsky Market (Bessarabka), Bessarabs'ka pl., at the end of Khreshchatyk; Tsentralny Gastronom (food store), opposite Bessarabka.

ALMA ATA

Travel Essentials: Aeroflot Information, Tel. 338-921; Railway Information, Tel. 56-262; Taxi, Tel. 676-711; Intourist Office, ul. Gogolya 65, Tel. 330-045; Sputnik Office, ul. Komsomolskaya 67, Tel. 681-092.

Museums: Central State Kazakh Museum, at the corner of ul. Karla Marxa and ul. Gogolya; Museum of Natural History, ul. Shevchenko 28; Arts Museum, ul. Satpaeva 30a.

Performances: Kazakh State Theater of Opera and Ballet, ul. Kalinina 112, Tel. 695-671; Auezov Academic Drama Theater, prosp. Abaja 103, Tel. 677-826; Circus, prosp. Abaja 50;

Places of Interest: Funicular Railway, Mt. Kok-Tyube; Medeo tourist complex and skating rink; Park of the 28 Panfilovtsev; Government Houses on Lenin Square.

Sports: Central Stadium and Swimming Pool, prosp Abaja 48-50; Dynamo Swimming Pool, ul. Shalyapina 20; Hippodrome, ul. Lesnaya, 10a.

Shopping: Central Department Store.

ACCOMMODATIONS

Otrar (Intourist), ul. Gogolya 65, Tel. 337-789; **Zhetysu** (Intourist), Kommunistichesky prosp. 55, Tel. 392-222; **Ala-Tau**, prosp. Lenina 105, Tel. 691-716; **Alma-Ata**, ul. Kalinina 58, Tel. 620-943, 638-866; **Issyk**, ul. Kirova 140, Tel. 620-808, 620-4222; **Kazakhstan**, prosp. Lenina 52, Tel. 619-906, 619-9541; **Medeo**, tourist complex, Tel. 648-568, 648-752; **Campingsite Kazakhsky Aul**, Medeo complex.

EATING OUT

Alma-Ata, ul. Mira 152, Tel. 695-681; **Aul**, mt. Kok-Tyube, Tel. 616-554; **Demalys**, Gorky park, Tel. 610-9098; **Issyk**, ul. Panfilova 133, Tel. 630-931; **Samal**, Medeo complex, Tel. 648-747.

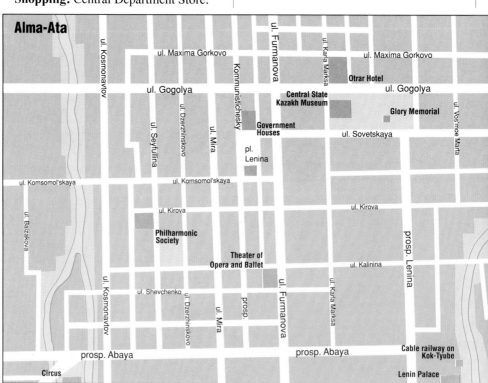

ASHKHABAD

Travel Essentials: Airport Information, Tel. 52-018; City Aeroflot Agency, prosp. Svobody 74, Tel. 54-857; Intourist Office, prosp. Svobody 74, Tel. 57-393; Sputnik Office, Tel. 53-342.

Museums: Museum of Fine Arts and Museum of Local Lore, prosp. Svobody 84; History Museum, ul. Pushkina 14; Museum of Regional Studies, ul. Khivali Babaeva 2; Kerbabaev Literary Museum, ul. Khivali Babaeva 1.

Performances: Pushkin Russian Drama Theater, ul. 1 Maya 19; Mollaneps Turkmenian Drama Theater, ul. Kemine 79; Makhtumkuli Theater of Opera and Ballet, ul. Engelsa 9.

Places of Interest: Botanical Garden, ul. Timiryazeva 16; Kurtli Lake; Kirov Park, prosp. Svobody 140; Mountain Ravine in Kopet-Dag Mts.; Nusoy (Nisa), ancient Parthian town ruins, 18 km/10.5 miles from Ashkhabad.

Sports: Kolkhozchi Stadium, ul. Belinskovo 32; Trudovye Rezervy Stadium, ul. Vilyamsa 2; Chess Club, prosp. Svobody 187, Tel. 41-217; Swimming Pool, ul. 1 Maya 47; Swimming Bath, ul. Sokolovskaya 80.

ACCOMMODATIONS

Ashkhabad (Intourist), prosp. Svobody 74, Tel. 55-191, 90026; **Turkmenistan**, ul. Gogolya 19, Tel. 55-810, -35; **Kolkhozchy**, ul. Engelsa 13, Tel. 53-426; **Oktyabrskaya**, prosp. Svobody 67, Tel. 57-082.

EATING OUT

Firyuza Restaurant, ul. Oktyabrya, Central Park; **Gulistan Restaurant**, ul. 1 Maya 8; **Yubileyny Restaurant**, 9th Mikrorayon (district); **Ajna Café**, ul. Timiryazeva-Botanicheskaya; **Parfia Café**, pl. Karla Marksa; **Kopet-Dag Café**, prosp. Svobody 4; **Molodyozhnoe (Youth) Café**, prosp. Lenina 22.

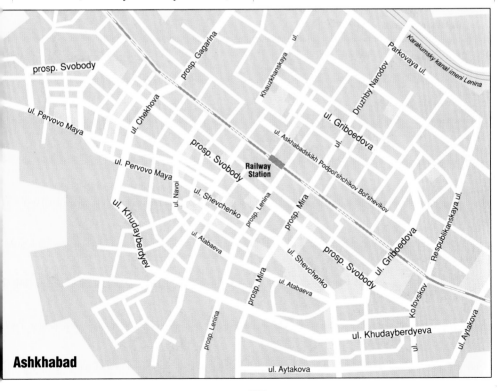

Ashkhabad

City GUIDE

BAKU

Travel Essentials: Aeroflot Information, Tel. 934-004; Intourist Office, Tel. 933-481; Sputnik Office, Tel. 987-963.

Museums: Azerbaijan History Museum, ul. Malygina 4; Mustafayev Museum of Fine Arts, ul. Chkalova 9; Museum of Carpets and Folk Crafts, Ichery-Sheker (the old city); Nizami Literary Museum, ul. Kommunisticheskaya 33.

Performances: Akhundov Opera and Ballet Theater, ul. 28 Aprelya 8; Azerbaijan State Theater of Song, prosp. Neftyanikov 36; Magomaev Philharmonic Society, Kommunisticheskaya ul. 2; Circus, ul. Sameda Vurguna 68;

Places of Interest: Shirvan Shahs Palace, Zamkovsky per. 76; Primorsky (sea-front) Park; Maiden Tower.

Sports: Neftchi Swimming Pool, Rabochy prosp. 25; Chess Club, prosp. Neftyanikov 26a.

Shopping: GUM Department Store, ul. Shaumyana 3; Central Market, ul. Sameda Vurguna 63; Sharg Bazary Market.

ACCOMMODATIONS

Azerbaijan (Intourist), prosp. Lenina 1, Tel. 98-7806; **Intourist**, prosp. Neftyanikov 63, Tel. 921-251; **Moskva** (Intourist), ul. Mekhti Huseinzade 1a, Tel. 393-048.

EATING OUT

Baku Restaurant, ul. Voroshilova 13, Tel. 986-163; **Gyandzhlik Restaurant**; **Legenda Restaurant** (coop); **Karavanserai Restaurant**, ul. Bashennaya 2, Tel. 926-668; **Tarane Restaurant**, ul. Alishera Navoi 22, Tel. 640-868; **Tbilisi Restaurant**, ul. Nizami 58, Tel. 935-118; **Yuzhny Restaurant**, prosp. Kirova 6, Tel. 987-111; **Beer Hall**, ul. 28 Aprelya 32; **Tasting (Wine) Hall**, ul. Zevina 3, Tel. 927-255.

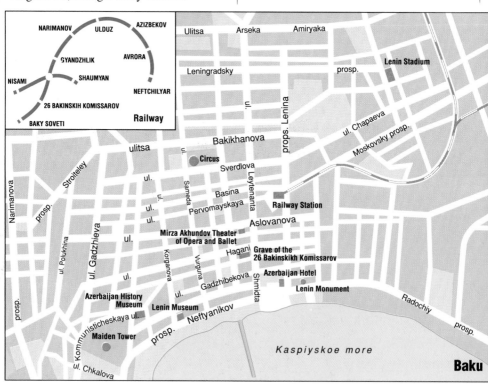

BUKHARA

Travel Essentials: Aeroflot Information, Tel. 32-644, 32-455; City Information, Tel. 33-322; Taxi, Tel. 33-669, 33-533; Intourist Office, Bukhoro Hotel; it can arrange a camel ride around the old part of the city.

Museums: Museum of History and Regional Studies, ul. Karla Marksa 2; Zindan Museum (former Emir jail), ul. Komsomolskaya 5; Museum of Folk Arts, Palace Sitorai Mokhi-Khosa; Picture Gallery, ul. Lewnina 41; Avicenna Museum, Peshkun district, Kishlak Afshona.

Places of Interest: Medrese of Ulug Bek; Medrese Kukeltash; Minaret Kalyan; Mausoleum of Ismail Samani; Mosque Magoki-Attari; Kirov Park; Ark Fortress, (the oldest construction in the town); Khodzha Zaynaddin Complex, ul. Vodoprovodnaya 5.

Performances: Ajni Theater of Drama and Comedy, ul. Teatralnaya 3.

Sports: Spartak Stadium, Tel. 32-758; Stroitel Stadium, Tel. 30-694.

Shopping: Central Department Store, ul. Ajni 8; Magazin Uzyuvelirtorga (jewelery), ul. Lenina, 2nd passage; Suveniry, ul. Kommunarov; Market Place, ul. Kommunarov 19 & ul. Ulyanova 7.

ACCOMMODATIONS

Bukhoro Hotel (Intourist), ul. 40 Let Oktyabrya 4, Tel. 32-276, 31-033; **Bukhara Tourist Camp**, ul. Gidzhuvanskaya 40; **Gulistan**, ul. 40 Let Uzbekistana 1; **Kukeldash**, ul. Pushkina 91, Tel. 43-481; **Shark**, ul. Bogdana Khmelnitskovo 2, Tel. 32-115; **Zeravshan**, ul. 40 Let Uzbekistana 1.

EATING OUT

Restaurants in the hotels and also: **Lyabi-Khauz**, ul. Tsentralnaya 7; **Saodat**, ul. Ulyanova 17/2; **Bakhor Café**, ul. Ulyanova 34/1; **Vstrecha Café**, ul. Avezovoy.

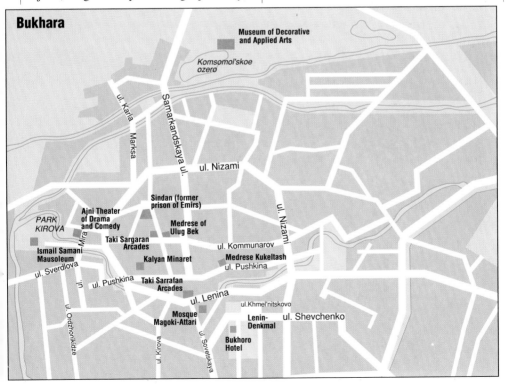

DUSHANBE

Travel Essentials: Aeroflot Information, Tel. 272-333; Railways Information, Tel. 294-646; Intourist Office, Tel. 274-973; Sputnik Office, Tel. 244-438.

Museums: Behzad Museum of History and Regional Studies, ul. Ajni 31; Museum of Education, ul. Ajni 45; Ajni House-Museum, ul. Khamza Khakim-zade 1.

Performances: Ajni Tadjik Theater of Opera and Ballet, prosp. Lenina 28, Tel. 222-871; Lakhuti Tadjik Theater of Drama, prosp. Lenina 86, Tel. 227-843; Rudaki Philharmonic Society, Prosp. Lenina 36, Tel. 227-951; Circus, ul. Negmata Karabaeva 2, Tel. 334-364.

Places of Interest: Varzob Gorge; Ramit Gorge; Hissar Fortress; Nurek Hydropower Station.

Sports: Dynamo Stadium, ul. Shevchenko, 27; Frunze Stadium ul. Putovskovo 28; Swimming Pool, ul. Sportivnaya 7; Hippodrome, ul. Takhmos 1, Tel. 278-313.

Shopping: Market Places, ul. Lakhuti & ul. Putovskovo 1; Art Salon, ul Lenina 82.

ACCOMMODATIONS

Tadjikistan (Intourist), Kommunisticheskaya ul. 22, Tel. 274-513; **Dushanbe**, ul. Lenina 7, Tel. 291-150.

EATING OUT

Farogat Restaurant, Lenin Park, Tel. 243-120; **Gruzinskaya Kuchnya (Georgian Cuisine) Restaurant**, 10 km/6 miles along the Eastern Highway; **Nasimi Kukhsor (mountain breeze) Restaurant**, in Varzob Gorge, 25 km/15 miles from Dushanbe; **Orom Restaurant**, 30 km/18 miles along the Eastern Highway; **Pamir Restaurant**, ul. Kirova 155, Tel. 223-922; **Varzob Restaurant**, ul. Amirshoeva 1, Tel. 244-284; **Chaikhana (tea-house) Rokhat**, prosp. Lenina 84, Tel. 221-294.

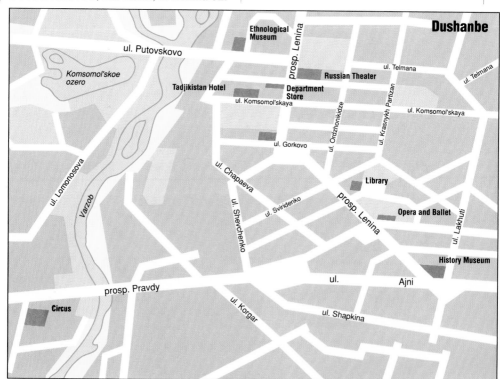

City GUIDE

FRUNZE

Travel Essentials: Intourist Office, ul. Dzerzhinskovo 1, Tel. 226-342; Sputnik Office, ul. Sovetskaya 175a, Tel. 265-547.

Museums: Kirgiz History Museum, ul. Pushkina 78; Museum of Fine Arts, ul. Sovetskaya 196; Mikhail Frunze Museum, ul. Frunze 362; Zoological Museum, ul. Pushkina 78.

Performances: Theater of Opera and Ballet, ul. Sovetskaya 167, Tel. 264-700; Kirgiz Drama Theater, ul. Panfilova 273; Satylganov Philharmonic Society, at the corner of Leninsky prosp. and ul. Belinskovo, Tel. 268-934; Circus, ul. Ivanitsyna 19, Tel. 221-536.

Places of Interest: Ala-Archa Gorge National Park, 42 km/26 miles to the south.

Sports: Swimming pool, prosp. Molodoy Gvardii 2; Hippodrome, ul. Termetchikova 1, Tel. 253-132.

Shopping: Department Store Ajchurek, ul. Kievskaya 114; Central Market, ul. Ogonbaeva 247.

ACCOMMODATIONS

Ala-Too (Intourist), prosp. Dzerzhinskovo 1 (opposite the railway station), Tel. 226-042; **Kyrgyzstan**, ul. Sovetskaya 191, Tel. 266-336; **Pishpek**, ul. Dzerzhinskovo 21 (at the corner of ul. Engelska), Tel. 221-323, 221-0321; **Sayakat**, ul. Dushanbinskaya 8a, Tel. 445-389; **Spartak**, ul. Togolok Moldo 17, Tel. 261-422.

EATING OUT

Ak Suu Restaurant, prosp. Dzerzhinskovo 2, Tel. 226-476; **Kyrgyzstan**, ul. Sovetskaya 185, Tel. 222-318; **Sejil Restaurant**, prosp. Dzerzhinskovo 37, Tel. 228-878; **Susamyr Restaurant**, ul. Toktogula 257, Tel. 255-440; **Ice Cream Parlor**, ul. Sovetskaya 95, Tel. 229-197; **Chinar Café**, ul. Kievskaya 95, Tel. 256-517; **Lagmannaya Café**, Kyzyl Asker, Tel. 252-896; **Chaikhana**, ul. Shopokova 120.

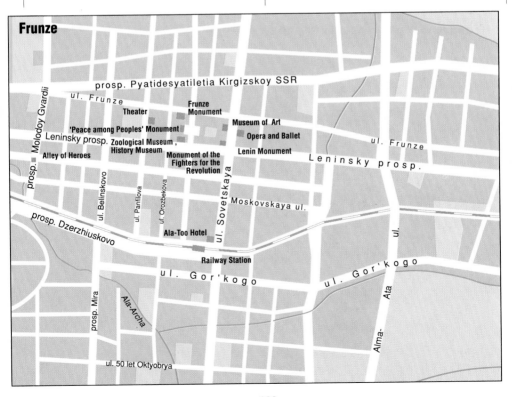

Frunze

prosp. Pyatidesyatiletia Kirgizskoy SSR
ul. Frunze
ul. Molody Gvardii
prosp. Molodoy Gvardii
Theater
Frunze Monument
'Peace among Peoples' Monument
Leninsky prosp.
Zoological Museum,
Museum of Art
Opera and Ballet
ul. Frunze
Alley of Heroes
History Museum
Monument of the Fighters for the Revolution
Lenin Monument
Leninsky prosp.
prosp. Dzerzhiuskovo
ul. Belinskovo
ul. Panfilova
ul. Orozbekova
ul. Sovetskaya
Moskovskaya ul.
ul.
Ala-Too Hotel
Railway Station
ul. Gor'kogo
ul. Gor'kogo
prosp. Mira
Ala-Archa
Alma-Ata
ul. 50 let Oktyobrya

IRKUTSK

Travel Essentials: Aeroflot Information, Tel. 42-535; Railways Information, Tel. 922-000; Taxi, Tel. 47-855; Intourist Office, ul. Sukhe-Batora 7, Tel. 44-686.

Museums: Museum of Regional Studies, ul. Karla Marksa 2; Decembrists House-Museum, ul. Dzerzhinskovo 64, Tel. 45-245; Fine Arts Museum, ul. Lenina 5; Mineralogical Museum, ul. Lermontova 83.

Performances: Okhlopkov Drama Theater, ul. Karla Marksa 14, Tel. 47-369; Musical Comedy Theater, ul. Lenina 23, Tel. 45-796; Philharmonic Society, ul. Dzerzhinskovo 2, Tel. 45-350; Organ Hall, ul. Sukhe-Batorta 1, Tel. 43-564; Circus, ul. Proletarskaya 13.

Places of Interest: Central Park, ul. Bortsov Revolyutsii 15; Planetarium, ul. Armii 8; Spasskaya Church (the Church of Our Savior); Lake Baikal environs; Bratsk Hidropower Station.

Sports: Aviator Stadium, ul. Shiryamova; Dynamo Stadium, ul. Barrikad 42; Hippodrome, ul. Kultukskaya 107.

Shopping: Lena Shop, ul. Uritskovo 2; Kulttovary (leisure goods), ul. Karla Marksa 35; Suveniry, ul. Karla Marksa 23; Market Place.

ACCOMMODATIONS

Intourist, bul'var Gagarina 44, Tel. 91-328; **Angara**, ul. Sukhe-Batora 7, Tel. 44-168; **Sibir**, ul. Lenina 18, Tel. 97-251; **Baikal** (Intourist), village Listvyanka, 70 km/ 42 miles from Irkutsk, Tel. 969-634.

EATING OUT

Almaz Restaurant, ul. Lenina 46, Tel. 45-006; **Arktika Restaurant**, ul. Karla Marksa 26, Tel. 46-229; **Baikal Restaurant**, ul. Bogdana Khmelnitskovo 1, Tel. 49-630; **Okean Café'**, ul. Lenina 25; **Petushok Café**, ul. Uritskovo 5; **Snezhinka Ice Café**, ul. Litvinova 2; **Sport Café**, ul. Karla Marksa 12.

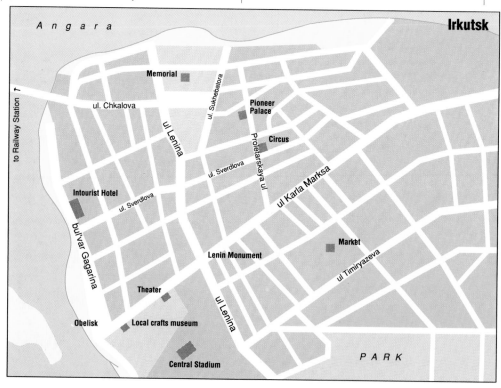

KHARKOV

From January 1918 till June 1934 Kharkov was the capital of the Ukraine. In 1934 the capital was moved back to Kiev.

Museums: History Museum, ul. Universitetskaya 10; Fine Arts Museum, ul. Sovnarkomovskaya 11; Grigory Skovoroda Estate-Museum (Skovoroda - Ukrainian teacher, poet and philosopher of the 18th century), village Skovorodinovka, 70 km/ 42 miles from Kharkov.

Performances: Lysenko Theater of Opera and Ballet, ul. Rymarskaya 21; Shevchenko Ukrainian Drama Theater, ul. Sumskaya 9; Musical Comedy Theater, ul. Marksa 28; Pushkin Russian Drama Theater, ul. Chernyshevskovo 11; Philharmonic Society, Sumskaya ul. 10; Krupskaya Puppet Theater, pl. Sovetskoy Ukrainy 24; Circus, pl. Uritskovo 8.

Places of Interest: Park Gorkovo; Funicular; Memorial Ensemble; Uspensky Cathedral, Universitetskaya Gorka (hill); Pokrovsky Cathedral on the bank of the Lopan River; Gosprom (Palace of State Industry, erected in 1928), the first skyscraper in the USSR, pl. Dzerzhinskovo.

Shopping: Kashtan (hard currency shop), prosp. Lenina 32.

ACCOMMODATIONS

Intourist, prosp. Lenina 21, Tel. 308-785; **Mir** (Intourist), prosp. Lenina 27a, Tel. 305-543; **Druzhba Motel** (Intourist), prosp. Gagarina 185, Tel. 522-091; **Kharkov**, ul. Trinklera 2; **Pervomayskaya**, ul. Sverdlova 52; **Spartak**, ul. Sverdlova 11; **Lesnaya camping site**, village Vysoky.

EATING OUT

Restaurants in the hotels; **Teatralny Restaurant** (Ukrainian cuisine), ul. Sumskaya 2; **Tsentralny Restaurant**, pl. Teveleva; **Lux**, ul. Rozy Luxembourg; **Vareniki Café** (Ukrainian cuisine); **Ice Café**, Park Gorkovo.

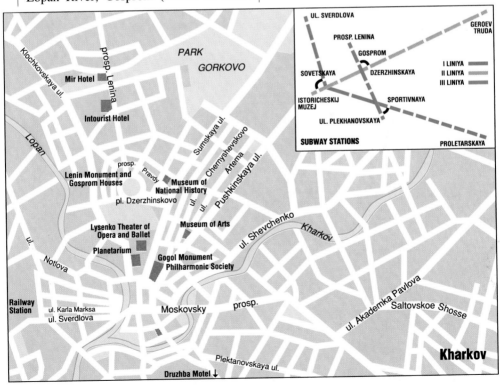

Kharkov

City GUIDE

KISHINEV

Travel Essentials: Intourist Office, prosp. Lenina 4, Tel. 529-066; Sputnik Office, Kerchenskaya ul. 7, Tel. 262-237.

Museums: Moldavian History and Local Lore Museum, ul. Pirogova 82; Archaeological Museum, Izmailovskaya ul. 41; Fine Arts Museum, prosp. Lenina 115.

Performances: Moldavian Opera and Ballet Theater, prosp. Lenina 150, Tel. 234-070; Pushkin Musical and Drama Theater, prosp. Lenina 79, Tel. 235-763; Chekhov Russian Drama Theater, ul.28 Iunya 75, Tel. 221-332; Philharmonic Society, ul. 25 Oktyabrya 78, Tel. 224-016; Organ Hall, prosp. Lenina 81, Tel. 237-262.

Places of Interest: Lenin Komsomol Park, ul. Sadovaya 77a; Planetarium, prosp. Lenina 164a; Botanika and Ryshkanovka Residential Areas; Cathedral, ul. Tkachenko 12; Vadul-luj-Vode Town.

Sports: Chess and Checkers Club, bul'var Negrutsi 5.

Shopping: Central Department Store, prosp. Lenina 136; Invalyuta (hard currency shop), bul'var Negrutsi 7; Art Salon, prosp. Lenina 64; Ilyinsky Market, ul. Kupriyanovskaya 22.

ACCOMMODATIONS

Aeroflot, next to the old air terminal, Tel. 525-452; **Intourist,** prosp. Lenina 4, Tel. 231-340; **Kishinev,** bulvar Negrutsi 7, Tel. 529-341; **Moldova,** prosp. Lenina 81, Tel. 235-781; **Tourist,** prosp. Molodezhi 13, Tel. 229-108; **Motel Sturugash** (Intourist), Kotovskoe shosse 230, Tel. 217-850.

EATING OUT

Butoyash (barrel) Restaurant, ul. Kuybysheva 71, Tel. 219-395; **Dolina Roz (rose valley) Restaurant,** Kerchenskaya ul. 7, Tel. 223-017; **Plovdiv Restaurant,** Moskovsky prosp. 6, Tel. 440-222; **Dnestr Café,** Komsomolskaya ul. 56.

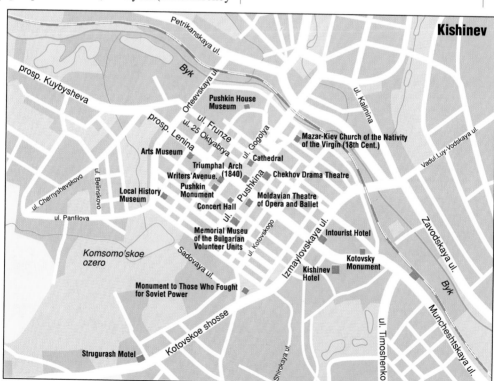

Kishinev

MINSK

Travel Essentials: Aeroflot Agency, ul. Karla Marksa 28, Tel. 006, 221-882; Railway Station, Tel. 297-151; Taxi, Tel. 260-501; City Information, Tel. 068; Intourist Office, Yubileynaya Hotel, Tel. 298-018, 236-014; Sputnik Office, Omsky per. 15, Tel. 334-674.

Museums: Museum of World War II History, Leninsky prosp. 25a; Yanka Kupala Literary Museum, ul. Yanki Kupaly 4; Museum of Folk Architecture, ul. Pashkevich 3.

Performances: Byelorussian Academic Bolshoi Theater of Opera and Ballet, ul. Pashkevich 23, Tel. 341-041; Kupala Academic Theater, ul. Engelsa 7, Tel. 221-717; Philharmonic Society, Leninsky prosp. 50, Tel. 334-974; Circus, Leninsky prosp. 32, Tel. 222-445.

Sports: Palace of Sports, prosp. Masherova 4, Tel. 234-483; Swimming Pool, ul. Surganova 2a, Tel. 662-816; Dinamo Stadium, ul. Kirova 8.

Shopping: GUM Department Store, Leninsky prosp. 21; Yubileyny Market, ul. Ratomskaya 10.

ACCOMMODATIONS

Planeta (Intourist), prosp. Masherova 31, Tel. 238-416; **Yubileynaya** (Intourist), prosp. Masherova 19, Tel. 298-835; **Minsk**, Leninsky prosp. 11, Tel. 292-199; **Tourist**, Partizansky prosp. 81, Tel. 454-031; **Motel Minsky** (Intourist), Brestskoe Shosse, 16th km, Tel. 296-814, 226-380.

EATING OUT

Kamenny Tsvetok (stone flower) Restaurant, ul. Tolbukhina 12, Tel. 663-793; **Neman Restaurant**, Leninsky prosp. 22, Tel. 227-879; **Paparats-Kvetka Restaurant**, ul. Sverdlova 2, Tel. 205-673; **Potsdam**, ul. Lenina 2, Tel. 220-523; **Cocktail Hall**, ul. Pulikhova 35, Tel. 364-110; **Cheburechnaya Café**, Partizansky prosp. 41, Tel. 450-522; **Beer Pub**, ul. Kharkovskaya 22, Tel.264-882.

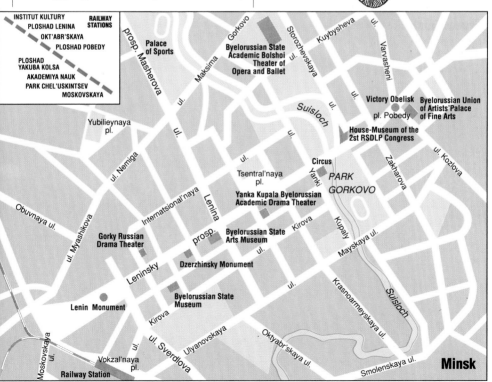

NOVOSIBIRSK

Travel Essentials: Aeroflot Information, Tel. 226-214; Railway Station Information, Tel. 298-581; Taxi, Tel. 298-982; Intourist Office, ul. Lenina 3, Tel. 221-366.

Museums: Regional Museum of Local Lore, Vokzal'naya magistral 11; Picture Gallery, ul. Sverdlova 13; Kirov House-Museum, ul. Lenina 35; Ethnography Museum, in Akademgorodok.

Performances: Academic Theater of Opera and Ballet, Krasny prosp. 38; Krasny Fakel Drama Theater, ul. Lenina 19; Puppet Theater, ul. Titova 25; Circus, ul. Chelyuskintsev 21.

Places of Interest: Akademgorodok - Akademichesky Gorodok (Academic Township).

Sports: Sibir Stadium, Tel. 760-586; Spartak Stadium, Tel. 291-735; Neptun Swimming Pool, ul. Bogdana Khmelnitskovo 25; Siberian Branch of the Academy of Sciences Swimming Pool, prosp. Akademika Lavrentieva.

Shopping: Central Department Store, prosp. Dimitrova 5; Malakhitovaya Shkatulka (jewelry), ul. Bogdana Khmelnitskovo 13; Central Market, ul. Michurina 12.

ACCOMMODATIONS

Intourist, Vokzal'naya magistral'; **Novosibirsk**, Vokzal'naya magistral' 1, Tel. 201-400; **Ob**, ul. Dobrolyubova 2, Tel. 667-401; **Severnaya**, prosp. Dzerzhinskovo 32, Tel. 771-347; **Tsentralnaya**, ul. Lenina 1 & 3, Tel. 227-660; **Zolotaya Dolina** (golden valley), ul. Ilyicha 10, Tel. 356-609.

EATING OUT

Druzhba (friendship), ul. Lenina 3, Tel. 225-998; **Dubrava** (oak grove), prosp. Karla Marksa 51, Tel. 461-967; **Orion**, ul. Vatutina 17/1, Tel. 462-120; **Sibirsky**, ul. Tenistaya 2, Tel. 649-261; **Snegiri** (bullfinches), ul. Kurchatova 3/4, Tel. 744-025; **Kartofel'noe Café**, ul. Poryadkovaya 4.

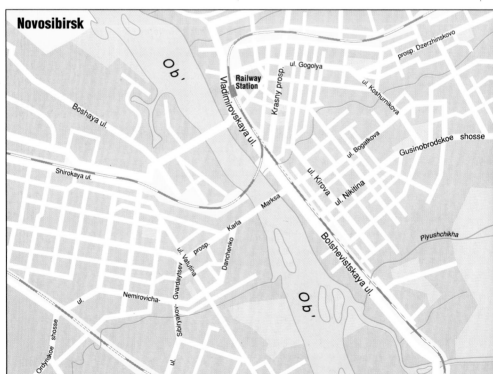

Novosibirsk

ODESSA

Travel Essentials: Aeroflot Information, Tel. 222-300; Railway Station Information, Tel. 221-227; Taxi, Tel. 004; Intourist Office, ul. Pushkinskaya 15, Tel. 227-085; Sputnik Office, Proletarsky bul'var 54, Tel. 224-610.

Museums: Archaeological Museum, ul. Lastochkina 4; Museum of History and Regional Studies, ul. Khalturina 4; Sea Fleet Museum, ul. Lastochkina 6; Arts Museum, ul. Korolenko 5a.

Performances: Academic Theater of Opera and Ballet, ul. Chaikovskovo 3, Tel. 252-408; Theater of Musical Comedy, ul. Karla Libknekhta 48, Tel. 224-851; Puppet Theater, ul. Pastera 62, Tel. 232-058; Circus, ul. Podbelskovo 25, Tel. 221-973.

Sports: Central Stadium, Shevchenko Park; Yacht Club, Otrada Beach.

Shopping: Central Department Store, ul. Pushkinskaya 72; Kashtan (hard currency shop), ul. Karla Marksa 6; Privoz Market.

ACCOMMODATIONS

Chernoe More (Intourist), ul. Lenina 55, Tel. 242-024; **Krasnaya** (Intourist), ul. Pushkinskaya 15, Tel. 227-220; **Bolshaya Moskovskaya**, ul. Deribasovskaya 29, Tel. 224-016; **Odessa**, Primorsky bul'var 11, Tel. 227-419; **Passazh**, ul. Sovetskoy Armii 34, Tel. 212-290; **Tsentralnaya**, ul. Sovetskoy Armii 40, Tel. 224-861.

EATING OUT

Bratislava Restaurant, ul. Karla Marksa 19, Tel. 221-432; **Kavkaz Restaurant**, ul. Khalturina 12, Tel. 250-395; **Kiev Restaurant**, pl. Martynovskovo 1, Tel. 229-631; **More Restaurant**, prosp. Shevchenko 8a, Tel. 225-158; **Ukraina Restaurant**, ul. Lastochkina 24, Tel. 227-479; **Yug Restaurant**, ul. Lenina 5, Tel. 620-087; **Fontan Café**, ul. Perekopskoy Divizii 61; **Chaj Café**, ul. Zhukovskovo 29; **Gambrinus Bar**, ul. Deribasovskaya 31.

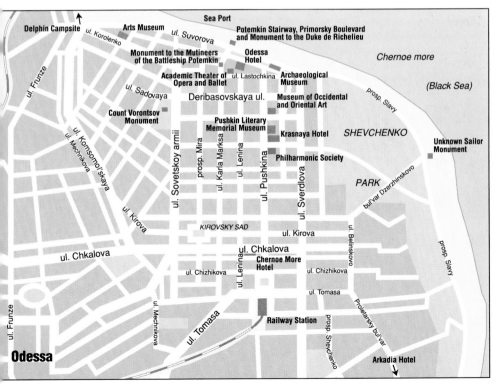

Odessa

RIGA

Travel Essentials: Aeroflot Information, Tel. 221-395; Railways Information, Tel. 007; Riga Information, Tel. 225-131; Jurmala Information, Tel. 48-910; Taxi, Tel. 334-041; Intourist Office, Tel. 213-843.

Museums: Latvian History Museum, pl. Pioneryu 3; Museum of Navigation and the History of Riga, ul. Palasta 4; Stradins Museum of the History of Medicine, ul. Paegles 1; Ethnographical Museum, Bergi Village.

Performances: Domus Cathedral and Concert Hall, pl. 17 Iyunya 1; Theater of Opera and Ballet, bul'var Padomju 3, Tel. 222-823; Upit Academic Drama Theater, bul'var Kronvalda 2, Tel. 322-759; Circus, ul. Merkelya 4.

Sports: Daugava Stadium, Augus ijela 1; Tennis Courts, bul'var Kronvalda 26; Yacht Club, ul. Bernudarza 19.

Shopping: Intershop, Teata ul. 9 & 12; Modes preces (for ladies); Central Market, ul. Negyu 7.

ACCOMMODATIONS

Latvia (Intourist), ul. Kirova 55, Tel. 212-525; **Atlantika**, ul. Atlantiyas 4, Tel. 340-178; **Metropol**, bul'var Padomju 36/38, Tel. 224-221; **Riga**, bul'var Padomju 22, Tel. 210-369; **Saulite**, ul. Merkelya 12, Tel. 224546; **Tourist**, ul. Slokas 1, Tel. 613-613; **Victoria**, ul. Suvorova 55, Tel. 272-305.

EATING OUT

Astoria, ul. Audeju 16 (on the floor of the Central Department Store), Tel. 213-466; **Daugava**, ul. Kutyu 24, Tel. 613-600; **Kavkaz**, ul. Merkelya 8, Tel. 224-528; **Kosmos**, Vienibas gatve 51, Tel. 615-874; **Ruse**, ul. Lokomotives 68, Tel. 263-525; **Tallinn**, ul. Gorkovo 27/29, Tel. 225-834; **Doma Café**, ul. Smilshu 1/3; **Kristine Café**, ul. Blaumanya 8; **Put Vejni Café**, ul. Jauniela 18/20; **Sigulda Café**, ul. Lenina 35; **Ligo** (beer pub), Majori, ul. Teatra 1.

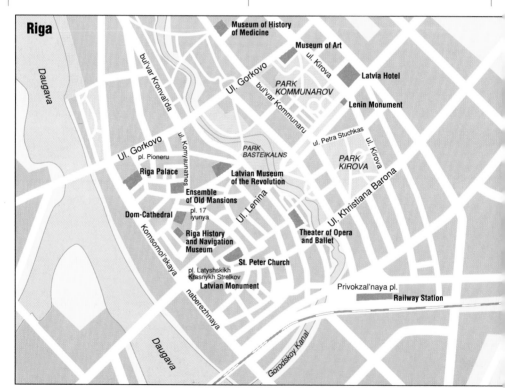

ROSTOV ON DON

Travel Essentials: Intourist Office, Moskovskaya Hotel.

Museums: Fine Arts Museum, ul. Pushkinskaya 115; Museum of Regional Studies, ul. Engelsa 79; Don Cossacs History Museum, Novocherkassk, 40 km/25 km from Rostov.

Performances: Gorky Drama Theater, Teatralnaya pl.; Musical Comedy Theater, ul. Serafimovicha 88; Philharmonic Society, ul. Engelsa 170; Puppet Theater, Universitetsky prosp. 46.

Places of Interest: Park on the bank of the Don; Memorial Ensemble in the Zmievskaya Ravine; Tourist Complex Petrovsky Prichal (Peter's Quay); Cathedral; House of Soviets.

Sports: Palace of Sports, Khalturinsky prosp. 112; Sports Center of Rostselmash Plant, ul. Pervoy Konnoy Armii 6; Hippodrome, at the end of Universitetsky prosp.

Shopping: Central Department Store, ul. Engelsa 46; Art Salon, ul. Beregovaya 10.

ACCOMMODATIONS

Intourist, ul. Engelsa 115, Tel. 659-082; **Moskovskaya**, ul. Engelsa 62, Tel. 388-700; **Don**, Gazetny per. 34; **Rostov**, prosp. Budyonnovo 59, Tel. 391-818; **Tourist**, Oktyabrsky prosp. 19; **Yuzhnaya**, prosp. Karla Marksa 20; **Camping site**, 14 km/8.5 miles from the city center along Novocherkasskoe shosse.

EATING OUT

Restaurants in the hotels and also: **Druzhba**, ul. Engelsa 90; **Kosmos**, ul. Engelsa 128; **Teatralny**, Park Oktyabrskoy Revolyutsii; **Tsentralny**, ul. Engelsa 76; Volga-Don, ul. Beregovaya 31; **Zolotoy Kolos** (Golden Spike), ul. Engelsa 45; **Molodyozhnoe (Youth) Café**, Teatralnaya pl.

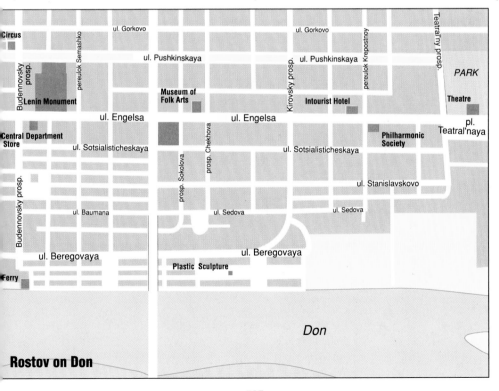

Rostov on Don

SAMARKAND

Travel Essentials: Aeroflot Information, Tel. 31-004; Railways Information, Tel. 30-011; Intourist Office, ul. sovetskaya 55, Tel. 33-493.

Museums: Ikramov Museum of Uzbek History, Culture and Art, Tashkentskaya ul. 1; Museum of History of Samarkand, Tashkentskoe shosse; Ulug Bek Museum, Tashkentskoe shosse; Sadriddin Ajni House-Museum, ul. Registanskaya 7b.

Places of Interest: Registan Ensemble: Medrese of Ulug Bek, Medrese Shirdor, Mosque & Medrese Tillya-Kari, Sheybanid Dakhma; Mosque Bibi-Khanym, ul. Choraga; Afrasiab Hill and Mosque Khasret-Khysr; Shahi-Zindah, ul. Dzhurakulova; Mausoleum Gur-Emir & Mausoleum Rukhabad, ul. Akhunbabaeva; (the burial vault of Tamerlane); Gorky Park, ul. Lenina 56; Park-Lake; Amankutan Town.

Performances: Alimdzhan Uzbek Theater of Drama and Comedy, Central Park; Russian Drama Theater, ul. Lenina 51; Summer Theater, ul. Vostochnaya 160; Opera and Ballet Theater, Krepostnaya pl.

Sports: Dynamo Stadium, ul. Karla Marksa 54; Spartak Stadium, ul. Akhunbabaeva 85; Tourist Club, ul. Karla Marksa 15.

Shopping: Central Department Store, ul. Gazovaya 2; Jewellery, ul. Tashkentskaya 47; Bagishamal Market, Kommunisticheskaya ul. 33; Siab Market, ul. 8 Marta 8.

ACCOMMODATIONS

Samarkand (Intourist), bul'var Gorkovo 1, Tel. 58-812; **Bagishamal**, ul. Mirsharapova 59; **Registan**, ul. Lenina 36; **Tourist**, ul. Gagarina 85; **Shark**, ul. Tashkentskaya 1; **Zeravshan**, ul. Sovetskaya 59.

EATING OUT

Restaurants in the hotels and also: **Uzbekistan**, ul. Lenina 52; **Zeravshan**, ul. Karla Marksa 79.

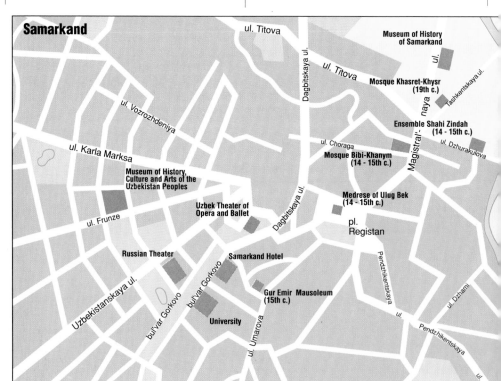

*City*GUIDE

SOCHI

Museums: Museum of Local Lore, ul. Ordzhonikidze 29; Ostrovsky Literary Museum, ul. Pavla Korchagina 4.

Performances: Letny (Summer) Theater, Park Frunze; Zelyony (Green) Theater, Park Riviera; Philharmonic Society, ul. Teatralnaya 2.

Places of Interest: Mt. Bolshoy Akhun; Dagomys Tea Farm; Krasnaya Polyana (red glade); Yew and Box Tree Grove; Yuzhnye Kultury (southern plants) Park; Mamay-Kale Fortress; Eagle Rocks (observational platform); Ritsa Lake; Novy Afon Monastery; Pitsunda Town and Old Cathedral.

Sports and Cure: Sochi is the largest balneologial resort in the USSR; next to Sochi is another spa, Matsesta, with popular curative baths and a famous source of mineral water. In the mountains around Sochi are marked walking routes.

Shopping: Beriozka (hard currency shop), Kurortny prosp. 50; Izumrud (jewelry), ul. Navaginskaya 12.

ACCOMMODATIONS

Kamelia (Intourist), Kurortny prosp. 91, Tel. 990-292; **Zhemchuzhina** (Intourist), ul. Chernomorskaya 3, Tel. 934-355; **Dagomys Intourist Complex** (Dagomys Hotel & Campingsite, Olimpiyskaya Hotel, Meridian Motel), ul. Leningradskaya 7, Dagomys, Tel. 322-994, 321-994, 322-987; **Khosta**, ul. Yaltinskaya 14, Khosta; **Magnolia**, Kurortny prosp. 50; Moskva, Kurortny prosp. 18; **Sochi**, Kurortny prosp. 50; **Svetlana Guest House**, Kurortny prosp. 75.

EATING OUT

Akhun, Mt. Bolshoy Akhun; **Kaskad**, Kurortny prosp. 31; **Kavkazsky Aul**, River Agura Valley; **Lazurny**, Kurortny prosp. 1030; **Staraya Melnitsa**, Bykhta Hill.

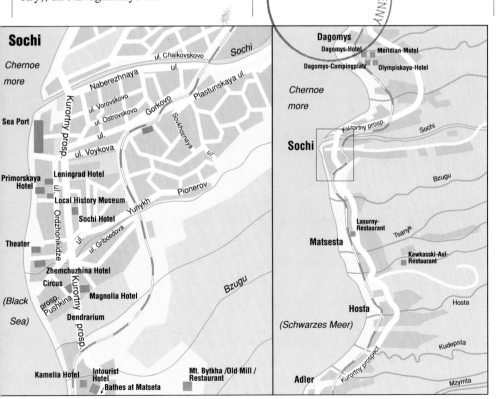

TALLINN

Travel Essentials: Airport Information, Tel. 060, 421-265; Railway Station Information, Tel. 446-756; Taxi, Tel. 603-044; Intourist Office, Viru väljak 4, Tel. 650-371.

Museums: Tallinn City Museum, Vene 17; Kiek in de Kök, Nôukogude 1; Park-Museum, Vabayhumuuzeumi tee 12; Museum of Fire Protection, Lai 29.

Performances: Estonia Academic Theater of Opera and Ballet, Estonia puiestee 4, Tel. 444-424; Kingisepp Drama Theater, Pärnu maantee 5, Tel. 443-378; Puppet Theater, Lai 1, Tel. 441-252; Niguliste Museum-Concert Hall.

Places of Interest: Singing Field; Olympic Center and Memorial in Pirita.

Sports: Kalev Swimming Pool, Aja tee 18, Tel. 440-545; Kalev Tennis Courts, Koze tee 4; Stadium, ul. Toompark; Hippodrome, Paldiskoe shosse 50.

Shopping: Market Places pl. Turu 6 & per. Turu; Art Shops, Hobusepea 2, Pikk 18, Vôidu väljak 10.

ACCOMMODATIONS

Kungla (Intourist), Kreutzwaldi 23, Tel. 421-460; **Olympia** (Intourist), ul. Kingiseppa 33, Tel. 602-438; **Tallinn** (Intourist), Gagarini puiestee, Tel. 450-474; **Viru** (Intourist), Viru väljak, Tel. 652-070.

EATING OUT

Gloria, Müürivahe 2, Tel. 446-950; **Kännu Kukk**, Vilde tee 75; **Nord**, Rataskaevu 3/5, Tel. 444-695; **Palace**, Vôidu väljak 3, Tel. 442-242; **Pirita**, Merivälja tee 5, Tel. 238-102; **Raeköök**, Dunkri 5; **Rataskaevu**, Dunkri 6; **Vana Toomas**, Raekoja plats 8, Tel. 445-818; **Gnoom Café**, Vana turg 6; **Kadriorg Café**, Narva maantee 90; **Maiasmokk Café**, Pikk 16; **Neitsitorn Café**, Nôukogude 1 (next to Kiek in de Kök); **Pegasus Café**, Harju 1; **Virmaline Ice Café**, Sauna 5; **Mündi Bar**, Mündi 5.

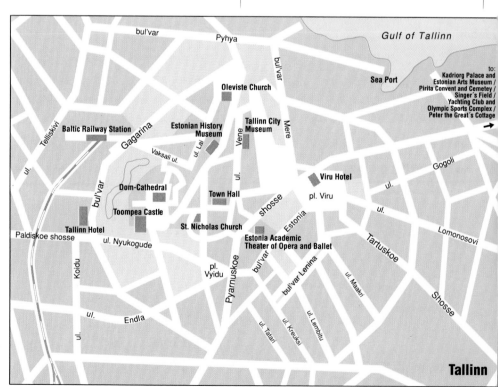

Tallinn

City GUIDE

TASHKENT

Travel Essentials: City Information Kiosks, Railway Station & ul. Samarkandskaya 30; Intourist Office, Uzbekistan Hotel; Sputnik Office, ul. Pakhtakorskaya 5.

Museums: Ajbek Museum of History of Uzbekistan Peoples, prosp. Lenina 30; Uzbekistan Fine Arts Museum, ul. Proletarskaya 16; Museum of Carpets and Syuzane (specially decorated covers), ul. Pravdy Vostoka 16; Museum of Natural History, ul. Sagban 16.

Performances: Navoi Theater of Opera and Ballet, ul. Pravdy Vostoka 31; Khamza Academic Theater of Drama, ul. Uigura 2; Gorky Russian Drama Theater, ul. Karla Marksa 28; Mukimi Uzbek Theater of Drama and Musical Comedy, ul. Almazar 187; Circus, ul. Lenina 42.

Places of Interest: Lenin Komsomol Park; Gorky Park; Dzhami Mosque; Sheikhantaur Ensemble; Mts. Chat-Kal.

Sports: Pakhtakor Stadium, ul. Sotsializma 21; Dynamo Stadium, ul. Pushkina; Palace of Water Sports, ul. 1 Maya 78.

Shopping: Central Market.

ACCOMMODATIONS

Uzbekistan (Intourist), ul. Karla Marksa 45, Tel. 332-773; **Intourist Hotel**, Ordzhonikidze village; **Moskva**, pl. Chorsu 1, Tel. 428-600; **Oktyabr**, ul. Tarasa Shevchenko 14; **Pushkinskaya**, ul. Pushkina 18; **Sayokhat**, shosse Lunacharskovo 115; **Tashkent**, prosp. Lenina 50, Tel. 332-735; **Zeravshan**, ul. Vysokovoltnaya 5a; **Bakht**, park Bakht.

EATING OUT

Restaurants in the hotels and also: **Chaikhanas**, in the park along prosp. Lenina & ul. Sagban 1; **Intourist Café**, on the shore of Lenin Komsomol Lake; **Pelmennaya Café**, ul. Lenina 44; **Yulduz Café**, ul. Shota Rustaveli 84a.

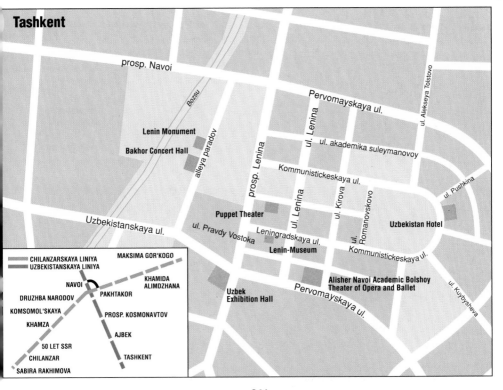

241

TBILISI

Travel Essentials: Aeroflot Information, Tel. 731-525; Railway station, Tel. 933-539; City Information, Tel. 933-714; Taxi, Tel. 953-606; Intourist Office, prosp. Rustaveli 13, Tel. 993-809; Sputnik Office, ul. Machabeli 11, Tel. 936-635.

Museums: Dzhanashia Museum of Georgia, prosp. Rustaveli 3; Museum of Georgian Art, ul. Ketskhoveli 1; Grishashvili Museum of History and Ethnography of Tbilisi (in the old Caravanserai), ul. Sioni 8.

Performances: Paliashvili Academic Theater of Opera and Ballet, prosp. Rustaveli 25, Tel. 997-586; Mardzhanishvili Academic Theater of Drama, ul. Mardzhanishvili 8, Tel. 954-001; Circus, pl. Geroev.

Places of Interest: Botanical Gardens of the Academy of Sciences; Ordzhonikidze Park; Mt. Mtatsminda; Svetitskhoveli Church; Mtskheta town (23 km/14 miles from Tbilisi).

Sports: Dynamo Stadium, prosp. Tsereteli 2; Swimming Pool, pl. Geroev; Hippodrome, ul. Guramishvili.

ACCOMMODATIONS

Adzharia (Intourist), pl. Konstitutsii 1, Tel. 369-822; **Iveria** (Intourist), ul. Inashvili 6, Tel. 930-488; **Tbilisi** (Intourist), prosp. Rustaveli 13, Tel. 997-329; **Ushba Motel** (Intourist), 9 km/5.4 miles along the Georgian Military Highway, Tel. 511-681; **Zolotoe Runo** (golden fleece) International Youth Camp, on the shore of Lake Tbilisi.

EATING OUT

Aragvi, Naberezhnaya (Embankment) 6, Tel. 934-423; **Iori**, the western shore of Lake Tbilisi, Tel. 664-110; **Kalakuri**, ul. Shavteli 13; **Krtsanisi**, ul. Gorgasali 39, Tel. 724-231; **Mtatsminda**, Mt. Mtatsminda, Tel. 999-735; **Mukhrantubani**, ul. Baratashvili 23, Tel. 995-904; **Dom Chaya** (tea house), ul. Kekelidze 2, Tel. 226-111.

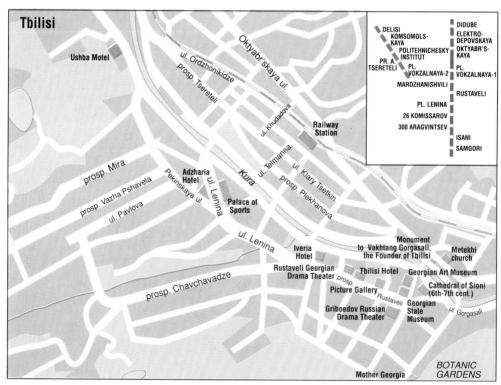

Tbilisi

City GUIDE
VILNIUS

Travel Essentials: Airport Information, Tel. 630-201; Railway Station Information, Tel. 630-086; City Information, Tel. 626-424; Taxi, Tel. 772-929; Intourist Office, Tel. 736-222.

Museums: Lithuanian Museum of History and Ethnography, ul. Vrublevskovo 1; Picture Gallery, pl. Gediminasa; Gediminas Castle, Castle Mt. (Piles); Literary Museum, ul. Subachyaus 124.

Performances: Lithuanian Academic Theater of Opera and Ballet, ul. Venuolisa, Tel. 730-303; Lithuanian Academic Drama Theater, ul. Basanavichüsa 13, Tel. 668-170; Philharmonic Society, ul. Gorkovo 69, Tel. 620-265.

Places of Interest: Castle mountain; St. Anna Church; Bernardinian Monastery.

Sports: Palace of Sports, ul. Ejdukyavichüsa 1, Tel. 750-212; Dynamo Stadium, ul. Kostyushko 9; Zalgiris Stadium, ul. Ejdukyavichüsa 3/11.

Shopping: Central Department Store, ul. Ukmyarges 16; Art Salon, prosp. Lenina 1.

ACCOMMODATIONS

Lietuva (Intourist), ul. Ukmyarges 20, Tel. 736-016; **Astoria**, ul. Gorkovo 59/2, Tel. 629-914; **Draugiste**, ul. Churlyonisa 84, Tel. 662-711; **Gintaras**, ul. Sodu 14, Tel. 634-496; **Narutis**, ul. Gorkovo 24, Tel. 622-882; **Neringa**, prosp. Lenina 23, Tel. 610-516; **Sportas**, ul. Bistriches 13, Tel. 748-953.

EATING OUT

Bochü, ul. Gedrisa 4/3, Tel. 623-772; **Dajnava**, ul. Venuolisa 4, Tel. 618-475; **Erfurtas**, ul. Architektu 19, Tel. 444-542; **Ladzinai**, ul. Architektu 152, Tel. 447-995; **Lokis**, ul. Antokolskovo 8, Tel. 629-046; **Palanga**, ul. Giry 10/16, Tel. 620-186; **Subatele**, ul. Subachyaus 3, Tel. 626-054; **Syanasis Rusis**, ul. Gedrisa 16, Tel. 611-137; **Aushra Café**, ul. Komjaunimo 40; **Bistro**, ul. Sodu 15.

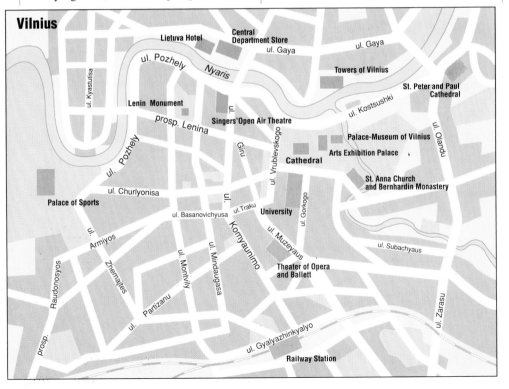

Vilnius

YALTA

Travel Essentials: Aeroflot Information, Tel. 22-491; Bus Station Information, Tel. 22-358; Trolleybus Station, Tel. 27-994; City Information, Tel. 27-938; Intourist Office, Tel. 22-034.

Museums: Museum of Local Lore, ul. Pushkina 25; Chekhov Museum, ul. Kirova 112; Lesya Ukrainka Museum, ul. Litkensa 8.

Performances: Chekhov Theater, ul. Litkensa 13; Circus, ul. Moskovskaya 27.

Places of Interest: Alupka Palace; Livadia Palace; Polyana Skazok; Mt. Darsan and Funicular Way; Lastochkino Gnezdo (Swallow's Nest); Miskhor; Simeiz and Baidarskie Vorota (Baidary Gate); Nikitsky Botanical Garden; Gaspra.

Sports and Cure: Pool for Swimming and Treatment, ul. Krasnoarmeyskaya 1, Tel. 27-838.

Shopping: Dom Torgovli (Department Store); Market Place.

ACCOMMODATIONS

Oreanda (Intourist), ul. Lenina 35, Tel. 25-794; **Tavrida** (Intourist), ul. Lenina 13, Tel. 27-784; **Yalta** (Intourist), ul. Drazhinskovo 52, Tel. 20-129; **Krym**, ul. Moskovskaya 1, Tel. 26-001; **Massandra**, ul. Drazhinskovo 50, Tel. 27800; **Primorskaya**, ul. Sverdlova 13, Tel. 24-425; **Yuzhnaya**, ul. Ruzvelta 10, Tel. 25-860; **Intourist Camping Grounds**, Polyana Skazok (Glade of Fairy Tales).

EATING OUT

Brigantina, ul. Karla Marksa 18, Tel. 20-171; **Gorka Restaurant**, Mt. Darsan, Tel. 24-076; **Dzhalita**, ul. Kievskaya 8, Tel. 25-548; **Lesnoy Restaurant**, Karagol Lake; **Leto Restaurant**, Gagarin Park, Tel. 27-652; **Priboy Restaurant**, Gagarin Park, Tel. 24-323; **Sochi Restaurant**, ul. Lenina 11, Tel. 27-705; **Vodopad Restaurant**, next to the Uchan-Su Waterfall, Tel. 23-531; **Yakor**, ul. Ruzvelta 5, Tel. 27-912; **Krab Bar-Café**, ul. Kommunalnaya 20.

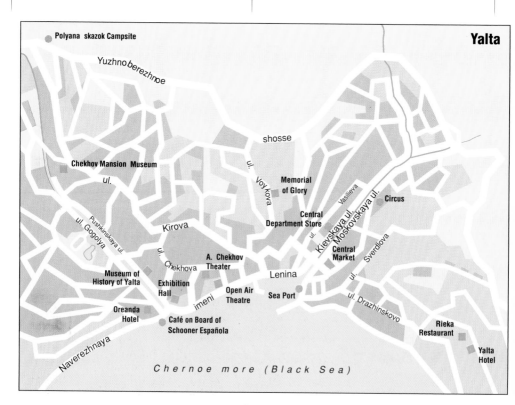

YEREVAN

Travel Essentials: Aeroflot Information, Tel. 007, 532-914; Railway Station, Tel. 004; City Information, Tel. 525-770, 565-122; Taxi, Tel. 009; Intourist Office, Tel. 525-373; Sputnik Office, ul. Moskovyan 31, Tel. 533-092.

Museums: Armenian History Museum, ul. Abovyana 2; Armenian Museum of Folk Arts, ul. Abovyana 64; Museum of History of Erevan, prosp. Lenina 12.

Performances: Spendiryan Academic Theater of Opera and Ballet, ul. Tumanyana 36, Tel. 566-302; Sundukyan Academic Theater, ul. Karmir Banaki 6, Tel. 527-670; Circus, ul. 26 Komissarov 1.

Places of Interest: Matenadaran (Manuscripts Depository), prosp. Lenina 101, Tel. 583-292; Razdan Gorge; Fortress Teishebaini, Karmir Blur; Fortress Arin-Berd, ul. Erebuni 38.

Sports: Chess House, Tel. 554-558; Razdan Stadium and Swimming Pool.

Shopping: Tsitsernak hard currency shop, ul. Amiryana 5, Tel. 586-374.

ACCOMMODATIONS

Ani (Intourist), prosp. Sayat-Nova 19, Tel. 520-724; **Armenia** (Intourist), ul. Amiryana 1, Tel. 525-393; **Dvin** (Intourist), ul. Paronyana 40, Tel. 536-343; **Sevan** (Intourist), ul. Shaumyana 8, Tel. 583-102; **Erevan**, ul. Abovyana 14, Tel. 581-392; **Sebastia**, ul. Leningradyan 46/1, Tel. 394-700; **Hotel of the Youth Palace**, ul. Komeritakan 1; **Tsitsernak**, Nork, Tretia ul. (3rd Street).

EATING OUT

Ararat, pl. Lenina, Tel. 524-633; **Masis**, ul. Ovsepyana 16/1, Tel. 652-090; **Praga**, prosp. Komitasa 54b, Tel. 233-729; **Aragats Café**, prosp. Ordzhonikidze 3, Tel. 560-821; **Araks Café**, Razdan Gorge; **Argishti**, prosp. Lenina 16a, Tel. 533-412; **Pizzeria**, prosp. Lenina 19, Tel. 535-143.

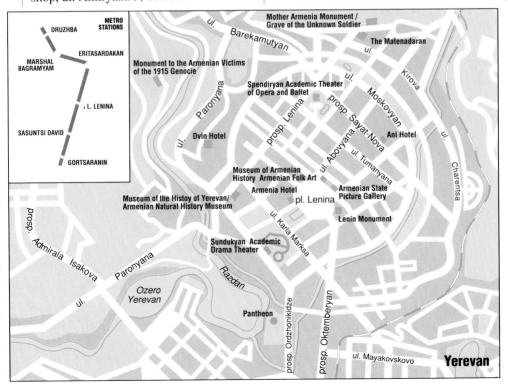

Yerevan

THE NATIVE LAND OF THE RUSSIANS

It is said that somewhere in far-off China there are words carved into one of the ancient rocks which run: "The fate of the Russian people is to die for others." Whoever wrote this might well be considered a crank. For how could an entire nation suffer for the sake of others? However it so happens that this statement is, historically speaking, by no means as groundless as it at first appears. If we take the ruinous invasions of the Mongols between the 13th and 15th centuries, then we will see that the major burden of repelling these invaders fell to the nascent Russian state. During the Russian-Turkish war (1877-1878), it was mainly thanks to the heroism of the Russian forces that the people of the Balkan peninsula were liberated from the yoke of the Ottoman Empire. The 20th century is also no exception, should we take into account the First and Second World Wars.

Internal political developments, the 1917 Revolution, the Civil War, and the events of the not so distant past, all raise the question: why is it that the Russians have either perished for others, or arbitrated in smoothing out international conflicts? All the same, this by no means implies that Russians have themselves chosen such an extraordinary destiny. Far from it.

Without a doubt, it has something to do with the character of the people themselves, who are somewhat reckless in their attitude towards themselves and often pay for it dearly.

When all is said and done, the Russians were, and remain the very core of a mighty state - the USSR - around which are collected hundreds of totally diverse nations and ethnic groups.

We have grown used to the fact that all Soviet citizens abroad are referred to as "Russians"; this is, however, by no means the case. Russians number only 148 million out of the Soviet Union's total population of some 286 million.

Indeed, the area populated by Russians is vast - in all some 17 million

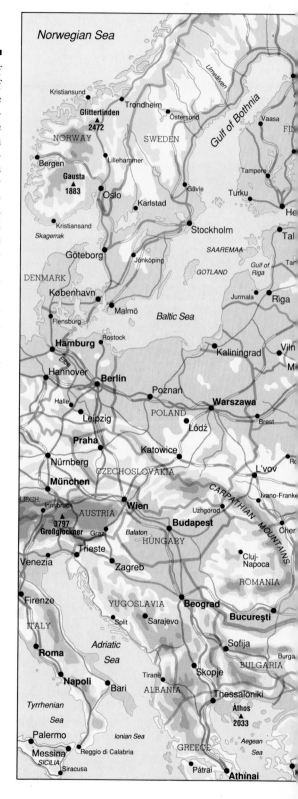

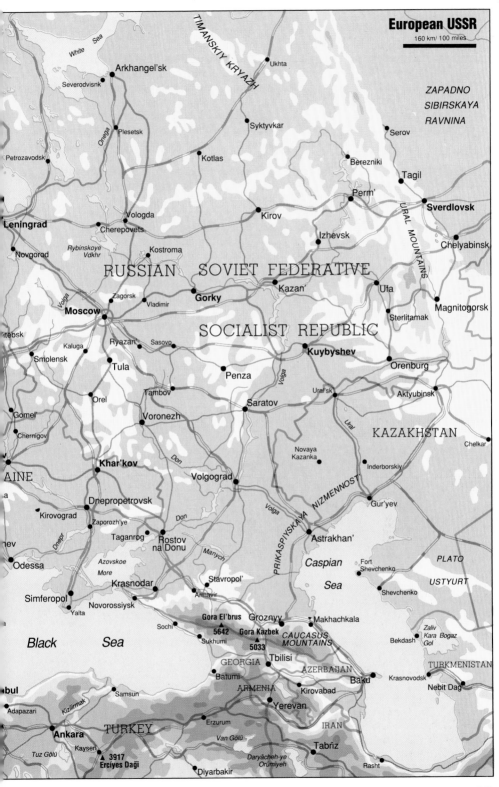

European USSR

160 km/ 100 miles

White *Sea*

Arkhangel'sk

Severodvisnk

TIMANSKIY KRYAZH

Ukhta

ZAPADNO
SIBIRSKAYA
RAVNINA

Syktyvkar

Serov

Plesetsk

Onega

Petrozavodsk

Kotlas

Berezniki

Tagil

Perm'

Sverdlovsk

Vologda

Kirov

URAL MOUNTAINS

Izhevsk

Chelyabinsk

Leningrad

Cherepovets

Rybinskoye
Vdkhr

Kostroma

Novgorod

RUSSIAN SOVIET FEDERATIVE

Zagorsk

Gorky

Kazan'

Ufa

itebsk

Volga

Vladimir

Moscow

SOCIALIST REPUBLIC

Sterlitamak

Magnitogorsk

Kaluga

Ryazan'

Sasovo

Kuybyshev

Orenburg

Smolensk

Tula

Penza

Volga

Gomel'

Orel

Tambov

Saratov

Ural'sk

Aktyubinsk

Chernigov

Voronezh

Don

Ural

KAZAKHSTAN

Chelkar

Khar'kov

Novaya
Kazanka

Inderborskiy

AINE

Volgograd

a

Dnepropetrovsk

Don

Volga

Gur'yev

Kirovograd

Zaporozh'ye

Dnepr

PRIKASPIYSKAYA NIZMENNOST

ev

Taganrog

Rostov
na Donu

Astrakhan'

Odessa

Azovskoye
More

Manych

Caspian

Fort
Shevchenko

PLATO

Krasnodar

Stavropol'

Sea

USTYURT

Simferopol

Novorossiysk

Armavir

Shevchenko

Yalta

Gora El'brus

Groznyy

Makhachkala

Black

Sea

Sochi

5642

Gora Kazbek

CAUCASUS
MOUNTAINS

Bekdash

Zaliv
Kara Bogaz
Gol

Sukhumi

5033

TURKMENISTAN

GEORGIA

Tbilisi

AZERBAIJAN

Baku

Krasnovodsk

Nebit Dag

Batumi

ARMENIA

Kirovabad

bul

Samsun

Yerevan

Adapazari

Kizilirmak

IRAN

Ankara

TURKEY

Erzurum

Van Gölü

Tabriz

Tuz Gölü

Kayseri

3917
Erciyes Daği

Daryācheh-ye
Orūmīyeh

Rasht

Diyarbakir

249

square kilometers (6.56 square miles), stretching from the Arctic Ocean to the steppes of Kazakhstan and from the Baltic to the Pacific. The territory of the Russian Federation, the largest republic in the Union, is usually divided into Siberia, the Far East, and European Russia whose Eastern border reaches as far as the Ural mountains.

The first colony of Eastern Slavs who formed the basis of a Russian nation appeared between the rivers of the Don and Dnieper. It was during the 6th century, on the central stretches of the Dnieper, that the first Russian state was founded under the name of **Kiev Rus**.

Even today, the origins of the word "Rus" are widely disputed. Some think that it comes from the Greek *rhos*, while others argue that it has its origins in the Finnish word *ruotsi*. But nonetheless, here in the territory of the middle Russian plains, through which lay the routes of the Varangians to Greece (i.e. from the Baltic to the Black Sea) the first Russian town emerged. Today, in this territory, apart from Moscow and towns

of the "Golden Ring" that surround it, a good ten more Russian regions have sprung up.

Let us take a closer look at this area, beginning in the west, with Smolensk, which lies at the center of an area sharing the same name.

Smolensk: For centuries Smolensk has been called "the key to Central Russia". Situated 338 kilometers (210 miles) west of Moscow, it has more than once suffered the effects of invasion. Since the 9th century Smolensk has been famous as the center of a colony of Krivichi (a Slavic tribe). At that time it was a major port, with a thriving trade and handicraft industry. It is no coincidence that the town is named after an ancient shipbuilding craft - *smolenia* (the caulking of ships) much later, at the end of the 14th until the beginning of the 17th century, Smolensk was transformed into a impenetrable fortress by the great Czar Boris Godunov. From 1609-1611 it withstood a two-year siege by a Polish army of 22,000 men.

The oldest, and rather crumbling part

Preceding pages, "Boatmen on Volga" by Repin. **Below,** Russian babushkas are loved by everybody.

of the city is around **Kashena Street** near the railway station. The austere architectural form of the domed **Church of St. Peter and St. Paul** (12th century) has to be seen with your own eyes. Nearby, the 17th century **Church of St. Barbara** is in typical Russian baroque style. On the hill on the other side of the Dnieper is the gray and green **Uspensky (Assumption) Cathedral** with its many cupolas. Its construction took an entire century, from 1677 to 1784. This is the city's major working cathedral.

There is a superb park in the city, named after the well known Russian composer Mikhail Glinka (1804-1857), who loved Smolensk and spent much time there. The city is also able to boast of its own Art Gallery, with works representing nearly all European schools of painting. Modern Smolensk is an important industrial center specializing in electronics and other branches of precision engineering. The ancient city has been given a new lease of life. The fortress has become an industrial center.

Klin: Northwest of Moscow lies the Kalinin administrative area (*oblast*). The road from Moscow passes through the city of Klin (97 km/60 miles away), a smallish local center where Pyotr Tchaikovsky (1840-1893) lived until he moved to St. Petersburg. Nowadays there is a museum in memory of the genius composer. It is in this building that he wrote the Pathetique and two ballets, *The Nutcracker* and *Sleeping Beauty* - and other works. Every year on the 17th of May and the 6th of November, traditional concerts are performed by the international Tchaikovsky piano competition which attract hundreds of admirers from all over the country.

Kalinin: From Klin we carry on northwest to the city of Kalinin (160 km/100 miles from Moscow). Kalinin lies on the confluence of the Volga and Tver rivers and has a history stretching back a thousand years. The town used to be known as Tver, but in 1931 was renamed Kalinin in honor of the former Soviet President Mikhail Kalinin. Indeed, the towns of central Russia have suffered, more than any others, from being given

Russian
mothers hold
the society
together.

away as "presents" to various "leaders of the proletariat".

In olden days, the town was a major trading center. And indeed, it was a Tver merchant, Afanassy Nikitin, who in the 15th century set off in search of rich eastern lands and became the first European to reach far-off India. Very few ancient buildings have survived; foreign aggressors, and not so foreign ones, have ensured this sad phenomenon.

Perhaps the most attractive architectural monument in Kalinin is the **Outer Palace of Russian Monarchs**, constructed between 1784 and 1786 by the architect Matvey Kazakov and completed in 1809 by Carlo Rossi. In its time, the palace was well known as a fashionable literary salon. Today it houses a museum and art gallery. Modern Kalinin is not only a major port on the Volga river, but also a center for the textile and chemical industries.

Valday: To the north-west of Kalinin begins the **Valday Mountains**, a region of lakes and impassible forests. It is difficult to find a place in the European part of the USSR so rich in fish, wild geese, berries and mushrooms. The region's most outstanding feature is **Lake Seliger**, or rather a whole cascade of lakes joined by streams and small rivers dating back to the Ice Age. Lake Seliger is one of the most popular recreational areas in central Russia.

Before we continue on our journey around ancient Russian cities, let's make a little deviation.

It is said that cities are the face of the nation. If you wish to understand how the Russian people live, it is better to look closely at Kalinin or Smolensk rather than at Moscow or Leningrad. Here the pace of life differs greatly from that of the capital, a different mood, a provincial atmosphere still exists in these towns. And, alas, the standard of living is lower than in the larger cities. The empty, sometimes dusty, shelves of the shops, and the less than clean streets, have become the calling card of the Russian provinces... But don't just take our word for it, judge for yourself.

Novgorod: 420 km (620 miles) to the

Peasants from Novgorod ca. 1880.

252

north of Moscow there lies the great city of Novgorod, as old as Russia itself; it was once given the nick-name "Lord". The origins of the "New Town", now abbreviated to "Novgorod", date back as far as the middle of the 9th century. Since that time Novgorod has become one of the centers of the Russian state. In the period between the 12th-17th centuries the Novgorodskaya Republic was completely independent, something which then was unique in Russia . Novgorod, like other towns in the northern part of Russian, has a completely different style of architecture from that of Central Russia. Indeed, only the oldest churches from the 11th and 12th centuries are reminiscent of the style of Kiev Rus, for instance, the **Novgorodian Sophia** (1045-1050), and the **Church of the Annunciation** (1103). First and foremost, they were built of limestone rather than from brick, and secondary, they were much simpler in form and their facades were often stripped of decoration as for example, the **Church of St. Peter and Paul** on Sinichya Hill (1185).

However, the 16th century witnessed an inflow of architecture more along the lines of the Moscow style like **St. Boris and Gleb Church** (1538). Peter the Great also left his mark upon the city when he prepared for a decisive battle with the Swedes. He ordered that the fortress walls be reconstructed around the city. Catherine the Great, who so much liked to travel, constructed an **Outer Palace** in 1771.

Alas, nowadays Novgorod cannot boast of its former beauty and historical significance for the Russian state. History has taken its course so that the once powerful and great city, that used to rival Moscow and Kiev has become more of a Mecca for tourists in search of antiques, than a cultural center of the Northern Russian lands.

There is an abundance of churches in Novgorod, even when compared to Moscow, and it seems that the people here are more conservative and inclined to appreciate the ancient history of their great city.

Pskov: Further up north, the road leads us to the outermost boundary of the Russian Federation, or to city of Pskov, another custodian of ancient Russian secrets. Pskov's history dates as far back as the 10th century. In those days the city faithfully defended Russia from Lithuanian and Swedish invasions. In spite of the frequent wars at that time the city was a major trading center, whose importance was enhanced by its favorably location at the confluence of the Pskove and Velikaya rivers which flow into Lake Chudskoye.

Any sightseeing tour of Pskov should start with its white Kremlin walls. A most impressive church within the **Pskov Kremlin** is the **Troitsky (Trinity) Cathedral** built at the end of the 17th century. It used to be a starting point for the numerous raids conducted by the Pskovian Grand Princes, and it was also here that foreign emissaries were received. It was also the burial site for Russian bishops and princes.

Middle city, a former marketplace, is now called **Lenin Square**. Here, next-door to the Main Post Office is the **Church of Archangel Mikhail**, (1339) the first stone-walled church of the city.

Moving up Sovietskaya Street you have a chance to see the **Vassily-na-Gorke Church** (1413) which is a typical example of Pskovian architecture with its trenched windows and its semicircular arcs that support the cupolas .Pskov has so many churches that it is impossible, and indeed, unnecessary to name them all.

110 kilometers (62 miles) away from Pskov is another attractive tourist site - the **Pushkin Museum**. It was here that the great poet Pushkin (1799-1837) was born and brought up. Pushkin's house was restored in 1949 to welcome all those who admire his talent. It is here, at not so great a distance from the small village of **Pushkinskiye Gory** at the foot of the Uspensky Cathedral wall, that the great Russian poet is buried.

Ryazan: The Ryazan region is the birthplace of Sergei Esenin, another great Russian poet (1895-1925). It is probably hard to find another place in Central Russia so rich in famous people. It was also the birthplace of Konstantin

Tsiokovsky (1857-1935), the founder of Russian space science, Ivan Michurin (1855-1935) a famous biologist and plantbreeder, and Ivan Pavlov (1849-1936), the world-famous physiologist. Ryazan, the contemporary provincial capital, was founded at the end of the 11th century between two rivers, the Trubezha and the Libeda, by prince Oleg Chernigovsky, the grandson of Yaroslav Mudry. Today only earthen ramparts remain of the fortified walls of the Riazan Kremlin. This is not surprising, since the city stood on the invasion route of the Tartar-Mongols.

The name Ryazan is most probably derived from the geographical name of *rozana* which describes the outlying area of a kingdom. You can discover the places' history in more detail by visiting the local museum located in the so-called **Oleg's Palace** on Kremlin Hill. There are more than ten historical and architectural monuments on this hill. The main one is the **Uspensky Cathedral** which dates from the 17th century, it was built in the traditional style of Moscow Cathedrals. The bell-tower, constructed in the mid-1800's imparts special features to this huge ensemble. To the north of the cathedral, right at the edge of the ravine is the **Rozhdestwensky Cathedral** built in the 15th century - which served as a burial site for Russian princes.

According to custom, the town, with its many centuries of history, played a significant role in the development of the Russian state. Today Ryazan is just the administrative center of the region which bears its name. It has a relatively developed industry; numerous problems and an unhurried, provincial way of life.

The decline of a culture: Concluding our short tour around the cities of central Russia, we should, perhaps, say a few words about the people who live there, their hopes and concerns. Since most of the population is Russian, it is here that we find remnants of a single, almost forgotten culture that exists under difficult socio-economic conditions.

Towns which once, in the former

The water in rivers is still clean enough to rinse clothes in it.

principalities, were independent and powerful, gradually became dead-end, provincial cities. They are now all looking towards a capital which attracts all talents and deprives them of their indigenous culture. It is hardly surprising that there is practically no real workforce in the villages of central Russia today, there are only old people and children. Farm work has lost its prestige, and has indeed become unprofitable. However, this alone doesn't constitute the tragedy of the Russian people it also stems from the three centuries when the proud and independent Slavic people were enslaved by Tartar-Mongol conquerors.

The obedience forced upon them by their new masters became after some time a natural state of mind. Cultivated by almost all the rulers who followed, it became so deeply seated in the consciences of the people that with time they were not able any more to understand the degree of injustice and humiliation brought upon them.

Democracy and glasnost, introduced from above, placed the people in an ambiguous position, on the one hand it became clear that democracy would not stop people going hungry while on the other hand, it turned out that the people had already forgotten how to enjoy their work and do it properly. The result is a vicious cycle - an eternal striving towards freedom but at the same time an incapacity to deal with it.

Along the Volga and the Don: "The bread basket and drinking well" of Russian towns, and the "mother of the Russian land" is how the longest European river (3,530 km/2,192 miles) has been described. Known even by the ancient Greeks as the *Ra* (generous), the river is famous for its beauty. It is from the ancient Slavs, living on her banks, that the name of "Volga" from the Slavonean *vlaga* (moisture) is derived.

Today, the river still generously continues to offer her gifts. In her waters live more than 70 types of edible fish, including carp and sturgeon, the producer of caviar - one of the world's great delicacies.

Winterscape at Kostroma in Central Russia.

The river's surroundings are multi-faceted: dense pine forests by its source, rocky mountains ridges rising to meet the Urals, lush meadows and harsh steplands, found half way along the river, as well as the shifting sands of her tributaries. The Volga is not just Russian's main waterway, it was the medium that united the Russians and other peoples, who used to inhabit the area: the Udmurty, Tartars, Muri, Chuvash, Mordva, Kalmyks and Germans.

Kazan: We begin our river tour with Kazan - the ancient and present capital city of the Tartar Autonomous Republic. In spite of the fact that Tartaria was united with Russia in the 16th century, there is still a strong national tradition that is as strong as in former times. This is not surprising since the overwhelming majority of the population (about one million) are Tartars.

Kazan, with good reason, is considered to be a great cultural center. Way back in 1758, the first provincial gymnasium in Russia was opened here, as was Russia's fourth ever university, in 1840 (after Moscow, Tartu and Vilnius) where, incidentally, Lenin studied.

Please note the town's exotic architecture where the national element is combined with Russian tradition. The traditional **white-bricked Kremlin** of the 16th century, the work of the Pskov masters, together with the orthodox **Annunciation Cathedral**, unexpectedly adorned with a khan's minaret. The Tartars worshiped Islam in ancient times. These days the territory of the old Kremlin is "occupied" by the republican government.

74 kilometers (46 miles) downstream, to the west of Kazan, the Kama tributary (1,809 km/1,123 miles) flows into the Volga. Since ancient times, the Kama and its tributaries were the most important waterways, connecting Rus with Siberia and Central Asia. The meeting point of the Kama and the Volga is in the **Kyibyshevsky Lake**. It is 40 km (25 miles) from one bank to the other, and in places is 40 meters (130 feet) deep.

Ulyanovsk (known as Simbirsk until 1924) is visible from the other side of

Unearthing memories of hard times...

256

the Kuibyshevsky Lake. It is the cultural and industrial center of central Povolzhye (central Volga). It was renamed after the death of Vladimir Uljanov (Lenin) who was born here on April 22, 1870.

Down the Volga beyond the village of Usolye we arrive at the most beautiful place on the whole river. This place is called **Zhiguli** which is the only mountain range on the Volga, it extends for 75 km (46 miles) along the right bank of the river. It is said that in former times it served as a veritable defense fortress for Cossack liberty.

Our boat leaves the gigantic **Volga Car Plant in Togliatti** behind and sails past the "Tsarev Hill" which was visited by Peter the Great, and pushes through the so-called "Zhigulevsky Gates" between the Zhiguli and Sokolya mountains, until it finally approaches the ancient custodian on the Volga banks - the city of **Kuibyshev** (called Samara until 1935, when the name was changed in honor of Valerian Kuibyshev (1888-1935), also a Bolshevik leader.

Kuibyshev: The city, which was founded in 1586 near the point where the river Samara flows into the Volga, served as a military look-out post on the south-eastern borders or Russia. It had become a center of commerce as early as the end of the 16th century.

Today Kuibyshev is a large town with a population of over 1.5 million people. It has a highly developed industry, which includes aircraft construction, petrochemicals, and since 1987, it also has a metro system in operation. The chocolate factory's products are a welcome delicacy on every Russian table.

If you sail up the Volga towards Saratov, you will see on the left the not so particularly noteworthy town of **Marx**. The only remarkable fact about the town is that it was founded in 1767 by settlers from Germany and Austria, who named it Ekaterinstadt after the lady who enticed Europeans to Russia. Incidentally, the Autonomous Republic of Povolzhye, inhabited by Germans, was one of the first to become part of the USSR. Its economic development came to a sud-

..and life
:hells.

den halt in 1941 when, at Stalin's despotic will, the German community, accused of treason and of "undermining the state", was liquidated and its population split up and resettled in Kazakhstan and Siberia. Let's hope that historical justice will be restored.

Saratov: On the right bank of the Volga basin, surrounded by three high mountains, extends the town of Saratov. As you might guess, the town was founded at the same time as the fortress, i.e. in the late 16th century. On more than one occasion, it was the center of peasant uprisings and revolutionary activity. The famous Russian writer and democrat, N. Chernyshevsky (1829-1889) was born and brought up there. The future prime-minister of Russia P. Stolypin (1862-1911) began his glittering career here, as local governor.

His agrarian reforms are still referred to by modern Soviet economists, and not just in passing, either. For under Stolypin's government, Saratov was able not only to feed its own people, but half of Russia. Now, however, its inhabitants are forced to go to Moscow to buy foodstuffs.

Volgograd: The last town on our journey along the Volga is the "Hero City of Volgograd". There are few cities that happened to change their names thrice, and each time differently. From the day of its foundation in 1589 it was called Tsaritsyn, after the local river, from 1925 Stalingrad, to immortalize the name of the tyrant, and from 1961 simply Volgograd. Unlike all the previous cities it has no Kremlin or anything like it. It is not even rich in churches. Here, the monuments are of a different type - those of grief and sorrow. They mourn those who gave their lives in the war with the Nazi fascists in an attempt to break through General Paulus' closed "steel" ring. After liberation the town had practically no house that escaped destruction. Even the ruins here carry the names of the hero soldiers as for instance the house of Sgt. Pavlov on Lenin square. The highest point in the city is **Mamayev Kurgan**. It is here that the severest battle raged for full five **Industry comes in big size.**

258

months. It was later calculated that every square yard was covered with 1,200 splinters and fragments of shells and bullets. On the summit, the 52-meter (170-foot) **Motherland Monument** is a unique Pantheon of those who died in the Second World War.

Where the Don meets the Volga: Already back in ancient times people have wanted to join the waters of the Don and the Volga. We know that Turkish Sultan Selim II attempted this huge task in the 16th century. In the 18th century Peter the Great tried it, and if it hadn't been for the war with the Swedes, one of the rivers could have been done for; finally GIDROPROEKT (not any great personality, but a research institute) developed and approved the master plan for the gigantic project. In a record time of two and a half years a 10 km (6.2 miles) canal joined the two mighty rivers. The Don started to flow into the Volga. Shall we, perhaps, follow the route, but in the opposite direction.

There is no other river in Russia which was so profusely praised in folk songs and legends. This area gave birth to and raised many genuine fighters for popular freedom such as Stepan Razin and Yemelian Pougachev. It was during their heyday that free Cossacks started their war raids from here.

Rostov: The city of the Rostov stands in the center of that land, 48 km (30 miles) from the delta where the Don flows into the Sea of Azov. It is normally referred to as the "Gate to the Caucasus". It is here that all roads from Russia to Transcaucasia and the Black Sea pass through.

You start sightseeing from the Don Embankment. Rostov is a major industrial center, a river and sea port. In the center of the city, in the pedestrian area, are many small restaurants and cafeterias which specialize in a variety of fish dishes. There is also the **St. Mother of God Cathedral** which dates back to the 19th century.

It is famous for its outline which repeats Moscow's Christ The Saviour Cathedral that was destroyed in the 1930s. In a way it is its miniature double.

Amateur folk singers are still very popular.

THE BALTIC STATES

"Freedom and independence!" This fighting slogan of numerous rallies and marches, has become the symbol of the past year or two in the life of Lithuania, Latvia and Estonia, the three Soviet Baltic republics. These magic words caused thousands of people to join hands in an unprecedented, 600 kilometer-long (372 miles) human chain extending from Vilnius (capital of Lithuania) to Tallinn (capital of Estonia) on August 23, 1989: half-a-century ago on that same day, Molotov and Ribbentrop signed the Soviet-German non-aggression pact, which, as the protesters now claim, "legitimized the forced annexation" of the Baltic States by the USSR.

There is no hiding the fact that their protests have ample justification, for Lithuania, Latvia and Estonia had been independent countries in the period between the two World Wars, until Stalin and Hitler decided their fate. Separatism is further fueled by the impractical system of false unitarianism that has hitherto been the Soviet Union's substitute for true federalism. One way or the other, more and more Lithuanians, Latvians and Estonians are nowadays leaning towards national isolation and even secession from the union.

Typically, little thought is given to the socio-political consequences of such an act for both the Baltic states and the country as a whole. Many serious experts think that since the three republics are at present unable to face competition in the world market, they are not ready for economic and, consequently, political, separation from the Soviet Union. The nationalist euphoria that holds many Lithuanians, Latvians and Estonians in its grip today blinds them also to the interests of non-natives, who account for almost 50 percent of the population in Latvia and 40 percent in Estonia.

The problem is far from being a simple one, and the rapid development towards independence in Lithuania is **Preceding pages, Estonia: striving for independence. Below, 16th-century cityscape of Riga.**

ample proof. We must realize that there is a certain amount of difference between the three nations in terms of culture and traditions - Estonians, are not like Latvians, let alone Lithuanians. Yet they have much in common: the Baltic Sea, their climate, and, of course, their history. It is difficult to name a neighbor that has not, at one time or another, conquered their lands. Danes, Germans, Poles, Swedes, and Russians have all left a trace in the history and culture of the Baltic nations and have all contributed to their lifestyle, which, seen from the Soviet Union, is strikingly close to that of Western Europe. It is not for nothing that the ancient Lithuanian, Latvian and Estonian towns, for all their originality, are an architectural blend of Gothic, Romanesque, baroque and classical styles.

Characteristically, the three republics are not far from one another in both the current level and orientation of their economic development. Industry is dominated by instrument-making, electronics and electrical engineering (along with light and food industries). It may be that because of this, the shops of Tallinn or Riga offer more products than you can find in, for instance, Kiev or Leningrad.

The Baltic republics are, however, resource-poor, and most enterprises work exclusively with imported raw materials. Yet meat and milk products (amongst other products) are exported to other republics.

Another thing that all three nations have in common is their respect for old customs. Their traditions live on in arts and crafts, pottery, amber jewelry, and woolen garments, in folk songs and tales (which one hears in everyday life, and not just at formal festivals).

Traditionally, nature is an extension of the home to the locals. There are preserves and natural parks, to say nothing of resort areas. Finally, there is no other place in the USSR where the tourist industry is developed to such a degree, from ubiquitous and cozy cafés and restaurants to good roads and comfortable hotels.

Vitautas Landsbergis.

Estonia

If you ask any of the numerous tourists who come here from other parts of the country whether they like Estonia, you are likely to hear in reply, "Oh, yes... Estonians live better." As indeed they do. Most of the credit goes to themselves. Estonians are diligent and industrious at work, wise with property, and true to their word in business. They are cultured and well-educated.

In the eyes of people from any other part of the country, the obsession with cleanliness you encounter in Estonia (and in the other Baltic republics) borders on a mania. Where, for example, the Ukrainian housewife will whitewash the walls of her cottage, and where her Russian sister will give the house a fresh coat of paint, the Estonian woman will scrub the walls with a soapy brush. Estonians decorate their houses, yards and streets with impeccable taste. Flowers and English lawns are everywhere.

A country of 1,500 islands: The republic is one of the smallest in the USSR. It is

240 kilometers (150 miles) long from north to south, and 350 kilometers (217 miles) from east to west. It can be crossed in any direction in an automobile in a matter of hours. The population is just above 1.5 million. Almost 10 percent of the territory consists of islands, which are over 1,500 in number. This gives Estonia a longer sea borderline than that of neighboring Lithuania and Latvia put together.

Besides the climate (cool summers and mild winters), the Baltic Sea shapes the image of the republic's cities, of which the foremost is Tallinn, the capital city with a population of 500,000.

Tallinn: Seen from the sea, the ancient town of Tallinn (founded in 1154, but archaeologists say that people lived here in the first millennium B.C.) resembles a seagull in flight. Its sharp-roofed skyline gives it a fairytale quality as it rises from the waters.

Tallinn has its share of modern structures - the tall buildings of two hotels, **Viru** and **Olympia**; the pretty sea terminal; and the **yachting center** in Pir-ita, which looks very much like a large white ship (the Olympic Regatta was held here in 1980). But Tallinn is above all an old town, which, thanks to the restorers, stands today as a single historic-architectural ensemble.

Old Vyshgorod: You should see old Tallinn on foot, only in this way, as those who live here will tell you, will you absorb its essence. The old town has remained almost totally unchanged over the past 600 years. The castle on **Toompea Hill** was built on the order of the King of Denmark (13th to 14th centuries). The tallest surviving tower of the castle (50 meters/165 feet) is known as **Long Herman**. As you stroll through the streets of medieval **Vyshgorod**, as you take in its atmosphere, marveling at its Gothic churches, peculiar windows, and iron lampposts, you can't shake off the feeling that these streets look too much like stage settings for some fairytale to be real.

Pikk-Yalg ("Long Leg") Street leads down into the Lower Town. Until the 17th century, this rather steep street

Festival of medieval customs in Tallinn.

was the only one connecting the two parts of the city. In those days, you really had to be an expert to get a cart up or down the hill.

Town Hall Square is at the center of the Lower Town. Back in the 12th century there was a market here. The Town Hall excels all similar structures in Northern Europe in both dimensions and architectural accomplishment. It took 30 years to build. The tall 17th century spire carries **Old Toomas (Vaana Toomas)** - the symbol of the city.

The square is framed by a perfect rectangle of old houses, whose ground floors are given over to abundant cafés and shops. As you see, the square is still a significant center of trade today. Locals will tell you (not without pride) that you could buy pharmaceuticals here before America was discovered.

It is plainly impossible not to admire the **Oleviste Church** (late 15th-early 16th centuries) with its 120 meter-high (395-foot) spire, which served for a long time as a beacon for ships. The same goes for the city's most beautiful church,

Niguliste (13th-15th centuries), and the **Theater of Opera and Ballet**, which was built in this century.

A cozy resort on the Baltic: From Tallinn, the way lies 124 km (77 miles) to the south, to **Piarnu**, a cozy resort that doubles as a port and industrial center. These three parts are isolated from each other and those who come to the Baltic shores to rest frequently do not even suspect that there is industry nearby.

The resort of Piarnu is first of all famous for its magnificent sandy beaches (almost 2 km/1.2 miles long) and the wonderful park on the seashore. The profusion of greenery, the quiet, orderly rhythm of the place, comfortable paths for walking or cycling, and the incredibly pure air of the Baltic make Piarnu pleasant at any time of the year.

Turbulent history has wiped clean nearly all traces of ancient culture. It is a miracle that **Punane ("Red") Tower** has survived from the 14th century (it used to be a part of a fortress). There are also a few structures from the 18th century, notably the baroque **Tallinn**

Gates, and two churches, **St. Elizabeth's** and **St.Catherine's** - both are wonderful examples of local baroque architecture.

Estonia's second largest town, **Tartu**, lies in its southeastern part (160 km/100 miles from Tallinn). It is a place of academic fame. The town is the home of one of Europe's oldest universities, founded in 1623 by the Swedes. Tartu is a town of students and takes everything that has to do with the university very seriously. Right in the center of the town, on **Toomemyaga Hill**, there are numerous sculptures and obelisks, erected in honor of professors and graduates of the university.

Parts of the **Domsky Cathedral**, a Gothic wonder, founded in the 13th century, are still there. Its gallery was remodeled to accommodate the university library in the beginning of the 19th century. Today, the library owns several unique manuscripts and first editions, along with letters and autographs of famous scientists and cultural figures. There is also a collection of graphic art.

Viliandi: (62 km/38 miles west of Tartu). In the 13th century, this ancient fort of the Ests was besieged by the Order of the Sword-Bearers. The knights then founded a castle, whose ruins are still there. The castle stood in the middle of a park, which is crisscrossed by deep gorges spanned by bridges. The memories of anyone coming to the town in spring will always evoke the nightingale's song and the scent of bird cherries, shrouding the bottom of the gorges, as well as the glittering moonpath on the dark waters of **Lake Viliandi** near the mysterious ruins of the ancient castle, the silent witness of events long past.

Latvia

Biographers of the Baron of Münchhausen are seldom in agreement. One of the rare occasions when they do see eye to eye is when they say that five of the good baron's 17 years in Russia were spent in Riga, where he served the Czar in the Russian Cuirassiers. He got mar-

Mockery of the Hitler-Stalin pact in Vilnius.

ried in Riga. When he left Russia, he often remembered the beauty of Riga and his wonderful adventures there. Maybe so, maybe not, but the streets of Riga, the capital of Latvia, really do retain memories of the distant past.

Locals call Latvia *zale zeli* - "green land". Oak stands, groves, parks and forests cover almost half of its territory. There are also many lakes - nearly four thousand in total. The breath of the Baltic is felt both in nature and in the everyday life of the people. The feats of the sailors and the fishermen are immortalized in folk songs (*dainas*), tales and various legends.

Even though the total territory of Latvia (64,000 square kilometers or 24,710 square miles) and its population (2.7 million) are greater than those of its northern neighbor, Estonia, Latvia is still minuscule next to the vast expanses of the USSR, with a mere 0.3 percent of the country's territory and approximately 1 percent of its population.

Riga: Its population is 915,000. Skarnia Street is the center of the old town (favored by Münchhausen in his days) with its remnants of the wall that used to surround old Riga (**Vestriga**, as the Latvians call that part of the city). The city's oldest structure - the 13th century **Yura (St. George's) Church** - stands here. Nearby, in Ian Street is **Ian (St. John's) Church**, one of the best examples of medieval Gothic architecture in the city (its stepped facade is something rare in this part of the country).

Ian Street also has **St. Peter's Church** (built in the 13th-early 14th centuries), which is famous for its wooden tower, the tallest in Europe at 120 meters (395 feet). The tower was burned down in 1941 but was rebuilt and now stands again in its former splendor. The spire is tipped by a gold rooster.

Domsky Cathedral is Riga's greatest architectural monument. Construction was started in 1211. Rebuilt many times, it combines many architectural styles today. Fortunately these changes were invariably introduced with great tact. In the 18th century a baroque spire was added. The cathedral owes its reputa-

Left, Estonian shops offer a greater variety of goods than anywhere else in the USSR. **Right**, future currency of Estonia.

tion to the organ, one of the best in the world, built in 1833-1884 by Valker Co. of Württemberg. To this day organ music fills the vaults of the cathedral in the evenings.

Riga's only church with a Gothic spire is the **Yekaba (St. Jacob's)**, built in the 13th century outside the city wall for the ordinary people. The first Latvian school was opened at this church in the 16th century. Needless to say, the building was rebuilt many times; it now combines many styles.

Situated on the banks of the Daugava River not far from the Baltic, Riga enjoys the double advantage of access to the sea and, via the river, to the east. In fact its geographic position shaped both the history and the appearance of the city - Riga started out as a town of merchants and artisans. The merchants left an interesting architectural monument (13th to 15th centuries) in their part of the city.

On the outskirts of the old town are the ancient walls of the **Livonia Knights' castle**. Erected in the 15th century, it was rebuilt on several occasions. There is a museum of art history here today. Just a mere 15 kilometers (9 miles) to the west of Riga, lies the largest resort area in the Soviet Baltic republics - **Jurmala**. Stretching along the Riga Coast for over 30 km (18 miles), Jurmala is a continuous string of small villages. The resort was "discovered", by, of all people, Russian army officers - veterans of the battle at Borodino in 1812 who probably liked the dozens of kilometers of sandy beach and the waters of the Baltic, which in summer, are warmed to 20°C/68°F. But even when the sun does not shine, no one is bored in Jurmala. There is the *Uras perle* (sea pearl), a restaurant which stands out from a multitude of similar establishments owing to the beautiful view of the sea it offers. The village of **Dzintari** attracts lovers of classical and contemporary music with a philharmonic orchestra and a summer theater.

A short distance away from Riga (18 km/11 miles), shrouded from head to toe in the foliage of century-old maples,

Lenin's busts have been removed from many towns because "they have no historical or cultural value."

stands the town of **Salaspils**. The place owes its sad fame to the concentration camp that the Nazis built here during World War II. More than 100,000 people were killed here - from the Soviet Union, Czechoslovakia, Poland, Austria, the Netherlands, Belgium and France. There is a memorial to the victims of terror on the site of the former camp. It is visited by almost everyone who comes to see Riga.

One of the roads out of Riga leads northwest, to the ancient Russian towns of Novgorod and Pskov. In the past it was called the Great Route. Numerous trade caravans followed it in the middle ages and, of course, the proximity of this trade artery led to the rapid growth of many Latvian towns.

One of these towns is the small but breathtakingly beautiful **Sigulda**. The resort town stands on the Gaua River. One of the hills which offers a view of the town is known as Artists' Hill. Many come here to capture on canvas the romantic landscapes for which these parts are famous.

Other tourist attractions include thick mysterious forests, natural sand caves and abundant monuments of ancient architecture. It is known that Sigulda was founded in 1207, when the first stone of the **Turaid Castle** was laid. The main tower of this fortress has been carefully restored.

From Sigulda, the way leads back to the coast, to **Ainazhi** (116 km/72 miles to the north of Riga, on the Estonian border). The place is known for its shipbuilders. The town museum has documents which prove that no less than 50 sailing ships were built here, mainly out of pines, prior to World War I. It was also here that Russia's first merchant marine school was opened in 1864. Anyone, regardless of age or education, could study there free of charge. The school had given the Russian fleet of merchantmen over a thousand navigators and captains by 1915; its graduates carried the school's fame across the equator and the Arctic Ocean.

On the way from Riga to Ainazhi lies **Saulkrasty** (sunny shores), a quiet and picturesque place that attracts holiday-makers from all over the country. They say that Peter the Great traveled along this road more than once on his journeys to and from St. Petersburg. Once, when the Czar was crossing a small river, his carriage broke and damaged the bridge. His entourage was at a loss. But Peter rolled up his sleeves and fixed both the carriage and the bridge in half a day. Since then, the stream has been known as Peterune - Peter's River.

Lithuania

Legend says that Nero, the Roman Emperor, used to send expeditions to the Baltic coast. They were sent to procure "sunstone" - amber. For months Roman slaves wandered in the forested wilderness and, exhausted, greedily peered ahead for signs of the elusive amber coast. That is what Lithuania was called in the old days - "Amber Coast". Amber, the stone that absorbed the mellow light of the soft and gentle Baltic sun, has been a symbol of the land from time immemorial. Lithuanians call it

Estonian girl in national dress.

"gintaras" and treasure it as their national pride.

Lithuania has existed within its current borders since 1940. It is the largest of the Baltic republics (65,000 square kilometers/40,390 square miles) and most populous (around 3.7 million). The Lithuanian coast has wonderful beaches with sand so fine that it could have been sieved, and ports which are never blocked by ice (the main reason why an independent Lithuania would be an irreplaceable loss for the USSR). "Continental" Lithuania may appear less attractive with its dark forests, marshes, lakes, and small rivers with boulder-strewn banks. But that would only be a first - and erroneous - impression.

Lithuanian architects can be proud of such modern creations as the theater of opera and ballet, the palace of sports and the palace of weddings, all of which are in Vilnius, the capital of the republic (582,000 inhabitants). The new buildings do not interfere with the harmony of the old streets; in fact, they add a new dimension to their venerable beauty. This is also true of the new residential areas - Zirmunai, Padsinai and Karolin-sikes. They are probably the best in the entire Soviet Union. Seeing them, you can't help thinking that these projects must have been created in a joyful and festive spirit.

Vilnius: This city became the capital of Lithuania in 1323. In those times the oldest structures - the Gothic cathedrals - were built in the old town, the heart of modern Vilnius. The ruins of the **Upper Castle** on Castle Hill are topped by the **Tower of Gediminas**. A symbol of Vilnius, the tower gets its name from the Grand Prince who moved the capital here from ancient Trakai. One of the squares in the old town also bears his name. It is framed by a bell-tower with a clock and an 18th-century cathedral (now a gallery) on the one side, and the building housing the government of Lithuania on the other.

On holidays, memorable days and, recently, during times of social upheaval, people come to Gediminas Square by the thousand. The square sees rallies, popular festivals, and, when Christmas comes, Lithuania's largest holiday tree.

Many people love to stroll about an unknown city without a predetermined route or a guidebook. They prefer to discover things for themselves, and to decide what is worthy of attention on the basis of their own tastes. Vilnius has a lot to offer such people. You will hardly remain indifferent, for example, to the Gothic **St. Anne's Church** in Tesos Street (it is five centuries old), or the baroque **Peter and Paul Cathedral** in Antakalne Street, with its two thousand sculptures. The buildings of the **V. Kapsukas State University** occupy an entire city block. The university is one of the oldest in Europe (over 400 years old, in fact) and was built in the 16th to 18th centuries.

A mere 20 kilometers (12 miles) separate today's capital of Lithuania from its original capital city - **Trakai**. This ancient residence of Lithuanian princes is situated on a long and narrow peninsula amid three lakes. It was founded in 1241 and is, without doubt, one of the most beautiful corners of the republic. Its main charm is the lofty forbidding castle, which stands on an island, a worthy specimen of medieval architecture.

Trakai is connected to **Kaunas** (85 km/53 miles to the west of Vilnius) by a very good highway. It takes less than an hour to reach the city without which it would be impossible to understand the history, culture and contemporary problems of the land.

Kaunas abounds in cultural and historical monuments. Most date to the 17th-19th centuries. Pretty squares and cozy streets do wonders for the old-town atmosphere. The interiors of many cafés and shops have been reproduced in their original form.

What could be nicer than sitting on a bench in Rotushes Square? There is Lithuania's first classical building, the town hall, whose spire seems to hover over the square. Not far away, there is the huge cathedral. The old houses framing the square are in perfect shape.

The people of Kaunas are proud of the collection of paintings by Mikalous

Churlionis (1875-1911), which are exhibited in the state museum (named after the artist). Many experts call the art of this great Lithuanian genius "musical" because he tried to synthesize music and painting and was as gifted a composer as he was a painter.

There is another museum in Kaunas that must be visited. It doesn't contain outstanding masterpieces, but it produces lots of fun. **The Museum of Devils** has all kinds - clay devils, bronze devils, glass devils, rag devils; sad devils and merry devils, singing devils and dancing devils; devils from Europe, Asia, Africa and America. There is genius and humor in every one of them.

From the port of Kaunas, the road goes up the Nyamanus to the resort town of **Druskininkai**. It is famous for its climate, mineral waters, picturesque forests and therapeutic muds.

Local herbs are also famous for their healing properties. Not many people know that their fragrance can heal, too. The herbs in Druskininkai park have been planted for this very purpose.

Kaliningrad

Kaliningrad does not belong to the Baltic republics, it is a part of the Russian Federation and would be disconnected from the Russian mainland should the Baltic republics secede from the Soviet Union. **Königsberg** (as the city was known until 1946) was founded by the Prussians in 1255. For many centuries it served as a beachhead for countless wars.

Today, the city fathers want Kaliningrad to be a place where East meets West. As a first step, they plan to restore the city cathedral with its **grave of Immanuel Kant** - a project to be financed by the Russian Orthodox Church and the Union of Evangelical Churches of West Germany. After restoration, the building will be used for solemn religious services, conducted and attended by followers of various religions.

As for secular occasions, they will be celebrated in the neighboring cultural center. The center will also house the **Kant Museum**.

The ruins of the cathedral are a reminder of war years in Kaliningrad, the former Königsberg.

THE WESTERN REPUBLICS

It is difficult to think of a time and place where the Biblical commandments of loving your enemy, turning the other cheek, and doing unto others as you would unto yourself have ever been fully adopted as a way of life. If the more fortunate lands failed to observe Biblical law, what is there to say of the peoples of Byelorussia, Ukraine and Moldavia, united (in spite of historical, cultural and even ethnic differences) by something much greater than common territory - by the unprecedented oppression of national self-consciousness and wholesale genocide perpetrated by the Stalin regime and, later, by the Nazis, who killed millions and left the land in ruins. After collectivization swept across the land like the black plague in the 1920s and the early 30s, Moldavia, the Ukraine and Byelorussia were "reunified" with their western territories in 1939-1940 and yet another wave of Stalin's repressions, aimed against virtually all sectors of society.

Add the persistent efforts of party bureaucrats to regulate the language problem (that is, the relationship between Russian, the official language of the USSR, and the national languages) with administrative measures, recall how difficult it has been for national movements and fronts to win official recognition in the last few years, and you'll see why the growth of national self-consciousness in these republics engendered separatism and strife. In fact, Moldavia and Western Ukraine suffer from separatism as much as the Baltic republics, though the situation is less tense in Byelorussia.

Even the first year of *perestroika* brought the land only woes. Chernobyl took its terrible toll on human lives. A full fifth of Byelorussia's arable land was lost. 1,500 square kilometers/580 square miles of Ukrainian territory were contaminated. It is no wonder that the national movements in these republics owe most of their popularity to the ecology-over-economy nature of their pro-

grams. One-shot measures won't work in Byelorussia, the Ukraine or Moldavia, just as they won't work in the rest of the country. It is therefore clear that the success of Gorbachev and his team will largely hinge on how soon the national movements can be made to take the plunge from destabilization to promotion of *perestroika*. Hopefully, every step in this direction will be governed by the feeling of responsibility for the future of this land and its people.

Byelorussia

In 1989, when Soviet television first showed the documentary newsreel of the joint parade of Red Army and Nazi Wehrmacht units, held in September 1939 (soon after the Molotov-Ribbentrop pact was signed), the people of Byelorussia (which lost 2 million lives to the Nazis in World War II), experienced a shock as, indeed, did all Soviet people: the parade was held in the Byelorussian city of Brest! Known as Brest-Litovsk before 1939, the city had been a symbol of heroism for Soviet people - its garrison met the first blows of the Nazi invasion on June 22nd, 1941, and held out against incredible odds for almost a month.

There is a reason why we started our acquaintance with Byelorussia (population 10.2 million) in **Brest**, the city on the Polish border. It is one of the USSR's major railway/autoroute junctions; figuratively speaking, the country's gate into Western Europe. Here (as indeed in all of Byelorussia) many things remind you of the past war. The city's main highlight is the grandiose memorial to the defenders of the Brest Fortress.

The highway from Moscow to Byelorussia (1,054 km/632 miles), most of which passes through Byelorussian territory, is probably the most popular route among the thousands of tourists who flock by car from all over Europe. Let's follow their example. But before we do, a bit of history.

The "free land" of the flaxen haired: "Byelorussia" derives from two words - *Belaya Rus* ("White Russia"). Historians still argue about where this land, which resembles a heart on the map, got its name. Some are inclined to link the name with the blond hair or the snow-white flaxen clothes of the Byelorussians. It would seem that those who associate the epiteth "white" with notions of "freedom" and "independence" are closer to the truth, because the part of Western Rus which did not fall to the Mongols in the 13th century could well have been called "white" to distinguish it from the enslaved - "black" - lands further to the east.

As a sovereign Soviet republic, Byelorussia dates to January 1, 1919 (it had not been recognized as a nation under the czars). However, Western Byelorussia, Brest included, was lost to Poland in 1921 and reclaimed by the Soviet Union only in 1939.

And now, let us get on with the trip along the Brest-Moscow highway. As is easy to see, Byelorussia is a land of forests (30 percent of the territory), and of marshes (20 percent of the territory), as well as of plains and hills. By the way,

there is a unique preserve in the Brest Region: **Belovezhskaya Puscha**. This ancient forest (85,000 hectare in area/ 210,000 acres) has a rich fauna; its fame comes from the herd of buffaloes, a contemporary of the mammoth, which still survives there.

You can't help noticing the ubiquitous monuments, memorials and obelisks in the streets and squares, along the highways and in the forest clearings and rye fields of Byelorussia. People cherish the memory of those who fell in history's most terrible war. People also cherish their customs and traditions, above all, their folklore, their tales, legends and songs. Their ancient art of straw-over-wood inlay is certainly original; in fact, you won't find anything of the kind anywhere else in the Soviet Union.

The language: Although Byelorussians account for 80 percent of the population, although there are radio and TV broadcasts in Byelorussian, the public is alarmed over the plight of the Byelorussian language which, accord-

Rally in Minsk for democratic elections.

276

ing to some experts, is today "on the brink of extinction". On the whole, modern Byelorussian is so close to Russian that Byelorussians easily understand Russians, and vice versa.

Continuing on the way to Moscow, let's make a short stop in **Baranovichi** (208 km/129 miles from Brest) - a relatively young, up-and-coming industrial center. Several highways of national importance (to Vilnius and Rovno) pass through and this has, of course, influenced the way the city looks today.

Another hundred or so kilometers on (62 miles) and we are in **Minsk**, the capital of Byelorussia. Before we go there, however, let's stop at the village of **Vyazynka**, 45 km/28 miles to the west of Minsk, where the classic writer of Byelorussian literature, Yanka Kupala (1882-1942), lived.

The first thing you see as you approach Minsk (population 1.6 million) are the light-colored highrises. And yet Minsk is one of the oldest towns in the country; it is over 900 years old. It was founded on the upper reaches of the

Svisloch River, near the portage (a place where boats were hauled over land) that connected the basins of the Black Sea and the Baltic Sea. The route from "the Varangians to the Greeks" determined the importance of the town and its name too: in the chronicles, it is called Mensk (from the word *menyat* meaning change).

Unlike the towns of ancient Rus, Minsk has no architectural monuments - the city was almost totally destroyed during World War II. The only buildings that remain include several 17th-century structures in Bakunina Street and Ostrovskogo Street, and, of course, the ruins of the 12th-century **Zamchische Cathedral**. Here we are in the oldest part of the town.

The people of Minsk are proud of their city. They usually tell you the legend about the beautiful flower that brings happiness. Try as the forces of evil might, they cannot destroy the magic flower with frost, wind, heat or rain, because after each new trial, it blossoms even more prettily than be-

Sports complex in Byelorussia.

fore. As you have probably surmised, it is Minsk they are talking about.

Roughly 100 km (62 miles) of highway divides Minsk from **Borisov**, the ancient town on the Berezina River (tributary of the Dnieper). Like Minsk, it has had its share of suffering in the many centuries of its history. In November 1812, the approaches to the town became the site of the final defeat of Napoleon's hapless invasion of Russia. Today, Borisov is known for its tapestries and musical instruments.

A little more than 100 km (62 miles) away, there's **Orsha**, another old town. It is the center of the Vitebsk Region. Here, on the banks of the Dnieper, the Moscow-Brest highway crosses the Leningrad-Kiev-Odessa route. If you haven't yet tried the Byelorussians' favorite dish, *dranniki* (grated potatoes fried in vegetable oil and served with sour cream), do it here, because you are leaving Byelorussia and crossing into the Smolensk region of Russia. This region has 14 towns, but you'll only pass four on your way, including **Smolensk** (384 km/230 miles from Moscow) and **Vyazma** (13th century). There, be sure to see the **Church of Odigitrya Smolenskaya** and the **Trinity Cathedral** (16th century). You'll also see **Gagarin**, (Gzhatsk before 1968), the birthplace of Yury Gagarin (1934-1968), the first man in space.

You have already read about Smolensk itself in another chapter, so let us move on to Moscow. We shall stop, of course, at the **Borodino Museum** near the field of Borodino: it was here that the two Russian armies robbed Napoleon of any hopes he might have had of capturing Russia in August 1812. The place is quite close to **Mozhaisk** (109 km/68 miles from Moscow), the last large town before the capital.

A final word about Byelorussia and Byelorussians. As the traveler is certain to notice, life in the republic (as in the rest of the country, for that matter) is, putting it mildly, not easy.

Many Byelorussians still believe that the changes perestroika brings will transform their land (and other places in our country too, it is hoped) into that legendary flower, whose beauty is impervious to hardships.

Moldavia

Some Moldavians consider themselves close to Italians; others identify with the southern Slavs. Be that as it may, the best way to get to know real Moldavians is at their country festivals; here the eye is dazzled by the women, the colorful ribbons on their headdresses flying as they dance; here the head spins from the swirl of the bright embroidered national costumes and from the always flowing traminer, the Moldavians' home-made wine. Dark wavy hair, eyes reminiscent of ripe black cherries, and sparkling-white teeth make up the portrait of the inhabitant of this land, the traditional home of breadgrowers and winemakers.

Moldavia (population 4.3 million) may not look large on the map but to the eye of the traveler, it offers huge expanses, variety and beauty of landscape. As they carry their waters towards the Black Sea its two rivers, the Dniester and the Prut, seem to tie in all of the republic's natural zones: the green oak groves of the north, the forest-covered Kodry Hills and the endless flat steppes of the south.

The territory of contemporary Moldavia was conquered and turned into a province of Rome by the legions of Emperor Trajan; it was then, in the early 2nd century AD, that the Latin language first came to these lands, later to serve as the basis for the Moldavian tongue.

Moldavia rose to the apex of its economic and cultural development under Gospodar (King) Stephan III (1457-1504). Called Stephan the Great, he defended his realm against would-be conquerors by entering a military-political union with Muscovy.

After his death came troubled times. The country fell under the Turkish yoke for over three centuries. When the Russian troops achieved several victories over the Turks in 1812, the territory between the Dniester and the Prut (then known as Bessarabia) was added to the Soviet Union and remained a part of the

Spontaneous demonstrations are not the first-page news anymore: Rally in Kishinev.

278

empire until 1913.

As a republic, Moldavia dates to 1940, when Bessarabia became part of the USSR (before 1940, the part of Moldavia that belonged to the Soviet Union was included in the Ukraine). Moldavia was thus the last republic to join the Soviet Union.

Kishinev became its capital city (its population 665,000). Compared to most republican capitals located in the European part of the USSR (Tallinn, Riga, Kiev, Moscow), Kishinev is fairly young: it has recently celebrated its quincentenary and is first mentioned in one of Stephan III's deeds, dated 1466. Kishinev entered the 19th century as a large village, even though it was already famous for its artisans and merchants. Yet by the second half of the 19th century, it was already one of the largest towns in the south of Russia.

The most memorable architectural monuments in Kishinev include the late 18th-century **Mazarakiev Church** and **Ryshkanov Church**, both of which are wonderful examples of old Moldavian architecture, which had absorbed the Byzantine style. There are also a few more recent creations, such as the **St. George's Church** (1819) and the **Cathedral Church** (1835). Even though huge new sectors have been added to the city, it retains its old charm thanks to its picturesque hills, the unpredictable turns of its streets, the calming green of its limes and acacias, and the Italian architectural silhouette.

Roughly 25 km/15 miles to the east of Kishinev, on the bank of the Dniester, lies the resort village of **Vadu-lui-Vode**. In its park, which stretches along the right bank, there are sanatoria, a motel, and a camping site. Vadu-lui-Vode is famous for its sandy beaches and its unique whitestone quarries.

Its main highlight, however, is the famous subterranean **Krikovskoye reservoir**, the republic's largest. In the nearby restaurant, you'll be served a very good sparkling wine from the Labyrinth - an underground store 40 kilometers/24 miles long.

Traveling south along the Dniester, you see many cozy, quiet creeks - a haven for fishing buffs. You'll also see many sunny orchards and shady villages before you reach **Bendery**, the pearl of the lower reaches of the Dniester. The town's history is tied in with the history of the fort in its northern environs. No one knows exactly when the fort was founded, but some believe that it was built by Genoans in the 14th century, after they conquered the Slav town that stood on the spot.

In 1538 the town, along with the entire country, fell to the Turks. The Pasha gave the town a new name - *Ben-dere* (I want), which reflected his smugness. The fort itself has an intricate system of bastions which date to different times. The fort has had an eventful military history. Its walls have played host to Stephan the Great and Charles XII, the King of Sweden, who escaped beyond the Dnieper with what remained of his army after his defeat at Poltava (1709).

Before they started erecting the modern blocks of flats, the **Preobrazhenskaya Cathedral** (19th century) was the architectural center of the town. It is said that it was built on the site of an old wooden church founded by Stephan the Great himself. Today Moldavia is one of the republics where the growth of national self-consciousness (triggered by perestroika and democratization) is particularly manifest.

Another language problem: And even though things sometimes get out of hand (for the Moldavians, as all southern peoples, are very emotional), the healthy trends, based on the recognition of the need for the republic to pitch in along with the entire country, are there for all to see. The desire for self-determination is further fueled by the language problem. The Moldavian language is the only "major" Roman-based language in the USSR but was for decades been based on the Cyrillic alphabet (it was transformed to the Latin alphabet only at the end of 1989).

Late in 1989, the Supreme Soviet of Moldavia established Russian as the language to be used for communication among different nationalities; the Moldavian language was declared the official language of the republic. This provoked quite a reaction in some quarters, because there are towns (Tiraspol, for example), where Moldavians account for only 20 percent of the population.

But whatever takes place in Moldavia, its people are invariably hospitable and friendly. They are always ready to dance and to sing and that says quite a lot about a nation's soul.

Ukraine

For many long centuries, ever since it was founded as a fort in the mid-13th century by Prince Daniil of Galicia and named after his son, Lev (Leo), the town of **Lvov** has been a haven of nationalism. The Poles and the Austrians, who controlled the city for six centuries, did their best to suppress the national self-consciousness of the West Ukrainians and to assimilate them. Yet the Ukrainians persevered and came through as a nation. Their national sentiment survived the vicious times of Stalin's terror, when even the statue of Neptune in front of the Town Hall became a victim:

they took away his trident on orders from the "fighters against Ukrainian nationalism". The trident - that symbol of the once proud and prosperous Kievan Rus - and the yellow-blue colors of independence are still with us today: both are used by *Rukh*, the Ukraine's popular pro-perestroika movement.

Today, Rukh has its organizations in all the regions of the republic; it has finally won official recognition (the authorities regard it - and with good reason - as a threat to single-party rule). Rukh originated in Lvov and Kiev. Even before the movement was officially registered, it proved its power when hundreds of thousands of sympathizers formed a human chain along the Lvov-Kiev highway (540 km/325 miles) in January 1990.

Let us take this route ourselves: it is probably the best choice for the tourist traveling from Europe to Moscow (via Poland). Yet let us first tour the city. The town's troubled history has left its mark on the architecture. Lvov is called an architectural museum: the styles range

The epicenter of the Chernobyl disaster, the reactor after meltdown on April 26, 1986.

from Gothic, Renaissance and baroque to Empire and modernist; at times one sees a mixture of all these. Be sure to see **Rynok (Market) Square** and the nearby district. It has quite a few ancient structures, of which the most notable are **St. Nicholas Church** (late 13th century) and the **Armenian Cathedral** (late 14th century). Another church - the 15th-century **Latin Cathedral** - is the best Gothic creation in Lvov. Then, of course, there's **Lychakovskoye Cemetery** - a pantheon to Ukrainian writers and public dignitaries.

Approximately 200 km/120 miles away, there's another ancient Ukrainian town: **Rovno**. They say that the town got its name from the flatlands on which it was founded seven centuries ago (*rovny* means even or flat). The place was visited by the great Frenchman, Honoré de Balzac.

The next regional center on our way to Kiev is **Zhitomir** (187 km/112 miles from Povno). Before getting there, make a stop in the town of **Novograd Volynsky** (87 km/52 miles from Zhito-

mir), the birthplace of the Ukrainian poetess, Lesya Ukrainka (1871-1913).

Zhitomir, one of the oldest cities in the Ukraine, is situated on the rocky banks of the Teteriv River. The scenic banks and numerous mineral-water springs attract tourists from all over the USSR. It was here that Yaroslav Dombrovsky (1836-1871) of Paris Commune fame and Sergei Korolev (1906-1966), the father of Russian space exploration, were born.

Kiev is a short two hours away (130 km/78 miles). Anyone who gets to see Kiev once, usually dreams of going back. The way from the capital of the Ukraine to the capital of the USSR (858 km/515 miles) leads through the Chernigov Region, and the Russian regions of Kursk, Orel and Tula. The highway from Orel to Moscow (340 km/205 miles) lies on the way to Simferopol.

On the Dnieper

"You haven't seen the Ukraine if you haven't sailed the Dnieper," Ukrainians

Arkadia Beach, Odessa, Black Sea.

282

say. And this is probably true. The Dnieper is much more than just a transport artery for the republic. It is the history of a nation immortalized in legend and song. In fact, the Dnieper can be called the cradle of Eastern Slav culture. It was on its banks that the first ancient Russian state - Kievan Rus - once stood; since time immemorial, the river has acted as a settling axis for the Eastern Slavs, who called the Dnieper *Slavutich* (Son of Glory).

The Dnieper (2,200 km/1,320 miles) is not as long as the Volga or the Danube. We shall not see its upper part on this itinerary - the 132 km/80 miles of forest-lined banks from the riverhead to Kiev. But we will see its central part (555 km/333 miles from Kiev to Zaporozhye) and the lower reaches (410 km/246 miles from Zaporozhye to the estuary), which are situated in the steppe/forest and the steppe zones.

From Kiev to the estuary: Calm and majestic, the river carries its waters past the ravine-cut banks. The slopes of the **Kanev Hills** are crisscrossed by gullies and landslides. They look like veritable mountains from the river, especially after all the plains of western Russia.

The first stop is in **Kanev** (140 km/87 miles from Kiev). It is one of the oldest towns on the Dnieper. In the 12th century, the chroniclers described it as a sturdy fort on the south border of Kievan Rus. The **St. George's (Assumption) Cathedral**, built here in 1144, survives to this day, along with the ruins of the city wall.

From the deck, there are nice views of **Taras Hill**, on top of which is the grave of Taras Shevchenko (1814-1861), the father of Ukrainian literature. Even though he died in St. Petersburg, friends brought his remains back to the Ukraine.

Heading downstream, the boat passes through the Cherkassy and Poltava Regions. The landscape changes as the river makes its way past the flat lowlands with their meadows and an occasional stand of trees. As we head south, the forests disappear altogether, and the river grows wider and wider: we are

Hydroelectric scheme on the Dnieper.

entering the **Kremenchiug Reservoir**. On its right bank, 60 km/36 miles from Kanev, there is another thousand-year-old town - **Cherkassy**, a large industrial center of the republic.

The next stop will be another large industrial regional center - **Dnepropetrovsk**. There are still 270 km/162 miles to cover and two sluice-gates to negotiate by means of locks: one at the Kremenchiug hydroelectric-power station, and the other at the Dneprodzerzhinsk power station. Its dam helped create the large **Dneprodzerzhinsk Reservoir** which is between two (1.2 miles) and ten km (6 miles) wide. As the landscape changes once more, you can hardly make out the villages on the banks - they are awash in greenery.

Dneprodzerzhinsk is Leonid Brezhnev's home town, where he went to school and started working at an iron-and-steel factory. While he was still alive, a monument was erected here in his honor, and worshiped as an idol by the local party bosses. Brezhnev understandably took a liking to bureaucrats who came from Dnepropetrovsk and Dneprodzerzhinsk, because he had worked there for a long time in various party posts. Consequently, the two towns presented the country - or, more accurately, the apparatus of the CPSU Central Committee and the Council of Ministers - with many of their sons. The people promptly dubbed them the "Dnepropetrovsk Mafia". Founded in 1776 and known as Yekaterinoslav (in honor of Catherine II) until 1920, today's Dnepropetrovsk is a major national industrial center.

Another 80 km/48 miles downstream, you will see, even on a sunny day, a red shimmering cloud and smoke rising from the stacks of numerous metallurgical enterprises, which stand smack in the middle of residential areas. The place is called **Zaporozhye**, a major center of ferrous and non-ferrous metallurgy. Lovers of black humor will appreciate the local joke, which claims that Zaporozhye is a city of eternally young and eternally laughing people. They are young because no one gets to

Left, Orthodox cross dating to the 16th century. Right, icon of St. Nicholas, 13th century.

live to old age. And laughing? Well, when the wind blows from the north, those in the south can't breathe and those in the north laugh at them; and when the wind changes, it's the other way around. Unfortunately, this joke is too close to the truth for comfort. The ecological situation is alarming.

Perestroika gave rise to numerous green movements, which demanded the closure of these factories. But economic interests and central ministries are still too strong for the greens. So, if the wind is from the west or the southwest, you'll get a good view of **DneproGES**, one of Europe's largest hydroelectric power stations. Another 12-15 minutes and the ship will pass the station's single, 300-meter (984 feet) long lock, descend to the water level on the other side (50 meters/164 feet), and continue on its way down the lower Dnieper. Looking back, you can see the majestic panorama of the power station. In the old days, shipping between Dnepropetrovsk and Zaporozhye was blocked by rapids (*porog* means rapid, *za* means behind,

hence the name "Zaporozhye"). The dam elevated the water level and made the river navigable. Cheap electric power from DneproGES, and the proximity of Donetsk coal, Krivoi Rog iron ore (120 km/72 miles away) and Nikopol manganese (70 km/42 miles) determined the destiny of this town. In addition, the Soviet Union's largest nuclear-power station was built downriver.

The best view of the town and the dam can be had from the **island of Khortitsa**, which is without equal on the river in terms of size, beauty and historical significance. In the 15th and the 16th centuries, Khortitsa, along with other islands behind the rapids, became a refuge for runaway serfs. Gradually, the free settlers evolved into some of the greatest military men known to history - the Cossacks. For a long time, they had their headquarters on Khortitsa. The island was turned into a preserve in the years of Soviet power. There is a **Cossack museum** here today.

Several kilometers away, is the last reservoir on the Dnieper (Kakhovskoye

Ukrainian peasant woman in Odessa.

Sea), which stretches for 240 km/144 miles and ends at the dam of the Kakhovskaya power station. It is up to 23 km/14 miles wide and its waters wash the lands of three regions - Dnepropetrovsk, Zaporozhye and Kherson - as well as irrigating hundreds of thousands of hectares of Tavria land. Making a detour you can visit the young (late 19th century) industrial city of **Donetsk**.

Contemporary Donetsk reflects, in a nutshell, the industrial structure of the region: coal-mining, iron-and-steel, machine-building and chemicals. Naturally, it also has all the problems that go with such super-industrialization. There are some 40 mines within the city limits. Some of them are over 100 years old; in others, coal is mined at a depth of 1,000 meters (3,280 feet). And where there are mines, there are the refuse heaps - hideous mounds that can be seen from far away. The miners here were among the first in the USSR to go on strike (summer of 1989). The ad hoc government committee did more to smother than to resolve the conflict, which resulted from the miner's socio-economic plight.

But back to the Dnieper. After we pass the lock at the power station, we dock in **Novaya Kakhovka**. The town was founded by the builders of the power station, who established the happy tradition of planting fruit trees, lilacs and roses around each new house. The place is also famous for its juicy watermelons, cherries and grapes.

Askania-Nova lies to the southeast. This is one of the Ukraine's marvels, a unique corner of the steppe, the place to go to see bisons, llamas, buffaloes, zebras, antelopes and ostriches. There are only 80 km/50 miles to go before the boat reaches the estuary of the Dnieper, of which 60 km/37 miles separate us from the first seaport, **Kherson**. The town derives its name from the ancient Greek colony of Hersones (near Sebastopol); for a long time, it was a Russian naval base and shipyard.

Kherson still retains the flavor of a shipbuilders' town. It produces ocean-going dry-cargo ships, tankers and mo-tor vessels. Many think that the local beaches are the best in the Ukraine. The Dnieper estuary is more of a coastal lake than a proper sea, which is still 96 km/58 miles away. The Dnieper divides into three channels here, allowing us to admire the marshlands in-between.

It is only once you pass **Ochakov** (the former stronghold of the Turks on the Black Sea that was conquered for Russia by Count Alexander Suvorov in 1788) that you will find yourself on the open sea.

Another 60 km/36 miles on and you enter the port of a city that we have no right to pass by: if you love Russian music and if you've been to a Russian restaurant in Europe or America, half of the songs you've heard there must have been dedicated to this town - **Odessa**. The city gets its name from Odessos, the Greek settlement that disappeared in the 4th century B.C. It was Suvorov who picked the site for modern Odessa at the end of the 18th century. The town boomed in the times of the Duke de Richelieu, who fled to Russia from the French Revolution and was appointed Governor General of the region (1805-1814). The Duke turned the town into a zone of free trade and enterprise, which gave (as the locals who honored the Duke with a monument in downtown Odessa believe) a powerful boost to economic and cultural growth and ensured that the traditional unbending spirit and sparkling humor would pass on from generation to generation of local inhabitants.

Forming an amphitheater along the sea bay, Odessa was built in accordance with a master plan - hence the no-nonsense layout of its central part. Be sure to visit the **Theater of Opera and Ballet** (founded in 1809), where Fyodor Shaliapin and Pyotr Tchaikovsky gave performances. Take a stroll along the **Morskoi (Sea) Boulevard**, where young Pushkin used to wander in the shade of the pines (he was exiled to Odessa in 1823 and wrote some of his best poetry here).

And if, God forbid, you don't like Odessa - don't say so out loud: your views are not likely to be understood. **National festival in Ukraine.**

TO THE CRIMEA

When a prominent Moscow journalist called it "death road", he wasn't kidding. Or maybe only a little bit. The fact is that the **Simferopol Highway**, which links Moscow and the administrative center of the Crimea, Simferopol, can hardly be called the auto-tourist's dream: on his way to Yalta, the hapless journalist was driven to exasperation by potholes, near-total absence of gas, and, to top things off, by a memorable encounter with racketeers. The Simferopol Highway leads to the wonders of the Crimea, its Black Sea coast, the breathtaking scenery and such roadside attractions as Yasnaya Polyana and Spasskoye Lutovinovo. But before we reach it there's almost 1,400 kilometers (870 miles) to cover. The road crosses two Soviet republics: the Russian Federation and the Ukraine. The Ukrainian part, self-proclaimed experts say, is the better of the two.

Traditionally, the first stopover is just after the town of **Tula**. There, on the 195th kilometer of the highway, a right turn will lead you to the museum-estate of the great Russian writer Leo Tolstoy (1828-1910), **Yasnaya Polyana**. Here the writer was born; here he lived for more than six decades; here, he wrote *War and Peace* and *Anna Karenina*. The museum displays authentic furniture and Tolstoy's personal belongings. His grave is in the nearby forest.

Another hundred or so kilometers (60 miles) along the highway, there lies the former country seat of the Turgenevs. It was here, in **Spasskoye**, that another classic Russian author, Ivan Turgenev (1818-1883), spent his childhood and several adult years. The next stopover will be the nightstop at a motel to the south of **Orel** (361 km/224 miles). Still heading south, one has to pass **Kursk** (521km/323 miles), whose main attraction is the **Sergiyevo-Kazanssky Cathedral** (18th century), built by the famed Rastrelli. Cutting across the Belgorod region, you enter the Ukraine after a 700-kilometer (435-mile) long trip.

Slowly, the landscape begins to change as Russian hills and tree-covered plains give way to Ukrainian table-flat steppes. It is warmer here, and fruit orchards are everywhere. It seems that Ukrainians are better off than Russians. At least their homes are sturdier, made of brick, and they have, more often than not, a Russian bath or a garage attached.

The next night should be spent in a motel near **Kharkov** (743 km/461 miles away from Moscow), a major industrial center of the Ukraine. From here the highway leads on to Simferopol. You can also get to the Caucasus, via Rostov-on-Don, from Kharkov.

The major part of the journey is covered when you pass the **Zaporozhye exit** (1,030 km/640 miles), where there is also a fairly good motel a little to the north. Here lies the shallow **Lake Sivash**. We then enter the Crimea via the **Chongar Bridge**.

The Crimea, a joy for the eye: Since there is really not much to see in **Simferopol**, which is still off-limits for foreigners, it is best to move directly on to the south coast, and then to the east coast, towards "the Black Sea pearls", as the poets quite truly refer to the local towns.

The Crimean landscape has a contemplative quality. Its steppes, proud peaks and long rocky beaches, with stretches of sand here and there, arouses the desire to take a closer look, to stop and think. The realist thrives on food for the eye; the dreamy, romantic yearns for imagination-stirring isolation. But the Crimea has far more ways of stirring the imagination than its landscapes.

Where the Taurians once lived: The people of Moscow are proud because their town is over eight hundred years old. Yet Moscow is just an upstart next to the Crimea's Feodosia, Kerch or Sudak. They are 25 centuries old. When Moscow-founder Yury Dolgorukiy's ancestors in the fiftieth generation weren't even born yet, the inhabitants of Greek colonies on the Crimean coast had already built the houses and harbors they needed to engage in trade. The Taurians - a primeval race of hunters and fishermen - the ancient Greeks, the enigmatic Alans, the Byzantines, the

Hazars, the Scythians, the Polovtsians, the Genoans, the Turks, the Tartars - the Crimea has seen them all.

Since the times of the Golden Horde (1233), the peninsula was populated by Tartars, who influenced its development and gave names to many local villages and mountain peaks (happily, the names survive to this day).

The fate of the Tartars: The Tartars accounted for the majority of the Crimean population until 1944, when they were forcibly evacuated on Stalin's orders into the internal regions of the country, ostensibly as punishment for their collaboration with the Nazis, who occupied the peninsula in 1941. Untold thousands of innocent people were literally thrown out of their home. The "Father of All Peoples" attached the Crimea to the Russian Federation as an administrative-territorial unit (the lands of the Crimean Khans were proclaimed a part of Russia by Catherine II in 1783); later, in 1954, the Crimea was made part of the Ukraine. Today, the place is mainly populated by Ukrainians and Russians, who feel - why beat about the bush - quite comfortable in the lands developed by the Tartars for centuries.

All this amounts to another illustration of Stalin's "humane" national policy, the root cause of the national strife we have been witnessing in the past few years, when democracy and the freedom to express their will have become a vital factor for the people. The descendants of exiled Tartars demand that the Crimea be returned to them. But what about the Russians and the Ukrainians who have come to love the Crimea as their home in the past few decades? In short, the problem is going to be there for a long time to come.

The south coast: An hour and half's trolley ride along a scenic mountain route over the **Angarsky Pass** (725 meters/2,200 feet above sea level) leads over the main range of the Crimean Mountains, past the small resort town of **Alushta**, past the great brownish bulk of the **Au-dag** ("bear mountain" in Tartar), past the scattered roofs of coastal **Gurzuf** and the colonnaded gates of the

Tartarian school ca. 1888.

292

Nikitsky Botanical Garden, to the end point of the journey, a spot much favored by Soviet and foreign holiday-makers - **Yalta**.

The town of Yalta was founded by the Byzantines in a sheltered place on the coast. It is situated, by the way, on the parallel which is equidistant from the equator and the North Pole. This makes its climate, which resembles the climate of the Mediterranean with its rainy winters and dry, hot summers ideal. Yalta is protected from cold winds by an amphitheater of mountain slopes. This hollow, enclosed on three sides by the mountains, is dominated by sea breezes - ventilation that you will be particularly thankful for in the summertime. All these factors combine to give Yalta its unique microclimate, known far and wide for its healthiness.

Today, the town (its population is over 90,000) is one of the Soviet Union's best resorts. It has nearly 150 sanatoria and pensions where hundreds of thousands of visitors come every year from all around the country.

Come summer, Yalta is invaded by millions of "savages", as those who prefer to arrange their vacations themselves, without the aid of tourist agencies, are known. In the hot season, the beaches, the quays and the parks (not to mention the cafés and restaurants) are packed with young people.

The town has been an attraction for celebrities throughout its history. It was visited by the geniuses of Russian literature. Alexander Pushkin, who passed the "happiest moments of life", as he put it, in nearby Gurzuf. Maxim Gorky came here several times. But the best-loved of Yalta's famous residents was Anton Chekhov, who came to live here, on the advice of his doctors, in 1898. Today, his house (Kirova Street 112) is the town's most popular museum.

It was near Yalta (on a state dacha in the village of Oreanda) that Leonid Brezhnev liked to pass his vacations. And the newly elected president, Mikhail Gorbachev, comes here, too.

Unfortunately, there aren't many hotels worth the name in Yalta. Foreigners

Worshipping the sun.

as a rule stay at the comfortable **Orianda Hotel** or in the 17-storied **Yalta** on the east side. These hotels have everything to make a stay pleasant. Comfortable suites, well-equipped beaches, seawater swimming pools, saunas, bars and even a good restaurant or two.

Yalta gets crowded during vacation season. The best escape is to visit the peace and quiet of the **Uchan-Su Falls** or the picturesque **Lake Karagol**, lying 7-9 km (4.3-6 miles) to the north.

It takes half-an-hour by boat to reach the **Swallow's Nest**, the symbol of the southern coast. This mini-castle was built on top of the absolutely vertical **Ai-Tudor Rock** in 1912 by the well-known architect A. Sherwood.

There are traces of antiquity nearby in the ruins of Harax, a Roman fortress (1st-3rd century A.D.), built on the site of an even older, Taurian fort.

Where the Yalta Conference took place: From the boat, you get a nice view of the **Livadia Palace** the summer residence of Emperor Nicholas II. The palace stands in a huge park, one of the best in

the Crimea. In February 1945 the heads of the three leading Allied countries - the USSR, the USA, and Britain - came here for the Yalta Conference, the results of which have influenced the life of millions of East Europeans during the past decades. Today the Livadia Palace is a museum.

Alupka (16 km/10 miles to the west of Yalta) is a must. This small village behind the Ai-Petri was the site chosen by Prince Mikhail Vorontsov for his palace, a unique architectural creation constructed during the first half of the 19th century. The palace was built by Edward Bloar, the architect who also participated in the construction of London's Buckingham Palace.

Before saying goodbye to the south coast, you should pay a short visit to **Gurzuf**, 16 km (10 miles) to the east of Yalta. This is a very poetic and charming place, much-favored by the great singer, Fyodor Shaliapin (1873-1938) and Konstantin Korovin (1861-1939), the artist who painted his inspired landscapes here.

Aboard the cruise ship Taras Shevchenko.

The Koktebel spirit: As many people will tell you, the east coast of the Crimea is at least as beautiful as the south. They are probably right. It is certainly different. In **Koktebel** there are low sand or grass-covered hills to the left and shrub-covered hills to the right. The village lies on the shores of a small harbor; behind it lies hilly, sun-scorched steppe. It may not be much, but there is something about Eastern Crimea that soothes the eye and makes your dreamy.

These parts have given three great talents to the USSR: painter Ivan Aivazovsky, writer Alexander Grin, and poet Maximilian Voloshin. It was probably thanks to the latter that the village acquired that fleeting, precious quality which is to this day known as the Koktebel spirit.

Here, you find minstrels singing on the quay, violin or flute players giving improvised concerts on a hillside, young artists participating in endless exhibitions - all this is quite commonplace.

But the greatest local wonder is the **Kara-Dag** ("Black Mountain" in Tar-tar). Some call it a mountain system; some a range. The highest peak is only 580 meters (1,800 feet) above sea level.

The Kara-Dag is Europe's oldest extinct volcano. There is, perhaps, no other place on the face of the Earth as diverse and full of expression as this theater of stone. Among the stone sculptures two of nature's creations deserve special attention: the **Devil's Finger** and the **Black Gates**, two rocks which rise right out of the sea.

There is much more to be seen in the Crimea: **Bakhchisarai** ("Palace of Gardens"), the ancient capital of the Crimea Khans, 30 km (18.6 miles) to the west of Simferopol with its magnificent palace; **Sevastopol** with its tragic war history and last, but for some, not least, the **Gurman**, Yalta's cozy cooperative restaurant (on the quay near the Sea Terminal).

Anyone who sees the Crimea for the first time is certain to cherish its memories forever, as we cherish the memory of our first love, longing to return to it again and again.

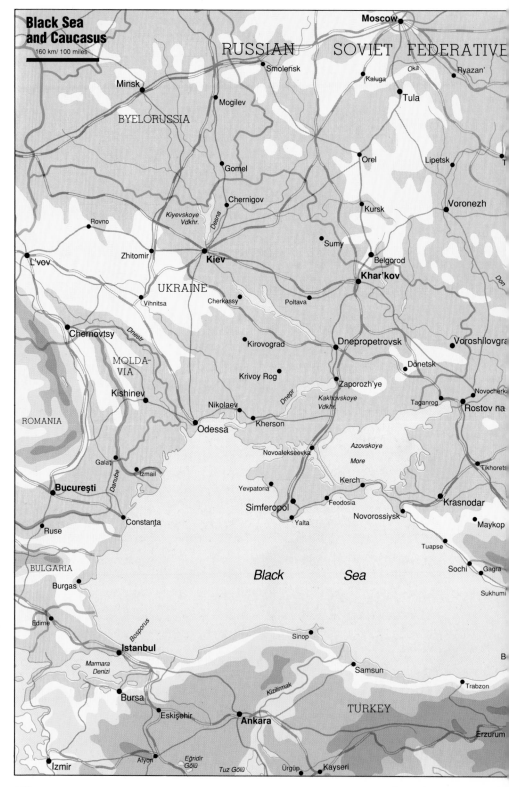

Black Sea and Caucasus

160 km/ 100 miles

RUSSIAN   SOVIET FEDERATIVE

Moscow

Smolensk
Kaluga   Oka   Ryazan'
Minsk   Tula
Mogilev

BYELORUSSIA

Orel   Lipetsk   T
Gomel

Chernigov   Kursk   Voronezh
Kiyevskoye
Vdkhr.

Rovno
Sumy
L'vov   Zhitomir   KIEV   Belgorod

Don

UKRAINE   Khar'kov

Vihnitsa   Cherkassy   Poltava

Chernovtsy   Kirovograd   Dnepropetrovsk   Voroshilovgra

Dnestr

MOLDA-   Krivoy Rog   Donetsk
VIA
Kishinev   Nikolaev   Dnepr   Zaporozh'ye   Novocherka
Kakhovskoye
Vdkhr.   Taganrog   Rostov na
ROMANIA   Odessa   Kherson

Azovskoye   Tikhorets
Novoalekseevka   More
Galati   Yevpatoria   Kerch
Izmail   Krasnodar
BUCUREŞTI   Simferopol   Feodosia
Novorossiysk   Maykop
Ruse   Constanţa   Yalta
Tuapse
BULGARIA   Sochi   Gagra
Burgas
Black   Sea   Sukhumi
Edirne
Bosporus   Sinop
Istanbul
Marmara   Samsun
Denizi
Bursa   Trabzon
Kizilirmak
Eskişehir   TURKEY
Ankara
Erzurum
Eğridir
İzmir   Afyon   Gölü   Tuz Gölü   Ürgüp   Kayseri

298

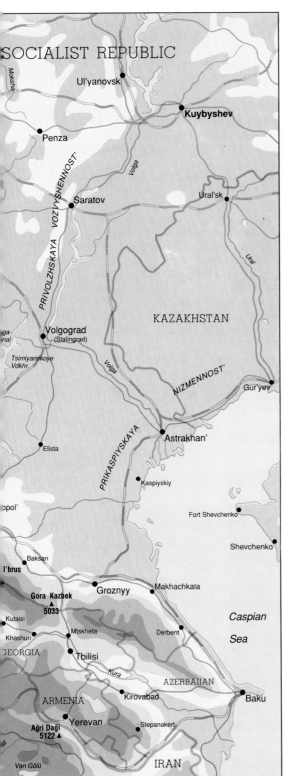

THE CAUCASUS

There are not many places which we could describe as having been specially created for love, esthetic pleasure and relaxation, where nature displays harmony, endless diversity and rare beauty. The Caucasus is one such blissful corner of the earth, a region of fresh mountain air, of a warm and gentle sea basking in the bright southern sun.

The Caucasus is, of course, first and foremost a mountain region. From time immemorial, the majestic Caucasian peaks (higher than those of the Swiss Alps), the blue, wooded gorges and valleys in bloom have lured both poets and travelers.

To the north lies the 1,500 kilometer-stretch (930 miles) of the Great Caucasian mountain range, and to the west and east are two seas, the Black Sea and the Caspian Sea, located as if they'd embraced the three Caucasian republics - Georgia, Armenia and Azerbaijan.

A rare people: Each of these countries has a history of its own. Nevertheless, Georgians, Armenians and Azerbaijanians alike have preserved (and the inimitable Caucasus is probably to "blame" for this) what has become a rare ability: to love profound and take exceptional joy in life.

Visitors are all but taken aback by how tenderly and attentively the locals treat their old folk and their children, how loyal they remain to their homeland and how tirelessly they drink their delicious wines amidst agreeable company. It is no coincidence that many believe the thing worth seeing most of all in the Caucasus is the local inhabitants themselves with their inherent generosity, hospitality and emotionalism.

The Caucasus is a fountain of ancient culture, with innumerable stories and legends to its name which are still alive today. Let us recall, for example, the Argonauts: Thirty-three centuries ago, the Greek ship Argo, captained by Jason, dropped anchor at the shores of Colchis (Kolkhida, West Georgia). Jason took from there the Golden

Fleece and the beautiful woman Medea, the daughter of the Kolkhidian king. Equally well known is the myth of Prometheus whom Zeus chained to one of the Caucasian mountains as a punishment for having stolen fire from the gods and brought it to man. It was here also that Heracles performed some of his labors.

A glorious past and a difficult present: The Caucasus is crammed with monuments of hoary antiquity. Throughout their centuries-old history, the Georgians, Armenians and Azerbaijanians have created remarkable monuments of architecture, frescoes and jewelry, all of which are breathtaking in their originality and delicacy of touch. Some of the towns are carved into the rocks and old churches and fortresses are scattered all over the Caucasus to tell of a glorious past and of the people who inhabited it.

Today the Caucasus, the "land of love" as one poet once called it, is, to put it mildly, not going through the best of times. Moreover, it is considered to be one of the "hot spots" on the country's political map. A bloody wound that is yet to heal, Karabakh has provided the setting for a fratricide conflict between what were once brotherly peoples, the Armenians and the Azerbaijanians.

The terrible earthquake in Armenia took the lives of thousands upon thousands of people. And then there were the tragic events that shook Tbilisi (tragic indeed for all of Georgia), when on the night of the 8th of April, 1989, innocent people were killed through the fault of those in power.

This crisis has stricken literally all aspects of the life of the Caucasian peoples. And yet, there is that characteristic Caucasian faith and patience, that will overcome the difficulties and the day may not be far off when everything will fall again into place and the "land of love" will, as before, greet its visitors with joy and, as so many affirm, with a type of hospitality that is without equal anywhere else.

Approaching the Caucasus: Let us start a tour of the Caucasus, be it at the wheel of a car or seated in a coach. First,

Preceding pages, ancient caves at Gori. Below, Mtskheta, the former capital of Georgia.

however, we will have a look at the region bordering Georgia, the region of **Krasnodar Territory**, for it is precisely from here that one of the most interesting car journeys begins - along the Great Caucasus Ring Road.

From Moscow, you have to journey along the "road of death", the Simferopol highway, to Kharkov, then almost 650km/400 miles to the south (via Rostov-on-Don) where the motorway reaches Krasnodar, the industrial and administrative center of the Krasnodar Territory. We will not linger here. To be honest, it's not really worth it. Instead, we'll press on southwards to the shores of the Black Sea. After a couple hours' driving we find ourselves in **Novorossiisk**, the major center of the Soviet Union's cement industry and a Black Sea port. During World War II, Novorossiisk became the site of bitter fighting. This, incidentally, was the case everywhere, in virtually every Russian town and village reached by the Nazis. However, unlike many other cities, Novorossiisk was awarded in 1971, at

the behest of Brezhnev, the prestigious title of "Hero city", while the site of the Soviet landing on Malaya Zemlya - a part of the Miskhako peninsular not far from Novorossiisk - was named "the greatest of battles". And all because in the autumn of 1943 one colonel Leonid Brezhnev fought at Malaya Zemlya, who, decades later rose to the rank of marshal and then became General Secretary of the Communist Part of the Soviet Union.

A little to the side of Novorossiisk lies the town of **Abrau-Dyurso**, famed in many countries for its fine wines and champagne. Tourists who come to Abrau-Dyurso are always happy to visit the local vintage museum and to sample its produce.

Thirty-four kilometers (21 miles) to the south of Novorossiisk, located on the bank of a convenient bay, stands the cozy spa **Gelendzhik** to which every year up to 1.5 million people come in order to relax and to receive treatment. Along the bay of Gelendzhik people have settled since early times. The silent

Wedding in the mountains.

witnesses of the distant past are the enormous ancestral tombs - *dolmens*, thrown up three or four thousand years ago during the bronze age.

Ever since the 15th century, the ancient settlement site has been referred to by the name *Gelendzhik*, which, in translation from the Turkish, means "little bride". Beautiful slave girls were once taken from here to Turkey, Egypt and Arabia. Another, less dramatic, interpretation of the word "Gelendzhik" translates from the Circassian as "white bride", implying the whiteness of the gardens in bloom.

Continuing our journey along the Black Sea we pass by another health resort - **Tuapse**, some 160 km/100 miles from Novorossiisk, and move onwards to Sochi. Be sure not to miss out a visit to the Honey Caves in Bee Mountain on the outskirts of Tuapse. Perhaps in the whole world there is no such wonder of nature as this: in each of the three caves there is real bee's honey to be found trickling from the cracks in the wall. Millions of wild bees work at this self-styled "factory". Anyone who has tried the honey from these caves considers it to be one of the finest ever tasted.

An ancient spa: It's not long now, only 20 km/12 miles or so, to Sochi, when the traveler making his way along the road is greeted by a modern building accommodating a large tourist complex. This is **Dagomys**. It is here that most foreign visitors stay when they arrive in Sochi. The complex is reckoned to be able to accommodate 2,500 guests. Looking around, it is easy to spot that comfort has been combined with the beauty of the natural surroundings. The excellently equipped beach, comfortable hotel rooms, swimming pool, a cinema and concert hall, several restaurants and bars - everything is right at hand. It's no coincidence that the cream of Moscow and Leningrad elite try hard to secure a place in Dagomys. Vacationing here is a matter of prestige.

By the way, all the best land in Dagomys originally belonged to the czar's family and, except the luxurious Romanov Palace, there was never anything of any note here. In Soviet times, the Dagomys has been deprived of that, since a fruit farm has been created on the "base" of the czar's estate.

After half an hour's drive from Dagomys, the motorway brings us to Sochi. The city (population 350,000) is one of the best, if not the best health resort in the Soviet Union. However, Sochi, or to be more exact **Greater Sochi**, is an all-Union health resort uniting all the holiday resorts that extend along the Black Sea coast, 145 km/90 miles from the settlement of Magri, (some 12 km/7.5 miles from Tuapse) to the Psou River - the border with Krasnodar Territory and the Georgian SSR. Every year nearly 4 million people from all corners of the Soviet Union as well as 400 thousand foreign tourists come here for holidays.

The health resort functions all year round. Its "visiting card" is hydrogen sulfide mineral waters which have been given the name *Matsesta* waters (in the Andigean language it means fiery water). Their soothing effect on the human organism has already been known by the Romans and the Greeks. Matsesta provides a cure for those suffering from heart disease, troublesome organs and joints, weak metabolism and various other ailments.

But Sochi is naturally more than just Matsesta. It is an ever continuing park of evergreen vegetation which covers up to 82 percent of the city. It has a wonderful subtropical climate.

The mountains around Sochi form an amphitheater that shields the city from the cold winds. When winter reigns in the more northern Caucasian mountains, roses are blooming in Sochi. What may be better for the "peace of the soul" than roses of all colors and a gentle sea.

Good hotels such as "Zhemchuzhina" and "Kameliya" cater to foreign tourists. The town has numerous pleasant cooperative cafés and restaurants. However, to tell the truth, the number of hotels and restaurants is clearly not enough. The demand exceeds the supply. This is something understood by the local authorities who are striving to

This was a fortress once upon a time.

attract foreign firms and capital for the building of new hotels.

One thing not to be missed on any sightseeing tour of Sochi are the city's botanical gardens which boast of over 1,600 species of trees from all over the world, the **Agura falls** and the majestic mountain of **Bolshoi Akhun** with its view of towers and restaurant. The gardens are, as they say, the special local dish on Sochi's tourist menu.

Leaving Sochi, we pass through the small spa towns of **Khosta** with a unique boxwood forest that has been preserved since the Tertiary period and continue to **Adler** where the main airport of Greater Sochi is located. Shortly before reaching Adler, approximately 70 km/44 miles from the center of Sochi at a height of 550-600 meters (1,600-2,000 feet) above sea level there is a town which is unique for its mountain climatic conditions - **Krasnaya Polyana**. It is not without reason that the citizens of Sochi connect the future of their resort with its name. After all, Sochi has been put forward as a candidate to host the XVIII Winter Olympics in 1998. The idea of holding such an event on the shores of a warm sea might seem unusual. However, Sochi, or to be more exact, Krasnaya Polyana, is able to provide unique possibility for the games: the depth of the snow here is usually between 1.5 and 2 meters (5 to 6.5 feet) and stays this way for seven months of the year. It is planned that all skiing events will be held there in Krasnaya Polyana.

The Olympics would breathe new life into Sochi - new hotels and other modern facilities will have to be built. In short there is every reason to hope that "good days" lie ahead for Sochi.

Georgia

Leaving the Greater Sochi region behind us, we enter the territory of Georgia, or, more precisely, the **Abkhazian Autonomous Republic**, which forms a part of Georgia. The sea is still the same, but everything else surely is different.

A land of plenty: In Georgia (population 5.4 million) we find tea, citrus fruits, tobacco and grapes. Georgian grapes, wines and brandies are a welcome addition to every table in the USSR. Extremely popular at home, they are also in demand all over the world. The roots of the vine are the roots of Georgia itself. Vinegrowing is one of the most ancient of industries which, for ages, has exerted its influence on all aspects of the people's life. For numerous generations of Georgian wine merchants, the flowering vine has become a symbol of peace and happiness. Whenever an enemy invaded Georgia in the past, his first action was to cut down and burn the vineyards. Until this day Kakhetian peasants (Kakhetia is a historical district in East Georgia) continue to wear a black hat handed down to them by forebears, who, when coming out to the vineyards to work, equipped with tools but also with arms, donned this hat which served as a cap comforter.

In the country of the soul: The spiritual wealth of Georgia harmoniously combines ancient and modern traditions. There is *The Knight in the Panther's*

Left, confiscated arms after fighting between Abkhazians and Georgians. **Right,** there is no scarcity of beautiful girls.

Skin, the artistic creation of the great Shota Rustaveli (12th century), and the works of Niko Pirosmany (1862-1918), who at the turn of the century painted unsophisticated signboards which today are heralded as masterpieces. There is Koba Guruli, an outstanding master of modern chasing. There is golden enamel portioning and Georgian cinematography that is intently penetrating into the inner world of man.

Yet another characteristic feature of Georgia is its magnificent toasts. The *Tamada* - meaning in Georgian the person leading the festivities is a phenomenon which today is not only confined to the Soviet Union. The Tamada holds forth: "Let the steps leading to your home which are carved from the hardest of stone be worn away in a year by the tread of guests who come to enrapture your heart." Such is the land of the Georgians.

Our journey around it will begin from Abkhazia. The indigenous population of the republic, the Abkhazians, long ago gave their land the poetic name of "*Apsni*", which means "the country of the soul". Today people refer to Abkhazia also as "the country of long life". There are more people here who are over the hundred mark than anywhere else in the world.

They say that travelers in ancient times used to call the Black Sea "*Pontus Euxinus*" - "the hospitable sea". You will convince yourself of just how right they were when you visit **Gagra** (67 km/41 miles from Sochi), a wonderfully cozy health resort spread out along the shore of mirror-like bay. The ridge that shields Gagra from cold winds also opens it to the warmth of the sea.

With an average annual temperature of 15.5°C/60°F Gagra is the warmest spot in the European part of the USSR.

Our next step is in **Pitsunda** (19km/12 miles from Gagra), a picturesque resort, famous for its pine grove which has one of the best beaches on the Black Sea coast. Today they call Pitsunda the "people's resort", the origin of it's name, however, derives from the Greek word *pinthus* meaning pine.

It was from here, that Christianity spread throughout the Caucasus. It's 11th-century church is famous for its remarkable acoustics. A few voices are able to create the same impression as that of a full choir. The church also possesses one of the best organs in the whole of Europe.

Whilst traveling in Abkhazia, it would be unforgivable not to pay a visit to **Lake Ritsa** situated high in the mountains, 40 km/25 miles from Pitsunda, or to omit the Anacopia Cave at **Novy Afon**. A truly magical world opens up for all who come to see these wonders of nature. Traditional Abkhazian *shashliks* will bring everyone back from the world of wonder and beauty to the sinful earth, or to be more exact back to the astonishingly generous world of the Abkhazian people. At the Eshera Restaurant, eight kilometers (5 miles) from Novy Afon, national Abkhasian food is served in the traditional way.

A land where poets settle: The final stop on our tour of the Caucasian Black Sea coast will be **Sukhumi**, the capital of

Balancing acts are part of boys' education in the Caucasus.

Abkhazia, 163 km/101 miles from Sochi. The city lies on the latitude of Nice. This, however is not the only reason it is called the "Georgian Riviera". In Sukhumi, as the poet once said, you can forget about everything: its sweet smelling air and velvet sea, what else do you need for poetry.

Somewhat unusual surprises await visitors to Sukhumi. Among these there is the USSR's sole monkey nursery and of course the choir composed of men who average 100 years of age. Listening to these singing pensioners, it is difficult to believe that their ages range from 70 to 120, so infectious is their energy and so youthful their spirit. Five kilometers (3 miles) outside of Sukhumi are mud springs that were already used by Roman soldiers 2,000 years ago.

From here a road leads along the coast to **Batumi**, the capital of the Adzharian Autonomous republic (also a part of the Georgian SSR) close to the Turkish border. A newly opened checkpoint can now be used to cross from one country to the other. In Sukhumi we leave the Black Sea coast to drive through the interior of West Georgia, in the direction of Tbilisi.

Into the heartland of Georgia: The mountain Ukmerioni towers over **Kutaisi** (214 km/132 miles from Sukhumi) like a gigantic look-out post. From the terrace that stands above a 200 meter (650 feet) precipice, the second largest city in Georgia can be clearly seen: three thousand years old and one of the most ancient cities in Europe.

Kutaisi is a major industrial center. However it is not the factories and plants that attract the tourist. There is a cable-car to a beautiful mountain park situated on the hill above the city, and in the old part of the town there are ruins of the Bagrat church (12th century) which was destroyed in 1696. Alongside it there are the ruins of the ancient fortress of Ukmerioni.

We cannot leave out a visit to the 12th-century **Gelat monastery**, about 11 km/7 miles from Kutaisi - a monument to the age when ancient Georgian civilization was at its peak. Take note of the majestic ruins of the Gelat academy which in the early middle ages was the center of Georgian scientific thought.

Fifteen minutes drive northwest of Kutaisi lies the **Sataplia mountain forest nature reserve**, remarkable for the footprints left by dinosaurs and imprinted here on a clay strip of marl. On another 5 km/3 miles to the northwest stands the town of **Tskhaltubo** - the pearl of Georgia's health resorts. Its unique springs of curative waters, used in the treatment of rheumatism and skin diseases, brought fame to Tskhaltubo.

Whenever we find ourselves talking about health resorts we should not forget to mention **Borzhomi** stretched out along the shore of Kura a little to the south of the Great Caucasus Ring Road (approximately one hour's drive from Kutaisi). "This is one of the most lovely places I have ever seen", the great Russian composer Pyotr Tchaikovsky (1840-1893) wrote about Borzhomi. How true his words were. This is indeed a place of astonishing beauty. All the same, it is probably its springs that have brought Borzhomi fame. *Borzhomi* is also the most popular mineral water in the USSR, and all because it possesses not only excellent curative properties but is also a most pleasant drink. Then there is also **Bakuriani** (half an hour's drive from Borzhomi). This town is also a health resort but one located high up in the mountains (1,850 meters/6,000 feet above sea level). The Georgians claim that this resort has no equal where natural beauty and the purity of the air is concerned. Whatever the case may be, many of Moscow's skiers support this claim since Bakuriani is a mecca for Soviet skiing enthusiasts.

Back on the Kutaisi - Tbilisi motorway, 98 km/60 miles from Tbilisi, there is the old town of **Gori** where Stalin was originally from. The house where he was born and where he spent his childhood years is situated not far from the old fortress of **Goristsikka** whose walls gird the huge hill in the center of Gori.

When approaching Tbilisi (20 km/12 miles away), you will be able to spot the **Javri Church** (Church of the Holy Cross) in the distance, which was erected in the years 585-604 on a rocky mountain top at whose foot the Aragvi and Kura Rivers merge. This is **Mtskheta**, the ancient capital of Georgia. At night, when the Javri Church is illuminated from below by spotlights, it creates the impression of being suspended in midair.

Visitors to Mtskheta feel that they have arrived in an open air museum. Everything here is breathing history. In the very center of the town, surrounded by jagged stone walls, stands **Svetitskhoveli Cathedral** (11th-century). Not far from it is another outstanding 11th-century building, the Samtavro Church.

Inside the church are the tombs of Mirian, the First Christian king of Georgia, and his wife Nana.

One of the oldest cities in the world: From Mtskheta it's not far to the capital of Georgia, **Tbilisi** (population 1.7 million). Dozens of books have been written about this city, about its history and architecture, about the **fortress of Narikala**, squeezed in between the cliffs and the River Kura, whose first bastions were erected in the 4th century, about the ancient **Metekhi Church** (8th century) and the even older **Cathedral of Sioni** (7th century), about the opera and ballet theater founded in 1851, about the old streets and palaces, many of which are precious architectural monuments; about the constantly crowded Rustaveli Prospekt; about the poetry of olden days and the bold invasion of modernity. All of this is Tbilisi: a city that celebrated its 1500th anniversary in 1958, though archaeological evidence shows that it was already inhabited back in the Neolithic Age, in the 3rd millennium B.C.

Behind the city rises a hill, **Mtatsminda**, on top of which there is an observation point, a park and a restaurant that serves authentic Georgian food. From here, the view of the city and the Main Caucasian Range is superb.

Like no other city there is something of the theater about Tbilisi. They say things have always been a bit like that: spectacular, mysterious, rough, tender, truthful. Despite, or perhaps, thanks to this, visitors, as a rule, easily get accustomed to the atmosphere of the Georgian capital and leave it as if they were leaving behind something dear to them which they have known for a long time.

Lying ahead of us is a fascinating journey along the Georgian Military Highway which unites the capitals of Georgia and that of the North Ossetian Autonomous Republic, **Ordzhonikidze** (208 km/130 miles). It crosses the Main Caucasus mountain range at the point where the width of this greatest of mountain belts in Europe is at its smallest, only 110 km/68 miles.

Even the Roman historians Pliny and Strabo had something to say about this road. In modern times its indisputable fame lies in its being one of the most beautiful roads not only in the Caucasus but in the entire Soviet Union.

There are truly many wonderful places in Caucasus, the Georgian Military Road which connects many of them seems like the creation of a great artist. It is like watching a film reel where nothing is repeated or superfluous. The road on the approach to **Skalisty Khrebet** is particularly beautiful. Here the Terek valley forms a narrow similar to natural gigantic gates. To the right **Mount Stolovaya** (3,008 meters/9,870 feet) resembles the figure of a sitting giant, to the left is **Mount Araukhokh** (2,392 meters/7,845 feet). In winter the top of Mount Stolovaya is covered by snow and looks like a table covered with a white cloth.

From Ordzhonikidze one of the routes of the Great Caucasus Ring Road leads to the capital of Kabardino-Balkaria - **Nalchik** (115 km/71 miles), and on to the region of **Caucasian Mineral Waters**. Halfway from Nalchik to Pyatigorsk, left of the main highway and immediately behind the town of Baksan another road leads to **Prielbrusiye**, the all-Union center for mountaineering and mountain skiing. Prielbrusiye is a beautiful mountain valley stretching for about 50 km/31 miles. The verdure of a dense pine forest extends right to the glaciers of the **two-headed Elbrus**, the highest point in the Caucasus and in all Europe. The height of its peaks, divided in a wide arch, is **Honorables.**

5,604 meter/18,946 feet and 5,595 meter/18,356 feet respectively.

A few words about the "capitals" of the Caucasian Mineral waters, **Pyatigorsk**, **Yessentuki**, **Kislovodsk** and **Zheleznovodsk** or rather about the region as a whole. Here you can find crystal-clear air filled with the scent of alpine meadows, an extensive complex of mineral springs that help cure numerous illnesses, a mild warm climate and a gentle sun; excellent conditions for effective treatment and relaxation, picturesque landscapes and numerous natural, historical and modern sights.

Armenia

From Tbilisi our journey will now lead us to the capital of the Armenian SSR, Yerevan. But before we set off, a few words about Armenia and its people, the Armenians.

The population of Armenia is 3.3 million. People call the country "sunny Armenia". It is true. It is warm and bright, and yet nature is quite sparse here. Armenia's volcanic past has made it a country of stones. They are everywhere you look.

They are piled up around you in heaps that rise up on the horizon. The houses are made of stones both in cities and villages. For centuries they have been used to build strong and squat churches whose architectural uniqueness is known the world over.

"The stones of the motherland", as they say here without any hint of irony, have conditioned the peculiarities of the national character: stubbornness, industriousness and a strong will. In olden days hard work was the fate of the Armenian, whether he was plowing his field by hand or shaping and laying stones for his house.

Armenia is an ancient country and one of the places where human civilization originally took shape. It is not for nothing that over 4,000 unique examples of architecture are to be found spread across this small land.

The ancient alphabet of the Armenians: In the year 301, Armenia was the first

Armenian fighter on Azerbaijanian border.

310

country in the world to make Christianity its state religion. It has known periods of a powerful state and the flowering of its culture, it has known times when its people were all but threatened with total annihilation. Yet during the years of its most heavy trials, the Armenians' culture, fully reflected in the depth of their consciousness, proved to be a powerful weapon against the threat of assimilation and spiritual enslavement. Way back in 396, the outstanding scholar Mesrop Mashtots created the Armenian written language. This alphabet is so modern that in all its 16 centuries that it existed, it has not had to undergo any changes and serves to this day magnificently the Armenian language and its literature.

The past and present are intertwined in Armenia like nowhere else. The Yerevan of today, though a contemporary of Babylon and Rome, is in fact a young city. It was built totally under Soviet rule and yet at the same time bears features of centuries of Armenian national culture.

Where the family still reigns: The Armenians have one of the lowest divorce rates in the Soviet Union. The strength of the family is based on respect for one's elders, the warmth and depths of family feelings and love for the children. The flavor of Armenian culture is easily discernible not only on the canvases of their world-famous artists, but also in traditional national celebrations with their ubiquitous and noisy merrymaking and their exquisite national dishes, and in their love and knowledge of their history. It is quite typical that in front of the entrance to the Matenedaran, the place in Yerevan where ancient manuscripts are stored, the following words are inscribed: "To know wisdom and learning is to know the dictums of reason." These were the first words which Mesrop Mashtots wrote using the letters from the alphabet that he himself had created.

Setting off from Tbilisi towards Yerevan we pass the Azerbaijanian town of Kazakh (104 km/65 miles from Tbilisi) and after an hour's driving we

After the earthquake at Armenia's Spitak.

approach **Dilizhan**, a small mountain resort located in a forest gorge. Surrounding it are Armenian architectural monuments preserved from the 12th and 13th centuries. Among these is the **Nor-Getik monastery**, today called **Goshavank** in honor of the medieval Armenian scholar and writer Gosha thanks to whose efforts the monastery was originally built. Here we will also mention the **Agartsin monastery**. The most beautiful feature in its complex is the **Cathedral of the Holy Virgin** (in Armenian *Surp Astvatsatsin*).

South of Dilizhan the road rises up into mountains along the steep northern slope of the Pambak mountain range. We enter Seval Pass from where there begins a region that is almost totally deprived of trees. On the other side of the pass is the **Lake Sevan reservoir**, which is the biggest and highest mountain lake in the Soviet Union and also one of the most picturesque. The level of the lake, before it was artificially lowered, was 1,916 meters/6,285 feet above sea level, it occupied 1,416 square meter/15,236 square feet.

Twenty-eight rivers flow into the lake, the largest of which barely extends 50 km/31 miles, while only one river flows out of the lake, the River Razdan.

On the banks of the Sevan you can find traces of the Urartu civilization: cuneiform characters and fortress towns. Lovers of ancient culture will certainly find much of interest in the **Sevan monastery** (9th century).

From Lake Sevan it is only an hour's drive (69 km/43 miles) and we are finally in **Yerevan** (population 1.2 million). Situated approximately at equal distance from two mighty mountains - **the four-peaked Aragats**, the Armenians' "silent mentor of poetic thoughts", and the majestic **two-peaked Ararat**, the symbol of Armenia itself - is the many-sided, constantly changing, romantic city of Yerevan.

The city is extremely beautiful and picturesque. Architectural ensembles and monuments, houses made of multi-colored tufa, numerous boulevards with fountains - it all brings to the city its own special local coloring.

First of all there is the city's monumental building, the **Matenadaran**, the world famous library with some 13,000 Armenian manuscripts on parchment and paper as well as 100,000 ancient documents and a collection of Armenian miniatures. Not to see it is something to which visitors simply have no right. Outside Yerevan is the **Arin-Berd Hill**, with the ruins of the ancient **Urartu Citadel of Erebuni** which dates back to 782 B.C.

It is, however, also essential that you visit the old churches in the city, stroll the quiet streets of the old town, where you can see lamp-posts covered in vines and visit the new districts which are very green and, however strange it may seem, cozy. Lovers of sport will no doubt much appreciate the architecture of the "Razdan" stadium, one of the most beautiful in all the Soviet Union.

Most interestingly, Yerevan has on the map the appearance of a large flower. In its center, like an oval heart, lies the central square from which the city's new areas extend like petals in radical directions, getting wider as they near the outskirts.

No acquaintance with the city would be complete without a visit to a little restaurant along one of the many boulevards where you will have an opportunity to treat yourself to *kufta*. They are extremely delicious, made of meat, adding nuts, herbs, spices and the famous Armenian brandy.

To round off our visit to Armenia, let us visit the outskirts of Yerevan, where there is a genuine architectural monument which was created over the course of many centuries. We will begin with the small village of **Garni**, 28 km/17 miles to the west of Yerevan, a one-time formidable fortress and the summer residence of Armenian kings. Of great interest is a most unique monument of ancient architecture, a heathen temple dating back to not long after the death of Christ.

Twelve kilometers (7.5 miles) from Garni lies the village of **Gerand** where a 12th-13th century monastery is to be found. Its main part is cut into rock. The two cave churches are magnificent. It is **These Armenian eyes are full of wisdom and sorrow.**

312

the only building of its kind in the Soviet Union.

About two kilometers (1.2 miles) to the east of the Armenian capital is the **Echmiadzin Cathedral** (4th-century), the Armenian's first church built by Gregory the Enlightener, the first Patriarch of the country.

Azerbaijan

The Republic (population 7 million) sort of descends from the mountains of the Greater Caucasus to the Caspian Sea. The outlines of this land resemble an artist's palette on which nature put the white of cotton, the green of vineyards, the yellow of sand beaches, and the azure of the sea. The landscape of Azerbaijan resembles a motley and fantastic world. Evergreen pines and subtropics, mountains and plains, forests and steppes - such are the contrasts with which this land was endowed by nature. Azerbaijan is also rich in mineral resources. And not only in oil that brought world fame to Baku. The mineral waters of Isti Su and Badamly as well as naftalan, a unique medicinal oil, are known far outside the Republic.

The cultural palette of the Azerbaijanian people is no less rich in colors. It first of all features music and poetry sparkling like waterfalls in the mountains. And just think of the worth of what was made by Azerbaijanian craftsmen, old houses with carved balconies, the decorative patterns of the mosques, women's sides of the houses with windows locally known as *shebeke* which were made without a single nail or an ounce of glue, just of little wooden knots and pieces of color glass. Azerbaijan's unique jewelry, copper and ceramic items, and garments of silk and wool can be seen in many museums of Europe and America.

A land of fire and oil: Azerbaijan's history is rooted in antiquity. It is one of the oldest countries of the East. The first state known as Manna emerged in those parts already in the late 9th century B.C. Two centuries later another two major states, Media and Atropatene, emerged

Baku is the center of the Soviet oil industry.

on its ruins. Atropatene is one of the oldest names we find in our history books for what is now Azerbaijan.

The Persians pronounced it as "Aderobagadly" while among the Arabs it was known as "Aderbayutan" which means "a land of fires". There is ancient legend to explain the origin of this name. Once upon a time a lightning struck the sun-scorched land of the Apsheron Peninsula when tongues of fire burst out of the land and kept burning day and night.

Let us return from the past to the present and make a short tour of old and always youthful Azerbaijan. Our trip will start in Tbilisi, the capital of the Republic of Georgia. The distance to Baku, the capital of Azerbaijan, is 750 kilometers/465 miles along the route running across the Georgian towns of Gurdzhaani, Telavi and Kvareli.

The first major populated center on Azerbaijanian soil is **Belokana**. You can often see old citadel walls and the ruins of fortifications on hill slopes along the road. As if in contrast with the sad relics of the incessant wars against the Persians, Turks and Mongols, who plundered this extremely rich land, there is a string of hospitable *chaikhanas*, tea-rooms, strewn here and there by the roadside.

A half-an-hour drive takes us to **Zakataly**, a beautiful town with opulent greenery. Its streets are decorated with majestic plane-trees. Broad stone steps lead from the public garden in the downtown area to the ruins of **Shamil's fortress** dating back to the 19th century. In those days the fortress was manned by a garrison whose task was to put down, with brute force, uprisings against the czarist autocracy.

In the environs of the town lies the **Zakataly nature reserve** situated on extremely beautiful mountain slopes. Its area is 253 square kilometers/97 square miles. The reserve is remarkably rich in animal life. This and the unrepeatable beauty of the Zakataly nature reserve make it one of the gems of the Soviet Union.

Where Khans and Shahs once ruled:

Demolished bus after communal strife in Stepanakert.

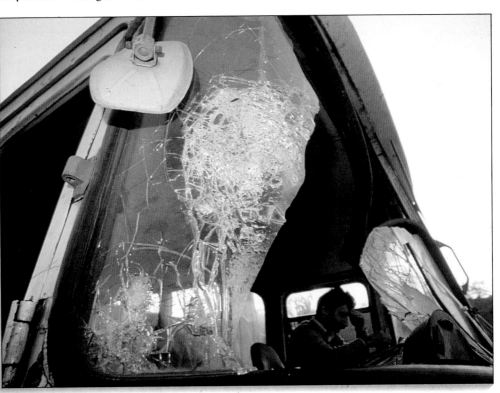

Another 100 kilometers/62 miles along the highway, and we are in **Sheki**, one of the oldest towns in Transcaucasia. Earlier, in the 18th and 19th centuries, it was the capital of the Sheki khanate.

Sheki is very picturesque - thanks to the Caucasus. The town is hemmed in by high mountain ranges on three sides.

Nevertheless, the main tourist attractions are the town's sites of historical and architectural interest. There is the **palace of the Sheki khans** (18th century) with patterned *shebeke* windows and walls decorated with paintings on the subjects of the poems by the great Nizami (1141-1209). Sheki also boasts old caravan-serais, mosques and minarets. The huge monumental caravanserais, the endless rows of traders' and artisans' shops, and large marketplaces made it possible to compare last-century Sheki with medieval Nuremberg also known for its rows of merchants' and craftsmen's shops.

Our next stop is in **Shemakha** (187 kilometer/116 miles from Sheki), the old capital of the Shirvan Shahs, the feudal rulers of Azerbaijan. But on our way to Shemakha, some 40 kilometers/25 miles before reaching the town, let us make a brief stopover at the **Akhedan Pass** (980 meter/3,215 feet above sea level). From here you have a remarkable panoramic view of the beautiful Shirvan valley.

Shemakha is widely known for its fine silk, beautiful rugs, dessert and table wines. Its environs are quite popular with holiday-makers and boast many country-houses.

The relics of antiquity are also quite impressive. This first of all applies to the ruins of **Gulistan**, a large citadel, where the palace of the Shirvan Shahs had been situated until it was destroyed in the 16th century.

The well-preserved **Yeddi Gumbez mausoleum** also dates back to the same century. The name means "Seven Domes". It is the sepulcher of the Shirvan Shahs. When you leave the town, you can see on your right the **Dzhuma mosque**, a masterpiece of the 10th-century architecture restored during the 19th century.

The pearl of the Caspian Sea: Finally, we come to **Baku** (population 1.75 million), one of the particularly beautiful Soviet cities. It is best seen from the sea. When the boat puts some distance between herself and the coast, you will see a beautiful view opening on the bay, the sharp arc of the **Apsheron Peninsula**, and the city which rises in terraces on the hills along the coast. It is enveloped by the green belt of Primorsky (Maritime) Boulevard.

There are tea-rooms standing in the shade of lush green trees. The tea-man is right here, he will at once serve you tea and sugar, cut in small pieces. That's the local tradition. You should not ignore it. A cup of tea, and your tiredness will vanish as if by magic.

The best thing to do in Baku is to go to the medieval Old City or the **Citadel** as the local people call it. In a maze of narrow Oriental streets and blind alleys the eye suddenly catches the majestic cylinder of **Kyz Kalasy**, the Maiden's Tower. It is a unique structure without analogous in architecture. Scholars are still racking their brains trying to guess who put up this tower up on the Caspian Sea coast in the 12th century. But the edifice guards its secret. This 28-meter/92-feet tower has become a symbol of Baku.

There were still quite a few local residents in the Citadel only a short while ago. At present it is a kind of tourist center. The former caravanserais have been turned to cafés where you are treated to *pival*, *kufta*, *piti*, and *dolma*, the amazing works of the Oriental cuisine rich in greens and spices.

The Citadel is the ancient nucleus of Azerbaijan's capital where a series of architectural masterpieces are carefully preserved. Among them are the **Synyk Kala minaret** (11th century) and the **Palace of the Shirvan Shahs** (15th century), to mention only two.

In Baku you can see interesting things at every step, so to speak. Even a week is too short a time to get to know the city more or less well. The atmosphere of this city of sunshine is open-hearted like any Caucasian, but also slightly mysterious and magnificent.

Azerbaijanian women in times of turmoil.

CENTRAL ASIA

"Praised be the living that die not." These words from *The Arabian Nights* could have been said about the peoples of Central Asia and Kazakhstan. This land has seen glory and decadence, victory and defeat, the glitter of wealth and the misery of squalor, the upsurge of creation and the blind rampage of destruction. This land spawned nations which have, throughout the long centuries, sought refuge from history's blows in the haven of ancient tradition. To this day, this land charms the eye with the creations of its ancient architects, the purple lyre of its poets and the mysteries of its philosophy, believed to hold the key to that secret "behind seven seals" which is the Orient.

Kazakhstan

It takes the sun three hours to travel across Kazakhstan. The republic (its population is 16.5 million) occupies a vast territory, from the Volga steppes and the shores of the Caspian Sea to the Aral, Central Asia and, to the south, to China. It has enough territory - 2,717 million square kilometers (1,050 million square miles) - to absorb Britain, France, West Germany, Spain, Finland and Sweden all together.

Kazakhstan is full of contrasts: fertile valleys border on dry and barren, endless steppes; snow-capped peaks and depths that reach to below sea level. The climate is sharply continental, with the difference between the coldest and the hottest day of the year at times reaching 90°C/162°F.

As a nation, the Kazakhs draw root from the Mongols, who conquered these lands in the 13th century and mixed with the various local tribes of nomads.

Even though Kazakhstan is not a territorial part of Central Asia, there has

Preceding pages: Turkmenian Lunar landscape; and Asians believe that a cup of good hot tea will always slake thirst.

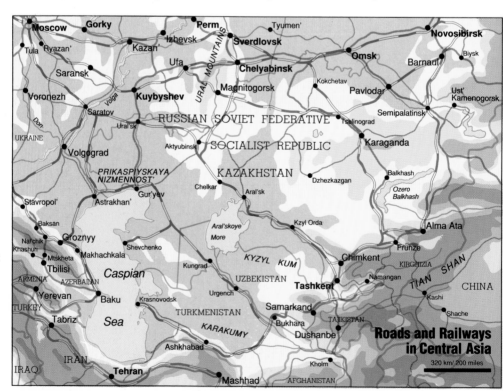

Roads and Railways in Central Asia

320 km/ 200 miles

always been an historical bond between the two. There is many a monument of ancient Asian culture to be found in its territory. Of these, the best known is the **Mausoleum of Hajji Ahmed Jasavi** (1105-1166), a poet and an avid preacher of Islam. The 15th-century mausoleum, decorated with azure tiles, is a sacred place for the Muslims of Central Asia and Kazakhstan.

The mausoleum, by the way, is in Turkestan, 184 km/110 miles to the northwest of Chimkent, the capital of the republic's southern territories. On the way there, be sure to sample local cuisine at one of the traditional *Aul* restaurants, where low Kazakh tables are set in tents called yurts and tended by beautiful girls in national dress. They will serve you *kumis* (mare's milk), a drink that prepares you for the spicy, rich and incredibly delicious food that follows in copious quantities.

Before the October Revolution, the Kazakhs were nomads. Animal husbandry had been their chief occupation. There were no schools, books or newspapers, for the Kazakhs did not have a written language of their own.

Today's Kazakhstan has a fairly well-developed industry and agriculture. It is one of the country's energy centers. Besides raw materials - coal, oil, gas, iron ore and polymetals - in addition Kazakhstan turns out industrial machinery, electronic equipment and radio sets.

Alma-Ata, the capital of Kazakhstan, lies at the foot of the Tien Shan. The city, which now has a population of over a million, was built on the site of a small *aul* (village) known for its apples. Not far away, is the **Medeo**, the world's fastest mountain skating rink - a holiday favorite with the locals.

Land of former Gulags: But let's return to yesterday. In Stalin's time - why let bygones be bygones? - the rich lands of Kazakhstan were studded with Gulag camps. (After the so-called "enemies of the people" were set free, many stayed on and settled in Kazakhstan.) The "Father of All Peoples" also exiled the nations unfortunate enough to have provoked his displeasure to far off Kazakh-

stan: the Volga Germans, the Meskhetian Turks, the Crimea Tartars and the Karachais, the people Stalin proclaimed "traitors to a man" during the war. Well, there was certainly a lot of empty land to send the "traitors" to.

The development of the virgin lands in the late 1950s-early 60s opened an important chapter in the history of Kazakhstan. As millions of hectares of these lands went under the plow, hundreds of thousands of enthusiasts flocked here from all over the country. They believed that the new lands would feed the country. But this was not to be. The project flopped. Yet many of those who came stayed on. That's why the majority of the population is Russian.

Atomic bombs and Cosmonauts: As we have already mentioned, the territory of Kazakhstan is vast. Yet it is sparsely populated. There are places where you won't see a soul for dozens of miles. That was one of the reasons why Kazakhstan was chosen as the location for the first Soviet nuclear test site. Until recently, the whereabouts of this hush-hush installation was kept secret. It was known that the site was near **Semipalatinsk**. Until 1963, surface tests were carried out there.

Then came the treaty prohibiting test explosions on land, sea and underwater, and the test site was moved below the surface of the earth. In 1986 the site fell silent for a full 18 months, but the United States refused to go along with the USSR's moratorium, and the site came back to life.

Now the earth shakes with the force of nuclear blasts once more, and the people who live here shudder as they think of the consequences for their children and for themselves. Foreign experts and journalists are frequent guests here now. Yet the explosions go on, despite the mounting demands for them to stop and for the Semipalatinsk test site to be closed, voiced by the public and the government of the republic.

There is another installation in central Kazakhstan that has been, until recently, off-limits to everyone but the military.

Baikonur: It was from here that the first man-made Earth satellite was launched in 1957. It was from here that the world's first cosmonaut, Yury Gagarin, embarked on his memorable voyage in 1961. Perestroika has now opened Baikonur to all nations out to explore cosmic space.

As former nomads, the Kazakhs are true to their ancient customs. In every home, rural or urban, you'll find special carpets on which you are expected to sit as food is served on the low table. The walls are usually adorned by two-stringed *domras*, the national instrument played by almost everyone here. When someone wishes to praise a man, they call him a *dzhigit* - horseman. Come the holidays, everyone gets into the saddle to take part in the races, which is a popular sport in the republic.

That is what Kazakhstan is like - a land of kind and industrious people, who have seen much grief in their lives. Yet their woes, formidable as they may be (take the Aral tragedy, for example), cannot deprive them of the hope for a better future.

The sea that man destroyed: Lake Aral, the pearl of Kazakhstan, God's gift of water in the deserts, is a full-sized sea that once had an area of 64,500 square kilometers/25,000 square miles. Kazakh lore calls it "Aral the gray-haired" and "Aral the mighty". For centuries, it inspired the desert traveler when it suddenly appeared shining on the horizon - a promise of respite from the heat, of cool shade.

The people lived in harmony with the sea. Its shores were still a haven for the tired traveler and for flocks of southbound birds, just as the Aral itself was a source of food for those who lived on its shores, and a giver of rain to the moisture-hungry lands. Its waves bore ships. But its calm was forever shattered by people greedy for the water of the two great rivers that give it life - the **Amu Darya** and the **Syr Darya**.

The fate of the Aral was planned with deliberate malice. In the early 1950s, there came the "great" canals. It was planned to channel the waters of the Amu Darya and the Syr Darya off to the fields of Kazakhstan, Uzbekistan and

Kazakh women in Alma Ata.

Turkmenia. Moisture-loving cotton had been proclaimed the king of Central Asia's agriculture, and the king required sacrifice upon sacrifice. Its victims included the endless thousands who toiled on the plantations from morning till night, and, of course, the Aral, shrugged off as "useless" and doomed to a dry death. "Competent" scientists showered the public with promises to transform "the lands surrendered by the Aral into new agricultural areas". As the Aral withered away, there was much back-patting, self-congratulatory talk about the "conquered desert", and the "man-made rivers" that were to "change its face forever". No one gave a thought to ecology. As they lauded "the triumph and omnipotence of human thought", people forgot what nature usually holds in store for rushing fools.

From sea to a salt lake: The Aral is getting shallow. The water recedes, exposing dozens of kilometers of sandy bottom. The water level has already dropped by 14 meters (46 feet) and the water volume by 65 percent. An entire industry - fishing - has ceased to exist. Today, only the skeleton-like remnants of ships, half-covered by sand, testify to the past existence of a fairly large fishing fleet. The desert advances. The people go away. The bottom of the Aral did not become the garden of Eden. Changes in the intensity of vaporization depressed what had been a low rainfall level to begin with.

The dry bottom produces salt, a source of vicious salt-dust storms, which at times reach the Volga, a thousand kilometers (620 miles) to the west. Uncontrolled use of mineral fertilizers transformed artificially irrigated lands into a deadly threat to everything - and everyone - around them. The waters of the Amu Darya and the Syr Darya contain toxic chemicals, high concentrations of hazardous heavy-metal components and cancerous substances. Since there is no other source of water, a large part of the local population (some three million people live in the Aral region) has no choice but to consume this deadly mixture. The region is on the brink of

Where there was once a lake there's desert now.

ecological catastrophe.

The Aral's death throes are a hazard to the people who drink the pesticide-poisoned water. Over the past two decades, the death rate has doubled. Over 80 percent of women of child-bearing age are afflicted with anemia. Typhoid is now contracted 30 times, and viral hepatitis 7 times more often.

How to avoid disaster?: The Aral tragedy has a long history. It is now in the center of attention of assorted organizations (official and "informal"), the public at large, and the government.

There is a government plan to save the Aral. The project will cost 37 billion roubles. It is planned to enclose the canals in concrete, thereby preventing the loss of badly-needed water, to install drainage-intercepting systems with outlets directly into the sea, and so on. Work has already started. But can the Aral be saved? Skeptics say that the unique lake will cease to exist by the end of this century, that it will turn into a lifeless desert, which will gradually engulf what many generations have worked so hard for. Such is the result of thoughtless playing with nature, which does not tolerate abuse.

On the other hand, there are also more optimisticaly-minded experts. But they are few in number.

Uzbekistan

The republic is a mecca for tourists, who revel in its artistic beauty and Uzbek hospitality. Your hosts won't allow you to leave the house until you've tried the pilaff, the fragrant melon and the golden peaches and, of course, until you've had some green tea which, drunk from the *piala* (wide-rimmed drinking bowl), quenches the weary traveler's thirst so well.

Uzbekistan is nothing without the peaks of the **Tien Shan**, whose snows feed the rivers which cascade to the valleys below and dress the orchards in the emerald attire of eternal spring. Then, of course, there are the endless deserts and semi-deserts, which occupy

Registan Square and Ulugbek Medrese in Samarkand.

two-thirds of the territory, the azure cupolas of eternal Samarkand, the fountains of Tashkent, the...

We could go on and on with these colorful touches, but they are not nearly enough for the full portrait of this unforgettable and unfortunate land between the steppes of Kazakhstan and the hot sands of Turkmenia. Uzbekistan produces two-thirds of the country's "white gold" (as cotton is called here), wonderful silks, and world-famous karakul firs. Uzbekistan also has a well-developed industry: airplanes, agricultural machinery (exported to many countries), complex radioelectronics. Finally, Uzbekistan is rich in natural gas, nonferrous metals, coal, and even gold.

The republic has a developed scientific base, capable of solving ultra-complex tasks, from earthquake forecasting and hydroturbine design to the development of novel food products. Its culture is ancient. Over the centuries, it gave the world a series of brilliant thinkers, scientists and poets: ai-Horesmi (787-850), Birundi (973-1050), Ulugbek (1394-1449), and Alisher Navoi (1441-1501). To top things off, Uzbekistan is a land where the modern arts, such as poetry, painting and cinematography are reaching new heights; as they do, they give another lease on life to the traditional arts and crafts - embroidery, carpet-making and jewelry.

25 years of totalitarian rule: It was in this way - and only in this way - that Soviet authors wrote about Uzbekistan for many years. Let us get one thing straight: they wrote the truth. The problem is that it wasn't the whole truth. At least half of the truth is missing from their pretty picture of a "rich and booming land" which did not, and indeed could not, have the slightest unsolved problem, and where everyone without exception was happy and well-off. It isn't really surprising, since everything written about Uzbekistan was measured in word and spirit against the prolific writings of Sharaf Rashidov, the "prominent Soviet Uzbek writer" (as they sometimes called him in the press), who served as the head of the republic's

The Gur Emir Mausoleum, Samarkand.

party organization and who, with Brezhnev's blessing, single-handedly ruled it for 25 years.

Rashidov's regime was a system of totalitarian power based on corruption, a mania for "reporting to the top" (or, in plain language, for lying), a flourishing black economy, cronyism and persecution of dissent in all its forms. Naturally, 25 years of this put the republic into dire straits. Raghidov's lop-sided economy emphasized raw material production and gave no thought whatsoever to the needs of the population, nearly half of which now ekes out an existence below the poverty line. Over a million people are unemployed (out of a population of 20 million). The worst part of it is that the living conditions in Uzbekistan are much worse than in the other regions of the country.

"The plan - at any price", Rashidov urged from year to year. Everything was cast aside as the republic waged its battle for "white gold" every fall. Millions of schoolchildren and students were sent to the fields.

Side-by-side with them, there were the old people working with the last shreds of their strength. But the crop varied from year to year. This gave rise to manipulations of their figures (oiled by bribery), which produced widespread moral degradation, and the degeneration of many - very many - honest people, including those with considerable power in their hands.

Yes, the USSR has to thank Uzbekistan for the country's "cotton independence" (which continues to elude the country in all other major agricultural spheres including the production of bread and meat). But at what a price?

Communal strife: Slowly perestroika is changing things for the better. But the past won't go away just like that, a truth confirmed by the tragic events in Fergana Valley in the summer of 1989. Egged on by religious fanatics and local mafiosi, Uzbek extremists started a bloody carnage of Meskhetian Turks, who had lived side-by-side with the Uzbeks in friendship for 45 years. (In November, 1944, 115,000 ethnic Turks

A smiling Uzbek in Tashkent.

were exiled from their native Meskhetia, in south Georgia, to eastern parts of the country, including Uzbekistan, on Stalin's orders). As things got totally out of hand, demands were voiced to banish the Meskhetian Turks (and not only the Turks) from Uzbekistan and to declare an "Islamic state" there. In part, they succeeded: the Turks were evacuated out of the fire and the ashes to Russia.

The tragedy in Fergana, which stemmed from socio-economic, rather than ethnic problems, was an alarming indication that the factions produced in Uzbekistan by the Rashidov regime were not, as the saying goes, dormant, and (predictably) not about to accept perestroika. These people are prepared to do everything to turn the republic around, back to the days of the feudalism and corruption of "the Uzbek model of socialism". Simultaneously, they are trying to divert the Uzbek nation to "Islamic fundamentalism". After all, "the goal justifies the means".

In the years of World War II, millions of Soviet people were evacuated from the regions occupied by the Nazis. They went to the east. Tashkent, which then had a population of half a million, took in another half-million people (it is 2.1 million now). "My home is your home." Many Russians, Ukrainians, Latvians and Byelorussians will remember these words of Uzbek hospitality for the rest of their lives. Whatever may happen, the words "the guest is the first person in the home" are still a law for the Uzbeks. And that, too, is part of the truth.

Turkmenia

It is only here, in Turkmenia, that one can see, over the infinite yellow expanse that is the desert, above the air shimmering in the heat of the sands, against the perfect azure skies, the sudden and fascinating images known as mirages. No other place in the country has as much sun and as little water. Most of Turkmenia (four-fifths) is covered by deserts, of which the largest is called the **Kara Kum** (black sands in Turkic). The name

Turkmenian women.

is uncannily accurate, for it is only in early spring that the thin rains breathe life into the desert, and it starts to glow with colors that only the carpets embroidered by Turkmenian women can match. But the magic spell is soon broken. The ruthless heat of the sun kills the colors, and the Kara Kum once more appears as lifeless and as barren to the eye of the rare airplane pilot as the surface of the moon. Neither the Caspean Sea, which washes the Turkmenian lands on the west, nor the once-plentiful Amu Darya can hope to quench the vicious heat of the Kara Kum.

"Where there is water, there is life", runs the Turkmenian proverb. In the middle of the desert, one can easily see its wisdom. Today, the republic gets most of its water from the Amu Darya and from the 1,100 km-long (680 miles) **Kara Kum canal**, which was built in the 1950s and the 60s to carry water from that river across the quicksand. True enough, where the blue artery of life cuts across the lifeless sands, orchards and plantations are now in bloom. But on the other hand, as we have seen, the canal is a major threat to the Aral. That's the dialectics of the situation.

The white gold of Turkmenia: Turkmenia's wealth is in its "white gold" - thin-fibre cotton. It also has more than the usual share of mineral riches - gas, oil and ores of non-ferrous metals. Mining and processing are important industries here. In addition, this Central Asian republic produces nitrogen fertilizers, textiles and clothing.

Carpet-making has always been the principle occupation of Turkmenian women. It can without reserve be called an art. Woolen Turkmenian carpets are matchless in terms of color and ornament. The fire of unfading (vegetable) reds, yellows and blues is emphasized by the traditional dark background.

Quite a few men and women wear national dress. It looks particularly smart on women: long bright silk or satin dresses with elaborate Oriental embroideries. Elegant brooches, stylish beads and earrings never seem to go out of fashion. Then, of course, there is also

Handmade Turkmenian carpets are the best in the USSR.

the jewelry made, as in olden times, of heavy silver.

The hardships of desert life are clearly no obstacle to animal husbandry, as the famous karakul sheep (bred here, in Turkmenia - their tracks everywhere) prove. But the special pride of the Turkmenians is the fine-legged horse, the Ahaiketian (if you doubt the breed's virtues, just go to an international auction, and look at the prices).

There's no hiding the fact that Turkmenia (it has a population of 3.5 million), as indeed the entire country, has its share of social woes. The republic has an alarmingly high infant mortality rate. There are other problems, such as rural backwardness and demographic lopsidedness. Finally, there's the plight of Turkmenian women.

Strange as it may sound, popular tradition is very much to blame for this. Most peasant families have between 7 and 9 children, who often go hungry and seldom see their parents, particularly their mothers, who break their backs on cotton plantations from morning till night. The husband, as the traditional head of the family, as a rule does not help around the house.

Generally speaking, the Turkmenian people never had it easy. Plagued by near-total illiteracy and tribal prejudice, fanatically dedicated to the dogmas of Islam, slaughtered in never-ending tribal wars, they were on the brink of extinction at the turn of the century. And this after Turkmenian soil saw civilizations comparable to ancient Greece and Rome in their grandeur! For it was here that the Akhemenides had their kingdom, which fell to Alexander of Macedonia in the 4th century B.C. It was here that the Parthian kingdom rose from the ashes of the great Macedonian's empire. You can still see what's left of the kingdom's capital, **Nisa**, 30 km (18 miles) to the west of **Ashkhabad**, today's capital of Turkmenia.

With 400,000 inhabitants, Ashkhabad is a relatively young city - it is a little over a century old. Its name is poetic: translated from the Turkmenian language, it means "land of love". But its history is tragic: on October 6, 1948, the city was leveled and totally destroyed by a force-ten earthquake.

Ashkhabad was rebuilt, of course. Today, it is a modern town, famous for its numerous parks and gardens. The most interesting of these is the **Botanical Garden**, where a unique collection of cacti and roses is on display.

It would be only just to admit that Turkmenia as a tourist attraction is far behind neighboring Uzbekistan. The fame of legendary Samarkand and Bukhara seems to overshadow that of ancient Turkmenian cities such as **Merva**, which was founded in the middle of the first millennium B.C. (30 km/18 miles east of **Maryi**, a regional center), with its ruins of a medrese, (an Islamic university) palaces, mausolea and temples, all of which are between 20 and 25 centuries old.

Experts in geography and botany revel in **Repetek**, the preserve that boasts a matchless collection of the region's flora and fauna. It is interesting for amateurs, too, for where else will you come across a crocodile-like monitor-lizard in its natural habitat, or a real black haloxylon "forest"?

A subterranean lake with wondrous properties: Finally, Turkmenia has another attraction that is a must for all visitors: the **Bakhardensk Cave**. Accurately speaking, it is a subterranean lake 30 km/19 miles to the west of Ashkhabad, which is known from ancient times for its wondrous medicinal properties. The warm mineral waters of the lake, lying a full 50 meters (165 feet) below the surface of the earth, cover an area of 2,500 square meters/26,900 square feet, and reach a depth of 13 meters (42 feet).

The cave serves as a home for the largest population of bats in both Europe and Asia. On a summer day, you will find 150,000 or so hanging, goodness knows how, from the walls or the ceiling of the cave.

Tadzhikistan

This is it: the home of the Yeti, the abominable snowman, who, they will tell you, was seen many times in the

Pamirs. So far, however, the crafty creature has managed to elude all dragnet expeditions organized by the USSR Academy of Sciences, and was therefore officially pronounced a myth. But the Yeti will have none of that: he keeps popping up from time to time, leaving huge tracks on an obscure mountain path here or presenting a fleeting glimpse of himself to the occasional tourist or mountaineer there.

For centuries, the mountains have been the blessing and the curse of the Tadzhiks. Mountains occupy 90 percent of Tadzhikistan, which is situated in the southeast of Central Asia and borders on China and Afghanistan. The highest ranges are in the Yeti's native Pamirs, the highest mountain system this side of the Himalayas. Predictably, the Pamirs are very much in fashion among the mountain-climbing portion of the world's population.

Even though the Tadzhiks love the rocky slopes as their home, wheat and corn won't grow there. River valleys were the only solution for agriculture. But every spring, the melting snows of the Pamirs swelled the rivers and turned them into fierce torrents, which brought huge rocks, chunks of ice and up-rooted trees crashing down onto the fields, flooding and destroying the crops. At times, the earth shook, destroying the peasants' clay huts, all their labors, and the peasants themselves.

Today, the Pamirs and the Pamiro-Altais stand as tall as before: but people are learning to harness the forces of nature to their benefit. Several hydro-electric power stations now stand on the turbulent rivers.

The largest of these is **Nurek Power Station** (it is, in fact, the largest in all of Central Asia), situated 80 km (48 miles) to the east of Dushanbe, the capital of Tadzhikistan. Spanning a hollow between two mountain ridges at the altitude of 600 meters (1975 feet) above sea level, the 300 meter-high (986 feet) dam of the Nurek Power Station tames the unruly waters of the **Vaksh**. Now the river gives light, power and heat to Tadzhik towns and villages; moreover, its temper is decidedly quieter.

It would only be just to admit that the construction of a string of power stations high up in the mountains created formidable problems. Fertile valleys, few and far between to begin with, had to be flooded. The ecological balance was upset. People had to move away from the areas designated for flooding. All this aggravated the republic's (by now traditional) social woes: a high death rate among children, unemployment, food shortages and lack of water. But problems, as the saying goes, are not the only pebble on the beach (or, in our case, in the mountains). So let's look on the bright side of things.

The Tadzhiks are accomplished cotton-growers, with a crop capacity unequaled anywhere else in the world. They plant wheat and corn in the mountain valleys. They grow fruit such as watermelons. Their apricots, by the way, are sweeter than the ones that come from Europe or America. There's animal husbandry in the mountains and in many places, they still breed the silkworm, just as they did eons ago. Tradi-

Left, there is an increasing demand for mullahs to call faithful to prayer. **Right**, mailbox.

tion rules everyday life, dress and even eating habits.

National dress is popular - embroidered dresses, skull-caps, white silks. Girls sport hairstyles with between 40 and 60 plaits. Tadzhik dances and mellifluous music make one think of India. The embroideries made by Tadzhik women are picture-perfect. This art is handed down from generation to generation; each territory of Tadzhikistan has something unique, a set of features characteristic of the composition, coloring, and pattern of that particular area. The skull-cap is part of the national dress. It is worn by men and women not merely as homage to tradition - it protects from the sun during hot summers. It seems that even prehistoric tribes favored the valleys of Tadzhikistan. Remains of Neanderthal man were found here.

Before the Roman Empire even existed, there was statehood in the territory of modern Tadzhikistan. The Tadzhiks gave the world the great scientist Avicenna (980-1037), and such wonderful poets as Rudaki (860-941), Firdousi (940-1020) and Omar Khayam (1048-1123). Even though the Tadzhiks preached Islam, they never oppressed their women as other Islamic nations. There were no veils or harems.

Dushanbe is the youngest among the 15 capitals of the union republics (it was founded in 1929). It is a city where the streets are straight, wide and green (something to be thankful for in summer). Many houses sport elements of national architecture. There are pools of water and fountains in the yards. There are almost no highrises in Dushanbe - the city lies in earthquake country.

Foreign visitors will like the **chaikhanas**, where you will be served such Tadzhik favorites as pilaff, shashlyk and, to quench the thirst, bitter green tea. There is also the bazaar, which is arguably the richest and most exotic in Central Asia.

Pendzhikent lies 150 km/93 miles to the northwest of Dushanbe. It is one of the oldest towns in Central Asia (over 20 centuries old). Its main attraction, ancient Pendzhikent (now in ruins), the center of the Sogdian Kingdom, was burned to the ground by Arab conquerors in the 8th century. Today, Pendzhikent is an archaeological preserve. Large-scale digs provide more and more evidence of the city's former glory, of the various sides of spiritual and material culture, and of the customs of the Sogdians - the ancestors of the Tadzhiks.

Every year, the ancient Tadzhik land surrenders more and more secrets. Time will probably shed light on the "Yeti phenomenon", too. But the Tadzhiks and everyone else who lives here in this land, have other things on their minds. How soon will perestroika reach each and every one of them? How soon will life become joyful and happy? Hopefully, it'll happen sooner than they find the snowman.

Kirgizia

Kirgizia is a land beyond the clouds. Over three-fourths of its territory lies at least 1,500 meters (4,950 feet) above sea level. Here, amid the snowy peaks of the Tien Shan (one of the USSR's highest mountain ranges), resembling a precious aquamarine stone in a silver setting, lies the **Issyk-Kul**, one of the largest (6,230 square kilometers/2405 square miles) and deepest (up to 700 meters/2,300 feet) mountain lakes in the whole world.

There's more sun in Kirgizia than anywhere else in the USSR. The northernmost point of the republic is on the same latitude as Rome, and the southernmost on the latidude of Lisbon. The landscape rarely changes here: the valleys are invariably sun-scorched, and the Alpine meadows are lush.

In most of Kirgizia the climate is perfect for growing grapes, cotton, apricots and tobacco. But there has never been enough water for that purpose here. The irony, however, is that there is more than enough water in the alpine glaciers to cover the whole of Kirgizia with a three-meter (10-foot) layer of water, if melted. But there is a golden means to everything, and the scientists in the employ of the republic's Academy of Sciences are

An honorable senior citizen.

presently searching for it.

Wresting water from the glaciers, they gradually breathe life into deserts, transforming them into blooming orchards and fields. Thanks to them, today's agriculture in Kirgizia combines the traditional breeding of fine-fleeced sheep with gardening and plant-growing, both of which were foreign to the Kirgizians and are only of recent origin.

In the years of Soviet power, the people of the republic have taken a step forward from artisan production to a highly developed economy. Kirgizia now produces machinery, metals, construction material and fabrics. There is coal, oil and gas, along with the USSR's largest deposit of lead and antimony which, by the way, was recognized as the standard of quality at the Brussels exposition, and is now exported to dozens of countries.

However, the economy is lop-sided, oriented exclusively towards mining and raw-material production. The 4.3 million people living in the republic face formidable social problems, for the consumer industries are weak, and at times you cannot find even the basic necessities in the stores.

There are also ecological problems, primarily in Frunze, the capital city (616,000 people), where the benzipyren concentration in the atmosphere exceeds the maximal allowed dose by more than 10 times. Talking about the capital, we should mention that, since 1926, the city has borne the name of one of its sons, the legendary military leader of the Civil War (1919-1922) Mikhail Frunze (1885-1925).

Formerly known as Pishpek, a desolate army fort 750 meters (2,470 feet) above sea level, Frunze has grown, in a matter of decades, into a rather smart, green and bustling modern city. It is here, in Frunze, by the way, that you can take a walk along the world's widest avenue - **Dzerzhinsky Prospekt**, which is 100 meters (328 feet) wide.

The land of the snow leopard: The **Tien Shan** still serves as a habitat for such rare animals as the snow leopard and the mountain goat. There are trout in the

The upper reaches of the Syr Daria in Kirghizia.

crystal-clear mountain rivers, and the hunting grounds enjoy an international reputation. Here, the connoisseur can take part in something as ancient and exotic as the golden-eagle hunt.

There are many legends and songs about the Tien Shan and the people populating its spurs. They include the poetical history of the Kirgiz people, a kind of an oral chronicle entitled Manas - the longest folk tale of its kind in the world. Manas was first mentioned in written sources of the 15th century (it was first published in Russian in 1885).

The tale relates the heroic deeds of Manas the Strong, who, together with his friends and his family, defended his homeland from foreign invaders. Manas also tells of the victorious march of the Kirgiz army into China - probably a true historical fact.

The people of Kirgizia are former nomads, for whom a newspaper (in the early 1920s) was such a rarity that they kept it as a talisman. But they welcomed enlightenment and knowledge. It is hardly surprising that this land gave us one of the world's best-known Soviet writers, Chingiz Aitmatov, whose books have been published in 70 countries. Be sure to read his novels if you want to know about the soul and the way of life of his people.

The pearl of Kirgizia - **Lake Issyk-Kul** - lies at an altitude of almost 2,000 meters (6,580 feet), it makes you think of paradise. The dark-blue skies, reflected in its bottomless depths, lend it heavenly beauty and grandeur. It is not surprising that people from all over the world come to the Issyk-Kul.

You must visit the ancient **nut-tree grove**, which still bears fruit despite the fact that it is getting on in years. It is one million years old. The grove stands in the vicinity of **Arslan-Bob** and extends to some 600 hectares/1,480 acres. People say that such wild and at once almost eternal beauty cannot be found anywhere else on the planet. Romantic spirits call Kirgizia a "heavenly land of legends and edelweiss". Now there is a rare case when the pragmatists among us won't argue.

Yourts serve as a reliable windshield for kirgiz families in the plain.

ALONG THE
ANCIENT SILK ROAD

Once caravans passed here from Western Asia to China. They carried porcelain, gold and jewelry, but most often they carried silk. That is why the route is known as "the Great Silk Road". It was used by Alexander of Macedonia in the 4th century B.C. and Timour (Tamerlane) in the 14th century A.D. as a conquest route. In the 13th century, Marco Polo, the famous traveler from Italy, used it to get to China. "And each caravan flashes as a link between the limbs of the great Orient's body", was the way the ancient poet described the Silk Road. It was here that all the trade routes from Europe to the Middle East and from China to India crisscrossed.

The Silk Road made Central Asia a prosperous land. This is confirmed by the greatness of the cities situated along the Silk Road: Samarkand, Bukhara, Khiva, Shakhrisabz, Tashkent, Margelan and the other ancient Asian towns, which have managed, despite their turbulent historical destinies, to preserve their former grandeur and the matchless beauty of their palaces, temples, and religious schools. Today, the marketplaces in these towns, with their diversity of color and their noise, resemble in part the bazaars of those ancient times, where merchants from practically all over the world sold and bought everything that could be bought or sold.

A young, 2000 year old city: The tour of the cities on the Great Silk Road is best started in the capital of Uzbekistan - **Tashkent** - which recently celebrated its 2,000th anniversary. The first thing that comes to mind when you ride along the streets of Tashkent is that you are, strange as it may sound, in a young city. In a way, it is true. Tashkent was rebuilt from scratch after the terrible earthquake of April 26, 1966, which all but destroyed the sleeping city. Today only several medrese buildings, mosques and old street names remind one of Tashkent's long history. For example, the central square is called **Chorsu**, which means "four ways"; it was here that the four caravan routes of the past converged. The square neighbors on the beautiful **Kukeldash Medrese** (16th century), whose colored tiles make a pretty combination with the uncovered red brick of the walls. Here, in the Old Town, you will find the Vatican of Central Asia - the residence of the Mufti, the spiritual leader of the Muslims of Central Asia and Kazakhstan (also found here is the **Barakhan Medrese**, the school of learning). Nearby, the rich **Tashkent market** is alive with the emotion-filled cries of the vendors, advertising their wares - melons, grapes, dried apricots and nuts.

One of the four roads from Chorsu takes you to the next town on the Great Silk Road - **Samarkand** which is 300 km/186 miles to the southwest. An hour's journey by plane or several hours by bus and you are in Samarkand, named by historians and poets as "the Rome of the Orient" and "the Muslim pearl".

Samarkand is 25 centuries old, the same age as Babylon and Rome. Alexander the Great dreamed of seeing the city, and when he did, he admitted: "I found Samarkand even more beautiful than I expected."

All the highlights of the city are within 10-15 minutes' walk of the **Samarkand Hotel**, where foreign guests usually stay. The first wonder to behold is **Registan Square** with its three majestic buildings. The first is the ancient **Ulugbek Medrese** (15th century). Opposite, with a largely identical facade, is the **Shir-Dor Medrese**, which is two centuries younger. Its walls carry images of tigers chasing llamas, hence the name, Shir-Dor, meaning "having tigers". In the middle of the square stands the **Tillya-Kary (decorated with gold) Medrese**. As implied by its name, it really does have the richest decor. **Registan** is the symbol of Samarkand. Without doubt it is one of the most exotic and poetic monuments of Islam.

Not far away, there is the **Bibi-Khanum Mosque** - the largest and most beautiful place of prayer in the Muslim world of the past. Legend says that it was built by the loving wife of ruler and

Preceding pages, the spirit of the thousand and one nights is still alive in Bukhara. **Left**, easily recognizable Islamic architecture in Samarkand.

conqueror Timour, Bibi-Khanum, to commemorate the return of her husband from a military expedition (1390-1404). Today the mosque is being rebuilt: an earthquake at the beginning of the century caused it serious damage. But even its ruins show how dearly Bibi-Khanum loved her roving husband.

Next to the mosque, is the noisy and multi-colored bazaar, which is, in its own way, another symbol of the city.

A little to the north of the bazaar and the Bibi-Khanum we find ourselves in the **Shakhi-Zinda (Living Shah) Mausoleum** complex, which dates to the 12th to 15th centuries. Here, says the legend, lie the remains of Kussam-ibi-Abbas, cousin to Muhammad the Prophet and one of the first preachers of Islam in Central Asia. A wide stairway leads up to the mausoleum.

A thirty-minute walk away from Registan, a huge blue dome reaches to the sky. They say that "should the sky disappear, the **Gur-Emir dome** will take its place". Under the blue hipped sphere is the tomb of the mighty con-queror Timour (Tamerlane) and his grandson, Ulugbek, the great scientist of antiquity. In the mausoleum there are the elegant marble grille, the walls (lined with transparent onyx) with their intricate gilded pattern, and Timour's magnificent jade tombstone.

From Samarkand, the route goes to the west, to **Bukhara** (271 km/168 miles away). It is called "city of legends", and with good reason: it is difficult to name an Oriental legend that does not mention Bukhara. The town remembers Scheherazade, Ali-Baba and the Forty Thieves, and, yes, even the Thief of Baghdad, who spent a part of his "career" here, at the Bukhara bazaar.

Bukhara is not large, but a single day is not enough for all its highlights. True enough, most of the historical monuments are concentrated in the Old Town, five minutes away from the **Bukhoro Hotel**. However, this does not make it easier to describe the numerous shrines of Bukhara.

Let us start our tour of the town near **Lyabi-hauz (near the pond) Square**.

Koran at the Khiva museum.

The largest medrese in Bukhara, **Kukeldash**, stands out from the architectural ensemble of Lyabi-hauz, which dates from the 16th to 18th centuries. The side gates of the medrese offer a rather grandiose perspective of barred windows under deep loggias running the entire length of the building.

To the west along Lenin Street, several blocks ahead, there is a peculiar structure on the right-hand side of the street - the blue-domed **Taki-Sarafon** (dome of moneychangers) - and, a little farther along the street, **Taki-Telpak-Furushon** (dome of skull-cap vendors), built in the 16th century like its neighbor. It has the shape of a hexahedron supporting the dome on a wide drum. The dome has five street passages as it stands on a crossroads of five streets.

To the north of these covered markets is the **Kosh Medrese ensemble** - two medrese buildings facing each other. The oldest of the two is **Ulugbek's Medrese**, which was built in 1417, a few years before its Samarkand namesake. It is not as large as the one in Samarkand, yet it is equally pleasing to the eye with its nobility of proportions, clearcut lines and flawless colored mosaics. The building in front of it, **Abdalazis Khan's Medrese**, is much larger. Its architecture is more luxurious, but it is two centuries younger.

Next to the Kosh Medrese, you'll find the **Mir-i-Arab Medrese**. This medrese is a functioning one. It is run by the department of Muslims of Central Asia and Kazakhstan and there are 80 students. Directly opposite is the **Kalyan Minaret**, without which one cannot imagine the Bukhara skyline. It dates to 1127. The height of the Kalyan (great) is 47 meters/155 feet.

To the east is **Balo-hauz** (standing over water), an ensemble created in the 18th to 20th centuries. It has a mosque, a minaret and a pond. The main attraction of the ensemble is clearly the mosque with its 20 elegant columns. Reflected in the waters of the pond, they gave the mosque its other poetic name - "the 40 columns".

To the north, almost directly opposite Balo-hauz, is the **Ark**, a fortress which is Bukhara's most ancient monument (6th century). It stands on a mound that is between 16 and 20 meters (52 and 65 feet) high. In the old days, a leather cat-o'-nine-tails - the symbol of the emir's power - used to hang near the main entrance of the fortress. The top of its wall, by the way, offers a magnificent view of Bukhara.

A few minutes away from the fortress, is the **city park** (founded in 1930). Deep in the park, an alley leads to the **Samanides' Mausoleum** (9th to 10th centuries). The mausoleum was built by the founder of the Samanide dynasty, Ismail Samani, over his father's tomb. He, too, was buried here later. The walls of the mausoleum, both inside and out, are adorned with an intricate burned-brick pattern. As the angle of the sun's rays falling on the walls changes in the course of the day, the ornament seems to alter its fanciful pattern. It is particularly impressive in the moonlight. No other architectural monument in the world has magic walls such as these. They appear to be carved out of stone.

Next stop on the Silk Road is **Urgench**, a regional center in Uzbekistan. Going there by airplane is better because the distance is considerable - 390 km/ 242 miles. But Urgench is just another town and does not have much worth talking about. It is just a stopover on the way to our real goal - Khiva - the third town in the famous "golden triangle of the Orient" (Samarkand-Bukhara-Khiva), 32 km/20 miles to the southwest of Urgench.

But first one should cross over to the Turkmenian side of the Amu Darya delta (150 km/93 miles to the west of modern Urgench) because that is where the ruins of **Kynia-Urgench** (*kunia* means ancient), the capital of medieval Khwarazm are. One of the routes of the Silk Road passed here in the old days. By some quirk of fortune, several wonderful and ancient architectural monuments have survived. They include the **Tekesh Mausoleum** (12th century), the **Farkh-ad-din-Razi Mausoleum** with its beautiful hipped roof and, of course, the cone-shaped, 60 meter-high (197 feet) minaret - the tallest surviving in

Central Asia. Then, of course, there is the domed **Turebek-Khanym Mausoleum**, which, although built later than its neighbors (14th century), easily rivals them in elegance.

Khiva: "I'd give two sacks of gold to see Khiva with one eye," they used to say in ancient times.

In the past, the town was the capital of the Khiva Khanate. It seemed to have come down from the heavens in the midst of the desert. The Khan's palace stood inside a fortress and, in fact, itself resembled a fortress with its sand-colored, windowless walls. Khiva, by the way, is first mentioned in a reliable source as dating to the 10th century.

Khiva, or to be more accurate, its upper part, **Ichan-Kala**, is a town-museum, the only one of its kind. Where the mosques and medrese buildings of Samarkand are lost among houses and streets, standing in groups only here and there, where the monuments of the past in Bukhara are "diluted" with modern structures, the monuments of Ichan-Kala are walled in - they stand in an architectural preserve. There are several palaces, a series of medrese buildings, minarets and prayer halls, baths, covered markets and dwellings. It is not only a museum: people still live there. The highest structure in Khiva is the **Islam-Hojja Minaret** (57 meters/187 feet). You get a good view of it from any place in the town. However, one of the Khans had planned to build a taller minaret - the **Kalta-minar**. Construction was started in 1855, but the Khan died, and work was stopped. The strange structure stands in the center of the town to this day. Even though half-finished, it astounds with its dimensions and the boldness of its design.

The most beautiful mausoleum in Khiva belongs to **Pakhlavan Mahmud**. Its blue dome resembles the vault of the heavens, with reflections of clouds running along its surface, much like the real skies. Mahmud's name is still remembered and respected here; pilgrims regularly make their way to his grave. Mahmud was a man of extraordinary strength, who found glory as a sol-

Parks are shelter against heat.

dier and a poet in the 14th century. For his strength, he was called "Pakhlavan", which means "strongman". Most of his poems are about love.

There is a well with holy water in the inner court of the mausoleum. Legend claims that anyone who drinks a cup of water from the well will live one hundred years longer. Another cup - another hundred years. The third cup, however, will kill you on the spot. So watch out!

Khiva has much more to offer, but most important of all is the atmosphere which you can only get a feeling for by walking through the ancient streets, mixing with the people and imagining the life as it once was in the heyday of the Silk Road.

Shakrisabz is 70 km/43 miles to the south of Samarkand. "In spring, the shine and opulence of greenery on its slopes make one believe that a heavenly carpet was unraveled here," wrote the poet about this ancient town (it's over 20 centuries old). This is probably where the name comes from: Shakhrisabz

means "green town". It was the birthplace of Timour (Tamerlane). Many architectural monuments are connected with his name - for instance, the **Ak-Serai Palace** (14th to 15th centuries). Unfortunately, only two supports of its main portal have survived. There is also the mausoleum of Timour's son, Dzhenkhangir, built in Timour's lifetime. The 19th-century mosque next to the mausoleum functions to this day. There is nothing special about this mosque, except for one of the plane trees, the one to the right of the entrance. They say it is a thousand years old!

The Silk Road passed through many other towns, which, in their time were places of might and delight, like Kokand, Margelan and Chimkent. Once traveling in the USSR is made easier they will also have their influx of tourists from all over the world and they, hopefully, will not have to pay the two sacks of gold that the ancients were only too willing to part with in order to see Khiva and the other jewels of the Great Silk Road.

Cooking shasklyk on the street.

THE WILD NORTH AND THE WILD EAST

The Far North: What secrets lie hidden in these forever-frozen lands? Patched with lichen and shrubs here, totally barren and lifeless there, they get the briefest respite only in the fleeting days of the Arctic summer when the barely warming rays of the life-giving sun appear over the horizon. Like a gigantic iceberg, which shows its tip but keeps its bulk away from the inquisitive eye, these lands jealously guard the treasures that lie waiting in their bowels.

It is probably this stubbornness to yield their secrets that traditionally attracted breakneck explorers to these savage parts. We do not know who'd been the first to set foot here. Was it the fearless Vikings, whose ships sailed all the known seas, or were it Novgorod and Pskov Princes, who discovered the way to the "midnight lands" eons ago? One way or the other, these lands were discovered, explored and civilized (if the word applies here); they are still being developed today, for the Soviet state needs their resources.

Discoverers and explorers: The exploration of the North has a long history. Late in the 10th century, Novgorod merchants appeared on the shores of the White Sea, and early in the 11th - on the Kola Peninsula. Those of their contemporaries who dared sail the high seas were even making their first voyages to Novaya Zemlya. By the 15th century, Russian ships could make their way through the ice of the White Sea into Western Europe. It was on this route that Ivan III's ambassadors reached Copenhagen in 1496. In the first half of the 16th century, they already sailed the western section of the Arctic Seaway between the Northern Dvina and the Ob (it was called *Mangasean* because of the "gold-filled" Mangasea, which was founded in those parts in 1601). The Mangasea Fair was one of the biggest. In a good year, up to 85,000 sableskins were sold there. There was also gold,

Preceding pages: factory in the Urals, early 19th century; and ice on Lake Baikal can sustain not only motor bikes, but also heavy trucks. Below, northern seascape.

"washed" in the northern rivers.

The search for the Arctic Seaway: Years of making their way through the perilous ice floes and reefs of the northern seas led the Russians to the ideal vessel for inshore sailing. It was called the *koch* - a kind of twin-mast boat, with a length of up to 17 meters/56 feet, a width of up to 4 meters/13 feet, and a draft of only 1.5 meters/5 feet. The vessel could carry 32 tons of payload and was able to avoid the crushing pressure of the floes, which it simply pushed out of the water due to its egg-shaped hull. On their long voyages, the Pomors (inhabitants of the northern shores) navigated by the Sun and the stars. As members of the Willem Barents expedition attested, they had even known the compass in 1597. All the main routes were marked with crosses installed atop the shoreline's highest rocks - beacons of a sort. The horizontal piece of these crosses always pointed from north to south.

The search for the Arctic Seaway occupied many an explorer's head. In the middle of the 16th century, Hugh Willoughby, the English captain, embarked on the search for a northern route into China. The bold explorer got as far as the Northern Dvina, where he died of hunger and scurvy. All the ensuing expeditions organized by the Dutch and the British were equally unsuccessful.

Ferdinand Vrangel (1796-1870), the Russian explorer, geographer, admiral and one-time minister of the navy, gave a large part of his life to the study of the northern shores and Chukotka. Vrangel was the first to give a scientist's description of the polar ice pack. He mapped the shoreline from the Indigirka to the Chukotka, and discovered an island which bears his name.

The first to make it through to the Bering Sea (1878-79) was a Swede, Niels Nordenskiold. It was a major victory. Yet it was too early to talk about commercial navigation in the Arctic ocean. First, someone had to make the entire voyage within a single season. It was only in 1932 that the icebreaker Sibiriakov, which was built at the turn of the century by gold magnate and pa-

Wooden church in Kizhi, built without a single nail.

tron of the arts Alexander Sibiriakov, finally conquered the ice floes and made it from the White Sea to the Bering Sea in one navigation season. The expedition was headed by the famous Russian scholar and explorer Otto Schmitt.

The European North: Today, the territories of the Soviet North are divided into several separate territories - usually the European part, Siberia and the Far East. Let us start in that order. **Murmansk** is the largest - and the youngest - city beyond the Arctic Circle. It dates to 1916, when it was decided to build a seaport on the shores of the non-freezing Barents Sea, and to toss a railroad into the bargain. The town lived through two difficult periods in its short history - the revolution in October, 1917, and World War II. And where the former passed more or less smoothly, the latter placed an enormous physical and mental strain on the defenders of the city, who staved off the German fleet for 40 months. The city, which occupies 17 km/10.5 miles of terraced shoreline (on lands that the receding sea surrendered),

came through and lived up to its proud title - the USSR's Northern Seagate.

Murmansk is still a port, but its main source of income is the processing and export of locally-mined raw materials (mainly non-ferrous ores and apatites) to other regions in the Soviet Union. There's also fish - the local fleet brings in a full sixth of the national catch.

If you arrive in the city in summer, you'll always see daylight. In winter, it's the other way around. It is never dark in the city during the short summer months because of the "white nights". In the winter months of December and January, the city plunges into the gloom of polar night. Average winter temperatures are slightly higher than in other Arctic towns thanks to the Gulf Stream, yet the vicious icy winds more than make up for this "drawback". The people who live here have it rough for most of the year. They say that their winter lasts for only 12 months, and the rest is summer. It is probably impossible to live here if you don't like winter.

It isn't difficult to guess what the most

Ecologists ringing an elder at the Barents Sea.

popular sports are. Every year, Murmansk hosts the traditional **Festival of the North** - the country's last winter sports competitions, complete with mass celebrations and deer races. The town fills with elite skiers, skaters and crowds of fans who come here just for the fun of it.

For all the problems Mother Nature faces beyond the Arctic Circle, there's a place in the Murmansk Region where one encounters a surprisingly abundant combination of primeval forests, mountainous tundras, marshlands and lakes, not to mention assorted species of local fauna. The place is called the **Laplandia Preserve**. It covers an area of some 160,000 hectares/395,000 acres not far from Monchegorsk. There's also a botanical garden in the region - the northernmost on the planet. It is situated on the shores of Lake Bolshoi Vudyavr.

Karelia: Between the south shores of the White Sea to Lake Ladoga, there lies the land of untouched forests and a thousand lakes - Karelia. The forests, which occupy 54 percent of the republic's territory, have always been its greatest asset. Karelia also has iron ores, decorative and precious stones, and even gold. The republic is populated mainly by Karels (150,000). There are also Russians, Vesies, Finns and many other nationals.

Petrozavodsk, the capital of Karelia, stands on the picturesque shore of Lake Onega. In 1703, Peter the Great gave the order to build a cannon foundry near the mouth of the Lososinka River. It was the starting point for the history of the city that eventually got the name of its founder. During the navigation season, you can take a boat from Petrozavodsk to the fairy-tale island of **Kizhi**. There's an outdoor museum of wooden architecture on the island. The prize of the collection is the 1714 **Preobrazhenskaya Church**. It has 22 cupolas - and not a single nail. The entire 35-meter/115-feet structure was assembled with simple joiner's tools made of straight-layered pine. There's a carved iconostasis inside. The church building is surrounded by very old wooden houses,

River fish exposed to summer wind.

typical specimens of the peasant's dwelling in the Onega region.

Karelia is washed by the waters of **Lake Ladoga** on the southwest. The lake is coldest and deepest here - up to 230 meters/755 feet. The place is very beautiful with its winding bays, long miniature peninsulas and innumerable rocky islands. A group of churches stands on one of these islands - the 14th century **Valaamsky Monastery**. The monastery got a new lease on life when it was returned to the Russian Orthodox Church in 1990.

Strange as it may be, the north of the republic and the coast of the White Sea were settled much earlier than its inland parts. The largest town on the coast is **Belomorsk**. It draws root from the ancient (12th century) Pomor village. Nearby, there's another ancient survivor - **Kem**. Kem still has its early 18th century **Assumption Cathedral**.

There's one more place, a place both famous and notorious - the **Solovetskiye Islands** near the Onega Inlet. In 1429, the monks Savvatiy, German and Zosima founded a monastery here. Even though the islands lie on the 65 parallel 160 km/100 miles from the Arctic Circle, there's enough sunlight and warmth here for watermelons to grow. Solovetskiy Monastery was a wealthy landowner. It actively engaged in trade and protected, on more than one occasion, the Pomors from assorted invaders, whether Swedish, British or Dutch. Its granite walls and turrets survive to this day, along with the monumental **Preobrazhensky Cathedral** and the Mess in the Kremlin. Late in the 17th century, the monastery becomes a haven for *raskolniki* - rebels against Patriarch Nikon's church reforms. From ancient times, the monastery-fortress served as a prison for those who dared to provoke the wrath of the powers that be. It has seen the likes of Father Silvestr, Ivan the Terrible's adviser, Count Pyotr Tolstoi, Peter the Great's favorite.

Early in this century, the monastery got the czar's dungeons, and in 1923 a death camp for Stalin's victims, code-named SLON (Solovetskiye Special

Red flags is an attribute of festivities in Petrozavodsk as well as in other Soviet cities.

Camps). Now it has been turned into a museum preserve.

The Archangelsk region: The last part of the European North before the Urals is the Arkhangelsk Region. It is the least-populated, which isn't really surprising considering that a lion's share of its territory is taken up by marshy tundra and impenetrable taiga. Even though it lies to the south of the Arctic Circle, winters are harsh and summers - short.

The largest river in the region is the Northern Dvina which is second only to the Volga in terms of freight turnover, even though it is navigable for only 160 days a year.

One of the oldest towns in the region, **Solvychegodsk** stands on a Northern Dvina tributary, the Vychegda. It owes its existence to salt. The town grew around the salt factories built by the famous Stroganovs - merchants and industrialists. Solvychegodsk Fairs used to be famous all over the country. One of the fair's main attractions was folk art - jewelry, gold-thread embroidery, icons. The latter were particularly prized. To-

day, they are known as the Stroganov School. There are architectural monuments in the city - the 16th century **Blagoveschensky Cathedral**, generously decorated by the artists of the Stroganov School, and the baroque cathedral of the **Vedensky Monastery**. The lower reaches of the Northern Dvina are breathtakingly beautiful. There, in the Kholmogory Floodlands, an ice-age glacier left a fascinating combination of islands, streams and sand bars.

Arkhangelsk: The capital of the region is relatively young. It was founded in 1584 on the site of the former Mikhailo-Arkhangelsky Monastery at the time when the sea link to Britain was established. Up to the foundation of St. Petersburg, the city remained Russia's sole port in the North Sea.

Arkhangelsk was built on marshland, which is why it has such a peculiar layout. The areas suitable for housing construction stretch along the dry banks of the Northern Dvina and the innumerable islands of its delta for dozens of

Karelia is not as hot as Turkmenia, but a glass of cool soda-water is worth drinking.

kilometers. This is in fact perfect for the timber industry, which is currently booming in the city. Every year, over 1.5 million cubic meters/2.10 million cubic yard of timber gets to the city over the Northern Dvina. In terms of dock length, the port of Arkhangelsk is one of the largest in the world. As all the other northern cities, Arkhangelsk had until recently been almost totally made of wood. Which was reasonable, of course: wood holds warmth well, and it's always there. The historical center of the city occupies several kilometers of the Northern Dvina's bank. Lenin Embankment along the river bend is one of the central thoroughfares. From the quay, one sees the sea terminal and the river terminal, the yacht club and the man-made beach. Thirty kilometers away, on the right-hand bank of the river, there stands the ancient village of **Lyavlya**. It is the favorite resting place of locals and tourists in summer. There is a museum of wooden architecture there, with the oldest wooden church in the Dvina basin - the tent cathedral was built in 1589.

The northeastern part of Arkhangelsk Region is taken up by the **Nenetsky National District**. It is one of the USSR's deer-herding centers. Most of the district lies in marshy tundra and forest tundra. The reindeer are usually put to pasture in the coastal areas come summer; as winter sets in, the herds go south. Long and harsh winters with an average temperature of -25°C/-13°F, frozen topsoils and scarce manpower impede industrial and agricultural development here.

Nomad country: Since time immemorial, the district was populated by the Nentsy nomads. Today, they account for 14 percent of the population (5,000 people). Novgorod and Pskov potentates came here in the 12th century. Early in the 16th century, Moscow military chieftains built the Pustozersky Fort on the lower Pechora - the place where tribute was brought from all over.

The traditional occupations for Russians and natives were fishing and hunting. The Nentsy lived in the chum - a cone-shaped tent made of doubled deer-skin on a fir-pole carcass. The national dress, too, features double layers of fur. The men wear the long *malitsa* - a shirt of young deerskin lined with fur. The women follow the same principle, but pay more attention to decor - their clothes are embroidered and adorned with different furs. For footwear, they use *pimy* - fur boots made of skins taken off deer's legs. The diet consists of deermeat and wild birds, with fish in summer. Those of the Nentsy who live in cities wear European clothes and have a balanced diet. However, they prefer to use their national dress when hunting or deer-herding.

Over 1000 km/620 miles off the northeastern coast lies the two-island archipelago of **Novaya Zemlya**. There's practically no vegetation there. As far as the eye can see, there's permafrost and mountain ranges. But the off-shore waters abound with fish and sea animals. The island's most remarkable feature is its "bird bazaars". Millions of gulls, eiders and other sea birds nest during the summer on the sheer cliffs of the western coast of **Yuzhy Island**. On this is-

Life in Siberia is simple, but there are charming corners.

356

land the Nentsy have a settlement, mostly of hunters and fishermen.

There are several monitoring stations on the islands. **Severny Island**, sad as it may sound, has been a nuclear test-site for nearly half a century now. Today, the site has been moved underground, but the prospects for shutting it down altogether are as grim as they are for Semipalatinsk.

Franz Josef Land is another archipelago in the Arctic. It is situated in the Barents Sea near Spitsbergen. The archipelago has over 190 islands, almost all of which are covered with glaciers. The polar day lasts over 4 months here. The sun never sets - it just goes around in circles. A long polar night starts in wintertime (over 130 days). Temperature drops to -55°C/-67°F in winter, and rises to zero (32°F) in summer. There are numerous monitoring stations on the islands.

The Siberian North: The modern port of **Dudinka** on the Yenisei River was founded in 1667 by Pomor hunters on the way to Mangasea. At the end of the last century, there were not even a dozen houses in the entire village. Today Dudinka is a well-developed city and a large sea and river port. There is one amusing thing about this town: come spring, the port suddenly comes alive, gathers all its belongings down to the railway tracks, and climbs up the mountain in anticipation of the moment when the ice on the river starts drifting. Because when the ice starts to go, it crushes everything within the reach of its huge, several-meter thick chunks, leaving the banks looking like a well-ploughed field. When the water falls from its incredible spring level of 15 meters/50 feet, the port once again descends to where it should be.

Norilsk is just over five decades old. In the early 1920s, huge deposits of copper-nickel ores were discovered on the Taimyr. The geologists founded the original settlement, which later developed into the town which has the USSR's largest mining/metallurgical complex. There are over 100 enterprises - mining, ore-dressing, power genera-

tion and so on - in the area. The town stands on permafrost. The houses rest on concrete piles hammered into the ground to prevent it from raveling out.

Living and working conditions are terrible - suffice it to mention that there isn't a single tree left in the entire area! What is there to expect when sulfurous anhydride is dumped into the atmosphere every day?

To attract manpower, the town, as most of the other areas in the Arctic, provides special state-sponsored privileges, such as higher wages, guaranteed living space in any region of the USSR (obtainable immediately, without waiting in line, upon completing the required tour of duty in Norilsk), and several others. Unfortunately, not many make use of this opportunity, because when you reach retirement age in Norilsk, your health usually precludes long voyages.

There is one unique feature there - the streetlamps burn so brightly, that you can comfortably read a newspapers, which is more than can be said about the streets of even our big cities.

The plight of the "small peoples": All was well when suddenly, right in the middle of perestroika, thunder struck: the public found out about the plight of the "small peoples" of the Soviet North and Siberia. Who could have thought that the dozens of small nations that populate these vast and - to us - ecologically safe expanses, are in mortal danger? And why would they want to set up an **"Association of Small Peoples of the Soviet North"**, the foundation of which was announced at their first congress in March, 1990? Don't they benefit from the grandiose railroad and highway construction projects, the appearance of new cities, the continued exploration of the Arctic seaway, the gas and oil pipelines? Shouldn't all this serve to improve the lives of people who hitherto eked out a miserable existence in reindeer tents, knowing nothing of modern technology, of civilized housing?

Unfortunately, it isn't technological progress (or lack of it) that lies at the root of their problems - it is their very nature, the lifestyle and way of thinking of these nations who, although few and far between, are nevertheless the rightful masters of their land. As century-old forests fall under the relentless ax, as crystal-clear rivers and lakes are polluted, as fish and beast - their main sources of food - disappear, as their souls ache at the sight of the innumerable atrocities daily committed against nature "for the greater glory" of union ministries and "national interests", the death rate among them skyrockets. Life expectancy remains twenty years or so below the national average, and an all-encompassing apathy holds them in its viselike grip. How can they fight when everybody who is anybody in these parts represents the almighty "national interests", and does not care at all for the local populace?

There are many reasons why the nations of the North are today staring death in the face - historical, economic, social. Yet there is one more reason, which no one has ever really contemplated. Psychologists speak about "national mentality" - the traditional way of thinking prevalent in every nation. But has anyone ever asked a Nentsy, an Evenky, a Chukchi, a Yakut or all the rest of them how they want to live, instead of the usual, "This is how you should live to have a better life"?

The circle takes us back to technological development. Something has to be done about the railroad across the Yamal Peninsula, the nation's No.1 gas supplier, the Turukhansk Power Station on the Lower Tunguska, the joint ventures in Yakutia, on the Yamal and the Krasnoyarsk Region and the new tourist projects with licensed hunting and fishing for foreigners. Should all this be sacrificed to the "egotism" of the natives' stone-age way of life? Every decision must reflect the interests of the native population.

So far, their life is regulated by a series of "do not's": don't hunt for yourself, all the firs are for export; don't fish for yourself; don't even think about how much money (earned through the sale of your natural resources) disappears in state coffers... The only "do's" include the privilege to breathe polluted air and eat tinned food from the "mainland". **A Buriat woman from the Lake Baikal region.**

358

Perestroika has uncovered scores of acute social problems, and will probably unearth a great deal more. Yet there is now hope that there will be no more stillborn declarations, no remonstrations, that the pain of the few will become the pain of all, and that the abstract "national" interest will bow to the concrete businesslike interest of the owner.

The history of the arctic land: Separated from Europe - and the turmoil of European politics - by the Urals, the native population of ancient Siberia - **Autokhons** - went through stage after stage of cultural development as the centuries went by.

Early in our era, Siberia was populated by nomads from the steppes - the **Ugors**, and some time later - by Samodian tribes. The latter mixed with local tribes and produced today's Siberian nations: **Khanty**, **Mansi**, **Nentsy**, **Evenky**, **Yakuts** and **Buriats**. In the era of the Great Migration, the Huns drove them out of Central Asia further to the north. In the 6th to the 9th centuries, there was another clash with new invaders - Altai and Central-Kazakhstan Turks. Then, in the 13th century, came the Mongols (Tartars), and took over great chunks of what we know as Siberia today.

Siberian Tartars had a strong feudal state - the Great Tiumen Principate with the capital in Chingi-Tura (future Tiumen). As the Golden Horde fell apart in the 16th century, the lands of the Great Tiumen became part of the Siberian Khanate, a new political union. The word "Siberia", by the way, is derived from the word *Sabers* - an Ugor tribe. But there are also different opinions, as always in such cases. Exploration of the lands in the Kama region and near the Urals is associated with the famous salt magnates, the Stroganovs.

In 1515, Anika Stroganov built the first saltworks which 50 years later evolved into a large town, Solvychegodsk, that rivaled even Velikii Ustiug itself. The czar freed the Stroganovs of all taxes for 30 years. They were even allowed to have their own men-at-arms. The Stroganovs became Soviet Union's richest industrialist merchants.

Yermak's historic expedition: Further movement to the east is connected with Yermak's expeditions. The Ataman (Cossack chief) himself was shrouded in legend. The only thing known about him beyond doubt is that he was highly successful as a robber - his "team" caused so much trouble on the northern rivers that Ivan the Terrible ordered the brigand caught and hanged. Fleeing the czar's wrath, he escaped to the Kama, where the Stroganovs took him under their wing in exchange for a promise to guard their lands.

Yermak's historic war in Siberia started in September 1581. He spent the winter on Kokuya Islands and set out for Tagil. There, he repaired his fleet, which had incurred considerable damage after being dragged over land from one river to another, sailed down the Tura and the Tobol, and, fighting all the way, finally reached the Irtysh.

Here, on the right bank near Chuvashsky Mys (Cape), the decisive battle against Kuchum Khan's army took place in 1582. Victory was total, yet it did not result in the definitive addition of Siberia to Russia, since the new territories could only be held with a chain of forts and settlements.

Such forts (they were known as *ostrogs*) were built for two purposes: defense and collection of tribute.

Roughly until the end of the 18th century, furs were the only thing Siberia was considered good for. Every year, it gave 40,000 sables, over 50,000 ermines, and millions of squirrel skins.

The Siberian gold rush: Then came the 19th century, and signaled the end of the unhurried life. When huge gold fields were discovered in Siberia, the age of the "gold rush" came roaring in no less turbulently than in California.

Gold was mined in Russia starting from the end of the 18th century in the Urals, after a gold-rich quartz deposit was found not far from Yekaterinburg (Sverdlovsk) in 1745. But those mines could not keep up with the treasury's growing demands.

And so, when the gold fields in the **Yermak conquering Siberia.**

upper reaches of the Lena were discovered in 1846, when the fantastically rich field on the Vitim, a tributary of Lena, was found in the 1860s, they outshined all previously discovered gold mines and fields, and, naturally, triggered further frantic searching. And once again, success: gold beyond the Baikal, gold on the Amur, gold in Primorsk. Russia started to mine 40 percent of all the gold in the world.

There was nothing sophisticated about the process itself: tons of sand were washed in search of the small grains. Many of the arguments that arose among the gold hunters were often resolved with fists, and at times even with guns. Working conditions were impossible, and people died at their workplaces. They lived in wooden huts that were precariously assembled from anything that chanced to lie underfoot. The *starateli* ("hard triers" as they were called in Russia because of their difficult working conditiones) were followed by well-financed and equipped search parties with mining engineers and builders.

Gold, tin, uranium and diamonds: The golden trail led north, beyond the watershed and towards the Kolyma. But World War I interrupted the gold hunt. After the revolution, in 1923, gold was discovered on the Aldan. The theory that America's gold belt continues on the Asian Continent proved correct.

The modern gold-hunters live in normal houses. At work, they operate huge machines, which mill tons of precious rock each day. The search for gold also unearthed huge deposits of tin, which lie in the earth in the near-exact pattern of the gold belt from the Chukotka to the Baikal. Also discovered was uranium ore and, of course, the Yakutia diamonds. The first diamond was found in Siberia in 1949 on the Vilui River. A year later, Yury Khabardin found a three-carat stone on the same river. A survey of its banks led to the discovery of a large Kimberlite diamond deposit that was called *Mirnaya* (Peaceful). As members of the expedition said later, they sat on the diamonds for days with-

Natural gas will come to house kitchens in Western Europe.

out suspecting anything.

One day, a geologist decided to take a walk and discovered a freshly dug fox hole near the sheer wall of the bank's cliffs. There was a mound of greenish clay nearby - Kimberlite. It was covered with earth on top, and its presence would have eluded the geologists forever if not for the fox's timely intervention.

It would not be an exaggeration to say that Siberia, particularly Eastern Siberia, owes its developed present to these rare minerals.

Then World War II came and turned further development in Siberia full circle. Starting from the autumn of 1941, Siberia becomes, figuratively speaking, one huge munitions factory. In the first five months of the war, 244 enterprises were evacuated to Western Siberia, and 78 to Eastern Siberia. In the second year of the war, Siberia produced a third of the nation's pig iron, over a fourth of its steel and rolled articles, and half of its coal. It also produced tanks, airplanes, and self-propelled artillery.

There were hospitals all over the land.

Nearly all the theaters of Moscow, Leningrad, Kiev and Minsk were evacuated here. Even the world-famous Tretiakov Art Gallery was loaded onto a train in July, 1941, and embarked on a long voyage on the Trans-Siberian Railway. The treasures of the museum were given shelter by the Novosibirsk Opera and Ballet Theater until 1944.

Siberian oil: Siberia was reborn in the 1960s. It all started in 1953, when the decision to terminate the search for Siberian oil had already been made. But the unbending, confident oil hunters finally came through - they discovered Siberia's first gas field near the village of Berezovo. Then came Ust-Balyk, Samotlor, Urengoi, Medvezhye, and, further to the north, Yamburg and Arkticheskoye. The first oil field was discovered in 1960, near the small village of Shaim.

Siberia produces over 360 million tons of oil every year. It gives the nation three-quarters of its gas. Today, it is clear that Eastern Siberia is as rich in oil as Western Siberia, but no serious pros-

Summer in Siberia.

pecting has been contemplated as yet.

The problems facing Siberian miners are the same everywhere: poor housing, bad transportation, difficult working conditions, and terrible frosts - at -50°C/-58°F even metal grows brittle as glass, and rubber tires crumble like dry toast.

The Siberian Far East: Early in the 17th century, three routes for river boats (they were dragged over land when necessary) took the explorers of Eastern Siberia and the Far East from the Yenisei to the Lena. The Far East was settled by small parties of the czar's officers, runaway serfs and tax collectors. The local populace - Yakuts, Burats and Evenky - often gave them voluntary assistance, acting as guides.

In the late 1740s, parties headed by Ivan Moskvin, Vasily Poyarkov and Yerofei Khabarov reached the Pacific shore, thereby terminating the addition of Siberia and the Far East to Russia. It took less than five decades for the Russians to cross Siberia and wash their faces in the surf of the Pacific.

Early in the 18th century, **Okhotsk** was established as the main port of the Far East. Sailors and shipbuilders were brought here in horse-drawn wagons from Arkhangelsk and Central Russia on Peter the Great's orders. Construction of a huge wharf was launched. A special school for navigators was opened in 1740. Okhotsk became the base of the Russian-American Trade Company, the prototype of today's joint venture companies.

The great explorer Bering: In 1725, the first Kamchatka Expedition, headed by Vitus Bering, a Danish captain in the employ of the czar, set out through Siberia towards the Pacific Ocean. In 1728, the expedition boarded the "Svyatoi Gavriil" in Nizhne-Kamchatsk, and that same year St. Petersburg newspapers informed Europe that a sea passage between Asia and America was discovered. In 1733, Bering organized the second Kamchatka expedition, which lasted a decade. He explored the shore of the Arctic Ocean, the rivers Pechora, Ob, Yenisei, Lena, Yana, Indigirka, Kolyma. In 1741, his "St. Peter" hope-

"Disarmament is the demand of our time." <u>Right</u>, life is hard in the northern mining city of Vorkuta.

lessly stuck in the floes for the winter, the famed commander died of scurvy, sharing the fate of most of his men.

The Far East was still being settled late in the 19th century, mostly with the aid of sea transport. In the 20 years after 1883, over 3 million people were transported in this manner from Odessa to the Vladivostok area. Soviet power was established relatively quickly in the Far East - in December, 1917 - a mere two months after the Petrograd uprising. Six months later, however, it fell, to return only in the mid-20s.

Providence Bay: Some ports are especially dear to sailors. Providence Bay is one of them - just ask anyone who sails the Arctic. There is yet to appear a ship that would sail the Arctic seas and pass it by. When Bering Strait is still blocked by heavy ice, a string of ocean-going vessels makes its way into the port. The bay is more than a port - it is the regional center of the **Chukotka**. Today, Providence is a quite civilized city, with a network of automobile roads, educational establishments and commercial enterprises.

There are hot springs 67 km/42 miles away from the city. Their temperature is 90°C/194°F. The surrounding area has a microclimate of its own. Practically every plant found in Central Russia grows there. The hot water is used to heat the towns in the area.

The **Komandorskie Islands** include the island where what remained of Vitus Bering's expedition landed. This event is commemorated by the tomb with the wooden cross, which was erected by the Russian-American Company in 1874. There is the legendary Orlov-Rock here, as well. Legend has it that on the island, there lived the beautiful Alevtina, the daughter of a warlock. A simple village lad, called *Orel* (Eagle) for his bravery and easy-going nature, fell in love with her. But the warlock would have none of the peasant boy, and turned him into a huge rock. Meanwhile, Alevtina ran away from her father, saw the great rock, and understood her father's villainy. She threw herself into the sea and became the wave which caresses

the foot of Orlov-Rock.

Kamchatka is a continuation of the volcanic Kuril Archipelago, which stretches for 1200 km/745 miles and occupies an area of 350,000 square kilometers/135,000 square miles, which roughly equals the area of England, Holland, Belgium and Switzerland.

Kamchatka is enormously rich in mineral resources - oil, coal, mercury, silver. There are over 150 hot springs - geysers. With a temperature of some 70°C/158°F, many of them are used for economic purposes.

The main part of Kamchatka is covered with mountainous forest, which mostly consists of the rare "stone birch", called thus because of its incredibly hard wood. The forests swarm with valuable fur animals. The peninsula is populated by Koryaks and Russians.

Petropavlovsk-Kamchatsky, the capital of the peninsula, forms an amphitheater from the coast to the tops of the hills on the western shores. Founded in 1740, the city derives its name from the "St. Peter" (of which we already

know), which once spent the winter here. The city has made its way from God-forsaken one-horse village, the most backward province of old Russia with a population of 300 to an administrative, industrial and scientific center. It also has a developed fish industry.

Avachinsk Bay is the largest deep sea harbor in the world. You could stick all the naval vessels - and all the merchantmen - owned by all countries all together in here. The bay has a round form and cuts 24 km/15 miles into the mainland. Built almost entirely of wood, the city has changed into stone dress, which protects it from the elements and the destructive salt vapors. The city is linked to the mainland by sea and by air. It is roughly 9,000 kilometers/6,000 miles away from Moscow.

Sakhalin: Lore calls it "the black pearl of the Far East". Nature has been extremely kind to this fairy-tale island, which has an area of 74,000 square kilometers/28,500 square miles. There's oil, and gas, and non-ferrous metals, and rare minerals. The coldness of the Sea of

A hunting party on Sakhalin.

Okhotsk and the warmth of the Sea of Japan give diversity to its flora and fauna - from permafrost and tundra dwellers in the north to near-tropical forests in the south.

The first Russian Cossack parties headed by Ivan Moskvin and Vasily Poyarkov came to the island in the middle of the 17th century, to find numerous tribes of Amur peoples and Nivkhs, who lived on the island from time immemorial. Then the island started to turn into Russia's largest *katorga* - prison camp.

Everything that followed was marked by constant territorial bickering on the part of Russia and Japan. In 1855, the island was the joint property of Russia and Japan. In 1875, it went over to Russia. In 1905, southern Sakhalin was claimed by Japan. In 1945, it went back to the USSR.

The capital of the island, **Yuzhno-Sakhalinsk** (Toyohara before 1946), lies at the foot of **Mt. Bolshevik**, the top of which offers a nice view of the Sunai Valley and the sandy beaches of An-

visky Bay. The city was founded in 1881, but there is not a single house from those days left.

Many places in the city are connected with the name of Anton Chekhov, who visited it in the 1990s. You can find out more about the history of the island at the historical museum, which occupies a Japanese pagoda.

In the last few years, life has changed for the 150,000 of the city's inhabitants, going from sleepy-calm to industrious and businesslike. Cooperation and self-employment, not to mention perspectives of doing business with Japan, have wakened the long-dormant island.

Along the Lena: The river with the poetic woman's name - the Lena - is by right considered the main waterway of Eastern Siberia. Third in length after the Yenisei and the Amur, the Lena originates on the western slopes of the Baikal hills. The narrow mountain streams meet and form a powerful waterway. Flowing across 4500 km/2800 miles of Yakutia territory, the river gives its waters to the Arctic Ocean. A mere 500

Koryak worker in Kamchatka.

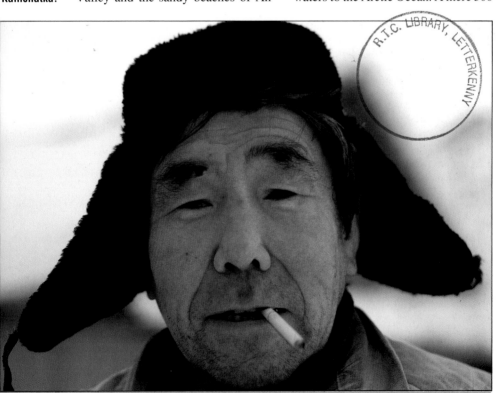

meters/1650 feet wide in its upper reaches, it attains a width of 5-10 km/3-6 miles in mid-stream, and 15-20 km/9-12 miles below Yakutsk. Here, the river is torn into shreds by large and small islands.

The upper reaches and the mid-stream of the river are the natural scientist's dream: century-old evergreen forests, abundance of bird and beast, valuable fishes (omul, nelma, and khatys - a relative of sturgeon). In its lower reaches, the land of eternal cold (-60°C/-76°F), nature is bleak and unexpressive.

Yakutsk, the capital of modern Yakutia, was founded in 1632 as the colonization center of Siberia and the Far East. It has seen many a famed explorer, gold and diamond hunter. As time went by, the purpose of the city changed - it became a place of exile for political prisoners. Famous exiles included writers Nikolai Chernyshevsky, Bolsheviks Georgy Ordzhonikidze, Viktor Nogin, and others.

Today's Yakutsk is one of the few suppliers of fresh vegetables and meat in the Far North, a metal-processing center and a producer of construction materials.

The city stands on permafrost. Until recently, it was entirely composed of two-storey wooden houses. Among the older structures are the **watch tower of the Yakutsk Fort** (17th century), and the former **Military Governor's Chancellery** - an administrative establishment in Czar Mikhail Romanov's day. It's not only that you cannot dig in permafrost; you cannot plant anything, either. For this reason, there isn't a single tree in the city. But if you leave dusty Yakutsk, you'll come to a green oasis - the botanical garden of the **Permafrost Institute of the USSR Academy of Sciences**. The grandeur of its pines, green meadows and entire fields of flowers are a memorable contrast to the lifeless tundra around it.

For several dozen kilometers beyond Yakutsk, there lies the Lena valley with its innumerable islands. The river is 10-12 km/6-8 miles wide here; the banks rise high above the water, their rocky slopes are barren here or studded with mighty ageold pines. Further downstream, you see the **Lena Posts** - probably the greatest wonder on the river. They are limestone rocks of up to 200 meters/650 feet in height. To the unprepared tourist, they appear as awe-inspiring as the mighty warriors from folk legends. For millions of years, the rocks stand exposed to rains, frosts and winds. During the day, they have a yellowish-grey color; in the rays of the setting sun, they acquire a bronze hue. These rocks stretch for 180 km/112 miles on the way to Olekminsk.

On the steep right bank, there stands the town of **Lensk**. In the old days, there was a 20-house village here called Mukhtuya. Today, Lensk is a major river port, which handles all freight shipped to the northern cities where diamonds are mined. The town is connected with the largest of these towns, **Mirny**, by an automobile route.

Ore is milled to a very fine dust at the diamond mines. Diamonds cannot be broken, since they are harder than steel. Then they are sorted, and the large transparent ones are sent to the jewelers for inspection.

Further upstream, where the Lena meets the Vitim, there is the border between Yakutia and Irkutsk Region. The flat banks are covered with dense taiga. The notorious Lena gold mines are situated on the Vitim. In 1912, 270 workers were killed here in the course of a peaceful manifestation, unleashing a wave of resentment and hatred of the czarist regime. Before the revolution, the Vitim Fort was frequented by gold diggers. There were many saloons and assorted other amusement establishments. Life boiled around the clock. Recently, the restorers of an old house that used to be a saloon found a trap door in the floor. The trap door led to a deep well, which in turn went down to the river. The hapless fortune-hunters, mellowed by drinking, were robbed and tossed into the water.

Today, life in the provincial town proceeds at an unhurried pace. When it is not frozen, the people live off the river, they fish, float timber and transport heavy freight on it.

Many races found their home in Siberia.

THE TRANS-SIBERIAN RAILWAY

"To Siberia, to prison": These were the opening words of the Imperial Command which spelled, for hundreds of thousands of Russia's freethinkers, the beginning of a difficult life in the land of impenetrable forests, wild animals and bloodthirsty mosquitoes. From the time of Ivan the Terrible until the recent reign of Brezhnev, Siberia has "gratefully" received all those who fell out of favor with the powers-that-be (not to mention the ordinary, common-or-garden-variety of criminals, as well).

History tells us of the first Siberian exile: his tongue was torn out, his ears were cut off, and he was given twelve lashes. But the culprit was not a thief or a murderer. It was an alarm bell from Uglich. The bell was punished for having warned the people of Uglich of the murder of baby Czarevich Dmitry, Ivan the Terrible's son.

Nearly thirty thousand townspeople, who were sentenced to exile in Siberia, dragged the bell along the Tobolsk road. Two centuries passed before the bell was pardoned and allowed to return to its native parts.

The Siberian "Shackle Route" dates to 1735. It was built by local peasants and prisoners, who felled trees, uprooted stumps and built crossings over rivers and bogs. The road took thirty years to build. Prisoners walked along the road, heads shaved, chains clanking, in a never-ending stream. Those wives and children who chose to accompany them shared all the perils of the exhausting journey.

Exile turned Siberia into the melting pot of Russia. The first foreigners to be exiled to Siberia were probably the Swedes who had taken part in the Northern War against Russia (1700-1721). Many of them married local women and accepted Orthodoxy and Russian citizenship. Then came the Poles, the Frenchmen, and, in the middle of this century, the German POW's whom Stalin sent to the east.

All this does not mean, of course, that when you arrive today you will be immediately thrown into the camps or forced to live side-by-side with the dregs of society; for the tourist, the worst part of Siberia is probably getting there. The 160 or so hours spent in a train may seem, at times, worse than the camps. Still, the wild beauty of the stern land and the amiable nature of its people more than compensate for the dreariness of the 9300 km/5775 mile journey on the world's longest railway.

Those bold enough to take the plunge will pass through seven time zones and cross practically three-fourths of Eurasia. The journey takes in nearly all types of natural zone, from the rather monotonous northern lands of the European part of the country, and the mountains of the ancient Urals, to the forest-covered plains of Western Siberia, the ranges and the endless tunnels cut through the Baikal mountains, and the Pacific shore. Dozens of old cities, and hundreds of young towns, as well as six of the country's largest rivers, will flash past the window. You will discover how these lands were settled and, hopefully, come to understand the people that the rest of the nation calls "*Sibiriaki*" - Siberians.

The history of the Transsib: The first plans to connect Europe and Siberia date approximately to the middle of the 19th century. By 1857, there already existed at least three such projects - the Russian, the British, and the American. However, the green light was given only in 1891. The grandiose project included inarguable advantages for the state: commercial and industrial development, fantastic mineral riches, and greater military security at the country's eastern border.

On May 19, 1891, the ambitious and, as it turned out later, ill-starred project, got under way in Vladivostok. The first stone of the foundations of the station-house was laid by the heir to the Russian throne, the future emperor Nicholas II. The project was managed by Sergei Vitte, Russia's minister of finance.

In 1894, the first section of the railway, Vladivostok to Iman (404 km/250 miles), came into operation. Almost at the same time, construction began in the west to east direction, from Cheliabinsk to the River Ob; work proceeded at a snail's pace, however, owing to the scarcity of materials and manpower. To speed things up, rails were lightened, ties were shortened, and the ballast layer thinned.

In terms of national composition, the worker body was non-homogenous. The railway workforce was multi-national in composition. Native Siberians accounted for only 29 percent, while the rest came from other regions of Russia and from foreign countries - China, Korea and Japan.

The workers of the Ussuri section were mostly Chinese. Prisoners were also widely used as manpower. Needless to say, they worked with primitive tools, and had no clothes suited to the harsh climate.

Yet the project progressed at a fantastic pace. By 1903 the builders had installed 12 million ties, moved 100 million cubic meters of earth, and finished nearly 100 km/62 miles of tunnels and bridges. In 1896, the Cheliabinsk to Krasnoyarsk section was ready. This was followed, three years later, by the Baikal section. In 1903, trains could go from Cheliabinsk to Vladivostok (6503 km/4000 miles). The road did not yet provide the much-desired access to the gold and diamonds of Western Siberia. Meanwhile, the thought of its immense riches spurred big business on.

Soon after the Transsib came into operation, the Americans offered to build a railroad that would start in Alaska, pass under the Bering Strait by means of a tunnel, cross the ranges of Eastern Siberia and link up with the already operational Transsib. They proposed to do all that for free, in exchange for a long-term concession to the territory running the length of the railroad. It is difficult to know what motivated the government to say "no". It was either a false sense of self-esteem or fear of an American "presence". But one thing is beyond dispute - six decades ago, we lost a priceless opportunity to develop some of our richest land.

The BAM: In the early 1930s, the BAM (the Russian abbreviation for the Baikal-Amur Railway) project came into being. This project included the construction of the town of Komsomolsk-on-Amur (1932) and the BAM Village at the 7280th kilometer of the Transsib. The plan envisaged the construction of several additional railroads, branching off from the Transsib and extending several hundred kilometers to the north, where the BAM could then be built in the western and eastern directions. BAM Village, known in every Soviet household, was located on one of those projected Transsib branches.

World War II froze the project. It was only much later, in 1951, that the first eastern section of the BAM, Taishet to Bratsk, was finally opened. The Bratsk to Ust-Kut line was completed in 1961. The most active period of construction started in 1974, when the 17th Congress of the Komsomol declared the BAM a "crash Komsomol construction project". As people joked at the time, everything started rolling when the delegates were hit over the head with a heavy rail, giving off a loud "Bam!". The Komsomol leaders went off to faraway Siberia to manage the project directly. Soon the railroad was completed from Ust-Kut to Komsomolsk through Tynda, Zea and Chegdomyn.

What is the BAM today? Approximately 3200 km/2000 miles of track, nearly 150 bridges (ranging between 500 and 1000 meters/1600 and 3200 feet in length), 600 km/370 miles of bogs and 2000 km/1240 miles of permafrost, along with the 15 km/9.3 mile long Severomuisky Tunnel.

It is also the product of a chronic lack of manpower resources, and deplorable living conditions. It has been finished, at a final cost of 11 billion roubles (some Western experts say 80), yet problems remain, with social problems chief among them. But the vast expanses of Siberia - the main obstacle in the way of further development - have now been conquered.

Along the Transsib: Let us start our journey in the last city on the western

The Transsib gives plenty of time to think and create.

side of the Urals - **Kirov** (957 km/594 miles from Moscow).

Known as Khlynov before 1870 and Vyatka until 1934, the city was renamed after party and state leader Sergei Kirov, who was assassinated in 1934. It is believed today that his death was plotted by the ruthless Big Brother himself.

The town was first mentioned in the 15th century. It was a place of exile for many decades before the revolution. Alexander Herzen spent three years, and Saltykov-Schedrin spent eight years here. Felix Dzerzhinsky, the future first director of the Cheka was also exiled to this town for several years.

Today, the town is a major railway junction and an industrial center producing computer technology, metal products, measuring devices, and agricultural machinery, notably the Kirovetz supertractor. Today's Kirov is six times larger than Vyatka used to be. The only reminders of the town's past are Vyatka toys - earthenware dolls, handpainted jewelry and cigar boxes - which are known far and wide, even abroad.

Rivers of stone: The train follows the left bank of the **Cheptsa River**, the largest tributary of the Vyatka, to the border of the Kirov Region. Ahead lie the Urals, which the train usually traverses in 24 hours.

The **Urals** are over 300 million years old. This mountain range stretches from the Karskoye Sea in the north to the Kazakhstan border 2000 km/1240 miles to the south. The Urals are more than just a mountain range - they are a country unto themselves, the "stone belt" of Russia, inhabited by a people with a unique culture and traditions.

Territorially, the Urals are administered by the Russian Federation. Its climatic and natural conditions make it possible to divide the region into three areas - the Polar (north), Middle and Southern. The mountains are like nowhere else in the world: veritable "rivers of stone" descend from the low jagged crests. The bright bronze of pine forests gives way to sun-speckled mountain springs. The dark-green of the taiga fir and the red of clay cliffs.

Left, carriage attendant and friend. **Right**, railway official.

These lands were known in the 11th century to the people of Novgorod and Pskov, who found a river route to the Urals. The mountains were then inhabited by Udmurts, Bashkirs, Mansi, Khunts, and later by Tartars.

The region is fantastically rich in natural resources. In the old days many legends and fairy-tales were told about mighty warriors who drew their strength from the lofty peaks of the mountains, about the keepers of underground treasures, about witches and warlocks. Ural stone was used for the walls and floors of Russian churches; metal mined in the Urals was used for casting cannons and church bells, while the gold and jewels that came from the region adorned the clothes of Russia's foremost aristocrats. Nor has the area lost its significance today.

Further on, beyond Kirov, our way passes through Udmurtia into the **Perm Region** (near the Kama River). "The proud beauty", "the river of ancient legend", "the rival of Volga" are three of the river's folklore titles. The river

Kama really does lend a special kind of beauty to the town of Perm standing on its left bank.

Founded in 1781, Perm became an industrial center. Its advantageous geographic position promoted trade and made the town an important river port by the mid-19th century. The railroad which linked Perm with Moscow in 1899 further boosted industrial growth. Today, more than a million people live here. They work in machine building, wood processing, oil-mining and other industries. In 1945, the town opened a choreography school, which gave the world Nadezhda Pavlova, the future prima ballerina of the Bolshoi. The Perm opera and ballet theater is called "the laboratory of Soviet opera".

Into Asia: An important event for every Transsib traveler occurs at the 1777th km (1110th mile): here, the train leaves Europe and enters Asia. This symbolic border is marked by a 4-meter/13-foot tall obelisk.

Forty kilometers (25 miles) ahead lies the city of **Sverdlovsk**. Peter the Great

A Buriat Lamaist monk.

wanted the town to help him create Russia's first navy and merchant fleet. The city was built roughly simultaneously with the northern capital of Russia, and where St. Petersburg was planned as "a window into Europe", the town on the River Iset, which was founded in 1723 as **Yekaterinburg** (and changed to Sverdlovsk in 1924), was intended as the nation's "window into Asia". Despite the inarguable importance of this function, the city owes its entry into the history books to another event - the brutal and senseless murders of Russia's last emperor, Nicholas II, and his family including the children and his doctor, of all people in 1918. Today, some believe that the murders were committed on the personal orders of Sverdlov or Lenin; others say that it was an arbitrary act on the part of the local authorities.

Sverdlovsk is the capital of the Eastern Urals, the third largest junction in the nation (after Moscow and Leningrad). Railroads run out of the city in seven directions. It is a city of machine-builders who work in the URALMASH Factory. The Sverdlovsk Polytechnic trains engineers for all branches of the national economy in the Urals, Siberia and the Far East.

The Urals is the birthplace of the inventor of the first Russian bicycle, Artamonov, of the Cherepanov Brothers, who invented the locomotive in Russia, of the chemist Mendeleev and the writer Mamin-Sibiryak, not to mention our distinguished contemporaries - Boris Yeltsin, Nikolai Ryzhkov and Yegor Ligachev.

Our acquaintance with Siberia starts with Tiumen Region. There are many legends about the history and wealth of Siberia. One says that when God was creating the world, He was flying over Siberia with a sackful of treasures. His hands grown stiff from Siberian cold, He dropped the sack, which contained diamonds, gold, precious stones and other minerals. This made God angry, and He cursed Siberia with permafrost, bogs, tundra, impenetrable forests and terrible frosts. Yet as any Siberian will

Snow roads near Lake Baikal are not easy.

tell you, to a native, 40 kilometers is no distance, 40 degrees below zero isn't frost, and 40 per cent of alcohol in a beverage isn't vodka.

Siberia's oldest town: Tiumen Region occupies an area of 1435 square kilometers/554 square miles, or 60 percent of Western Siberia. It is crossed from the south to the north by the mighty rivers **Irtysh** and **Ob**.

Tiumen is the oldest town in Siberia. It is graciously called "Mother of Siberian cities". The town was founded on the site of the former capital of the Golden Horde, Chingi-Tura, in 1586, with the blessing of Boris Godunov's crony Danila Chulkov. Yet it developed slowly, and the first monastery was founded only in 1616. The monastery - Troitsky - stands to this day. Like most other Siberian towns, Tiumen stands on a large river - the **Tura** - which is a tributary of the Tobol. Some 500,000 people live there today. Tiumen Region produces 75 percent of the USSR's oil and natural gas.

The next large city is located at the junction of the Irtysh and the Om Rivers. It is called **Omsk**. It is the second largest town in Siberia. Founded as a fort in 1716, it was soon transformed into a prison - the fate of many towns here. Fyodor Dostoyevsky spent four long years in the local hard-labor camp, immortalizing its horrors in his "Notes from the Dead House".

The city was also the capital of the Supreme Governor of Siberia, Adm. Kolchak. The story goes that Kolchak (who was an officer in the Czar's army and a perfectly honest man) is connected with the mysterious disappearance of a portion of Russia's gold reserve (some 500 tons of gold nuggets) which he impounded in 1918 from the bank of Kazan.

Most of the gold was recaptured by the Red Army, a part of it went to finance Kolchak's army, and a part disappeared without trace. Approximately one ton was stolen from the train (chartered exclusively to transport it) somewhere on the Transsib by one of Kolchak's senior officers. It has not been recovered yet, although reliable proof exists that it is hidden somewhere.

Novosibirsk, the largest town in Siberia with a population of over 1.5 million people is situated 672 km/417 miles away from Omsk. The city was founded in 1893 at the point where the Transsib, crosses the river Ob (the river is 600-800 meters/1970-2620 feet wide within the city limits).

The town grew as only Siberian cities can. Lunacharsky, the People's Commissar of Education, called Novosibirsk "the Chicago of Siberia", because both cities, when they were still young, doubled their populations every 10 years; today, Novosibirsk is the only town on earth to have reached the 1 million population mark in 70 years. The town is a huge industrial center, which alone produces more machinery than all of pre-revolutionary Russia. It is also the only Siberian city to have a metro. Novosibirsk boasts an opera and ballet theater that is called the "Bolshoi of Siberia". In 1957, **Akademgorodok (Academic Town)**, the scientific center of Siberia, was founded in a picturesque location on the shore of the Ob Sea 25 km/15 miles away from Novosibirsk. The center consists of a variety of research establishments which investigate the riches of the land.

The Siberian Meridian: Eastern Siberia starts with **Krasnoyarsk**. The plate that bears the name of the city, which is installed on its outskirts, has the number 3182, which represents the number of minerals sites discovered here in the Soviet era. This territory, which covers one-tenth of the USSR, has eight times more forests than Japan. It also has the longest rivers in the country - the Lena, the Amur and the Yenisei. The latter is justly known as the "Siberian Meridian" since it divides the country into two nearly equal halves.

Krasnoyarsk is the home town of Vasily Surikov, the painter, and has a world renowned song and dance ensemble. The town is a center of the sciences and seems like one big campus - there are some 11 higher schools here. Changes are coming. The foundation of an international center for space studies based on the Krasnoyarsk Radar Station is an event of world significance.

The Siberian Sea: The territory of the Irkutsk Region covers an area of 775,000 square kilometers/300,000 square miles. The main asset of the region is timber, but its greatest attraction is, without doubt, Lake Baikal. When they say that the Siberians have a sea of their own, they mean the Baikal. The water in the lake is pure; it amounts to 80 percent of the freshwater reserves in the USSR and 20 percent in the world. Scientists say that if all other sources of freshwater disappear tomorrow, the planet can drink water from the Baikal for 42 years.

The length of the lake is 636 km/395 miles and the width is 80 km/50 miles (which gives it an area larger than Belgium). The lake is 1637 meters/5370 feet deep. It has some 30 islands, five of which are flooded at regular intervals. The only inhabited island is the largest - Olkhon. The largest peninsula of the lake is the Svyatoi Nos (Holy Nose), which owes its name to its original outlines. Three hundred and thirty-six rivers and streams flow into the Baikal, and only the Angara flows out of it. The lake is situated at an altitude of 456 meters/1500 feet above sea level and is the oldest on the earth, dating back to between 25 and 30 million years. The water of the lake is kept crystal-clear through the efforts of the "sanitation police" - crustacean micro-organisms.

In November, the lake is covered with ice; by May, it is already totally ice-free. In 1904 a railroad operated on the surface of Lake Baikal (between February 17 and March 14), which tells a story of its own about the strength of the Baikal's ice cover.

But Baikal also has its share of woes. The gigantic pulp and paper mill on its shore kills more and more of the surrounding territory with each passing year. The issue of its closure has been discussed repeatedly at the highest level. But the resistance of the central ministry bureaucrats is still too strong.

The city of **Irkutsk** was founded by the Cossacks in 1661 at the point where the River Irkut falls into the Angara. The

Lake Baikal contains 20 percent of the world's freshwater.

city's coat of arms bears the image of an ancient - and extinct - carnivore, which used to have its habitat in the Sayan Mountains. The image symbolizes Siberian power and might. "The might of Russia with Siberia will multiply," said Mikhail Lomonossov.

The distance between Moscow and Irkutsk is 5191 km/3223 miles. There are 600,000 people here - along with the first power station of the four on the Angara River. The town is also the place where all the furs are collected before they are auctioned off in Leningrad, Leipzig and London.

Then there is the **Znamenskaya Church**, near which "the Russian Columbus" - Grigory Shelekhov of Irkutsk, who founded the first settlement on American shores - lies buried.

Ulan-Ude is 5646 km/3500 miles from Moscow. The capital of modern Buriatia lies at the foot of forest-covered mountains, on terraces descending to the picturesque Uda River. Ulan-Ude is a fortunate town: all industrial enterprises are outside the city limits. The air is wonderfully clean here.

The city is first mentioned in 1666 - a small winter settlement existed where the modern town now stands. It was known as Verkhneudinsk. The city is a scientific and cultural center. It produces railway cars, powerful engines and other goods. There is a national opera and ballet theater in the city.

Buriats are Buddhists, or, more accurately, Lamaists. Carved pagodas with roofs curving towards the skies are typical for these parts.

Khabarovsk is the capital of Khabarovsk Region (named after the explorer Yerofei Khabarov). The city was founded in 1858 on the high right bank of the Amur. Once the only industrial enterprise in the city was the cigarette factory. The 20th century has seen intense industrial growth, and today there are 200 enterprises producing powerful pumps, turbines and compressors. The local airport is one of the country's largest. The mighty river ties the city with many other towns in this country.

Nature, here, is diverse to the extreme, with its virgin taiga and permafrost, tundra moss and even northern jungles, which surround the cities in a tight ring. Winter lasts nearly 6 months here, and the earth in the northern areas freezes more than 2 meters/6.5 feet below the surface. Even so, Manchuria walnuts, Amur marigolds, poplars, limes and many varieties of fruit-trees grow on the city's boulevards.

Primorye is the southernmost region of the Far East and is situated on the shores of the Sea of Japan. It has an area of 165,900 square kilometers/64,000 square miles. It is a land of fascinating beauty, under which nearly every mineral known to man is found. Mountain ranges and hills make up the country of Sikhote-Alin, which rivals the Urals in terms of mineral deposits. The soft warm climate has created a floral cornucopia here. Over a fourth of the territory is covered by Ussurian taiga, with its Siberian stonepines, wild grapes, oaks and ancient yews.

Vladivostok is the center of Primorye. Located at the bustling cross-roads of human destinies and ways, Vladivostok was founded in 1860 on the Muraviev-Amursky Peninsula as the fortified port of Russia in the Far East. The founders were soldiers, brought to the spot by the schooner "Manchzhur". Today, a replica of this ship stands on a column near the entrance to the city as a reminder of its origins. The port, with its 800,000 inhabitants, is the country's largest in the Pacific basin. A third of the population consists of sailors and fishermen. The port is the liveliest place in town. Vladivostok is also a superb resort which combines a sunny climate, beautiful forest-covered mountains, and medicinal muds.

Nakhodka, with 200,000 inhabitants, is the second largest port in the Far East and the embarkation port for Japan. Called the eastern seagate of the country, it receives over 20 million tons of freight every year, and processes 20 percent of the national fish catch. The Transsib takes the city's produce to all corners of the USSR. The port dates to the middle of the 19th century, when it caught the attention of the crew of a Russian corvette on a research mission.

Happy lovers found a lonely place on Angara river bank in Irkutsk.

382

TRAVEL TIPS

GETTING THERE

As the USSR covers 1/6th of the earth, there should be lots of ways to reach its vast territory. But, until recently, foreigners could only penetrate the country behind the "iron curtain" through special entry points whose number could be counted with the fingers of one hand. Although today the quantity of these "doors" is almost the same, all the procedures, including customs formalities are now much simpler.

BY AIR

Thirty-four international airlines connect Moscow with the rest of the world. Flights take about 9 hours from New York, 4 hours from London, Paris and Rome; from Frankfurt it takes 3 hours, 2 hours from Stockholm, 6 from Delhi and 8 hours from Peking. In addition to Moscow, some international carriers fly also to Pulkovo-2 in Leningrad and to Borispol in Kiev.

BY SEA

Several Soviet ports accept international passenger liners. Tallinn and Leningrad on the Baltic Sea are connected with London, Helsinki, Gîteborg, Stockholm and Oslo. Odessa on the Black Sea is on the itinerary of liners from Marseilles, Istanbul, Naples, Barcelona, Malta, Piraeus, Varna, Dubrovnik, Alexandria and Constanca.

Ismail is a Dunai river port connected with Passau, Vienna and Budapest. Nakhodka on the Japan Sea coast is connected with Yokohama, Hongkong, Singapore and Sidney.

Additional information about sea routes, schedules and bookings can be obtained from Intourist or Morflot offices.

BY RAIL

Within the European part of the USSR, railways are the most important means of passenger transportation . Railways connect the largest Soviet cities (Moscow, Leningrad, Kiev, Minsk) with Western European capitals. Travelers who can spare the time, can travel in a comfortable 1st class sleeping-car, the pride of the Soviet Railways. From Western Europe the train takes about three days to Moscow, with a change of gauge when reaching the railway system of the USSR.

The most popular among rail routes between the west and the USSR is the Helsinki-Leningrad route (departure 1 p.m., arrival 9 p.m.) and Helsinki-Moscow (departure 5 p.m. and arrival 9.30 a.m. next morning).

But there are also transcontinental rail routes, such as those from Moscow to Vladivostok and from Moscow to Hanoi. They demand an adventurous spirit and a week spent in the train contemplating the endless Siberian and Transsiberian (Baikal) landscapes. Food for the trip should be taken along since the buffets on the stations offer food that is often not to the weary travelers' liking.

BY ROAD

During the last few years marked changes have taken place in the quality of services along Soviet roads. Moscow now boasts new service and repair stations for non-Soviet cars. But you should still be cautious of the state of Soviet roads. Diverting from the highways (which is still not permitted if not on your officially approved itinerary) might get you into some unexpected adventures.

Entry points on the Finnish border are Brusnichnoe and Torfyanovka; Brest and Shegini on the Polish; Chop when coming from Czechoslovakia and Hungary; and Porubnoe and Leusheny from Rumania. You can bring your own car by sea through Leningrad, Tallinn, Odessa and Nakhodka.

Below are the routes to Moscow which you can use driving your own car. You will, however, have to stick to your schedule, staying overnight only at the hotels or campsites booked. You are not permitted to leave the planned route either. Intourist will make the necessary arrangements.

From Finland: Torfyanovka-Vyborg-Leningrad-Moscow

From Western Europe: Brest-Minsk-Smolensk-Moscow and Chop-Uzhgorod-Lvov-Kiev-Orel-Moscow.

There are no international bus lines to the USSR, but special bus tours operate from the UK, West Germany and Finland.

TRAVEL ESSENTIALS

VISAS & PASSPORTS

You will need a valid passport, an official application form, confirmation of your hotel reservations (for both business travelers and tourists) and three passport photographs, to get your visa from a Soviet embassy or consulate. If you apply individually, rather than through a travel agency, you should allow ample time, as it might take a month or so to check your papers.

According to the new regulations, this term can be shortened to 48 hours if an applicant is a business traveler or if he or she has a written invitation (telex and fax are also accepted) from a Soviet host. However, it might take the Soviet counterpart some time to have the invitation stamped by the local authority.

The visa is not stamped into the passport as is the norm, but onto a separate sheet of paper consisting of three sections. The first part is removed when a person enters the country, and the last is taken out when leaving the country.

There are several types of visas. Transit visas (for not more than 48 hours), tourist, ordinary and multiple entry visas (for two or more visits).

If you go to the USSR on the invitation of your relatives or friends, you get a visa for a private journey which presupposes that no hotel reservation is needed. Individual tourists should have their trip organized through Intourist or their Soviet hosts. They need an itinerary, listing in detail, times, places and overnight reservations.

You should carry your passport at all times while you are in the USSR. Without it you might be prohibited entry to your hotel, the embassy of your country and many other places.

Intourist hotels will give you a special hotel card that serves as a permit to enter the hotel and use its restaurant and currency-exchange office.

HEALTH REGULATIONS

Visitors from the USA, Canada, European countries and Japan need no health certificate. But for visitors from regions suspected to be infected with yellow fever, especially from some territories in Africa and South America, an international certificate of vaccination against yellow fewer is required. If necessary, a cholera and a tetanus vaccination may also be required. Visitors from certain AIDS-infected regions who are going to stay in the USSR for a longer period of time can be subjected to an AIDS test.

CUSTOMS

When entering the USSR you fill in the customs declaration which must be kept as carefully as a passport during the whole period of your stay on Soviet territory. This must be returned to the customs office, along with another declaration, which you fill in on leaving the country.

USSR customs regulations have been revised several times in the last 2 years. Customs authorities want to find a compromise between conforming to international standards of customs regulations in the epoch of openness and preventing the export of large batches of multifarious cheap goods bought in Soviet shops for resale in other countries.

The latest edition of the Soviet customs regulations prohibits the import and export of weapons and ammunition (excluding approved fowling-pieces and hunting-tackle), and also drugs and devices for their usage. It is prohibited to export antiquities and art objects except for those which the visitor imported to the country and declared on entry.

It is permitted to import free and without limitation: 1) gold and the other valuable metals except for gold coins, whose import is prohibited 2) materials of historic, scientific, and cultural value 3) articles approved by the licensees of V/O Vneshposyltorg 4) foreign currency and foreign currency documents 5) personal property except for computers and other technical devices (see limited duty-free import).

Limited duty-free import: 1) gifts with a total value less then 500 roubles (about 770 US$). Gifts, highly appreciated among the Soviet people, can be ballpoint pens, elegant business notebooks, calculators, electronic watches and other inexpensive items. You are recommended not to have more than 10 units of an article if you want to escape time-consuming questions from customs officers 2) cars and motorcycles approved according to International Traffic Convention, no more than 1 unit per family, with the obligation to export the vehicle 3) spare parts of the vehicles insured by the Soviet international insurance company Ingosstrakh and approved by the documents of Ingosstrakh or Intourist (for the other spare parts duty must be paid) 4) medicines not registered in the list of the Soviet Ministry of Health Protection must be approved by the Soviet medical institutions 5) personal computers, photocopying apparatus, video-recorders, TVSat systems with the obligation to export (if the obligation is broken and the article is sold in the USSR, duty must be paid) 6) alcohol (limited to persons over 21): spirits - 1.5 liters, wines - 2 liters 7; tobacco (limited to persons over 16): 200 cigarettes or 200 grams of tobacco per person.

Duty-free export: 1) articles imported by the visitor 2) articles bought in the Soviet hard currency shops or in rouble-shops for legally exchanged Soviet currency (with some limitations - see below) 3) food stuffs with a total value of no more than 5 roubles 4) alcohol (over 21): spirits - 1.5 liters, wines - 2 liters per person 5) tobacco (over 16): 100 cigarettes or 100 grams tobacco.

It is prohibited to export the following articles bought in rouble-shops: electric cable, instruments, building materials, fur, cloth, carpets, leather clothes, linen, knitted fabric, socks and stockings, umbrellas, plates and dishes, medicines and perfumes, sewing machines, refrigerators, bicycles, cameras, vacuum cleaners, washing machines, children's clothes and boots, all articles produced abroad, valuable metals and jewels.

Some of the customs officers are indeed quite severe in their observation of these regulations. Therefore when you enter or leave the country, you must expect a careful examination of all your luggage and you will be asked if any personal items are intended for sale in the USSR (if yes, you will have to pay duty).

WHAT TO WEAR

Today the Soviet Union is visited by many visitors who demonstrate the caprices of fashion of many different countries. Therefore, the old guide-book phrase: "when going to the USSR, follow a modest and classic style of clothes" is somewhat outdated. You may dress as you would dress at home.

Coming to the USSR in the cold months (November to March) you should not be surprised to meet temperatures of 25°C to 30°C below zero (minus 13°F to minus 22°F). Water-proof shoes are also a necessity in winter, since the traditional Russian frost is not as frosty anymore and is often interrupted by periods of thaw. For business meetings, formal dress is obligatory. The dress code is as rigorously enforced as in the west and compliance with it is an important matter of status.

MONEY MATTERS

Roubles can neither be imported nor exported to or from the USSR. The newly established exchange rate for tourists has more or less abolished the former black market. There is no limit to the import of hard currency, which, however, has to be declared on entry. The amount exported should not exceed the amount declared when entering the country. Officially documented but unspent roubles can be reconverted at the airport bank. If you intend to do this, you should reckon on spending at least half an hour, since there always seem to be long lines at the bank counters.

All Intourist hotels have an official exchange counter where you can buy roubles with hard currency cash, traveler's cheques and credit cards. You need your customs declaration form where all your money transactions have to be recorded. You will need this form when leaving the country and you should, as with your passport make sure not to lose it. Most major hotels have bars, restaurants and shops where you can only pay with hard currency, and these transactions do not need to be recorded on your exchange certificate. Leaving the country, customs will check that you have officially exchanged money for the goods you bought and export from the country and that you are not exporting more hard currency than you have imported.

CREDIT CARDS

Most tourist related businesses accept major credit cards. American Express runs two cash dispensers in Moscow where card holders can either receive roubles or US$ traveler's cheques. AMEX: at 21 A Sadovokudrinskaya St. and at the Sovincentr, Mezhdunarodnaya Hotel, 12 Krasnoprenskaya Embankment.

Intourist hotels, restaurants and cooperative cafés that accept credit cards usually have a notice to this effect at the entrance. As well as American Express, Diners Club, Visa, Eurocard and Mastercharge are also accepted.

LOCAL CURRENCY

Banknotes in the USSR are available in the following denominations: 1, 3, 5, 10, 25, 50, and 100 roubles. 25, 50 and 100 rouble notes cannot easily be changed. One rouble is divided into 100 kopecks and they are issued in denominations of 1, 2, 3, 5, 10, 15, 20 and 50 kopecks. Platinium and golden coins of 150 and 200 roubles are more the object of numismatists than a matter of real circulation. You should not neglect small coins of 5, 3 and 2 kopecks. You will need 5 kopecks to go by Metro to any distance and any direction; for 3 kopecks you can drink a glass of water from the "*automat*" and for 2 kopecks you can make a telephone call.

The story of the word "*rouble*" (from the verb "*rubit*" - to chop) comes down from the early days of Russia. In Novgorod, long bullions of silver were used as coinage, but sometimes, for services and goods that cost less than the whole bullion, approximately equal pieces were chopped of the block of silver. These pieces were then called "roubles". ·

The present Soviet exchange rate (1 US $ to 6 roubles) which is called the "commercial rate" is quite reasonable and has nothing in common with the "official rate", according to which only 0.7 roubles were paid for each US$. The "official rate" is still used in "Beriozka" shops and in restaurants where you have to pay in hard currency (all the prices here are according to the "official rate", which is also called the "*invalutny rouble*" and the "foreign currency rouble").

Foreign visitors are still exposed to propositions from black market dealers, the most active of whom are taxi drivers and waiters in the restaurants. The black market rate at the beginning of the 1990 was some 14-15 roubles per 1 US$. The black market rate is published regularly by the newly established non-governmental newspaper "Kommersant".

In spite of the fact that rouble banknotes carry an inscription saying that they are accepted for "all fees within the USSR's territory" porters and taxi drivers sometimes demand hard currency payment. You should remember that currency black market activities are unlawful and culprits can be punished severely.

YOUTH TRAVEL

The USSR does not have an extensive system of youth hostels. Only big cities have youth hotels belonging to **Sputnik**, the Bureau of International Youth Tourism, once a part of Comsomol but now acting independently. During the summer months, when demand exceeds ʼhostel capacity, Sputnik falls back on unused, inexpensive university dormitories.

An inexpensive way to visit the USSR (circumventing Intourist) is through institutes that run Russian language courses: **Lomonossov** and **Lumumba Universities** and the **Pushkin Institute of Russian Language** in Moscow, the **Shevchenko University** in Kiev, the **University of Leningrad** and other universities and newly sprung-up linguistic cooperatives. They are all able to arrange visas and inexpensive accommodation during the period of studies. To communicate directly with the universities you should contact the cultural attaché of the Soviet embassy or consulate. It is rather more difficult to communicate with the cooperatives since they are not represented abroad.

PHOTOGRAPHY

The diplomat services agency (UPDK) and some newly appearing cooperative laboratories develop Agfa, Kodak and Fuji films (E6 process). But these services are only available in a few large cities. Hard currency shops usually sell Ektachrome and Fuji films. Kodachrome, which needs a special development process, is officially not available.

At the following addresses you can buy slide and print film and have your films developed.

Mezhdunarodnaya Hotel (hard currency), Tel. 253-1643;

prosp. Kalinina 25 (Kodak, Fuji; a rouble shop), Tel. 203-7307;

ul. Gporkovo 1, Tel. 203-5462;

Universitetskaya Hotel, 1st Floor (Kodak);

Salyut Hotel, 1st Floor (Kodak);

National Hotel, 1st Floor (Kodak).

You should not take photographs of military installations or from airplanes and it is also not recommended to take them from the train.

The interpretation of what is a military installation rests with the officials. You will have to be cautious and if possible ask your guide or interpreter before you take a picture of a bridge, a railway station, an airport or anything else that might be assessed as a special security object.

GETTING ACQUAINTED

CLIMATE

The USSR spans all climatic zones. It covers arctic and subarctic zones (including the Pole of Cold, Oymyakon, Verkhoyansk), where the average winter temperature is minus 50°C (minus 58°F) and where lowest temperatures reach minus 70°C (minus 94°F).

By contrast, in the Crimea, the Caucasus and the deserts of Central Asia, summer temperatures of 45°C (113°F) are not uncommon. But then, the short Subarctic summer can also be quite hot (around 38°C (100.4°F).

The main tourist routes lead through the European territory of the USSR. This has a typical continental climate with hot summers (30°C/86°F) and cold winters (minus 25°C/minus 13°F). Maritime European regions are characterized by smaller temperature extremes, with comparatively mild winters (although not so in Leningrad and Arkhangelsk), cool summers in the Baltic states and hot summers on the Black Sea coast. The Caucasus has a lot of rain while at the same time the Crimean steppe and the southern part of the Russian Federation suffer because of low rainfall.

Mountain regions of this country include the Carpathian mountains in the Western Ukraine and the Caucasus where the climate is similar to that of the Alps. The highest mountain ranges of Asia include the Pamirs and the Altai. These regions have a typical continental climate.

Mild summers, a rich vegetation and cold winters are typical for the Far East and Kamchatka; that region belongs to the Pacific zone of volcanic activity.

AVERAGE TEMPERATURES

Moscow: minus 10.8°C to 18.5°C (12.6°F to 65.3°F)
Leningrad: minus 7.7°C to 17.5°C (18.5°F to 63.5°F)
Sochi: 16°C to 23°C (60°F to 73.4°F)

TIME ZONES

Moscow time is GMT plus 3 hours. Officially, Moscow time is adopted nearly everywhere west of the Urals, although Western Ukrainians and the people of the Baltic states prefer to use the Mean European Time (GMT plus 1 hour) in their daily life to demonstrate their independence from Moscow. Moscow time is also shown on the station clocks along the whole Transsiberian Railway.

If the radio announcer tells you that it is 3 p.m. in Moscow, it means that it is 4 p.m. in Baku, 5 p.m. in Ashkhabad, 6 p.m. in Karaganda, 7 p.m. in Novosibirsk; in Irkutsk it is then 8 p.m., in Chita 9 p.m., in Vladivostok 10 p.m. and in Yuzhno-Sakhalinsk it is 11 p.m. The inhabitants of Petropavlovsk-Kamchatsky have at that time just started a new day and the polar bears walking amongst the heaped blocks of ice of the Chukchi Sea are already a whole hour into the new day.

DURATION OF A HOTEL DAY

The duration of a hotel day is counted from noon to noon. Especially in hotels that cater for large groups exceptions are seldom made. Still, ask your receptionist or the house-lady responsible for your floor if you want to stay longer; maybe the next group is not due until the evening.

ELECTRICITY

Electrical current in tourist hotels is normally 220 V AC, but don't count on it. In some remote places you will also find 127 V. Sockets require a continental type plug, but no Schuko plug. It is best to have a set of adaptors with you. The same is true for batteries. If your appliances depend on a supply of batteries, bring plenty with you, they might not be available in the USSR, not even for hard currency.

OFFICIAL HOLIDAYS

January 1, New Year Holiday
February 23, Soviet Army Day
March 8, International Women's Day
May 1 and 2, Day of International Solidarity of Working People
May 9, Victory Day
October 7, Constitution Day
November 7 and 8, October Revolution Anniversary
On February 23, May 1, May 9, November 7 and April 12 (Cosmonauts Day), there are fireworks in the evenings.

RELIGIOUS HOLIDAYS

The greatest religious holidays of the year include Christmas (celebrated by the Orthodox Church on January 7), Easter (a movable holiday usually celebrated in March-April), Moslem Ramadan and others. Religious holidays are still not acknowledged officially, but they are recognized by many people participating in religious services, as during the recent celebrations for the *Millennium of Russia's Baptism*.

Nowadays local factory and government administrators negotiate with believers, offering compromises like shifting the days off to the days of religious festivals or granting free time which can be worked later, etc.

RELIGIOUS SERVICES

In the Russian Federation and the eastern region of the Ukraine and Byelorussia, the Russian Orthodox Church is the most influential faith. The western region of these and the Baltic republics are under the influence of the Roman Catholic Church. Baptists, Adventists and the other Protestant branches are also quite influential. In Central Asia and Azerbaijan, Islam is the main faith. The following churches are all in Moscow.

Russian Orthodox:
Bogoyavlensky (Elokhovsky) Cathedral, ul. Spartakovskaya 15, Tel. 261-6913; **Troitsky Cathedral**, Svyato-Danilov Monastery, Danilovsky Val 22; **Uspenskaya Church**, Novodevichy Convent, Novodevichy proezd 1, Tel. 245-3168; **Voskresenskaya Church**, ul. Nezhdanovoy 15/2,

Tel. 229-6616; **Vsekh Svyatykh Church**, Leningradsky prosp. 73, Tel. 158-5515. Services: Mon.-Sat. 8 a.m. & 6 p.m.; Sun. & holidays 7 a.m. & 10 a.m.

Greek Orthodox:
Church of Archangel Gabriel, Telegrafny per. 15a, Tel. 923-4605; Sun. mass at 10 a.m.

Bulgarian Orthodox:
Uspenskaya Church, ul. Volodarskovo 29, Tel. 271-0124.

Catholic:
St. Louis, Malaya Lubyanka 12; Sun. 8 a.m., 11 a.m. & 6 p.m.; Mon.-Fri. 8 a.m.; Fri. & Sat. 6 p.m.; **Chapel of Our Lady of Hope**, Kutuzovsky prosp. 7/4, korp. 5, kv. 42, Tel. 243-9621; Mon.-Wed. & Fri. 8.30 a.m., Thurs. 7 p.m., Sat. 6 p.m.

Baptists:
Maly Vuzovsky per. 3, Tel. 297-5167; Sun. 10 a.m., 2 p.m. & 6 p.m., Thurs. 6 p.m.

Protestant and Anglican:
US Embassy, Tel. 252-2451, 143-3562.

Evangelische Gemeinde:
German Embassy, services twice a month at 10.30 a.m., Tel. 238-1324.

Old Believers:
Cathedral, Rogozhsky per. 29.

Mosque:
Vypolzov per. 7, Tel. 281-3866.

Synagogue:
ul. Arkhipova 8, Tel. 923-9697.

STATISTICS

General Profile
Area: 8,649,498 sq. m. (22.4 million sq. km.)
Population 1988: 286,435,000
Population Density: 33 per sq. m.
GNP per capita: US$8,734, (cf. USA, US$18,951)

Demographics
Population Growth: 0.80 %
Population 2000: 315,175,000

Age Distribution:
Under 15   26.0 %
15-65   64.9 %
Over 65   9.1 %

Health
Life Expectancy (M): 65 years
Life Expectancy (F): 74 years
Infant Mortality: 25.4 per 1000

Politics
Type of a State: Union of Republics
Government Leader: President Gorbachev, Mikhail Sergeyevich Major Parties: Communist Party of the Soviet Union, Democratic Platform (Social-Democracy), Russian People's Front, Rukh, Sayudis.

Languages: Russian, Ukrainian, Turkish and Caucasian languages.
Ethnic Groups: Russians 52%, Ukrainians 16%, Other 32%.
Religions: Orthodox 18%, Muslim 9%, Jewish 3%, Atheists, 70% (including other confessions like Buddhists, Hare Krishnas etc.).
Natural Resources: Crude Oil, Natural Gas, Coal, Timber, Manganese, Gold, Lead, Zinc, Nickel, Potash, Phosphates, Mercury.
Agriculture: Wheat, Rye, Oats, Potatoes, Sugar Beets, Linseed, Sunflower Seeds, Cotton, Flax, Cattle, Hogs, Sheep.
Major Industries: Mining, Metallurgy, Fuels, Building Materials, Chemicals, Machinery, Aerospace.

PEOPLE WHO GAVE THEIR NAMES TO THE STREETS

Looking at the map of any Soviet city you will find a standard set of names. Streets under these names can be found in almost every city. These names have been changed in different periods of the short but intensive Soviet history. During Lenin's government, streets were named after Karl Marx and revolutionaries from all epochs and ethnic groups. The more exotic the revolutionary to be immortalized in a street name, the better it was. Stalin's time was also marked with the compulsory use of the name of Karl Marx. But then a new standardization was used since some foreign revolutionaries were suspected to be the followers of heresies. The champions during this period were

Lenin and Stalin himself (the names of the final points of a tram route that crossed Kiev looked like this: Stalin sq. to Stalinka) and the members of Stalin's gang: Voroshilov, Kaganovich, Zhdanov, Beriya etc. The present tendency is to bring back the original pre-Revolutionary names.

Who were the men immortalized on Soviet city maps? Leading names are Lenin, Marx and Engels. They are known by people the world over. In addition there are:

Chernyshevsky, Nikolai (1828-1889) - revolutionary-democrat, publisher and literary critic. The author of novel "*What to do?*" revered by Lenin.

Dzerzhinsky, Felix (1877-1926) - revolutionary, the associate of Lenin. After the revolution he became chief of the VeCheKa, the Bolshevik's special department, the forerunner of the KGB.

Gogol, Nikolai (1809-1852) - famous Russian writer, the author of the prose poem "*Dead Souls*" and a series of stories in which Ukrainian mythological plots are used.

Gorky, Maxim (1868-1936) - well-known writer, the author of the novels "*The Life of Klim Samgin*" and "*Mother*" and romantic short stories. Proclaimed as the father of so-called "socialist realism" in literature.

Kirov, Sergei (1886-1934) - revolutionary, after the Revolution the 1st Secretary of the Leningrad Regional Party Committee. His assassination, instigated by Stalin, became a cloak for starting the repressions of the 1930s.

Ordzhonikidze, Sergo (1886-1937) - revolutionary, associate and friend of Stalin. After the Revolution the People's Commissar of Heavy Industry. Shot by Stalin.

Pushkin, Alexander (1799-1837) - famous Russian poet and writer, author of "the novel in verses", "*Evgeny Onegin*", and of many poems, essays and stories.

Shevchenko, Taras (1814-1861) - famous Ukrainian poet, writer and painter, revolutionary-democrat.

Sverdlov, Yakov - revolutionary, the associate of Lenin. After the Revolution the chairman of the Executive Committee. He is believed to have given the order to shoot the Czar's family and developed the policy of exterminating the Cossacks.

GETTING AROUND

INTOURIST

Intourist cooperates with more than 700 foreign firms who are agents for Intourist in their respective countries. It offers services in more than 200 cities in all the 15 Soviet republics and runs numerous hotels, motels, campsites and restaurants. On Intourist's itinerary are more than 600 different tours within the USSR. They include local sightseeing trips, thematic tours for history, art and nature lovers, as well as arrangements for recreation and medical treatment, sporting and hunting tours. A visit to the nearest Intourist office will give you a good overall impression of their diversified offerings.

In addition to its tours Intourist also runs a car rental service, with and without driver in the larger cities. Lada, Chaika and Volga cars as well as Ikarus coaches, LAZ, PAZ and RAF buses for 9 to 42 people can be hired.

Intourist also manages 110 hotels, motels and campsites for 55,000 guests. A variety of hotels are now built and reconstructed in cooperation with foreign partners like Moscow's Savoy Hotel and Leningrad's Astoria which are operated jointly with the Finnish INFA Hotel company and Finnair.

Over 5,000 guide-interpreters, speaking more than 30 languages work for Intourist.

Since cooperatives are now permitted, Intourist is no longer a monopoly tourist agency; a few small and independent firms have sprung up during the last few years which now serve special interest groups. But since the itinerary of a journey to the USSR has to be handed in in advance, together with the visa application, Intourist, with its worldwide net of sales agents is still carrying out most of the business.

Besides group tours, Intourist also arranges individual journeys to the USSR. These trips must be planned on a day by day basis in advance, and Intourist arranges transport, accommodation and food. Judging by accommodation prices in those Intourist hotels that are available to foreigners, such individual travel is, however, not inexpensive.

Intourist offices:

Amsterdam:
Honthorststraat 42, Tel. 020-798964;
Athens:
Stadiou 3, Syntagma Sq., Tel. 323-3776;
Berlin:
Friedrichstr. 153A, Tel. 229-1948;
15 Kurfürstendamm 63, Tel. 880-070;
Budapest:
Felszabadulas ter.1, Tel. 180-098;
Brussels:
Galerie Ravenstein 2, Tel. 02-513-8234;
Copenhagen:
Vester Farimagsgade 6, Tel. 01-112-527;
Delhi:
Plot 6/7, block 50-E, Njaja Marg Chanakiapuri, Tel. 609-145;
Frankfurt:
Stephanstr. 1, Tel. 285-776;
Helsinki:
Etela Esplanaadi 14, Tel. 631-875;
London:
292 Regent Street, Tel. 071-631-1252;
Montreal:
1801 McGill College Ave. Suite 630, Tel. 849-6394;
New York:
630 Fifth Avenue, Suite 868, Tel. 212-757, 212-3884;
Paris:
7, Boulevard de Capucines, Tel. 474-24740;
Prague:
Stepanska 47, Tel. 267-162;
Rome:
Piazza Buenos Aires 6/7, Tel. (06) 863-892;
Sydney:
Underwood House, 37-49 Pitt Street, Tel. (02) 277-652;
Tokyo:
Roppongi Heights, 1-16, 4-chome Roppongi, Minato-ku, Tel. (03) 584-6617;
Vienna:
Schwedenplatz 3-4, Tel. 639-547;
Zurich: Usteristr. 9, Tel. 23-296.

ALTERNATIVE TOUR OPERATORS

Sputnik, International Center for Youth Tourism: 15 Kossygin St., 117946 Moscow, Tel. 139-8665; International Center MIR: pr. Nepokoryonnyh 74, 195273 Leningrad, Tel. 249-9400. Specializes in inexpensive group travel, accommodation and international group exchange.

BY CAR

CAR RENTAL

Two western car rental companies have recently opened offices in the USSR: Hertz in Moscow and Tallinn (Estonia) and Budget Rent-a-Car in Moscow. The addresses are: Moscow, Hotel Cosmos, Tel. 215-6191, Tallinn, Maealuse 3a, Tel. 528-727.

Car rental services are also offered by Eurocar, Moscow, Krasnopresnenskaya nab. 12, Hotel Mezhdunarodnaya-1, 1st Floor, Tel. 253-1369, and Nissan, Soviet-Japanese joint venture, Moscow, ul. Petrovka 15/13, Tel. 927-1187.

ROUTES

If you intend to visit the USSR by car you should first get into contact with Intourist as they have worked out a number of routes in the European part of the Soviet Union which can easily be negotiated with your own vehicle. Road conditions in the other parts of the USSR do not permit you to go there (unless if you participate in the Camel trophy!).

The ideal route through European Russia means entering from Finland, driving via Leningrad and Moscow to the Caucasus and the Black Sea, ferrying the car across to Yalta or Odessa and crossing the Ukraine to Czechoslovakia or Poland.

Details for this and other routes (across the Baltic States, Byelorussia or Moldavia) can be found in the book "Motorists' Guide to the Soviet Union" (Progress Publishers Moscow, 1980). It gives details about fueling stations, repair shops, overnight stops and emergency procedures.

Since crossing the border into Turkey is now possible, you can also exit or enter to or from Anatolia.

Sovinterautoservice, Institutski per., 2/1, Moscow, Tel. 101-496, are the specialists for car travel in the USSR. They solve nearly every problem a foreigner can have on Russian roads.

RULES OF THE ROAD

The USSR is a signatory to the International Traffic Convention. Rules of the road and road signs correspond in general to international standards. The basic rules, however, are worth mentioning.

1) In the USSR traffic drives on the right.

2) It is prohibited to drive a car after consuming any, even the smallest amount, of alcohol. If the driver shows a positive alcohol test, the consequences may be very serious. It is also prohibited to drive a car under the effect of drugs or drastic medicines.

3) The driver must have an international driving license and documents, verifying his right to drive the car. These papers must be in Russian and are issued by Intourist.

4) Vehicles, except for those rented from Intourist, must carry the national registration code. All must have a national license plate.

5) The use of the horn is prohibited within city limits except in emergency situations.

6) The use of seat belts for the driver and front seat passenger is compulsory.

7) The speed limit in populated areas (marked by blue colored signs indicating "town") is 60 km/h (37 m/h); on most arterial roads the limit is 90 km/h (55.5 m/h). On highways the limit can differ and is marked by corresponding road signs.

8) You can insure your car in the USSR through Ingosstrakh, the national insurance company.

9) Foreigners still need a permit to drive more than 40 km/25 miles beyond city limits, and must follow the routes established by Intourist. Permits may be checked by traffic police when exiting the city.

BY TRAIN

With some 90,050 miles/145,000 km, the railway system of the USSR is the longest in the world. It is a means of transport used for 4 billion individual trips per year. The busiest lines in the European USSR connect Moscow with Leningrad and Kiev, where a train leaves almost every hour. In overnight sleeping cars, tea is always served and trains traveling for more than 8 hours have a restaurant car attached during daytime.

You should make your reservation several days ahead since, as with everything else in the USSR, reserved train seats are in short supply, especially 2nd class tickets that are cheap but do offer a comfortable journey.

You can reserve your seat through Intourist or at the Intourtrans Office (situated in Moscow, ul. Petrovka 15). There is also an Intourist booking office in the railway stations of every major city. The ticket must have a cover and a coupon (it is only valid with both these components).

The price of a 1st class ticket from Moscow to Kiev is 32 roubles and Moscow to Leningrad costs 30 roubles.

Intourist provides an English language telephone information service in Moscow: Tel. 921-4513.

BY BOAT

Many rivers in the European USSR are open to navigation during the spring to autumn seasons. You can travel along the Dnieper, Volga, Oka, Moskva, Don, Dniester, Neva and other rivers. The cities on the banks of the rivers are connected by passenger ships and hydrofoils. (Raketa and Kometa Class).

If you plan a trip along one of these routes you can make a reservation through Intourist or directly at the Moscow River Station (Rechnoy Vokzal).

River Stations:

Moscow: Severny Rechnoy Vokzal, Leningradskoe shosse 51, Tel. 457-4050;

Leningrad: Rechnoy Vokzal, prosp. Obukhovskoy Oborony 195, Tel. 262-1318 (information), 262-5511 (booking office);

Kiev: Rechnoy Vokzal, Poshtova pl., Tel. 416-1268 (information).

Cruises: Intourist offers organized river cruises on comfortable river liners which are relaxing and informative but quite expensive. These cruises are sold through foreign travel agencies that sell Intourist tour packages. Just recently Intourist has started to offer trips along the Lena and soon the Ob and the Yenisei will also be on their itinerary.

BY PLANE

Aeroflot is the world's largest airline, transporting more than 110 million passengers per year. It flies to 97 countries worldwide and more than 3600 cities and villages in the USSR; many of them in remote and outlying areas which are serviced with helicopters and small hopper planes. Its fleet of aircraft has been designed primarily for military purposes and lacks the comfort of western carriers. There are no statistics yet available of how many aircraft the national carrier has in service but it is estimated to be a few thousand. Aeroflot is now buying the European Airbus which will soon be in service on certain international routes. Forty percent of all foreign tourists who visit the USSR arrive on Aeroflot.

Fares within the USSR are very reasonable, though flights have to be booked far in advance since there is a far greater demand than there is capacity. Check-in at Aeroflot counters starts one and a half hours and ends half an hour before departure. Foreigners have to pay for their tickets in hard currency.

Aeroflot offices in the USSR are:
Moscow:
4, Frunzenskaya Naberezhnaya, Tel. 245-0002;
Leningrad:
7/9 Nevsky Prospekt, Tel. 211-7980;
Kiev:
66, Boulevard Shevchenko, Tel. 774-4223;
Minsk:
18/28, Karl Marx St., Tel. 224-232,
Yerevan:
2, Tumanyan St., Tel. 582-422;
Tbilisi:
2, Javakhishvily St., Tel. 932-744;
Vilnius:
21, Lenin Prospekt, Tel. 756-175;
Khabarovsk:
5, Amursky Boulevard, Tel. 332-071;

International:
Amsterdam:
Singel, 540, Tel. 245-715;
Athens:
Ksenofontis 14, Tel. 322-1022;
Bangkok:
7, Silom Rd, Tel. 233-6965;
Berlin:
Unter den Linden, 51/53, Tel. 229-1592;

Budapester Str. 50, Tel. 261-8250;
Bombay:
7th Brabourn Stadium, Vir Nariman Rd., Tel. 221-682;
Brussels:
Rue des Colonies 54, Tel. 218-6046;
Bucharest:
35, Boulevard Nicolae Balcescu, Tel: 167-431;
Budapest:
4, Waci, Tel. 185-892;
Copenhagen:
1/3, Vester Farimasgade, Tel. (01)126-338;
Delhi:
18, Barakhamba Rd., Tel. 40-426;
Frankfurt:
Teaterplatz 2, Tel. 230-771;
Helsinki:
Mannerheimintie 5, Tel. 659-655;
Lisbon:
Av. Antonio Augusto de Aguiar 2H-3E, Tel. 561-296;
London:
69-72, Piccadilly, Tel. 492-1756;
Madrid:
25, calle Princesa, Tel. 241-9934;
Milan:
19, Via Vittor Pisani, Tel. 669-985;
Munich:
Ludwigstr. 6, Tel. 288-261;
Paris:
33, Avenue des Champs Elysees, Tel. 225-4381;
Peking:
2-2-42, Jianguomenwai, Tel. 523-581;
Prague:
15, Vaclavske Namesti, Tel. 260-862;
Rome:
27, Via Leonida Bissolati, Tel. 475-7704;
Singapore:
55, Market St., Tel. 96-711;
Sofia:
2, Russky Boulevard, Tel. 879-080;
Tokyo:
Tatsunuma Bldg. 3-19, 1-chome Yaesu, chuo-ku, Tel. 272-8351;
Vienna:
10, Parkring, Tel. 521-501;
Warsaw:
29, Allee Jerozolimskie, Tel. 281-710;
Zürich:
9, Usteristr., Tel. (01) 211-4633.

LANGUAGE

FORMS OF ADDRESSING

Modern Russian has no established and universally used forms of addressing. The old revolutionary form "tavárishch" (comrade), still used amongst some party members, lacks its popularity in the rest of the population.

One way is to say: "Izviníte, skazhíte pozhálsta..." (Excuse me, tell me, please...) or "Izvinite, mózhna sprasít'..." (Excuse me, can I ask you...).

If you want to look original and to show your penetration into the depths of history of courteous forms, you can appeal to the man "súdar'" (sir), and to the woman resp. "sudárynya" (madam). Many people want to restore these pre-revolutionary forms of address in modern Russian society. If you know the name of the father of the person you talk to, the best and the most neutral way is to use these both when addressing him (her): "Mikhál Sirgéich" to Mr. Gorbachev and "Raísa Maxímavna" to his spouse.

In business circles you can use forms "gaspadín" to a man and "gaspazhá" to a woman. The English forms of address "Mister" or "Sir" will also be accepted quite well.

You can hear common parlance forms "Maladói chilavék!" (Young man!) and "Dévushka!" (Girl!) to a person of any age and also "Zhénshchina!" (Woman!) to women in the bus, in the shop or at the market. These forms should be avoided in the conversation.

TRANSLITERATION

There exist some 4 systems of transliteration of Russian words into English (see: J.T. Shaw, *The Transliteration of Modern Russian for English Language Publications*. The Univ. of Wisconsin Press, 1967). If it is necessary, the systems can be combined so that one letter or a group of letters is transliterated according to one system and the other according to another.

To transliterate some Russian letters, English letter combinations are used: ж = zh, x = kh, ц = ts, ч = ch, ш =sh, щ = shch, ю = yu, я = ya, ё = yo. The Russian letter combination кс is transliterated both as *ks* and as *x*. Some Russian letters are transliterated with a few exceptions in a similar way: й, ы = y, e, ё = e.

To transliterate Russian soft sign between the consonants and before no-vowel, the apostrophe " ' " is used, or the soft sign is ignored, as before vowels.

The transliteration of nominal inflections has some peculiarities: ый, ий = y, ие, ье = ie, ия = ia.

If the traditional English spelling in names differs from their letter-by-letter transliteration they are mostly translated in their English shape: Moscow (city), but river Moskva.

The Genetive inflections in the names of the streets and the other objects are translated according to their pronunciation, and not their spelling: площадь Горького, (*ploshchad' Gór'kogo*) = pl. Gorkovo in this book.The transliteration in this section shows the way to pronounce Russian words and therefore does not correspond exactly with their spelling.

The city maps and their captions use Russian words and abbreviations: "ul." (*úlitsa*), means "street"; "per." (*pereúlok*) - "lane"; "prosp." (*prospékt*) - "avenue"; "pl." (*plóshchad´*) - "square"; *alléya* - alley; *bul'vár* - "boulevard"; *magistrál* - "main line"; *proézd* - "passage"; *shossé* - "highway"; *spusk* - "slope".

Some local names (especially in the capitals of Baltic republics) are given as they are in local languages: so, *väljak* in Estonian means "square".

The Russian system of mentioning house numbers is used, *prosp. Kalinina 28* stands for 28 Kalinin Avenue.

ENGLISH/RUSSIAN

Russian is one of the 130 languages used by the peoples of the USSR. It is the mother tongue of some 150 million Russians and the state language in the Russian Federation

(RSFSR). Talking to anybody in the USSR in Russian, you will be understood by most Soviet citizens.

From a linguistic point of view, Russian belongs to the Slavonic branch of the Indo-European family of languages, English, German, French, Spanish and Hindi are its relatives.

It is important when speaking Russian that you reproduce the accent (marked here before each stressed vowel with the sign ') correctly to be understood well.

Historically Russian can be called comparatively young language.

The appearance of the language in its present shape on the basis of the spoken language of Eastern Slavs and the Church-Slavonic written language, is attributed to the 11th to 14th centuries.

Modern Russian is tolerable to foreign words and they form a considerable group within the Russian vocabulary. Very few tourists will be puzzled by Russian words like telefon, televizor, teatr, otel, restoran, kafe, taxi, metro, aeroport.

The thing usually intimidating people resolved to make their first aquaintance with Russian is the Russian alphabet. The apprehension is quite vain because the alphabet is remembered easily in a few repetitions and the difference with the Latin alphabet is only minimal. Understanding the Russian alphabet permits to make out the names of the streets and the shop sign-boards.

The Russian (or Cyrillic) alphabet was created by two brothers, philosophers and public figures, Constantine (St. Cyril) and Methodius, both were born in Solun (now Thessaloniki in Greece). Their purpose was to facilitate the spreading of Greek liturgical books in Slavonic speaking countries. Today the Cyrillic alphabet with different modifications is used in the Ukrainian, Byelorussian, Bulgarian, Serbian and in some other languages.

THE ALPHABET

printed letter	sounds, as in	Russian name of a letter
А а	a, archaeology	a
Б б	b, buddy	be
В в	v, vow	v
Г г	g, glad	ge
Д д	d, dot (the tip of the tongue close to the teeth, not the alveoli)	de
Е е	e, get	ye
Ё ё	yo, yoke	yo
Ж ж	zh, composure	zhe
З з	z, zest	ze
И и	i, ink	i
Й й	j, yes	jot
К к	k, kind	ka
Л л	l, life (but a bit harder)	el'
М м	m, memory	em
Н н	n, nut	en
О о	o, optimum	o
П п	p, party	pe
Р р	r (rumbling, as in Italian, the tip of the tongue is vibrating)	er
С с	s, sound	es
Т т	t, title (the tip of the tongue close to the teeth, not the alveoli)	te
У у	u, nook	u
Ф ф	f, flower	ef
Х х	kh, hawk	ha
Ц ц	ts (pronounced conjointly)	tse
Ч ч	ch, charter	che
Ш ш	sh, shy	sha
Щ щ	shch (pronounced conjointly)	shcha
ъ	(the hard sign)	
Ы ы	y (pronounced with the same position of a tongue as when pronouncing G,K)	y
ь	(the soft sign)	
Э э	e, ensign	e
Ю ю	yu, you	yu
Я я	ya, yard	ya

NUMBERS

1 adín		один
2 dva		два
3 tri		три
4 chityri		четыре
5 pyat'		пять
6 shes't'		шесть
7 sem		семь
8 vósim		восемь
9 d'évit'		девять
10 d'ésit'		десять

11 adínatsat'	одиннадцать	maí (plural)
12 dvinátsat'	двенадцать	мой/моя/моё/мои
13 trinátsat'	тринадцать	
14 chityrnatsat'	четырнадцать	Our/Ours
15 pitnátsat'	пятнадцать	nash/násha/náshe/náshy (resp.)
16 shysnátsat'	шестнадцать	наш/наша/наше/наши
17 simnátsat'	семнадцать	
18 vasimnátsat'	восемнадцать	Your/Yours
19 divitnátsat'	девятнадцать	tvoj etc. (see My)
20 dvátsat'	двадцать	vash etc. (see Our)
21 dvatsat' adin	двадцать один	твой/ваш
30 trítsat'	тридцать	
40 sórak	сорок	His/Her, Hers/Their, Theirs
50 pidisyat	пятьдесят	jivó/jiyó/ikh
60 shyz'disyat	шестьдесят	его/её/их
70 s'émdisyat	семьдесят	
80 vósimdisyat	восемьдесят	Who?
90 divinósta	девяносто	khto?
100 sto	сто	Кто?
101 sto adin	сто один	
200 dv'és'ti	двести	What?
300 trísta	триста	shto?
400 chityrista	четыреста	Что?

GREETINGS & ACQUAINTANCE

500 pitsót	пятьсот
600 shyssót	шестьсот
700 simsót	семьсот
800 vasimsót	восемьсот
900 divitsót	девятьсот
1,000 tysicha	тысяча
2,000 dve tysichi	две тысяч и
10,000 d'ésit' tysich	десять тысяч
100,000 sto tysich	сто тысяч
1,000,000 milión	миллион
1,000,000,000 miliárd	миллиард

Hello!
zdrástvuti (neutral, often accompanied by shaking hands, but it is not necessary)
Здравствуйте!

alo! (by telephone only)
Алло!

PRONOUNS

zdrástvuj (to one person, informal)
Здравствуй!

I/We
ya/my
я/мы

priv'ét! (informal)
Привет!

You
ty (singular, informal)/
vy (plural, or formal singular)
ты /вы

Good afternoon/Good evening
dóbry den'/dobry véchir
Добрый день/Добрый вечер

He/She/They
on/aná/aní
он/она/они

Good morning/Good night
dobrae útra/dobraj nóchi (= Sleep well)
Доброе утро/Доброй ночи

My/Mine
moj (object masculine)/
mayá (object feminine)/
mayó (neutral or without marking the gender)/

Good bye
dasvidán'ye (neutral)
До свиданья

chao! (informal)
Чао!

paká! (informal, literally means "until")
Пока!

Good luck to you!
shchislíva!
Счастливо!

What is your name?
kak vas (tibya) zavút?/kak váshe ímya ótchistva? (the second is formal)
Как вас (тебя) зовут?/Как ваще имя и отчество?

My name is.../I am...
minya zavut.../ya...
Меня зовут.../Я...

It's a pleasure
óchin' priyatna
Очень приятно

Good/Excellent
kharashó/privaskhódna
хорошо/отлично

Do you speak English?
vy gavaríti pa anglíski?
Вы говорите по-английски?

I don't understand/I didn't understand
ya ni panimáyu/ya ni pónyal
Я не понимаю/Я не понял

Repeat, please
pavtaríti pazhálsta
Повторите, пожалуйста

What do you call this?
kak vy éta nazyváiti?
Как вы это называете?

How do you say...?
kak vy gavaríti...?
Как вы говорите...?

Please/Thank you (very much)
pazhálsta/(bal'shóe) spasíba
Пожалуйста/(Большое) спасибо

Excuse me
izviníti
Извините

Where is the...?
gd'e (nakhóditsa)...?
Где находится...?

beach
plyazh
...пляж

bathroom
vánnaya
...ванная

bus station
aftóbusnaya stántsyja/aftavakzál
...автобусная станция/автовокзал

bus stop
astanófka aftóbusa
...остановка автобуса

airport
airapórt
...аэропорт

railway station
vakzál/stántsyja (in small towns)
...вокзал/станция

post office
póchta
...почта

police station
...milítsyja
...милиция

ticket office
bil'étnaya kássa
...билетная касса

marketplace
rynak/bazár
...рынок/базар

embassy/consulate
pasól'stva/kónsul'stva
...посольство/консульство

Where is there a...?
gd'e z'd'es'...?
Где здесь...?

currency exchange
abm'én val'úty
...обмен валюты

pharmacy
apt'éka
...аптека

(good) hotel
(kharóshyj) atél'/(kharoshaya) gastínitsa
...(хороший)отель(хорошая)гостиница

restaurant
ristarán
...ресторан

bar
bar
...бар

taxi stand
stayanka taxí
...стоянка такси

subway station
mitró
...метро

service station
aftazaprávachnaya stantsyja/aftasárvis
...автозаправочная станция

newsstand
gaz'étnyj kiósk
...газетный киоск

public telephone
tilifón
...телефон

hard currency shop
val'útnyj magazín
...валютный магазин

supermarket
univirsám
...универсам

department store
univirmák
...универмаг

hairdresser
parikmákhirskaya
...парикмахерская

jeweler
yuvilírnyj magazin
...ювелирный магазин

hospital
bal'nítsa
...больница

Do you have...?
u vas jes't'...?
У вас есть...?

I (don't) want...
ya (ni) khachyu...
Я (не) хо чу...

I want to buy...
ya khachyu kupít'...
Я хочу купить...

Where can I buy...
gd'e ya magú kupít'...
Где я могу купить...

cigarettes
sigaréty
...сигареты

wine
vinó
...вино

film
fotoplyonku
...фотоплёнку

a ticket for.....
bilét na...
...билет на...

this
éta
...это

postcards/envelopes
atkrytki/kanv'érty
...открытки/конверты

a pen/a pencil
rúchku/karandásh
...ручку/карандаш

soap/shampoo
myla/shampún'
...мыло/шампунь

aspirin
aspirn
...аспирин

I need...
mn'e núzhna...
Мне нужно...

I need a doctor/a mechanic
mn'e núzhyn dóktar/aftamikhánik
Мне нужен доктор/автомеханик

I need help
mn'e nuzhná pómashch'
Мне нужна помощь

Car/Plane/Train/Ship
mashyna/samal'yot/póist/karábl'
маъшина/самолёт/поезд/корабль

A ticket to...
bil'ét do...
билет до...

How can I get to...
kak ya magu dabrátsa do...
Как я могу добраться до...

Please, take me to...
pazhalsta atvizíti minya...
Пожалуйста, отвезите меня...

What is this place called?
kak nazyváitsa eta m'ésta?
Как называется это место?

Where are we?
gd'e my?
Где мы?

Stop here
astanavíti z'd'es'
Остановите здесь

Please wait
padazhdíti pazhalsta
Подождите, пожалуйста

When does the train [plane] leave?
kagdá atpravl'yaitsa poist [samalyot]?
Когда отправляется поезд (самолёт)?

I want to check my luggage
ya khachyu prav'érit' bagázh
Я хочу проверить багаж

Where does this bus go?
kudá id'yot état aftóbus?
Куда идёт этот автобус?

SHOPPING

How much does it cost?
skól'ka eta stóit?
Сколько это стоит?

That's very expensive
eta óchin' dóraga
Это о чень дорого

A lot, many/A little, few
mnóga/mála
много/мало

It (doesn't) fits me
eta mn'e (ni) padkhódit
Это мне (не) подходит

AT THE HOTEL

I have a reservation
u minya zakázana m'esta
У меня заказана комната

I want to make a reservation
ya khachyu zakazát' m'esta
Я хочу заказать место

A single (double) room
adnam'éstnuyu (dvukhmestnuyu) kómnatu
одноместную (двухместную) комнату

I want to see the room
ya khachyu pasmatrét' nómer
Я хо чу посмотреть номер

Key/Suitcase/Bag
klyuch/chimadán/súmka
ключ /чемодан/сумка

AT THE RESTAURANT

Waiter/Menu
afitsyánt/minyu
официант/меню

I want to order...
ya khachyu zakazat'...
Я хочу заказать

Breakfast/Lunch/Supper
záftrak/ab'ét/úzhyn
завтрак/обед/ужин

the house specialty
fírminnaya blyuda
фирменное блюдо

Mineral water/Juice
minirál'naya vadá/sok
минерал'ьная вода/сок

Coffee/Tea/Beer
kófe/chai/píva
кофе/ чай/пиво

What do you have to drink (alcoholic)?
shto u vas jes't' vypit'?
Что у вас есть выпить?

Ice/Fruit/Dessert
marózhynaya/frúkty/disért
можо еное/фрукты/дессерт

Salt/Pepper/Sugar
sol'/périts/sákhar
соль/перец/сахар

Beef/Pork/Chicken/Fish/Shrimp
gavyadina/svinína/kúritsa/ryba/kriv'étki
govädina/svinina/kurica/ryba/krevetki

Vegetables/Rice/Potatoes
óvashchi/ris/kartófil'
овощи/рис/картофель

Bread/Butter/Eggs
khleb/másla/yajtsa
хлеб/масло/яйца

Soup/Salad/Sandwich/Pizza
sup/salát/butyrbrót/pitsa
суп/салат/бутерброд/пища

A plate/A glass/A cup/A napkin
tar'élka/stakán/cháshka/salf'étka
тарелка/стакан/чашка/салфетка

The bill, please
shchyot pazhalsta
Счёт, пожалуйста

Well done/Not so good
fkúsna/ták sibe
вкусно/так себе

I want my change, please
zdáchu pazhalsta
Сдачу, пожалуйста

MONEY

I want to exchange currency (money)
ya khachyu abmin'át' val'yutu (d'én'gi)
Я хочу обменять валюту (деньги)

Do you accept credit cards?
vy prinimáiti kridítnyi kártachki?
Вы принимаете кредитные карточки?

Can you cash a traveler's check?
vy mózhyti razminyat' darózhnyj chek?
Вы можете разменять дорожный чек?

What is the exchange rate?
kakój kurs?
Какой курс?

TIME

What time is it?
katóryj chas?
Который час?

Just a moment, please
adnú minútachku
Одну минуточку

How long does it take?
skól'ka vrémini eta zanimáit?
Сколько времени это занимает?

Hour/day/week/month
chas/den'/nid'élya/m'ésits
час/день/неделя/месяц

At what time?
f kakóe vrémya?
В какое время?

At 1:00/at 8 a.m./at 6 p.m.
f chas/ v vósim utrá/f shés't' chisóf v'échira
в час/в восемь утравшестьчасоввечера

This (last, next) week
eta (próshlaya, sl'édujshchiya) nid'elya
эта (прошлая, следующая) неделя

Yesterday/Today/Tomorrow
fchirá/sivód'nya/záftra
вчера/сегодня/завтра

Sunday
vaskris'én'je
воскресенье

Monday
panid'él'nik
понедельник

Tuesday
ftórnik
вторник

Wednesday
sridá
среда

Thursday
chitv'érk
четверг

Friday
pyatnitsa
пятница

Saturday
subóta
суббота

The weekend
vykhadnyi dni
выходные дни

SIGNS & INSCRIPTIONS

вход/выход/входа нет
fkhot/vykhat/fkhóda n'et
Entrance/Exit/No Entrance

туалет/уборная
tual'ét/ubórnaya
Toilet/Lavatory

Ж (ZH) / М (M)
dlya zhén'shchin/dlya mushchín
Ladies/Gentlemen

зал ожидания
zal azhidán'ya
Waiting hall

занято/свободно
zánita/svabódna
Occupied/Free

касса
kassa
booking office/cash desk

медпункт
mitpúnt
Medical Services

справочное бюро
správachnae bzuro
Information

вода для питья
vadá dlya pit'ya
Drinking Water

вокзал
vakzál
Terminal/Railway station

открыто/закрыто
atkryta/zakryta
Open/Closed

запрещается/опасно
zaprishchyaitsa/apásna
Prohibited/Danger

продукты/гастроном
pradúkty/gastranóm
Grocery

булочная/кондитерская
búlachnaya/kan'dítirskaya
Bakery/Confectionery

закусочная/столовая
zakúsachnaya/stalóvaya
Refreshment room/Canteen

самообслуживание
samaapslúzhivan'je
Self-Service

баня/прачечная/химчистка
bánya/práchichnaya/khimchístka
Bath-House/Laundry/Chemical Cleaning

книги/культтовары
knígi/kul'taváry
Books/Stationery

мясо/птица
m'ása/ptítsa
Meat/Poultry

обувь
óbuf'
Shoe-Store

овощи/фрукты
óvashchi/frúkty
Green-Grocery/Fruits

универмаг/универсам
univirmák/univirsám
Department Store/Supermarket

ткани/цветы
tkani/tsvity
Fabrics/Flowers

EMERGENCIES

HEALTH

Like anywhere else, it is recommended that you wash fruits and raw vegetables before you eat them. Likewise, you should not drink tap water if you are not used to it, because a different and unfamiliar mineral composition can easily produce intestinal disorder. Bottled mineral water is available everywhere.

MEDICINES

During the last few years the USSR has experienced a shortage in the supply of basic medicines. It is quite common that simple aspirin or vitamins are not available in drugstores. If you need special medication it is best to bring it with you. Some medicines are still available, especially in Moscow which is better supplied with most daily necessities.

The following three drugstores in the capital are normally well stocked:

ul. 25 Oktyabrya 1, Tel. 925-1846;
ul. Kirova 32, Tel. 923-1388;
Kutuzovsky prosp. 14, Tel. 243-1601.

DOCTORS

Your hotel service bureau can get you a doctor to come to your hotel room or they will refer you to the next clinic. Medical standards in the Soviet Union are good and in the big cities there are specialists for every kind of illness available. Doctor's visits and first aid treatment is free of charge but medicines and hospital treatment must be paid in roubles.

The healing properties of the mineral waters in the **Rayon Kavkazskikh Mineralnykh Vod** (Caucasian Spa District) have been known for centuries. This area, and the customs of resort people, were described by Lermontov, one of the representatives of the Golden Age of Russian poetry. Like Pushkin, Lermontov was also killed in a duel in Pyatigorsk. Now duels are no longer in fashion but **Pyatigorsk** mineral waters are still used to treat the organs of movement, the neural system, dispepsia, pathological metabolism, vascular, feminine and skin diseases. Other spas in this region - **Essentuki**, **Kislovodsk** and **Zheleznovodsk** - are as famous as Pyatigorsk.

Sochi and **Matsesta**, are also in the vicinity of the Rayon Kavkazskikh Mineralnykh Vod, on the coast of the Black Sea. Not far away is another spa, **Tskhaltubo**. The movement of organs, vascular and neural disorders, feminine, urological and skin diseases are treated here.

EYE CLINIC

The world famous **Institute of Eye Microsurgery** headed by Prof. Svyatoslav Fedorov, treats many kinds of vision disorders and offers different operations: radial ceratotomie as a correction of myopia (shortsightedness) and astigmatisms; laser treatment of non-inborn forms of cataracts; laser treatment of glaucoma and laser treatment of complicated cases of high grade myopia.

Together with Intourist the Institute organizes treatment programs for foreigners including diagnostics, operation, accommodations, meals and excursions around

Moscow. The cost for diagnostics and an operation is 780 roubles (US$1170). Intourist services and accommodation are charged separately.

EMERGENCY NUMBERS

All Soviet cities have unified emergency telephone numbers. These numbers can be dialed free of charge from public telephones.

Fire Guards (Pozharnaya okhrana)	01
Police (Militsia)	02
Ambulance (Skoraya pomoshch)	03
Gas Emergency (Sluzhba gaza)	04
Information (Spravochnaya)	09

Officials responding to these calls will speak little English, so a minimal knowledge of Russian is needed to make yourself understood.

FOOD DIGEST

Most of the different ethnic groups populating the USSR pretend to have their national cuisine, and some of them do genuinely have them.

Within this diversity experts say Georgian, Ukrainian, Russian and Central Asian cuisines are the best.

Georgian: With perestroika Georgian food came to the rest of the USSR (like the traditional Aragvi restaurant in Moscow or the Kavkaz in Leningrad). Many cooperatives run by people from the Caucasus opened restaurants serving Georgian food. The Georgian cuisine is famous for its *shashlyk*, *tsyplyata tabaka* (chicken fried under pressure), *basturma* (specially fried meat), *suluguni* (salted cheese) and *satsyvi* (chicken). It can be served with *lavash* (a special kind of bread) or with *khachapuri* (a roll stuffed with cheese) flavored by various species like *tkemali* or with a delicious *bazha* sauce.

Ukrainian: Ukrainians have traditionally been known to eat a lot - but also tastily. Among different kinds of dishes they prefer *borshch* (beetroot soup with cabbage, meat, mushrooms and other ingredients), *galushky* (small boiled dumplings) and *varenyky zvyshneyu* (curd dumplings with red cherries served with sugar and sour cream). Known and served around the world is the *Kiev Chicken* (or Kiev Cutlet) prepared with different spices and garlic. Loved by everyone in the Ukraine is *salo* (salted raw lard spiced with garlic). It is served with black bread. Very popular is also *kovbasa* (different kinds of smoked sausages).

Russian: Famous are the beef Stroganov and Beluga caviar. Russian cuisine includes less refined but no less popular dishes like *bliny* (pancakes served with butter and sour cream, caviar, meat, jam etc.), *shchi* (sour cabbage soup with meat; gourmets prefer this with mustard), *pelmeni* (boiled dumplings with meat) and *kasha* (gruel or porridge of different grains).

Central Asian: The cuisine is represented by a variety of pilaws or rice dishes.

DRINKING NOTES

Everyone knows what they drink in Russia: vodka, and tea from the samovar. This is only half the truth. There are numerous other drinks within different national cuisines.

The Ukrainian traditional alcoholic drink is *gorilka* which resembles vodka. But more popular, and more refined, is *gorilka z pertsem*, i.e. gorilka with a small red pepper. The traditional non-alcoholic drink is *uzvar* (made of stewed fruit).

Georgians drink different dry and semidry wines. *Tsinandali*, *Mukuzani*, *Kinzmarauli*, *Alazan Valley*, and *Tvishi* (reported to have been the favorite wine of Stalin). Nonalcoholic drinks from Georgia are represented by the best in the USSR's mineral water such as *Borzhomi* and the so-called *vody Lagidze* (mineral water with various syrup mixtures).

In summer Russians prefer to drink *kvas*, an enigmatic refreshing drink prepared from bread fermented with water and yeast.

Central Asians drink *geok chaj* (green tea), the best treatment for a thirst in the hot Central Asian climate.

COMMUNICATIONS

MEDIA

Foreign-language press: *Pravda*, the official paper of the Communist Party of the USSR, appears in an English-language translation in the United States. Issues of the last few years are also available on CD ROM. *Moscow News*, an informative English-language weekly is a quite liberal paper published in Moscow. The first independent Soviet-American weekly newspaper is *We*, a joint venture between Izvestia and the Hearst Corp. The *Moscow Magazine* is an exceptionally well-made monthly magazine that every visitor to the city should read. It contains much information about the changing world of cooperative restaurants, etc. *Travel to the USSR*, is a bimonthly illustrated magazine, published in Russian, German, English and French, that carries many interesting tips and information about fast-changing travel conditions in the country.

Russian-language press, *Pravda* and *Izvestia* are the leading government newspapers. The monthly *Novy Mir* and the weekly *Ogonyok* are critical papers that thrive on the idea of glasnost.

COURIERS

Barry Martin Travel, Room 940, Mezhdunarodnaya Hotel, 12 Krasnopresnenskaya nab. 12, Tel. 253-2940.

The joint venture **Airservice-TNT Skypak** delivers mail to most countries of the world within 1 to 3 days. Open Mon.-Fri. 10 a.m. to 6 p.m., Tel. 578-9030. They charge 40 roubles for 0.5 kg/1 pound of mail and 8 roubles for each additional 0.5 kg/1 pound.

POSTAL SERVICES

The opening time of post offices varies, but most of them open from 8 a.m. till 7 p.m. or 8 p.m. during the week, from 9 a.m. to 6 p.m. on Saturdays. They are closed on Sundays. Some post offices, however, work only one shift a day, from 9 a.m. to 3 p.m. or from 2 p.m. to 8 p.m. The mail service in the USSR is constantly understaffed.

Not all post offices accept international mail bigger than a standard letter. Postal delivery is quite slow, and it may take some two or three weeks for a letter from Moscow to reach Western Europe and sometimes even a month or more to reach the USA. A standard letter up to 20 grams costs 50 kopecks and a postcard costs 35 kopecks to any country of the world.

CABLES & TELEGRAMS

Cables to addresses within the USSR can be sent from any post office or by phone. In Moscow the phone number for telegrams is 927-2000. To ask for the corresponding number in other Soviet cities, you have to dial 09. International cables can be sent from nearly any post offices, but not by phone.

TELEPHONE

From a pay phone a local call is 2 kopecks per 3 minutes. The coin must be inserted before dialing. If you hear a bip-bip tone during the conversation it's time to insert another coin.

For long distance calls within the USSR there are specially marked phones which accept 15 kopeck coins.

First dial 8, than the area code and the number. International calls must be booked in advance (the Moscow number is 8-190) or at the hotel service bureau.

TELEX & FAX

Area codes:

ALMA-ATA	327
ASHKHABAD	363
BAKU	892
BUKHARA	365
DONETSK	062
DUSHANBE	377
YEREVAN	296

KIEV	044
KISHINEV	042
KHARKOV	057
LENINGRAD	812
LVOV	032
MINSK	017
MOSCOW	095
NOVOSIBIRSK	383
ODESSA	048
RIGA	013
ROSTOV ON DON	863
SAMARKAND	366
TALLINN	014
TASHKENT	371
TBILISI	883
VILNIUS	012
YALTA	060

When calling the USSR from abroad, be prepared to try often; the lines are not too good and very busy.

The country code for the USSR is 007.

Some international direct dial numbers:

MOSCOW	007095
LENINGRAD	007812
MINSK	0070172
TALLINN	0070142

All official institutions and major business representatives have telex numbers and the majority of them by now also telefax. Moscow has a public fax and telex service, where you can send a fax or telex or register a number by which you can be reached if you plan to stay in the city for a certain period. Any incoming message will be forwarded either by phone or by local mail. It is the only way to beat the slow mail service. For further information call 924-4758 (Central Telegraph Office, ul. Gorkovo 7) or 925-1588 for the telex center.

The telex access code for the USSR is 871.

SHOPPING

The absence of a variety of goods, and sometimes the absence of even the most basic goods, determines very often the opening hours of shops. If there are no goods, the shop need not be open! At least in small towns.

Many small shops have a one hour lunchbreak sometime between noon and 5 p.m. Larger shops are continuously open, also on Saturdays. On Sundays all shops, with the exception of some food stores, are closed. In big cities, shops open between 7 a.m. and 9 a.m. and close between 8 p.m. and 9 p.m. In Moscow, Leningrad, Kiev and some other capitals of the republics certain food stores might be open until 10 p.m. Book shops and other specialities shops open around 10 a.m. or 11 a.m. and are open until 7 or 8 in the evening, with a break usually between 2 p.m. and 3 p.m.

Special shops for foreigners: For foreigners who seem horrified by the empty counters of Soviet shops, there are special shops where they can buy nearly everything for hard currency. There are now different chains of such shops in hotels, international airports and at certain points in the big cities called "*Beriozka*" (the birch tree), "*Sadko*", etc. The sales personnel in these shops usually speak English, French or German.

They offer Soviet goods of comparatively good quality. Furs, glass, ceramics, vodka, Crimean and Georgian wines, and many goods that are hard to come by in other city shops are all available if paid for in hard currency.

Beriozka prices are based on the so called "*invalyutny rouble*" and correspond with prices in Western European countries, though they are lower for Russian goods than for imported ones. These hard currency shops accept cash, traveler's cheques and most credit cards:

Moscow Duty Free, Sheremetevo-2 Airport Departure Lounge. Tel. 578-9012. Open 24 hours (liquor, tobacco, fashions, electronics, watches, perfume, food, crystal, porcelain, travel goods, fashion accessories, souvenirs).

Beriozka, (accept payment in Vneshekonombank coupons (cheques series D) only).

Gastronom, Ul. B. Gruzinskaya 63. Open 10-2, 3-7. Tel. 251-2589 (food supplies, cigarettes and drinks).

Exhibition Complex, Krasnopresnenskaya nab. Open 10-2, 3-7. Tel. 259-7380, 259-2583.

Clothing and Fur Shop, Ul.1812, Goda 12. Open Mon.-Sat. 11-8. Tel. 148-6976.

Department Stores: Rostovskaya nab., 5. Open Mon.-Sat. 11-8. Tel. 248-6664, 248-6508 (furniture, carpets, pianos, china, souvenirs, jewelry, radio, car accessories, wine and cigarettes).

Luzhnetsky proyezd, 25a. Open 9-8. Tel. 246-2742, 246-8755.

Leninsky pr. 60/2 & 86, Pr. 60-letiya Oktyabrya 12/1, Ul.Pyatnitskaya 39, Ul.Fersmana 5. All open Mon.-Sat. 9-8.

Sadko, Kutuzovsky prosp. 9, Tel. 243-7501 (consumer goods). Ul. B. Dorogomilovskaya, 16, Tel. 243-7501, 243-6601 (food and drink).

Vero-Moda, Ul. Chekhova 8, Tel. 209-7553 (Italian fashions).

La Pantera, Pr. 60-letiya Oktyabrya,10/1 (consumer goods). Open 9-8.

Stockmann-GUM, Red Square 3, 3rd line, ground floor, Tel. 921-1529.

Books, Ul. Kropotkinskaya 31, Tel. 203-9262, ul. Vesnina 8/10, Tel. 241-9587.

Jewelry-Salon, Grokholsky per. 30, Tel. 280-4706. Open Mon.-Fri. 9-6.

Motor Sales, Yuzhny Port, Tel. 279-4992. Open Mon.-Sat. 10-6, Varshavskoe shosse 21, Tel. 354-1001.

SOUVENIRS

Inexpensive souvenirs, toys and other knickknacks abound on Soviet streets. Many co-operatives prefer not to rack their brain with such difficult matters as food production or the maintenance of computers. They produce souvenirs, hair combs and belts. They also imitate the labels of designer jeans, so Soviet youngsters can sew them onto their pants to get an imitation feeling of freedom. All this cheap stuff is sold on the streets, in the vicinity of department stores and in cooperative markets.

The "must" street in Moscow is Arbat, where Moscow painters and wood carvers sell their works. Prices are quite high, but you needn't be in a hurry to buy a set of Russian *Matryoshkas* for 600 roubles (US$100). The same set may be found somewhere else for 150 roubles.

There are places similar to Arbat in Leningrad (Ostrovsky sq.), Kiev (on October Revolution Square) and other cities. Souvenirs abound also in special shops for foreigners, art-salons and curio shops. But beware of the problems waiting for you at customs: according to the new Soviet regulations, antiquities and art works may not be exported. The danger of confiscation is quite real. For all goods bought in a Soviet shop, including those you bought at "*Beriozka*", you must keep the receipt to show that you paid in hard currency and that the goods are not antique.

TIPPING

Though the Soviet Union has been a Socialist state for 70 years, tipping, one of the capitalist sins, is still an accepted practice. Waiters, porters, taxi drivers, especially in Moscow and Leningrad, have always appreciated tips.

As anywhere in the west, 10 percent is the accepted rule.

However, do not tip guides, interpreters or other Intourist personnel. If you want to show your gratitude they will surely appreciate a small souvenir or gift.

USEFUL ADDRESSES

SOVIET MISSIONS ABROAD

Argentina
1741 Rodriges Penya
Buenos Aires
Tel. (42) 1552

Australia
Griffis
70 Canberra Avenue
Canberra
Tel. (062) 956-6408

Austria
45-47 Reisnerstr.
Vienna
Tel. 721-229

Belgium
66 Avenue de Fre
1180 Bruxelles
Tel. 373-3569, 374-3406

Canada
Embassy
285 Sharlotta Street
Ottawa
Tel. (613) 235-4341

Denmark
3-5 Christianiagade
Copenhagen
Tel. (04) 125-585

Finland
Embassy
6 Tehtaankatu
Helsinki
Tel. 661-876

France
Embassy
16 Boulevard Lann 40/50
Paris

Tel. (45) 010-550

Germany
Embassy
2 Waldstr. 42
5300 Bonn
Tel. (0228) 312-086;
Consulate
76 Am Feenteich
2000 Hamburg
Tel. (040) 229-5301

Greece
28 Nikiforu Litra Street
Paleo Psyhico
Athens
Tel. 672-6130, 672-5235

India
Shantipath Street
Chanakiapury
Delhi
Tel. 606-026

Ireland
186 Orwell Road
Dublin
Tel. 975-748

Italy
Embassy
5 Via Gaeta
Rome
Tel. 494-1681

Japan
Minato-ku
Adzabu-dai 2-1-1 T-106
Tokyo
Tel. 583-4224

Netherlands
2 Andries Bickerweh
The Hague
Tel. (07) 045-130

New Zealand
Carory
57 Messines Road
Wellington
Tel. 766-113

Norway
2 Dramensveien 74
Oslo

Tel. 553-278

Singapore
51 Nassim Road 1025
Tel. 235-1834

Spain
6 & 14 Maestro Ripol
Madrid
Tel. 411-0706, 262-2264

Sweden
31 Ervelsgatan
Stockholm
Tel. (08) 13-044-044

Switzerland
Embassy
37 Brunnadenrein 3006
Bern
Tel. (031) 440-566

Thailand
108 Sotorn Nua
Bangkok
Tel. 258-0628

FOREIGN MISSIONS

Turkey
Embassy
Caryagdy, Soc. 5
Ankara
Tel. 139-2122

United Kingdom
5, 13 & 18 Kensington Palace Gardens
London
Tel. (071) 229-3828

USA
Embassy
1125 16th Street 20036
Washington
Tel. 628-7551, 628-8548, 628-6412;
Consulate
2790 Green Street
San Francisco (Calif)
Tel. (415) 922-6644

EMBASSIES IN MOSCOW

Argentina
Sadovaya-Triumfal'naya ul. 4/10
Tel. 299-0367

Australia
Kropotkinsky per. 13
Tel. 246-5012

Austria
Starokonyushenny per. 1
Tel. 201-7317

Canada
Starokonyushenny per. 23
Tel. 241-5070

China
Leninskie Gory
ul. Druzhby 6
Tel. 143-1543

Czechoslovakia
ul. Fuchika 12/14
Tel. 250-2225

Denmark
per. Ostrovskovo 9
Tel. 201-7868

Finland
Kropotkinsky per. 15/17

France
Kazansky per. 10
Tel. 236-0003

Germany
B.Gruzinskaya ul. 17
Tel. 252-5521

Greece
ul. Stanislavskovo 4
Tel. 290-2274

Hungary
Mosfilmovskaya ul. 62
Tel. 143-8955

India
ul. Obukha 6-8
Tel. 297-1841

Ireland
Grokhol'sky per. 5
Tel. 288-4101

Italy
ul. Vesnina 5
Tel. 241-1533

Japan
Sobinovsky per. 5a
Tel. 202-0061

Luxemburg
Khrushchevsky per. 3
Tel. 202-2171

Malaysia
Mosfilmovskaya ul. 50
Tel. 147-1415

Netherlands
Kalashny per. 7
Tel. 291-2999

New Zealand
ul. Vorovskovo 44
Tel. 290-3485

Norway
ul. Vorovskovo 7
Tel. 290-3872

Poland
ul. Klimashkina 4
Tel. 254-3612

Portugal
Grokholsky per. 3/1
Tel. 230-2435

Romania
Mosfilmovskaya ul. 64
Tel. 143-0424

Singapore
per. Voevodina 5
Tel. 241-3702

Spain
ul. Gertsena 50/8
Tel. 291-9004

Sweden
Mosfilmovskaya ul. 60
Tel. 147-9009

Switzerland
per. Stopani 2/5
Tel. 925-5322

Thailand
Eropkinsky per. 3
Tel. 201-4893

Turkey
Vadkovsky per. 7/37
Tel. 972-6900

United Kingdom
nab. Morisa Toreza 14
Tel. 231-8511

USA
ul. Chaikovskovo 19/23
Tel. 252-2451

CONSULATES IN OTHER SOVIET CITIES

BAKU
Iran: Bouniad Sardarof 4, Tel. 926-143
Iraq: ul. Khagani 9, Tel. 938-283

BATUMI
Turkey: prosp. Stalina 8, Tel. 33-909, 33-703.

IRKUTSK
Mongolia: ul. Lapina 11, Tel. 242-370.

KIEV
Bulgaria: ul. Hospitalnaya 1, Tel. 225-5119.
Cuba: Bethersky per. 5, Tel. 216-2930.
Czechoslovakia: Yaroslavov Val 34, Tel. 229-7269.
Germany: ul. Chkalova 84, Tel. 216-1477, 216-6794, 216-7854, 216-7498.
Hungary: ul. Reiterskaya 33, Tel. 212-4094, 212-4134.
Mongolia: ul. Kotsyubinskovo 3, Tel. 216-8891.
Poland: Yaroslavov Val 12, Tel. 224-8040, 225-7090.
Romania: ul. Kotsyubinskovo 8, Tel. 224-5261.

LENINGRAD
Bulgaria: ul. Ryleeva 27, Tel. 273-7347.
China: 3-Linia 12, Tel. 218-1721, 218-3492, 218-7953.
Cuba: ul. Ryleeva 37, Tel. 279-0492.
Finland: ul. Chaikovskovo 71, Tel. 273-7321.
France: nab. Moiki 15, Tel. 314-1443, 312-1130.
Germany: ul. Petra Lavrova 39, Tel. 273-5598, 273-5731, 273-5937.
Hungary: ul. Marata 15, Tel. 312-6458, 312-6753.

Italy: Teatral'naya pl. 10, Tel. 312-2896.
Japan: nab. Moiki 29, Tel. 314-1434/18.
Mongolia: Saperny per. 11, Tel. 243-4522.
Poland: ul. Sovetskaya 12, Tel. 274-4331, 274-4170.
Sweden: 10th line (VO), Tel. 218-3526/27/28.
USA: ul. Petra Lavrova 15, Tel. 274-8235.

LVOV

Poland: ul. Ivana Franko 10, Tel. 723-949.

MINSK

Bulgaria: Bronevoy per. 3, Tel. 225-500.
Germany (GDR): ul. Sakharova 26, Tel. 330-752.
Poland: Omsky per. 6, Tel. 331-313, 331-3601, 331-1114, 331-5109, 331-0260.

NAKHODKA

Japan: ul. Lunacharskovo 9. Tel. 56-371.
DPR Korea: ul. Vladivostokskaya 1, Tel. 55-310.

ODESSA

Bulgaria: ul. Posmitnovo 9, Tel. 662-015.
Cuba: ul. Tomasa 7/9, Tel. 251-469.
India: ul. Kirova 31, Tel. 224-333.

TASHKENT

Afghanistan: ul. Gogolya 73, Tel. 339-180.
Cuba: ul. Timiryazeva, Tel. 350-777.
India: ul. A.Tolstovo 5, Tel. 333-782.
Libya: ul. Engelsa 95, Tel. 352-009, 352-6103.
Mongolia: ul. Gogolya, Tel. 338-916.

AIRLINE OFFICES

MOSCOW

Air France, ul. Dobryninskaya 7, Tel. 237-2325, 237-3344, 237-6777, Mon.-Fri. 9-1, 2-6.

Air India, ul. Dobryninskaya 7,korp.1 (ground floor), Tel. 237-7494, 236-4440, Mon.-Fri. 9.30-1, 2-5.15, Sat. 10-3.

Alitalia, ul. Pushechnaya 7, Tel. 923-9840/56, Mon.-Fri. 9.30-1.30, 2-6, Sat. 9.30-1.

Austrian Airlines, Krasnopresnenskaya nab. 12, fl.18, Office 1805, Tel. 253-8268, 253-1670/71, Mon.-Fri. 9-6, Sat. 9-1.

British Airways, Krasnopresnenskaya nab. 12, fl.19, Office 1905, Tel. 253-2492, Mon.-Fri. 9-6.

Finnair, Proezd Khudozhestvennovo Teatra 6, Tel. 292-8788, 292-3337, Mon.-Fri. 9-5.

Japan Airlines, ul. Kuznetsky Most 3, Tel. 921-6448, 921-6648, Mon.-Fri. 9-6.

KLM, Royal Dutch Airlines, Krasnopresnenskaya nab. 12, fl. 13, Office 1307, Tel. 253-2150/51, Mon.-Fri. 9-5.

Lufthansa, German Airlines, ul. Kuznetsky Most 3, Tel. 923-0488, 923-0576, Mon.-Fri. 9-5.30.

Pan American, Krasnopresnenskaya nab. 12, fl.11, Office 1102A, Tel. 253-2658/59, Mon.-Fri. 9-5.30.

LOT, Polish Airlines, ul. Dobryninskaya 7, Office 5, Tel. 238-0003, 238-0313, Mon.-Fri. 9-6, Sat. 9-5.

Sabena, Belgian World Airlines, hotel Belgrade-II, fl.7, kom.721, Tel. 248-1214, 230-2241, Mon.-Fri. 9-1, 2-6.

SAS, Scandinavian Airlines, ul. Kuznetsky Most 3, Tel. 925-4747, Mon.-Fri. 9-6, Sat. 9-noon.

Swissair, Krasnopresnenskaya nab. 12, fl.20, Office 2005, Tel. 253-8988, 253-1859, Mon.-Fri. 9-6.

These airlines and others also have offices in Sheremetevo-2 Airport.

KHABAROVSK

Japan Airlines, Airport, Tel. 370686.
Chosonminhang, Airport, Tel. 348-024, 373-204.

LENINGRAD

Finnair, ul. Gogolya 19, Tel. 315-9736, 312-8987.

Pan-American, ul. Gertsena 36, Tel. 311-5819/20/22.

These airlines and Air France, British Airways, KLM, Lufthansa and LOT also have their offices in Pulkovo-2 Airport.

LAW FIRMS

International law firms that specialize in USSR trade problems: **Coudert Brothers**, Pan American Bldg., 200 Park Ave., New York, NY 10166, Tel. 880-4400; **Baker and McKenzie**, Aldwych House, Aldwych, London WC2B 4JP, Tel. 242-6531.
Locally, the USSR Chamber of Commerce has a consultation center that employs legal staff.

CHAMBERS OF COMMERCE

The USSR Chamber of Commerce and Industry, 6 Kuybyshev St., Moscow 101000, Tel. 923-4323; **US-USSR Trade and Economic Council**, 805 3rd Ave., New York, NY 10022, Tel. 644-4550. Moscow office: 3 Shevchenko Embankment, Moscow 121248, Tel. 243-5470; **British-Soviet Chamber of Commerce**, 2 Lowndes St., London SW1X 9ET, Tel. 235-2423. Moscow office: 1904, 19th Fl., World Trade Centre, 12 Krasnopresnenskaya Embankment, Moscow 123610, Tel. 253-2554; **French-Soviet Chamber of Commerce**, 22 ave Franklin D. Roosevelt, 75008 Paris, Tel. 422-59710. Moscow office: Apt. 3, 4 Pokrovsky Blvd., Moscow 101000, Tel. 207-3009; **Italian-Soviet Chamber of Commerce**, 5 Via San Tomaso, Milan, Tel. 481-6725. Moscow office: 7 Vesnina St., Moscow 121002, Tel. 241-5729.

INTERNATIONAL TRAVEL AGENTS

USA:
Four Winds Travel, 175 Fifth Ave., New York, N.Y. 10010
Lindblad Travel Inc. 1 Sylvan Rd. North, Westport, CT 06880
Russian Travel Bureau Inc., 245 E. 44th St., New York, N.Y. 10017

UK:
American Express Co. Inc., 6 Haymarket, London S.W. 1
P & O Holidays, 77 New Oxford Street, London W.C. 1

London Walkabout Club, 20-22 Craven Terrace, Lancester Gate, London W. 2, (specialist for Trans Siberian trips).

GERMANY:
Hansa Tourist, Hamburger Str. 132, Hamburg 76
Lindex Reisen, Rauchstr. 5, 8000 München
Intratours, Eiserne Hand 19, 6000 Frankfurt 1
GeBeCo-Reisen, Eckernförder Str. 93, 2300 Kiel

SINGAPORE:
Folke von Knobloch, 126 Telok Ayer, #02-01 Gat House, Singapore, (specialist for Sibera trips).

FURTHER READING

HISTORY

J.T. Alexander
Catherine the Great
Oxford University Press, 1989

K.N. Cameron
Stalin, Man of Contradiction
Strong Oak Press, 1989

E.H.Carr
History of Soviet Russia
Pelican, 3 vols, first published 1953

G. Hosking
A History of the Soviet Union
Fontana/Collins, 1990

L. Kochan and R. Abraham
The Making of Modern Russia
Penguin, 1983

H. Shukman (ed)
The Blackwell Encyclopaedia of the Russian Revolution
Blackwell, 1989

POLITICS

S. Cohen and K. van den Heuvel
Voices of Glasnost
Norton, 1989

Michael Glenny and Norman Stone
The Other Russia
Faber and Faber, 1990

M.S. Gorbachev
Perestroika
Fontana, 1987

M.S. Gorbachev
Towards a Better World
Richardson and Steirman, 1987

R.J. Hill
Soviet Union: Politics, Economics and Society
Pinter Publishers, 1989

A. Nove
Glasnost in Action
Unwin Hyman, 1989

Boris Yeltsin
Against the Grain
Jonathan Cape, 1990

BIOGRAPHY/MEMOIRS

G. Bailey
The Making of Andrei Sakharov
Penguin, 1990

Elena Bonner
Alone Together
Collins Harvill, 1986

A.G. Gross (ed)
An English Lady at the Court of Catherine the Great
Crest Publications, 1989

Olga Davydoff Bax (ed)
On the Estate: Memoirs of Russia Before the Revolution
Thames & Hudson, 1986

Eugenia Ginzburg
Into the Whirlwind
Within the Whirlwind
Collins Harvill, 1989

Irina Ratushinskaya
In the Beginning
Hodder & Stoughton, 1990

John Reed
Ten Days that Shook the World
Penguin, first published 1919

Alexander Solzhenitsyn
The Gulag Archipelago
Collins Harvill, 1988

Martin Walker
Russia: Despatches from the Guardian Correspondent in Moscow
Abacus, 1989

ART

A. Bird
A History of Russian Painting
Phaidon, 1987

J.E. Bowlt
Russian Art of the Avant Garde
Thames & Hudson, 1988

D. Elliott
New Worlds: Russian Art and Society 1900-37
Thames & Hudson, 1986

Rodimzeva, Rachmanov and Raimann
The Kremlin and its Treasures
Phaidon, 1989

D.V. Sarabianov
Russian Art from Neoclassicism to the Avant Garde
Thames & Hudson, 1990

V.Tolstoy, I. Bibikova and C. Cooke
Street Art of the Revolution
Thames & Hudson, 1990

The Art of Central Asia
Aurora Art Publishers, 1988

Folk Art in the Soviet Union
Abrams/Aurora, 1990

The Hermitage
Aurora, 1987

Masterworks of Russian Painting in Soviet
Museums
Aurora, 1989

TRAVEL, GEOGRAPHY & NATURAL HISTORY

Robert Byron
First Russia, Then Tibet
Penguin, first published 1905

Negley Farson
Caucasian Journey
Penguin, first published 1951

Roger Foxall
Sailing to Leningrad
Grafton, 1990

Algirdas Kynstautas
The Natural History of the USSR
Century Hutchinson, 1987

Fitzroy Mclean
Portrait of the Soviet Union
Weidenfeld and Nicolson, 1988

R. Millner-Gulland with N. Dejevsky
Atlas of Russia and the Soviet Union
Phaidon, 1989

Eric Newby
The Big Red Train Ride
Picador, 1989

Marc Polansky and Russell Taylor
The USSR: From an Original Idea by Karl
Marx
Faber and Faber, 1983

Laurens van der Post
Journey into Russia
Penguin, first published 1964

Colin Thubron
Among the Russians
Penguin, first published 1983

Peter Ustinov
Ustinov in Russia
Michael O Mara Books, 1987

Motorist's Guide to the Soviet Union
Progress Publishers, 1980

The Nature of the Soviet Union: Landscapes, Flora and Fauna
Mokslas Publishing, 1987

Russia
Bracken Books, 1989

USSR: The Economist Guide
Hutchinson Business Books, 1990

LITERATURE

John le Carré
The Russia House
Coronet, 1990

Fyodor Dostoevsky
The Brothers Karamazov;
The Idiot

Boris Pasternak
Doctor Zhivago

Anatoli Rybakov
Children of the Arbat
Hutchinson, 1988

Mikhail Sholokov
And Quiet Flows the Don;
The Don Flows Home to the Sea

Leo Tolstoy
War and Peace;
Anna Karenina

ART/PHOTO CREDITS

INDEX

A

B

L

N

T

431

V

W